Defining the Mission

STUDIES IN **CMR**
CIVIL-MILITARY RELATIONS

William A. Taylor, Series Editor

Defining the Mission

The Development of US Strategic Military Intelligence up to the Cold War

Scott A. Moseman

 University Press of Kansas

© 2025 by the University Press of Kansas
All rights reserved

Published by the University Press of Kansas (Lawrence, Kansas 66045), which was organized by the Kansas Board of Regents and is operated and funded by Emporia State University, Fort Hays State University, Kansas State University, Pittsburg State University, the University of Kansas, and Wichita State University.

Library of Congress Cataloging-in-Publication Data

Names: Moseman, Scott A., author.
Title: Defining the mission : the development of US strategic military intelligence up to the Cold War / Scott A. Moseman.
Other titles: Development of US strategic military intelligence up to theCold War
Description: Lawrence : University Press of Kansas, 2025 | Series: Studies in civil-military relations | Includes bibliographical references and index.
Identifiers: LCCN 2024030508 (print) | LCCN 2024030509 (ebook)
  ISBN 9780700638109 (cloth)
  ISBN 9780700638116 (ebook)
Subjects: LCSH: Military intelligence—United States—History—19th century. | Military intelligence—United States—History—20th century. | United States. Office of Naval Intelligence. | United States. War Department. Military Intelligence Division. | United States. War Department. Military Intelligence Service | Intelligence service—United States—History—20th century. | United States. Central Intelligence Agency. | Cold War. | Military intelligence—United States—Historiography. | BISAC: HISTORY / Military / Intelligence & Espionage | HISTORY / United States / 20th Century
Classification: LCC UB251.U5 M67 2025 (print) | LCC UB251.U5 (ebook) | DDC 355.3/4320973—dc23/eng/20241114
LC record available at https://lccn.loc.gov/2024030508.
LC ebook record available at https://lccn.loc.gov/2024030509.

British Library Cataloguing-in-Publication Data is available.

For my wife Paula and children Adam and Juliette

Contents

Series Editor's Foreword *ix*
Acknowledgments *xi*
Notes on Terminology *xiii*

    Introduction 1
1. 1882–1885: Emergence of ONI and MID 10
2. 1885–1895: Growing Pains of ONI and MID 30
3. 1895–1900: Operational Tests for ONI and MID 54
4. 1900–1915: The Nadir of ONI and MID 79
5. 1915–1919: The Resuscitation of ONI and MID 123
6. 1919–1929: ONI and MID Navigate the Rapids 153
7. 1929–1939: Storm on ONI and MID's Horizon 182
8. 1939–1941: ONI and MID's Inability to Warn 205
9. 1941–1945: ONI and MID Sidelined Again 234
10. 1946–1947: CIA Subordinates ONI and MID 260

Historiographic Essay *273*
Notes *281*
Bibliography *349*
Index *363*

A photo gallery follows page 110.

Series Editor's Foreword

William A. Taylor

In *Defining the Mission*, Scott A. Moseman analyzes the significant, yet understudied history of the Office of Naval Intelligence (ONI) and the Military Intelligence Division (MID). His novel contribution to our knowledge of these two institutions places much-needed emphasis on the morphing and uncertain nature of strategic military intelligence organizations in the United States over the lengthy span of sixty-five crucial years. Ranging from 1882 to 1947, this remarkable volume provides unique insights into how these two enterprises developed during an important epoch in American history. The result is an exceptional account of the evolution of strategic military intelligence organizations up to the emergence of the modern US national security structure forged by the landmark National Security Act of 1947. In doing so, this compelling explanation leverages the particular evolution of ONI and MID to reveal much larger lessons about military intelligence, American society, and the constant interplay between them.

A major theme of this comprehensive work is how the matter of elusive and fluid roles and missions, in this case vis-à-vis strategic military intelligence organizations, relates to civil-military relations and vice versa. Throughout the ensuing narrative, Moseman reveals the magnitude of both change over time and historical precedent for weighty themes that continue to resonate today. The creation of the Central Intelligence Agency (CIA), the most examined shift in the intelligence organization of the United States, did not simply emerge from a vacuum. Instead, the strategic military intelligence organizations that preceded it had been searching for purpose, often in vain, for many decades amid constantly shifting terrain, both military and civilian. Moseman makes clear that military leaders struggled to define their preferred roles and missions. Such ambiguity often led to large chasms between military and civilian leaders regarding the overall purpose of such endeavors.

By shedding new light on the intimate linkages between ONI and MID over a tumultuous historical era that led to the fundamental reforms of the intelligence community during the 1940s, Moseman reinforces the importance of these often-overlooked precedents. In a beneficial way, therefore, this book provides a superb institutional history that intersects with American history writ large. It reveals how various communities interpreted both the purpose and possibility of strategic military intelligence organizations in quite distinct ways that altered over time. As an added bonus, Moseman also situates these changing missions, and contrasting perspectives thereof, within the broader milieu of American society. The result is a layered story wherein these strategic military intelligence organizations searched for purpose at the same time that civilian leaders and American society grappled with their own discrete versions of the same dilemma.

The powerful relationship between civilians—both in government and within broader society—and military institutions often involves conflicting interpretations of roles and missions. In this case, Moseman provides useful comparisons between the way in which civilians defined strategic military intelligence organizations and how those institutions defined themselves, as well as the extent to which all these various understandings changed over many decades. Such matters are a valuable, and even indispensable, component of civil-military relations. Dissimilar actors—whether they be the government, military, or society—form palpable perceptions of one another, articulate rhetoric based on these impressions, and then act accordingly. Complicating matters, this dynamic process occurs in multiple directions simultaneously. The arena of constantly competing notions of roles and missions is therefore a major component of civil-military relations. In this excellent book, Moseman reminds us all that such differences are not simply binary between civilian and military individuals and entities but rather involve divergent sensitivities from a multitude of parties. Intelligence professionals, military leaders, civilian policymakers, and American society all had varying, and often diverging, ideas about what strategic military intelligence should be and in what way it could contribute to overall US national security. This enthralling account reveals how, out of this cacophony of dissonance, a general consensus formed by the middle of the twentieth century. Along the way, readers will benefit from the worthwhile discernments that strategic military intelligence organizations reveal, both about themselves and American society, when refracted through the analytical lens of civil-military relations.

Acknowledgments

Writing a dissertation and subsequent book was just as hard as I thought it would be, but the personal and professional rewards were well worth the time investment. I could not have done it without a little help from friends and family along the way.

During my initial research I had many supporters to help me. At Kansas State University, I extend my thanks to Dr. Mark Parillo for his experienced direction. I want to give a huge shout-out to the Department of History for the generous support of the History Department awards program. I want to thank the Colonel Peter Cullen Military History Scholarship program, Robin Higham Military History Graduate Student Research and Travel Fund, Florence Hamscher Graduate Student Travel Award program, and James C. Carey Research and Travel Award program for funding my many trips to the Washington, DC, region for archival research. I knew tackling such daunting organizational subjects as the Office of Naval Intelligence and the Military Intelligence Division would require reaching out to the command historians at ONI and the US Army Intelligence and Security Command (INSCOM) for assistance. ONI's command historian Dr. Randy Goguen and Mr. Michael Bigelow from INSCOM were more than helpful in providing source trails—primary and secondary—because they had been along that path before. The staffs at the Marine Corps History Division, the National Archives, the Manuscript Division at the Library of Congress, the Nimitz Library at the United States Naval Academy, the Navy History and Heritage Command, the Oral History Archives at Columbia University were all crucial in helping me obtain the valuable information I could turn into analysis on ONI, MID, and Marine Corps intelligence. I would be remiss in not recognizing key individuals in the discipline of history who have guided me: Dr. Patrick Bass, Dr. Mark Gerges, and Dr. Jon Mikolashek. Thank you, mentors!

As I have continued my intellectual journey from conducting college research to publishing this manuscript, I have also had precious guidance and support from colleagues and advisors. First, I want to express my appreciation to the editors at the University Press of Kansas. Editor in

Chief Joyce Harrison kept me informed every step of the way and was extremely patient with an author who was anything but patient (a flaw of mine) throughout the process. Civil-Military Relations series editor Dr. William Taylor also had some great advice for me on the publishing process, which I take to heart. Dr. Jonathan M. House and Dr. Kathryn Barbier thoroughly read one of my rough drafts in the peer review stages and provided excellent feedback to my manuscript, which I incorporated writ large. Finally, Mr. Brian Allen, a colleague at the Command and General Staff College and good friend, aided me tremendously in the scouring of archives and databases to find the insightful illustrations in this book. Thank you for helping a fellow shipmate out!

I would not be where I am at in my professional career without my family. To my kids Adam (eleven) and Juliette (eight), you still may not know why your daddy spent four months in our unfinished basement during the quarantine summer of 2020. Or you may not understand why he left for five separate trips to the faraway place, Washington, DC. Just know that I love you. You gave me the fuel to keep writing. To my wife, Paula, who allotted me the space to trap myself behind a computer for long periods of time and watched our kids while I went gallivanting to dusty, soulless archives, thanks for your encouragement. Your sacrifices to be in Wildcat (instead of Jayhawk) country and to pick up some random music gigs to support my academic dreams reconfirmed I am loved. I assure you, it's reciprocated and so much more.

Notes on Terminology

Military historians Jonathan M. House and Henry H. Ransom provided an excellent starting point for the terminology used in this book. House defined intelligence as "the product of systematic efforts to collect, confirm, evaluate, and correlate information from a variety of sources. The resulting conclusions are often subjective and tentative, representing the best-informed estimate of the analysts involved."[1] The word "information" in this study refers simply to unevaluated data. The term "military" also further delineates the research; there were civilian intelligence entities in the US government between 1882 and 1947, such as the Federal Bureau of Investigation and the Secret Service, in addition to State Department analysts. "Military intelligence" is a broad phrase. Used here, it refers to data on the armed forces of actual or potential adversaries as well as analysis of the terrain, weather, industrial production, weapons production, local diseases, and other factors that affect military operations.[2] The information-gathering apparatus in the United States military intelligence includes the Navy, Army, Marine Corps, Air Force, and Coast Guard. In traditional uses and even in some military circles today, "military intelligence" has been synonymous with Army intelligence. However, this has somewhat narrowed the phrase to the detriment of the other military services. Thus, when considering the Department of War's intelligence organization, we will refer to it as "Army intelligence." Likewise, the Department of the Navy has an agency that conducts naval intelligence work.

Different levels of military organizations practice military intelligence for separate echelons of customers. These levels (descending from the national level to the individual operators) include strategic intelligence, operational intelligence, and tactical intelligence. Strategic intelligence is concerned with the basic capacity of a nation to produce military forces, the missions of those forces, and the possible effects of an opponent's military forces upon the national and strategic objectives of the analysts' own nation in times of both peace and war. In the United States, the customers of such intelligence usually include the president, Congress, and senior civilian and military leaders of the Departments of War (pre-1947) and the Navy.[3] House described operational intelligence as "an intermediate level, in which a theater, field army, air forces, or corps/naval battlegroup commander seeks intelligence that will affect the campaign or contingency plan intended to accomplish strategic or national objectives. Examples of operational intelligence include the location, capabilities, missions, and movements of major enemy units—division or corps, air wings, or naval task forces."[4] Operational intelligence customers in the United States can include the senior military staffs of the departments, especially concerning contingency planning and locations of major units. Tactical intelligence seeks to understand the makeup, location, tactics, and intentions of small adversarial units.[5] We will not discuss tactical intelligence here because most of the narrative entails events that occur at the department-level or above. Hence, here the term "strategic military intelligence organizations" is used often.

A review of strategic military intelligence organizations uncovers other forms of intelligence functions: foreign intelligence, counterintelligence, and domestic security. Foreign intelligence is the product of systematic efforts to collect, confirm, evaluate, and correlate information that specifically targets another nation. Ransom calls counterintelligence a "phase of intelligence activity devoted to countering the effectiveness of hostile intelligence operations."[6] It is not inherently conducted at the strategic level, nor is it a traditional military intelligence duty. It is essentially a policy function. Besides counterintelligence, domestic security encompasses duties such as protection of installations, censorship, classification of information, operational security, security background checks, and port and base security.

Introduction

US strategic military intelligence organizations have had to adapt to several external and internal factors in finding their raison d'être. Indeed, military intelligence reflects the society it serves, as observed in the manner in which it handles intelligence used by military commanders and policymakers. From the creation of the first Navy intelligence outfit in 1882 to the formation of the CIA in 1947, strategic military intelligence organizations struggled to define their missions, as the American public, government and military leaders, and intelligence professionals had competing ideas of what strategic military intelligence should be and do. By the time of the post–World War II creation of the modern national security establishment, these actors had learned that the place for the armed forces' intelligence offices was often in operational intelligence, as part of a broad national intelligence community.

Strategic military intelligence organizations tried to find their voice in the expanding American military and maturing American society of the late nineteenth and early twentieth century, but their story usually stays in the shadows while scholars brush it aside as unimportant. Yet, as this book will show, we must revisit strategic military intelligence's place in the Department of War and Department of the Navy and understand the organizations' place in American society. To do so, the narrative begins in 1882 with the birth of strategic military intelligence organizations and ends in 1947 when the nature of military intelligence fundamentally changed from a focus on strictly strategic matters amid Cold War challenges. Throughout, we will explore how government leaders and American society defined strategic military intelligence organizations during this period, as well as how they described themselves in their service to the US military and American citizens.

To get at the root of the problem, one must ask a few key questions. First, what was/were the mission or missions of US strategic military intelligence between 1882 and 1947? To be more precise, the term "mission" is defined as tasks that indicate what actions an organization must take and the reasons behind them. There are few orders, directives, or other documents that specifically treat the missions or purpose of the Office of Naval Intelligence (ONI), Military Intelligence Division (MID), and Marine Corps intelligence. This is unsurprising, as the very nature of intelligence ensures classified information is often removed from open-forum discussions. At the same time, we know that these organizations were often fluid when considering policy, especially in peacetime.[1]

Certainly, the word "mission" has a temporal component, and military intelligence missions change over time. The American military of 1882 was not the same as the juggernaut of 1947. There were periods in this sixty-five-year window when intelligence missions changed dramatically. Factors such as wars, manpower, political environment, societal expectations, and fiscal restraints helped determine the areas of focus. At the same time, by the mid-1940s, the modern US intelligence apparatus had come to fruition, and national level decisionmakers used Navy and Army intelligence less frequently. The culmination of these developments was the creation of the Central Intelligence Agency (CIA), which inherited many of the strategic intelligence duties from military intelligence and proceeded to hinder military intelligence's access to national level customers.

Another important question is how strategic military intelligence missions reflected trends within US society, culture, economy, and politics during this period. These organizations did not operate in a vacuum. Social issues such as class conflict affected military intelligence's ability to survive and thrive. Citizens' understandings of morality, individual apathy, and national daily rituals affected the gathering of foreign intelligence and counterintelligence. The nation's political mood influenced whether American leaders wished to be outward-facing or inward-looking, and government leaders directed military intelligence in particular directions depending on the national context. Thus, strategic military intelligence missions echoed broader American trends such as professionalization, Progressivism, American exceptionalism and imperialism, and government bureaucratization.

Accordingly, this book asks: What did the strategic military intelligence organization leaders see as their reason for being? How they defined themselves shaped how they dealt with their superiors and related to society in general. What did the military departments and senior staffs expect from their military intelligence organizations? And finally, in broader terms applicable to our own era, how are the missions of military intelligence organizations influenced by the state of America? These are tough questions, but nevertheless we must answer them.

Specific overarching societal influences that affected ONI's and MID's search for purpose are evident in their respective eras. The managerial revolution of the 1870s and 1880s marked the age of centralization of authority and administration in American society, directly affecting the founding of the ONI and MID. On the one hand, the Hamiltonian impulse, where imperialism and free trade present themselves as an alternative to isolation and economic stagnation, showed itself whenever Americans entangled themselves in overseas affairs. ONI and MID excelled under the banner of looking beyond American borders because of their expertise gathering information about foreign powers. On the other, Progressivism (a political philosophy that, between 1890 and 1920, supported reform undertaken via government regulation) and Taylorism (a theory of management that sought to control and manage turmoil through efficiency) often tested strategic military intelligence organizations' cohesiveness and effectiveness, in particular through government overregulation. The rise of professionalization in a post–Industrial Revolution America and the related creation of general staffs within the armed forces impelled ONI and MID to continually readjust their positions within the Departments of Navy and War as early as the Progressive Era and as late as the 1940s. For its part, the organizational paradigm shift of the New Deal also had an impact on how ONI and MID conducted intelligence business in the 1930s. Finally, the increased growth and complexity of government emerges as a theme affecting the organizational structure and resources of these organizations from 1882 through 1947, often becoming more evident in times of America's involvement in war. These patterns continued to evolve and play out through the end of the narrative.

The function of intelligence is hard to conduct at any level. The first, and perhaps the most daunting, task is for intelligence professionals to understand what the customer wants from them, both in substance and the format. Then, they must figure out how to collect the information—if it is even feasible. Once the data arrive at an intelligence officer's desk, they have to decide what information is important and what can be discarded. An experienced analyst then takes multiple sources of information and turns it into intelligence, the "so what" answer to the question that has been posed. They then disseminate the intelligence to the customer, get feedback, and receive orders on what else the client needs. During the period examined in this book, the problem of navigating the constant intelligence professional–customer dynamics was compounded for ONI and MID by the need to learn the intelligence business from scratch, understand the political situation, and decipher the intelligence organizations' relationship to the society they served. It is no wonder that strategic military intelligence organizations often seemed behind the curve in respectability and usefulness. Intelligence is a difficult business to master.

In examining the growth of military, and indeed national intelligence, from a four-man office in 1882 to a multiorganizational operation numbering in the thousands of employees by the mid-1940s, this contribution to the existing scholarship attempts to tie strategic military intelligence's maturation process to the broader military and national trends occurring in American culture and society. We will investigate the nature of strategic military intelligence organizations, asking in part if they were truly strategic. The pages that follow show that ONI, MID, and Marine Corps intelligence grew and morphed to reflect the bureaucratic and professional expansion of the US government from the 1880s to the beginning of the Cold War. At the same time, military intelligence also sought to keep abreast of American cultural, economic, political, and international interests in constantly redefining strategic military intelligence missions, searching for the purpose of military intelligence in the American military and within the society it serves. Strategic military intelligence was not enough to fill the mounting governmental and societal requests for the national-level intelligence necessary for America's global position at the start of the Cold War. The civilian-led CIA and a strengthened intelligence community were the next evolutionary step.

For more than one hundred years after the signing of the Declaration of Independence, the United States of America did not possess a strategic military intelligence organization. The government did not even have an intelligence organization. This is not surprising, as professionalism in American society began to grow only in the later decades of the nineteenth century, meaning that large-scale organizations sprouted only in the 1870s and 1880s.[2] Throughout most of the nineteenth century, Americans did not feel an existential threat on their borders and certainly not from across the Atlantic. A flourishing, democratic republican government regulated a country unaffected by the Old World's practices of intrigue and alliances essential for keeping or discovering secrets. Gathering information for comprehensive war plans was not an American pastime. Its Navy and Army had neither a system to evaluate information gathered abroad, in the frontier regions, or on the borders, nor a place to store it. To be sure, the Navy collected information through naval warships and personnel who traveled abroad, and the Army had cavalry, scouts, and topographic engineers for such purposes. However, there was no centralized repository to direct these efforts within the Departments of the Navy and War. There simply were no urgent military threats necessitating such collection efforts. But as US foreign policy began to gaze outward, the simple intelligence system would need to change. But how? Even if the military had intelligence organizations, what specific missions would Americans and their representative leaders give to them? To answer this question, one must first explore the fits and starts of American intelligence efforts since colonial times.

Before the Gilded Age, the Army had a longer, more robust history of intelligence work than the Navy. Being on the frontier, American colonists scouted potential enemies and the topography just for basic survival. During the American Revolution, Gen. George Washington created an intelligence network, made mostly of spies, to monitor British Army activities. In Europe and the American colonies, a senior commander running his own information web was not an uncommon practice. Washington's networks penetrated the highest levels of British headquarters in New York City in 1778, and the same group uncovered Benedict Arnold's treason.[3] But this spy system nowhere near as complex as a military intelligence organization, a centralized agency for information gathering. Washington relied on scouts, such as Daniel Morgan, for reconnaissance missions that reaped a bounty of information. A prepared Washington often knew British locations accurately throughout much of the war.[4] Excellent intelligence manufactured from spies and scouts also allowed him to understand the weaknesses of his adversaries. Ultimately, although the Continental Army's intelligence apparatus was primitive, it served its purpose. The rudimentary Navy had a similar system for spying through its privateers and raiders, but it was less robust than the Army's network.

After the American Revolution, the spy networks broke up, and the military disbanded. For the next three decades, American political leaders focused on frontier expansion, with only a distracted eye toward external adversarial military developments. For example, when the new republic formed in 1789, the government created a small army under the secretary of war, whose role was to be an executive agent for westward expansion. This constabulary force's only duties loosely related to intelligence were scouting and mapping terrain. Military institutions and intelligence collections did not fit with America's core values of liberty, providence, and virtue during the early republic; quite simply, there was no need for these types of organizations.[5] As a result, "knowing thine enemy" was a practice lost just years after the Revolutionary War: neither the Army nor the Navy had intelligence agencies when the War of 1812 began.

Unsurprisingly, the American side was utterly unprepared for this conflict. Little accurate or timely information was available to military commanders for planning and operations.[6] In these circumstances, US forces made do with widespread employment of scouts, and the Department of War established the first topographical engineer unit with a mission to gather information to support military maneuvers. Still, in 1812 the Americans collected information as a matter of expediency rather than a coordinated effort at the department level to plan massive campaigns. The Navy again used privateers and raiders for simple intelligence, but they too were far from organized when gathering information.

The period between the end of the War of 1812 and that of the Civil War exhibited the same improvised methods of data collection that defined intelligence in the early republic. For example, the Navy assigned ships to patrols, exploratory expeditions, and hydrographic surveys, in the Navy's first true foray into information-gathering and intelligence for military value. On these missions, officers collected such data as foreign port facility layouts, channel and anchorage conditions, foreign coastline charts, and depth soundings.[7] Meanwhile, Army field commanders used reconnaissance as the chief source for data collection, but the information was only as good as the untrained staff's ability to analyze it. The government did not need intelligence, much less a military office for it, before 1861, as the country's only military pursuit was constabulary duties on the frontiers in a context of continuing continental expansion. The United States only required professional military intelligence against a world military or naval power; the wide Atlantic Ocean provided better protection than information.

However, there were promising developments for Army intelligence between 1814 and 1848. The Department of War began detailing officers to Europe as observers and students. When they returned, senior officers would debrief them on foreign technologies, doctrines, and procedures. Topographical engineers continued their mapping of the nation's interior. By 1838, this cadre of officers numbered thirty-six, and the new Corps of Topographical Engineers separated from the Corps of Engineers.[8] Still, in the Mexican-American War, the United States as usual lacked a centralized military intelligence agency either in Washington or in the field. Washington authorities did not anticipate information requirements at the start of the war, so military commanders made operational decisions on little to no intelligence. The data that did come from within the Department of War were misinterpreted often by senior officers and their staffs.[9] In short, there were some improvements to information gathering at the tactical level, but the American government still had no coordination mechanisms in the capital.

Before 1861, American officers continued trips overseas to collect technical information. For example, future commander of the Army of the Potomac Captain George B. McClellan was on the US Military Commission to the Crimean War in 1855 and 1856. These trips were meant to give American Army officers ideas about how a professional military fights in a larger war. But when war erupted within the American states, the peacetime Union Army clumsily scrambled into action without taking this new knowledge into account. The Department of War, without a general staff and with an army led by the aging Gen. Winfield Scott, again overlooked the need for a permanent intelligence organization. And while the Army of the Potomac formed a Bureau of Military Information in 1863 under Col. George H. Sharpe, the agency was not effective at coordinating information collection above the battlefield level. The lack of a national system on both sides led to awkward and counterproductive attempts at intelligence activities at the strategic level, with only local services in some commands proving effective.[10] Innovations and enhanced techniques in intelligence gathering did occur, including improved cavalry reconnaissance, observation balloons, interception of enemy semaphore messages by observers, telegraph line tapping, and more advanced codes and ciphers. But this all occurred at the tactical level. The Union's Corps of Topographical Engineers disbanded in 1863 to free up officers for what the Department of War deemed more important duty. Strategic intelligence did not play a major role in the Civil War.[11]

Army missions and functions normalized after the conflict; its ranks shrank to twenty-five thousand as the service returned to its traditional constabulary role in the West. The conditions once again best suited an Army commander who served as his own intelligence officer working from information gleaned by cavalry and scouts.[12] At least through the early part of the 1880s, Army intelligence activities largely consisted of reconnaissance and mapping and were confined to the territories in the western United States. Yet, with the frontiers beginning to close, the Department of War looked beyond American borders.

Reflecting this new trend, military observer activity increased, as more officers were sent on missions overseas. Senior Army leaders started to pay more attention to European armies' way of doing business, especially in organizational practices and doctrine. Major General William T. Sherman, the commanding general of the US Army from 1869 until 1883, oriented his senior officers' philosophies toward emulating European military thought. Army theorist Col. Emory Upton, best known for his views on Army reform and policy, had great influence on Sherman's way of thinking. According to his biographer Stephen E. Ambrose, "Upton's contributions to American military policy were essential to the development of a modern armed force in the United States."[13] Indeed, he helped bring European military thought back to the United States after a trip across the Atlantic, writing his observations for senior Army leaders such as Sherman. Later, twentieth-century Army reformer Secretary of War Elihu Root used Upton's ideas to form the Army's general staff. Crucially, to become like European military powers, the Department of War needed information: in short, it was time for a permanent military intelligence organization above the echelon of field commanders.

On the naval side of the equation, US naval forces deteriorated greatly between 1865 and 1882. In 1865, the Navy had seven hundred ships; in 1880 it could field only forty-eight aging vessels. Peacetime routines, a lack of interest in foreign affairs, reconstruction of the South, financial constraint, and a general American aversion to a standing Navy are reasons for this abysmal state of affairs. Congress provided miniscule budgets to build new ships, much less maintain the current fleet.[14] Ironically, as the United States remained stagnant, other nations copied many of the innovations the Americans made in their civil war and improved upon them. For example, the Industrial Revolution allowed European navies to work on armor plating, steam propulsion, rifled and breech-loaded naval guns, and iron and steel shipbuilding. In this context, fleet degeneration hurt some naval officers' morale as they watched the Navy decline and lose its technological lead to other navies. US naval officers who sailed to foreign ports or met foreign naval ships in the open ocean were embarrassed to be seen in their obsolete ships. These sentiments stirred an undercurrent of reformist agitation as early as 1869 for all-around improvements to equipment, training, doctrine, and organization, as officers reasoned that if Americans wished to protect budding financial interests overseas, they needed a strong navy.[15] This reformist movement led to more naval expeditions for scientific, economic, and military intelligence collection. Meanwhile, individual Navy bureaus sponsored trips of officers to Europe to observe foreign naval installations and operations.

In 1869, the Department of the Navy directed the Bureau of Navigation to collect information on foreign navies. This interest was due in part to the Prussian wars against Austria and then France. The bureau ordered Rear Admiral William Radford, commander of the European Squadron, to collect data on the war and other developments. This directive was different from any previous order for naval officers because it requested specific information.[16] Captain Christopher R. P. Rodgers, commander of Radford's flagship, directed information-gathering in Europe. Some of Rodgers's team, including his son Raymond, Ens. Theodorus B. M. Mason, and Midn. Albert G. Gleaves, would go on to man the first US intelligence organization. Separately, Chief Engineer James W. King made four trips to Europe between 1869 and 1878 to accumulate naval technical information, especially on engineering. In 1870, Captain Edward Simpson traveled to all major European countries to collect information on naval ordnance. Commander Francis M. Ramsay relieved Simpson in 1872 and became a de facto naval attaché to England ten years before the Navy had an official attaché system. These missions and others brought reams of data into the Department of the Navy's offices, but there was no centralized intelligence agency in the 1870s to collate and distribute it throughout the bureaus.

Even keeping up with South American countries in naval developments became an issue, as Chile, Bolivia, and Peru all bought naval equipment and ships from suppliers from the Old World. Rear Admiral Rodgers took command of the Pacific Squadron in July 1878, just in time for the kickoff of the War of the Pacific between Chile, Bolivia, and Peru. This conflict presented an eager Rodgers and his staff with an occasion to observe European-built ironclads in action. Could the US Navy defend the Western Hemisphere from European nations, as stated in the Monroe Doctrine? Much less, could they even go toe-to-toe with a South American nation?[17] Rodgers wanted to find out. At the same time, Rodgers was developing disciples within the next generation of naval officers to carry on reform in budding intelligence efforts.

Commodore John G. Walker, another pioneer of naval intelligence, became chief of the Bureau of Navigation in August 1881.[18] The former captain of the USS *Powhatan*, he had experience as a railroad operator throughout the 1870s, serving in such duties as secretary of the Chicago, Burlington, & Quincy Railroad. The railroad business taught Walker how to organize and manage information, a system he wished to instill in his bureau. Specifically, Walker recognized that while the observer system put together haphazardly after the Civil War had been beneficial, it did not comprise a systematic effort for filing intelligence and then reporting it to superiors. He believed it was time for a permanent military intelligence organization above the echelon of observers and individual ship captains. It was within this context, at the dawn of this information-gathering era in the early 1880s, that the Departments of the Navy and War launched their permanent strategic intelligence organizations.

Chapter One
1882–1885:
Emergence of ONI and MID

In his seminal *Arms and Men: A Study of American Military History*, Walter Millis marks the changing of the decades between the 1870s and 1880s with four events: the publishing of J. W. King's report *The Navies of the World* in 1877, the publication of Emory Upton's *Armies of Asia and of Europe* in 1878, Sherman's founding of the School of Application for Infantry and Cavalry in Leavenworth in 1881, and the beginnings of the Naval War College in 1884. Millis describes these junctures as the beginnings of the managerial revolution.[1] Indeed, this was the age of the centralization of authority and administration not only in the US military but also in American society in general. America began its industrial revolution, and economic, political, and societal forces coalesced to find order in the occurring changes.[2]

In 1880 the US military, intellectually nearly dormant for fifteen years, experienced the stirrings of reform and organization, spurred by a new generation of leaders. As discussed in the introduction, events such as the Franco-Prussian War and the modernization of European sailing fleets awakened American officers to fundamental changes in the art of war in the Old World that could affect American shores. Millis did not specifically write about the Army and Navy's yearnings to accrue foreign military information as part of this revolution, but he probably would have agreed with this assessment. There was a zeal for modernization among military reformers, as they foresaw a possibility of conflict with a world great power and increasingly demanded the transformation of the military from a decaying force to a formidable juggernaut.[3] But how does one prepare for the possibility of war with another country? The solution inevitably rested with the practice of gathering data on the armed forces and military strength of foreign powers. In 1882, the Navy established the Office of Intelligence (shortly thereafter renamed the Office of Naval Intelligence or ONI), and three years later the Department of War created the Military Information Division (MID). In the era of managerial and bureaucratic awakenings between 1881 and 1885, the establishment of strategic military intelligence organizations was a logical step for leaders of the Departments of the Navy and of War. Both the departments and these organizations' pioneers saw ONI's and MID's missions as strategic: information collection, data storage, and intelligence analysis to serve national security purposes.

The Department of the Navy and the Department of War were the prime movers in determining how ONI and MID would function. President Chester Arthur and later President Grover Cleveland probably knew that ONI and MID existed, but these extremely small offices were nearly invisible. Congress also had an idea that the Navy and Army began to collect military information, but this was only because the secretaries of the Navy and war started to request funds for such missions. The departments were instrumental in providing the funding, mission, personnel, and equipment to make these strategic military intelligence organizations viable. Military leaders were explicit in general orders and verbal instruction that ONI and MID had the task of data collection and management. And if these organizations' officers wanted to add analysis, that was acceptable as well.

The ONI and MID forerunners totally agreed with their superiors. After all, new officers of these strategic military intelligence organizations were cut out of the hide of the rest of the department. These plank owners—as sailors call the first crew of a ship—were reformers and organizational zealots who believed that the Navy and the Army had to learn more about the great and rising military powers of the world. And from a management standpoint, the military needed to figure out how to store this information. Their morale was high, as they had a purpose and a chance to start a fresh, new organization. They were the drivers of a new US Navy and Army that would perhaps one day rival European fleets and armies. The officers of these strategic military intelligence organizations thought of themselves as protectors of American society's economic and security interests.

Still, in the 1880s, American society barely knew ONI and MID existed. Except for some small newspaper clippings describing officers transferring to and from the fledgling intelligence offices, ONI and MID did not make the radar of American popular culture. Even the larger Navy and Army were inconsequential. The military was only needed for wars—the last one being fought fifteen years previously—and for coastal and frontier defense. If the populace felt protected from Native Americans and pirates, why worry about what Europeans were building an ocean away? Internationalist sentiment would not emerge until later decades. Though society was evolving, the American public remained largely rural. And as Gilded Age Americans were preoccupied with making money and coping with the effects this new industrial age, spies and secrets remained the Old World's milieu.

In 1879, war broke out between Chile and the alliance of Bolivia and Peru. The Department of the Navy sent observers to report on the naval engagements. The steel warships involved were impressive in the Americans' eyes; after all, they were built in Europe. One of the practical ways for the Americans to learn how the great powers build and operate their ships was to see them in action. What soon disturbed the naval observers was that these supposedly third-rate countries warships were superior to those of than the Americans. Even more worrisome, when one of the combatants threatened a US ship in one minor incident, the American captain had to back down for fear of being outgunned. Navy leaders in Washington realized that American naval affairs had to change.

The US Navy in the 1880s was a midsize world navy at best. It had forty to fifty ships manned by two thousand officers and seven to ten thousand enlisted men. Ships that were not in the yards were globally deployed to five forward squadrons: European, Asiatic, North Atlantic, South Atlantic, and Pacific.[4] But, then again, the Navy was not really needed abroad; its main missions were coastal defense and protecting American maritime commerce. Author Peter M. Swartz argued that the Navy did not have much to do at sea in the 1880s because of the relatively calm global environment, inward-facing state of the nation, and the tacit acceptance of inferior naval technology.[5] New naval leaders could fix the naval technology, though. It would take time, money, and motivation.

A small group of politicians, officers, and scholars became more vocal in the early 1880s. They argued that either the Navy would grow, or it would descend into uselessness. These "navalists" advocated adopting an expansionist policy on par with European powers and upstart Japan. The policy would require a strong fleet and perhaps overseas territory. The navalists were members of the East Coast social and economic elite and had a well-developed network of politicos, capitalists, academics, and the journalists in their ranks.[6] They shared a growing realization of the impotence of the Navy, especially when international tensions ratcheted up in South America and Europe: in the face of these developments, navalists felt action was needed as soon as possible.

The reconstruction of the Navy began in 1881 with President Chester A. Arthur's newly installed administration's advocacy of a naval rebirth. This renaissance would require managerial progress in the form of new, permanent agencies in the Department of the Navy's bureaucracy. Secretary of the Navy William H. Hunt led the charge for steel warships and an expansionist doctrine, creating an advisory board in July 1881 to establish shipbuilding requirements so that all the Navy's bureaus had a voice in the desired expansion. But the board could not properly advise Hunt without factual, objective information.[7]

Enter Lieutenant Theodorus Bailey Myers Mason. Fellow sailor Captain J. M. Ellicott called him "one of the most imperturbable officers I ever knew."[8] Calm but persistent, worldly, and motivated, Mason was the archetype of a navalist. Graduating in 1868 from the United States Naval Academy and by 1881 senior in his rank, Mason was one of Rear Admiral Christopher R. P. Rodgers's prize pupils. He carried on Rodgers' data collection initiatives in the Pacific Station even after the admiral returned for a second stint as superintendent of the Naval Academy. Mason had spent much of the 1870s researching the modernization of European navies. Both Mason and Rodgers were active members of the United States Naval Institute, founded in 1873, often contributing to its journal, the *Proceedings*. The institute was on the leading edge of the naval reformist movement, encouraging members to write about the profession's advancements in equipment, doctrine, and processes. By this point, Mason already had a few years of sea duty under his belt and knew the state of the fleet. He was also an instructor at the Naval Academy by 1877, as the Navy trusted him with teaching the next generation of officers the technical aspects of their new profession. Crucially, in that same year of 1877, Mason served in the Department of Ordnance and Gunnery, where he became quickly disgusted with the Navy's backwardness in ordnance and artillery drills. Based on his observation of European naval gun drills, he understood that Americans displayed none of their skill.[9] In 1878, he took a leave of absence in 1878 to travel to Europe and study naval progress. From this and other trips to Europe, as well as his observations during the War of the Pacific, he developed ideas for the future of naval intelligence, writing a report based on his travels titled "The War of the Pacific Coast South America between Chile and the Allied Republics of Peru and Bolivia, 1879–81." It is therefore not surprising that Mason seemed to be a perfect candidate to help Hunt and his board obtain information.

Upon returning from his overseas assignments, Mason sensed a new political atmosphere in Washington. Mason knew he was a qualified naval observer and understood where and how the foreign intelligence now desired by the state could be obtained. In late 1881, he politicked his views in the halls of the State, War, and Navy Building next to the White House to a receptive audience, advocating for naval attachés to embassies and legations abroad and the creation of a section for assembling, correlating, and distributing intelligence reports.[10] In so doing, he sought to assure himself a place within the managerial and bureaucratic awakening occurring throughout the military establishment.

Historians disagree as to whether his ideas fell on deaf ears or if he led the charge to get a strategic military intelligence organization started. According to naval historian Jeffrey M. Dorwart, in the months before ONI's founding, "Mason assumed that the U.S. Naval Institute was the most that could be expected in the direction of a bureau for naval information" and "no one bothered to consult Mason" on the specificities of such an organization.[11] Dorwart thought Mason was not aggressive in his lobbying in the winter months of 1881 to 1882. Historian Peter Karsten argues, on the other hand, that Mason and a group of young lieutenants—inspired by British views on naval intelligence—persuaded Commodore John G. Walker, chief of the Bureau of Navigation, to ask Hunt to create an intelligence office.[12] The truth is probably somewhere in the middle. Mason and his colleagues did lobby hard with the Bureau of Navigation but were not privy to the higher-level conversations occurring among Hunt, Walker, and other leaders about if and how a strategic military intelligence organization would come about. But in early spring he found out.

The reformers found their models for new organizations in the Department of the Navy from American businesses that responded to changing technologies, as the American public, especially capitalist tycoons, had by this point developed a new system for the collection and analysis of information: the managerial bureaucracy.[13] At the same time, the information explosion resulting from naval observers' trips to South America and Europe forced the Department of the Navy to build bureaucratic units within its organization to absorb the tremendous amount of data now coming into their offices. The result was the US Navy creating the first and oldest US government intelligence agency with headquarters in Washington, the Office of Naval Intelligence, established with General Order no. 292 on March 23, 1882.[14]

Though it was initially known as the Office of Intelligence, Navy leaders later called the new organization the "Office of Naval Intelligence," a name probably derived from the British Department of Naval Intelligence, though ONI was five years older than the follow-on British strategic military intelligence organization, the Naval Intelligence Division. It is debatable whether there were government intelligence organizations in the United States before 1882. The Secret Service of the Treasury

Department is older than ONI and had on occasion engaged in counterintelligence activities, but the mission of this organization was law enforcement and it only used spies for the wartime protection of the president.[15] ONI was a unique organization born out of this new bureaucratic age.

The Department of the Navy assigned ONI quarters in the State, War, and Navy Building. It had very modest accommodations, with a few tables, desk, chairs, and filing cabinets in one office. Secretary Hunt placed it under the Bureau of Navigation, a catch-all bureau that handled matters such as personnel. Hunt knew he would resign soon and realized that Walker, a navalist and supporter of Mason, would nurture the fledgling organization. He tied ONI to the Department of the Navy's library so that Mason and his office would have instant access to books and reports of foreign development already housed in the Bureau of Navigation.[16] For a couple of decades, the bureau would be a decent fit for an organization still trying to define itself.

The general order establishing the ONI was nonspecific about what type of information it was to gather or how its missions were to change during war and peace, so the potential targets of information collection were limitless. Given their limited resources, the officers of ONI set their own boundaries. One of the organization's first tasks was to centralize the information being collected independently by other Navy bureaus; they would need to gather that data for ONI files. This naturally became the first mission agreed upon by ONI's superiors and themselves: to become the depository and central management office for numerous reports regarding foreign navies. Specifically, the secretary of the Navy ordered ONI to gather reports on the great powers' technologies, strengths, and weaknesses, given that technology acquisition was especially important to the US Navy as it sought to build a new fleet.

By being vague about what intelligence to collect and for what customers, Hunt put ONI squarely into the strategic category. In the early 1880s, the Departments of the Navy and of War had just started to become familiar with the word "intelligence." The secretary of the Navy wanted general national-level naval information for national-level consumption. And because ONI was the only intelligence organization in the capital, the office naturally fit into the strategic realm. Initially, ONI did not have the capacity to reach out for or supply intelligence at the squadron- or individual ship-level. Indeed, the assignment to ONI to conduct national-level intelligence missions meant that the office would find it difficult to conduct operational missions for years to come.

General Order no. 292 established ONI with an ambiguous mission.

But the new office had neither a captain nor a crew. Certainly, the logical choice for ONI chief was Mason. He had many influential friends in Washington, including Rear Admiral C.R.P. Rodgers, Commodore Stephen B. Luce, and Walker. They probably persuaded the incoming secretary of the Navy, William H. Chandler, to meet with Mason in April 1882. After that meeting, the department cancelled Mason's orders for sea duty and assigned him to special duty in Washington.[17] The designation of "special duty" probably supposed that the Bureau of Navigation wanted to keep ONI's existence secret. This may also help to explain why American newspapers, and, by extension, the public had not heard of the strategic military intelligence organization in the spring of 1882.

Mason reported to the Bureau of Navigation in the second week of June. Incidentally, he also was assigned as naval aide to President Arthur. He was not unaccustomed to Executive Office exposure, as he had also served as an aide to President Ulysses S. Grant. Mason and his boss Walker got along extremely well, which was odd, given they had little in common at first glance. Still, despite their differences in age and careers and backgrounds, they established an immediate friendship and collaborated well. Dorwart describes the new partners as sharing the belief that they must promote naval progress and that an intelligence office would help sway public opinion in favor of this development.[18] They were both navalists and, more importantly for ONI, managers.

The new chief intelligence officer (CIO), as the Department of the Navy called Mason, had the daunting task of obtaining funding, refining his mission, and manning his workspace. The fact that the secretary of the Navy created ONI with a general order caused the first issue: because ONI was not established with legislative sanction, it did not have official funding. Second, the mission as defined by General Order no. 292 was unacceptable to Mason. Finally, Mason and Walker had to decide how to assign officers to ONI.

Complicating matters, the department would have to find inventive methods to move money from other bureaus and within the Bureau of Navigation to this new office. Walker and Mason devised inventive methods to transfer funds from other bureaus and from within the bureau to ONI, but they were more concerned about ensuring the new secretary of the Navy was on board with their ideas regarding ONI's mission. New Hampshire politician William H. Chandler replaced Hunt in April. He had no previous naval nor foreign affairs experience. Fortunately for Walker and Mason, Chandler immediately encouraged them to think of the new organization as important. On July 25, Chandler issued them a directive that came to serve as the Ten Commandments of naval intelligence.[19]

While the directive provided specific guidance, with a few updates and additions, it still defines an acceptable set of duties for naval intelligence today. The directive's numbered instructions laid out what type of products ONI would provide and much needed boundaries for data collection. Chandler recognized the need to have officers abroad to collect intelligence and in Washington to organize the data obtained. He introduced the idea of shipboard intelligence officers. The directive did not block other Navy bureaus from collecting information; they just had to ensure ONI received the information so that Mason's officers could collate it. Chandler also required ONI to keep tabs on the United States' own Navy, mercantile Marine, and coastal defenses. In today's US Navy parlance, this latter mission is "blue-force tracking," reserved for operators rather than intelligence professionals. Its inclusion among the ONI's responsibilities indicates how difficult it was to define strategic military intelligence organization missions.

New England politician Chandler was not steeped in naval lingo and technical skill; most likely Mason, with some advice from Walker, ghostwrote the July 25 directive, as evidenced by the fact that it articulated his philosophy of intelligence work and reflected his personal experiences.[20] For example, Chandler asked ONI to collect data on foreign naval facilities, a task Mason had performed in South America and Europe. Furthermore, for years, Mason had wanted official US Navy representatives in foreign countries as naval observers attached to American legations overseas, and Chandler directed Mason to organize an attaché corps to start work in Europe. The document solidified Mason as the unquestioned chief of naval intelligence.

The attaché system came to be in the summer and fall of 1882. In Europe, the idea of naval attachés in Europe was nothing new when ONI formed; on the Continent, the position emerged during the Franco-Prussian War in 1870 and expanded thereafter; by the time the United States sent naval representatives to Europe, every capital had at least thirty naval attachés. Although the US military often had sent representatives abroad, these officers had specific tasks with short mission timelines. In 1882, Mason proposed to keep permanent representatives in Europe with the main task of collecting information.

On July 3, 1882, Mason and Walker sent Lieutenant Commander

French E. Chadwick to London on special duty. Upon arrival, he operated without formal attachment to any American legation or official designation for three months. A go-getter, Chadwick was an intellectually gifted individual who specialized in languages, mathematics, and the physical sciences. Throughout his career, he demonstrated he was an "able researcher who possessed a keen eye for even the minutest detail," key traits for a naval attaché.[21] The West Virginian had previously gone to Europe under the auspices of the Bureau of Equipment to report on lifesaving and lighthouse systems, composing a subsequent study that would even be published as a Senate document. Chadwick's residency in Europe helped him establish foreign naval officers and officials as contacts. Notably, when Walker sent Chadwick in July, he emphasized that Chadwick represented and reported to the Department of the Navy, not to the State Department's ambassador in London.

Chadwick received official orders on October 28, 1882, making him the first formal naval attaché of the United States Navy. On the same day, he sent his first official report: "I have the honor to, from, and herewith for the Office of Naval Intelligence, notes upon the organization of the English Admiralty Office and upon the methods of promotion in the English Navy."[22] During his tenure, he would report on naval matters, the Coast Guard Service, the British Life Saving Service, the Lighthouse Service, Hospital Service, Meteorological Service, and the Board of Trade.

Such an array of collection priorities and organizations to monitor would be difficult for any officer to handle. For three years Chadwick was alone in Europe, traveling all over the continent. Inevitably, he faced many obstacles. Historian Brian T. Crumley notes that while Chadwick had only "rudimentary instructions," the Navy expected him to be a civil engineer, a diplomat, and a data collector—unaccustomed missions for a man used to giving orders.[23]

Chadwick was more than up to the task, setting the standard for future attachés and proving that the permanency of a naval attaché was critical to the core mission of collecting data. He sent daily dispatches back to Washington that filled numerous copybooks. Even more so than the information streaming in from ships abroad or bureaus in Washington, Chadwick's reports contained valuable technical data on the navies of Europe, information that the US Navy used to construct its own ships. Attaché and Director of Naval Intelligence Alfred P. Niblack later said, "It must be clearly understood that the Office of Naval Intelligence, from its inception, has been based on the proposition of having naval attachés abroad to collect information."[24] Chadwick admirably fulfilled this function.

Of note, the Department of the Navy ordered Lieutenant Junior Grade George Foulk to Korea as a naval attaché on November 13, 1883. The department gave him the title "attaché;" and though the Navy expected him to work through ONI, he did not perform the functions expected of that title. In 1883, Korea did not have a navy, so Foulk essentially was a chargé d'affaires, a diplomatic official who temporarily takes the place of an ambassador (whereas an attaché is a person on the staff of an ambassador, typically with a specialized area of responsibility). Meanwhile, the capital city's own *Evening Star* defended the naval attaché system from the criticism that it was dedicated only to maintaining diplomatic decorum.[25] Even early on, the US armed forces attaché corps was stigmatized in the public eye as officers who attended more galas than they produced reports on European military developments. Nonetheless, despite this reputation, naval attaché reporting would be the chief source of ONI's data through the end of World War II.

Now that the data was coming in, Mason assembled his staff and set up shipboard intelligence officers to it. Desiring navalists like himself to staff the office, Mason sought both go-getters and whatever officers the Bureau of Navigation could scrounge up. These eager young officers would later become prominent senior leaders in the Department of the Navy. The Navy did not issue public orders to the drafted officers; Walker told them just to show up at ONI. "I was taken out of the Hydrographic Office and simply told to report to Mason," Rear Admiral A. G. Berry later recalled.[26] Mason's other new assistants were M. Fisher Wright, Templin Potts, and Charles Rogers. When Berry reported to ONI in June 1882, Mason tasked him with analyzing foreign navies. Wright arrived two weeks later and was assigned translating foreign-language material. When Rogers joined the office in September, he began collating data on docking facilities in foreign ports. For his part, upon his arrival in February 1883, Potts helped Berry organize data on foreign navies.[27] To fill other staffing needs, Walker detailed clerks from other department bureaus or paid for their services via congressional appropriations under the "Increase of the Navy" fund.

ONI manned its office by the spring of 1883. The strategic military intelligence organization's first customers were the secretary of the Navy and the technical bureaus. Mason organized ONI along functional lines rather than geographic to ensure the bureaus received data in a timely manner. The data ONI distributed to their patrons coincided with Secretary

Chandler's directive: facilities of foreign navies, installations on foreign coasts and in foreign ports for the landing of men and supplies, cargo handling facilities in foreign ports, the capabilities and routes of foreign merchant steamers, and information on the US Navy.

ONI built routines for managing data. After copying a card catalogue system from the State Department, the ONI staff translated and compiled foreign publications from the Navy Library. Berry described the ordeal: "When I had to take up a subject in German, I did not know one letter from another, or a single word in that language, but by beginning with an English account, followed by the French, Italian, and Spanish and a big dictionary, I was able in about a year to make a fair translation from the German but could not pronounce a word."[28] They catalogued all military information, even data not related to naval matters. But this proved to be too tedious, especially in an organization with one room; once the Army leadership established MID, the ONI handed off military information to the Department of War.[29] The work was monotonous but necessary to building a centralized repository of a great mass of material.

Information came piling in, as data streamed into the Bureau of Navigation from shipboard officers. For instance, Walker thanked eager navalist Washington Chambers for his contribution: "I have the honor to acknowledge the receipt of your very interesting report and excellent drawings of the Alerte, Yarrow type, torpedo-boat."[30] Mason appreciated an energetic Albert Gleaves's information as well: "I have the honor to acknowledge the receipt of your excellent and very valuable report on 'Result of English Bombardment of Fort Mex, Alexandria, and Preparations for Flooding Lake Mareotis.'"[31] Chamber's and Gleaves's reports were only two of many from young officers in the fleet.

Mason was so impressed with Chambers's technical reports that he attempted to recruit the ensign.[32] Chambers was a studious shipboard intelligence officers who religiously filed intelligence reports, and Mason had taken a keen interest. On February 9, 1883, he replied to one of Chambers's reports:

> If you continue in the road which you are now travelling you will never have any trouble about duty. It has been my experience that men who apply themselves and make themselves usefull [sic] outside of their mere routine duties never need good places. The lazy fellows call such men coburgers and other such names. When you come to Washington, I shall be glad to see you and shall also be glad to receive any voluntary contributions which you may have from time to time for our work.[33]

Chambers eventually joined ONI in 1883. Knowing talent when he saw it, Mason leaned heavily on other talent in the office, such as his assistant Charles Rogers, to help promote ONI. Mason and Rogers knew each other well even before Rogers joined ONI. Rogers, a former student of Mason's at the naval academy, took on his new duties with enthusiasm. Among his first tasks was penning a monograph on recent British naval operations in Egypt and collating information on coastal defenses. Mason saw in Rogers's writing evidence of a talent that he could not let go to waste. Although protected by Walker, the CIO was frustrated by the indifferent attitude of the Department of the Navy to his office, brought on by the secrecy surrounding the Bureau of Navigation's new intelligence agency as well as the usual bureaucratic infighting. As such, he persuaded Rogers to publish an essay on naval intelligence for *Proceedings* to promote the fledgling office.[34] Rogers did so and the resulting paper, published in spring 1883, reiterated the July directive and laid out the purpose of ONI.

Rogers's "Naval Intelligence" article is a thirty-four-page treatise on the value of information to the Navy and the nation. He explained that the word "intelligence" does not carry the sense of immediate understanding, rather, it implies information.[35] Rogers also summed up ONI's designated mission: "Firstly, the collection, sifting, and arrangement of all information required by governments and naval authorities to enable them to take such measures in peace as will insure the rapid commencement and vigorous prosecution of any war, whether at home or abroad. Secondly, the diffusion of necessary or useful naval information through the navy and the country during peace or war."[36] He repeatedly mentioned that every naval officer needs to make it his business to study the science of naval warfare and that ONI could help him achieve that end. In one section of the paper, he mocked the Department of War for not having an intelligence branch, noting that General Upton had prescribed it in the late 1870s but the department had not acted upon the suggestion.[37] Rogers later expanded upon the directives of Secretary Chandler by outlining twenty-one duties that ONI must perform.[38] He also tried to alleviate concerns about ONI's political standing: "As to the administrative sphere of an Intelligence Department, its very essence is that it is in no sense executive. It robs no one of power; it encroaches upon no one's authority; it must ask for information from all and be ready to give information in return. It is a worker for all departments, all bureaus, and all officers of the Government, whether civil or military."[39]

In addition to naval intelligence, Rogers's article touched upon the broader duties of the Department of the Navy. For example, he referred extensively to general staffs and war planning, something practiced in European military institutions but had not yet translated well on American shores. Rogers believed that ONI was an important step to the creation of a general staff for the US Navy. The strategic military intelligence office would be that vital cog in the staff to provide information to planners. Naval commanders in turn could coordinate naval operations with strategic plans already on the shelf provided by the managers. It was as if "Naval Intelligence" had been written by Walker and Mason themselves.

The strategic military intelligence organization developed a battle rhythm as its staff received, collated, and reported information provided by the primary sources of intelligence: the naval attaché and the shipboard intelligence officer. In March 1885, ONI received its first correspondence from a young William S. Sims on sea duty. Walker appreciated the shipboard intelligence officer's information: "I have the honor to acknowledge the receipt of your much valuable report on the Panama Canal. . . . Please inform the Bureau from source the figures showing [how] the financial status were obtained. The information contained will be utilized by the Department. Your communication has been placed on file in the Office of Naval Intelligence where you can have access to it."[40] Sims's reporting was his first known communications with ONI, in a relationship that would last almost forty years. There is no denying the talent Mason recruited heavily from the young navalist officer pool.

Among those granted access to the accumulating collection of information was the US Naval Institute, which had been instrumental in getting ONI established. The institute flourished for years before naval leaders established ONI. Though only a semiofficial organization, it was home to the growing number of navalists in the Navy's ranks. The ONI and the Naval Institute quickly developed a symbiotic relationship that resulted in many *Proceedings* articles and ONI publications. Mason and Luce (a prolific writer with the institute) had a long-standing friendship, including jointly contributing articles to the early editions of *Proceedings*. Admirers of Luce and Mason also followed suit in publishing works in the Naval Institute's journal, a series of authors that included Chadwick, Richard Wainwright, Seaton Schroeder, William H. Beehler, W. W. Kimball, and Rogers. All these firm advocates of modernization were associated with ONI. The *Proceedings* was akin to blogs of the twenty-first century. Youthful lieutenants provided a fair share of the articles in the journal, mostly on emerging American naval power and coming naval technologies. For instance, in 1884 the Naval Institute awarded young officer Chambers the Best Essay prize.[41]

The institute and its periodical received a boost from the Chandler directive: naval officers came to rely on ONI for the data they included in their *Proceedings* articles.[42] ONI published a monthly bulletin, which helped lieutenants research articles for the Naval Institute. The organization also produced a series of reports, called *Information from Abroad*, centering on foreign navies and their recent operations. ONI's analysis assisted in some of the young officers' prize-winning essays, though Mason and his staff no doubt restricted access to the most sensitive information to senior Department of the Navy officers.[43]

ONI engaged in prolific writing and analysis through the US Naval Institute and in coordination with the institution it helped create: the Naval War College (NWC). Mason's views of war planning and the science of naval warfare dovetailed nicely with Luce's vision of a new navy. Luce believed that while ONI was the first step to the reality of a naval general staff, another preliminary move had to be the creation of a naval war college. The "visionary, prolific, and persuasive leader and writer" Luce reasoned that without an educated officer cadre, the Navy could never progress to great power status.[44] He expressed his ideas in an 1883 essay "War Schools," one of six articles he would write for *Proceedings* in the 1880s. In it he argued that ONI's potential success paved the way for a war college.[45]

ONI success translated into more political power for navalists within the department to push their agenda. For Luce, it meant the realization of the creation of a naval war college, as Commodore Walker instructed Luce to head up a board to make recommendations for such an institution, the first step in the establishment of the NWC in Newport, Rhode Island.[46] Luce and his fellow advocates believed that only good outcomes could come of this venture. For example, prominent naval theorist Alfred Thayer Mahan hailed the benefits of such an institution.[47] And, once the NWC began classes, ONI produced intelligence to provide factual conditions and realism to coursework. NWC students, in turn, considered solutions to strategic problems. This was the embryonic stage of the war planning mission. By providing lists of a nation's naval assets, describing port facilities and harbors, and giving the capabilities of foreign warships—known in more recent military circles as "preparing the battlespace"—ONI conducts this common function in even present-day war planning. Furthermore, the War College receiving intelligence to study war problems and create higher strategy remains essential to war planning.

As already suggested, Congress and society were not initially aware of ONI's existence. In 1882, the public barely observed that the Navy created a strategic military intelligence organization. On page 2 of a six-column inch review of Army-Navy news, the March 26 edition of the *New York Times* reported in the fourth paragraph that Hunt issued a general order for a naval intelligence organization and repeated his instructions verbatim.[48] There were otherwise no ripples of interest from news sources across the country. Intelligence and information gathering were a foreign concept to Americans outside of government circles. Why would a freedom-loving, democratic country need to spy on other countries?

Yet, as the ONI's successes mounted between 1882 and 1885, Congress and the media outlets took note. In his annual message to Congress, Secretary Chandler requested and received funds for his new organization in 1884, although a legislative body officially had not sanctioned ONI.[49] The *North American*, a Philadelphia newspaper, reported that it was a beneficial office in Washington: "One of the respects in which President Arthur's administration will prove to have been of permanent value to the country is in the establishment of the naval intelligence office. . . . This bureau has been in operation only two years, but its value, even in times of peace, has proved to be very great."[50] It was the first kudo ONI received from the media in its short history.

Yet, not everything was smooth sailing. The Bureau of Navigation quickly realized the need to protect the new organization from department predators. Mason ran into resistance from other Navy bureaus, whose personnel did not want to provide information they had gathered from abroad. For instance, in 1882 Chandler was forced to issue a circular to all bureau chiefs mandating the sharing of information freely among themselves. Mason would have to navigate the politics of the Department of the Navy in search of defining information collection as a mission, an issue he dealt with until his tenure ended in 1885.

ONI required some protection from these higher echelons, namely, the chiefs and senior officers from other bureaus who feared that ONI would trample on their jurisdictions. Who were these upstart junior officers telling old stalwarts of the establishment what they needed from their bureaus? Indeed, some of the information the Navy tasked ONI to centralize had to be gathered from these "independent and jealous bureaus." As Berry recalled, "Strange to relate, the idea, like nearly all new ideas, met with great opposition."[51] In short, Mason needed assistance in getting the rest of the department on board with ONI's mission.

In these circumstances, Walker stepped in as the previous secretary, Hunt, intended and protected ONI. Berry called him "a man of very strong character. . . . [and] a bad one to oppose."[52] Rear Admiral Gleaves, a shipmate who knew Walker firsthand, said in 1925 that he was "politically the most powerful man in the Service; he was one of the ablest administrators and executives the Department had ever had."[53] Walker had much invested in ONI politically and personally. Mason was a friend of his, and Walker defended the idea of an intelligence organization to higher echelons. Ultimately, Walker promoted ONI as beacon of the US Navy's rebirth. In the department, he used his weight to force other bureau chiefs to acknowledge ONI's bureaucratic authority. In the fleet, Walker directed commanding officers to appoint a crewmember to fill out blank intelligence forms of their observations while at sea starting in 1882. Despite captains' complaints that they had other pressing duties, most commanding officers complied so as not to cross Commodore Walker. Other bureaus' resistance to the ONI dwindled as Walker defended the organization's mission. Also, as ONI's finished products began circulating, bureau chiefs likely realized the information could provide value to their own planning and operations. But this did not mean ONI could ease up on promoting itself.

Mason rotated to another assignment in 1885 and handed over his CIO duties that April. Mason's legacy as a pioneer and innovator stemmed from his tenure at ONI, and he perhaps does not get as much credit as he deserves for the growth of the US Navy. During his term he designated the nation's first naval attachés, created a firmly grounded bureaucratic institution, and established long-lasting missions based on his own philosophy about strategic military intelligence. His accomplishments are that much more impressive considering ONI was treated like an unwanted stepchild by the bureau for much of his tour of duty. Future chief intelligence officers and innovators had nothing but praise for Mason and the institution he bequeathed to them. Admiral Seaton Schroeder would later note that his naval academy classmate Mason had "persevering initiative . . . to whom honor is due for his vision."[54] For his part, Rear Admiral Richard Wainwright argued, "Mason laid the foundations of the Office broadly and firmly. It immediately became of value to the service and has grown in value and importance with the growth of the Navy."[55] Some observers went as far as to state that Mason should be recognized as a founding father of the new navy alongside giants such as Luce and Mahan.[56] Indeed, Mason's influence was felt on the other side of the State, War, and Navy Building, where the Army had heard the buzz of success of the first permanent intelligence institution in the United States and considered copying ONI.

The Department of War had contemplated establishing organizations like those being established the Navy. In addition, as industrialization had ushered in professionalization and new bureaucratic institutions into American society, the Army responded similarly to the new age. At Fort Leavenworth in 1881, the Army set up its first of many professional schools. Army leaders often considered organizing information in a systematic fashion. For example, Upton and Sherman discussed the possibility of engaging in a war overseas. They and others realized how antiquated the Department of War organization and equipment was when Army observers traveled to Europe to witness the best war staffs, weapons, and technology in the world. The Army's inadequacy inspired a greater interest in foreign military developments and the desire to establish an agency to effectively manage the information observers gathered overseas.[57]

Significantly, Army leaders considered the long-term outlook. Foreign wars were a growing possibility as the frontier closed and American overseas interests expanded. The Franco-Prussian War brought to the forefront how valuable a well-organized general staff could be. Unsurprisingly, the Army's desire for a European-style general staff entailed accommodating the indispensable task of managing intelligence.[58] The creation of ONI accelerated Army leaders' decision to explore forming an information bureau in Washington.

The organizational foundations of Military Intelligence Division were laid in 1885, more than three years after the establishment of ONI. Indeed, MID's beginnings were a much more muddled affair than its Navy counterpart. On October 6, 1885, the *Evening Star* wrote:

> The statements of the formation of a bureau of intelligence in the War department, similar to the office of naval intelligence, are somewhat premature. Adjutant General (Richard C.) Drum is in favor of such a bureau, but its immediate organization is not thought of. The plan is, in receiving clerks in the department, to secure those who would be qualified for duties in a bureau of intelligence, as a foundation, and

gradually work to the desired end if everything proves favorable. With this object in view the War department recently applied to the civil service commission for two clerks of class one, who, in addition to passing the regular civil service examination, shall have a knowledge of nautical affairs. These clerks are to be assigned to the reservation division of the adjutant general's office and will form a nucleus for the intelligence bureau when the suitable time arrives for its formation.[59]

The newspaper was wrong; the statements were not "premature." Adjutant General Drum created a strategic military intelligence organization in October 1885. The reason for the confusion was MID's informal beginning, as it was generated not by general order or congressional act but on a whim from Brigadier General Drum.

The much-debated question of the founding of MID among historians and intelligence professionals focuses on the actual events leading to Drum's decision.[60] This is inconsequential. What is more important is that Army leaders planned MID since the late 1870s. Its establishment was part of American society's response to industrialization, something that European armies—challenged with the same issue—grappled with for decades. In America, this development was a natural progression spurred by theorists such as Upton. MID's formation signaled organizational innovation, as the organization provided information that would help transform the Army into a more professional force. MID was an "intellectual revival within the army inspired by European changes in military tactics and organization" but driven by changes in American society during the Gilded Age.[61] In short, the creation of a military intelligence bureau followed the evolution of the Army's bureaucratic and managerial revolution started by Upton in an era where American businesses were driving innovations in all office spaces.

The date of the MID's formation is not certain, but it most likely happened early to mid-October 1885. The word "information" was selected versus "intelligence" in the title, because in the 1880s "intelligence" meant the daily news, not something an Army organization would want to associate with the collecting, storing, and reporting of data.[62] Secretary William C. Endicott allowed Adjutant General Drum to house Drum's pet project in his office and gave him considerable flexibility in how to organize MID. In terms of specific organization, he buried it within the Military Reservation Division, Miscellaneous Branch. At first glance this would seem an odd fit. However, the division was responsible for all Army-owned lands, and Drum tasked MID to make maps not only of foreign countries but of the Army's land holdings. Many of MID's proponents, most of whom were in favor of European-styled Army renaissance, recognized cartography as a critical component of intelligence.[63] Maps in the 1880s contained more tightly held secrets than even a generation later, when businesses sold atlases commercially. In addition to information centralization and cartography, Drum assigned militia tracking to MID, indicating the wide range of MID's information-gathering boundaries. Just like ONI and its blue-force tracking responsibilities, MID initially had confusing missions.

Adjutant General Drum carved the MID out of his own office and manned it with somewhat qualified personnel. He delegated the details of its organization to Major William J. Volkmar, an Army observer recently returned from France. Volkmar fit the profile of Upton, an officer who witnessed European military maneuvers, perceived the Army's own weaknesses, and sought to correct them. Drum asked Volkmar for recommendations concerning MID, many of which would not receive formal action for another four years. For instance, Volkmar requested a captain from the Ordnance Department, a captain or first lieutenant each from the Engineers, Artillery, Cavalry, and Infantry, and a second lieutenant from the Signal Corps, but was rejected.[64] MID had only one or two officers and a few clerks detailed to it for the next five years. Drum and Volkmar ordered this skeleton crew to work gathering military items from all available sources, imitating the older strategic military intelligence agency in the building.

The relationship between ONI and MID started awkwardly. They had the same missions of collecting, compiling, and reporting information. MID admired ONI's organization by card index and copied it, just as they imitated other aspects of the office. But because ONI was MID's senior by three years and had more guidance and direction, Drum's personnel could not help but feel inferior. General orders and congressional acts making MID more official in the next fifteen years would alleviate some of the officers' sense of MID's inadequacy, but ONI's analytical capabilities were more proven through the next decade.

Rivalry aside, ONI's and MID's genesis came in an era where bureaucrats had to organize and manage traditional establishments more effectively, in order to keep up with increased data flowing into office spaces. The Navy and Army's answer was the rise of the professional intelligence officer to centralize the information with new strategic military intelligence organizations. By later standards, ONI and MID were extremely small and had simple missions.⁶⁵ Support for them from the Navy bureaus was tepid at best. And while ONI navigated a Department of the Navy still adapting to change, Army leaders hid MID within the Adjutant General's Office without directives. Americans had a vague idea that the Navy and Army had emerging intelligence organizations, but the significance was lost on the average rural person challenged with the consequences of the Industrial Revolution within the United States. The public thought of little more than what occurred in the acres around them; the concept of internationalism was still quite foreign. Something would have to change within these strategic military intelligence organizations, their leaders reasoned, to gain more recognition for their offices, when perhaps transformation could occur as per Rogers's essay on naval intelligence.⁶⁶ MID would take a different path than ONI in the next ten years, merely by needing to seek approval of its existence. ONI, through publications and policy support, experimented with public relations and war planning. Whichever road they traveled, the creation of strategic military intelligence organizations is an ideal example of Millis's managerial revolution.

Chapter Two
1885–1895:
Growing Pains of ONI and MID

The final decades of the nineteenth century saw a flare-up of the chronic struggle in American history between the Jeffersonian ethos and its Hamiltonian counterpart. Jefferson's vision for America was of an agrarian nation composed of white yeoman farmers who owned their own land. He viewed European societies as unethical, controlled by capitalism and afflicted by problems associated with urban settings, such as squalor and poverty. Jeffersonian democratic principles, such as equality for whites and frontier exploration, had dominated most of the century prior to industrialization. Once the latter occurred, the Jeffersonian backlash was soon to follow in the form of Populism, which historian Richard Hofstadter has described as an agrarian movement of the 1890s characterized by "provincial resentments, popular and 'democratic' rebelliousness and suspiciousness, and nativism."[1] In contrast, in his great disagreement with Jefferson, Hamilton predicted the United States emerging as an economic and military power that would surpass Great Britain and the other European powers. He tried to convince his fellow Americans to think of themselves as Americans, not citizens of a particular state. In the Gilded Age, Hamilton was revered by presidents and industrialists alike, as the rebellious elite of the 1880s and 1890s "intended to replace the Jeffersonian democracy with a more Hamiltonian republic," crafting an American nation where imperialism and free trade replaced isolation and economic stagnation as the dominant modus operandi.[2]

The battle for the philosophical direction of the country played out in the military as well. In the Navy, the traditional establishment favoring a coastal defense faced a challenge from outward-looking reformists. These navalists, such as Alfred Thayer Mahan and Theodore Roosevelt, took up Hamilton's banner and argued the nation's destiny was to be a great economic and military power. To rival Europe, America must have a blue-water navy capable of taking on top-of-the-line foreign warships. Because Mahan saw sea power as the tool guaranteed to make the nation a great power, these naval elitists viewed it as their particular duty to protect US business interests abroad.[3]

Progressive, outward-looking Army thinkers, such as General Emory Upton, faced more of a struggle to focus the Army establishment on overseas matters. Reorienting an ineffectual organization that no longer had Native Americans to fight into a force capable of waging a major war against a great power seemed to be a long-term Hamiltonian project and contrary to long-standing tradition.[4] Besides, why plan for a grandiose future against potential enemies overseas when Canada and Mexico were the historical rivals on America's doorstep? Nonetheless, there existed many Upton acolytes in the 1880s and early 1890s seeking to build a more professional army in order to be ready if and when Old World rivalries ensnared the United States.

In this contest for the direction of America, the Office of Naval Intelligence (ONI) and Military Information Division (MID) had to decide whether they would follow the Hamiltonian navalists and reformists' lead. The two intelligence organizations found their missions defined by the transitional era in which they existed. Between 1885 and 1895, the Atlantic Ocean still insulated Americans from fears of overseas powers, and the public believed the Native American problem was evaporating. Americans, although proud of the military's accomplishments and sacrifices and celebrating its revival, still pondered the Navy and Army's relevancy. Newspapers and magazines of the era barely mentioned the mysterious ONI and MID and even then, only in relation to how much the military was improving compared to European powers. Many Americans did not know what military intelligence was, much less understand the craft of intelligence.

Meanwhile, government officials used ONI and MID for their own political purposes. The complexity of government increased, and influential policymakers were savvy enough to use the new offices to control that complexity. At the same time, Presidents Grover Cleveland and Benjamin Harrison thought of them as miniscule offices in the military establishment and merely mentioned them in passing to support their pro-military agendas in addresses to Congress. The legislative bodies referenced ONI and MID in debates, particularly when fact-checking Army and Navy requests for appropriations in obtaining military information abroad, while the secretaries of Navy and War and senior military leaders below them still viewed ONI and MID as central information depositories. For their part, however, the Department of the Navy began to use ONI for public relations and war planning, and the Army wanted MID to continue to grow and for its staff to hone their craft as information holders and map makers. These goals were complicated by the fact that the strategic military intelligence organizations' supervisors saddled them with tasks to provide information to superiors and conduct public relations support to customers beyond the Executive Branch to support their policies.

ONI and MID leaders were eager to oblige as the managerial revolution raged on in receptive corners of the Departments of War and of the Navy. Intelligence officers were eager to help sharpen the swords of the republic that were the Navy and the Army. Historian Peter Karsten described ONI officers as "Young Turks" and part of the "naval aristocracy."[5] The office's morale was high (at least through the 1880s) because its staff knew they were helping build a great power. Meanwhile, MID was still catching up to its rival in the Department of the Navy and accordingly the mission simple. Its staff too had elitists and reformists in its ranks, but Army intelligence officers first needed recognition and guidance from the slowly modernizing, larger institution. The growing years of ONI and MID between 1885 and 1895 showcased their different levels of development but not differences in where they envisioned their role in the armed forces and in American society. Both offices willingly served strategic overlords leaning toward Hamiltonian policies.

Between 1885 and 1895, US strategic military intelligence organizations struggled to grow in structure to take on their missions. Like the adolescent stage of development experienced by the American nation, Navy and Army intelligence professionals grappled with how to grow up and centralize intelligence within the military establishment. It was imperative for them to figure out their organizational problems, in order to understand which missions they needed to focus on.

ONI organizational woes developed as talent in the office dwindled. But in 1885, prospects for a healthy staff and competent leadership were promising. In 1885, after CIO Lieutenant Theodorus B. M. Mason departed ONI for follow-on Navy duty, he bumped into his former student, Ensign John. M. Ellicott, and other friends in Panama. One officer asked him, "How is O.N.I. getting along?" Mason laughed and said, "They started me with a cubby hole for an office, a part time stenographer, and a stack of filing cases, but we gradually gained space and personnel. Raymond Rodgers relieved me and he is a go-getter, so I'm sure the Office has come to stay."[6]

Thus, a new era began as Lieutenant Rodgers became CIO on April 2, 1885. Rodgers had worked with Mason in Europe and during the War of the Pacific. In 1885, he was fresh from sea duty on the USS *Tennessee* as a shipboard intelligence officer, akin to Washington I. Chambers and

William S. Sims. In 1870, Rodgers had collected information on foreign navies under the watchful eye of his father, Rear Admiral Christopher P. R. Rodgers, while stationed in Europe. The Rodgerses belonged to one of the oldest cliques in the naval establishment, the Rodgers-Perry clan. Yet, Raymond Rodgers's actions as CIO over his four-year tenure indicated he was more of a navalist than reactionary traditionalist. He was the first naval officer to make a career of naval intelligence, serving as CIO from 1885 to 1889, as a naval attaché from 1892 to 1897, and as CIO again from 1906 to 1909. According to historian Jeffrey Dorwart, Rodgers was not as articulate or dynamic as Mason, but fellow officers respected him for his sincerity. Personnel flocked to ONI because he encouraged them to write to the US Naval Institute's *Proceedings* and their official products and unofficial essays circulated throughout the department.[7]

Ideally Mason and Rodgers wanted volunteers to join ONI but, given the choice between career-enhancing sea duty and a desk job in a fledgling office, volunteers were hard to come by. This was part of the emerging line-staff controversy in both the Navy and Army that the departments did not resolve until the middle of the twentieth century. The CIOs had to recruit by invitation or impressment. Rodgers's first conscripts were Lieutenants John Charles Colwell, Benjamin H. Buckingham, and Seaton Schroeder. They were all talented but quirky enough to keep them from more coveted jobs in Washington.[8] Schroeder became Rodgers's main lieutenant and publicity man. Ultimately, this articulate, assertive, and skilled staff was much improved from what Mason had recruited three years earlier.

ONI's accomplishments under Rodgers were impressive, as the CIO and his men reached out to scientists concerning the use of cameras for surveillance and reconnaissance; indeed, imagery production and analysis have been a part of ONI's functions ever since. The office also improved methods of data collection. According to Schroeder, "each officer in that office benefited by having to prepare an article each year, for publication in the Annual, bearing upon some important subject connected with naval development or some branch of professional knowledge; the study and research necessary with that in view could not fail to be beneficial."[9] Rodgers's team also helped develop a new Navy code for telegraphic messages between Washington and far-flung naval units. Higher echelons of the US government could not help but notice.

Tour rotations brought ONI capable officers. Navy scuttlebutt swirled in the fleet that ONI was conducting some transformational duties for the naval branch. The office's standing rose still more when, in September

1889, Bureau of Navigation Chief Comm. John G. Walker assigned to the bureau perhaps the most notable navalist of all: Captain Alfred Thayer Mahan, future author of *The Influence of Sea Power Upon History, 1660–1783*. Mahan was to serve as an advisor to Secretary of the Navy Benjamin F. Tracy and to prepare war plans. He had access to ONI files and consulted with the CIO often. Much of Mahan's correspondence while he was at the bureau was on ONI stationary.[10]

More personnel changes occurred in 1889. Walker left in October of that year, as probably the strongest advocate for the office among high-level officers. In December, Lieutenant William H. Emory relieved Lieutenant Commander French E. Chadwick as naval attaché in London.[11] A new CIO, Commander. Charles H. Davis, took over for Rodgers. Davis's higher rank spoke to the importance ONI's superiors placed upon its current and future missions: the CIO billet soared two ranks between Rodgers and Davis. Interestingly, the latter was the son of Admiral Charles H. Davis, a member of the traditional naval cabal. The senior Davis had a personal friendship with Secretary of the Navy Gideon Welles and his son wanted the same with Secretary Tracy. Complicating matters, while reformers sought for the new CIO to conduct public relations for a blue-water navy, Davis did not have the faculties for tact and inspiration necessary for such a task.[12] He demonstrated irritation at troublesome details such as messy attaché reports and illustrations. He guarded his Navy Secret Codebook and intelligence reports religiously. And he did not get along with MID. He had a tumultuous relationship with Assistant Secretary of the Navy James R. Soley, whom Secretary Tracy designated to watch over ONI once Walker was gone.

In these circumstances, ONI's prestige had plummeted by 1892, as talent drained from the office. In addition, the office's influence on Secretary Tracy abated. At the basic level, as queries about foreign naval technology innovation began to evaporate, so did the justification for an organization designed to conduct data management on this issue.[13] New missions—war planning and public relations—were not enough to justify appropriations to the small office in the Department of the Navy. Davis left ONI August 31, 1892.

After a disastrous tenure by the last CIO, the office staffers hoped that the selection of Commander Chadwick as the new chief would reinvigorate ONI. He had the credentials—maybe more than anyone else in the Navy. His résumé included holding the first attaché position in American history, a reputation for attention to detail, and having the respect of Tracy and Soley. It was therefore unsurprising that they picked him to change the morale of ONI. Leadership also thought that he could get his staff to perform effective public relations. For instance, in early 1893, Tracy asked ONI "to prepare a paper demonstrating how the Harrison administration had constructed a Navy that could compete with those of Germany, Italy, and Britain."[14]

There were signs that ONI's morale was rebounding. Early in 1893, President Harrison ordered the office through the chain of command to promote the value of the Hawaiian Islands to the American public. He needed ONI to provide evidence for him in his case with Congress for annexation.[15] In a further sign of reputational refurbishment, in January Chadwick welcomed to his staff First Lieutenant Lincoln Karmany, the first of many Marine Corps officers who would join ONI over its history. The Marine Corps did not have a strategic military intelligence organization until 1920, and even then, the Intelligence Section was not important. In general, Chadwick showed more interest in his staff's training than his predecessor; for example, he detailed them to the field to witness US Navy exercises and operations. The office also helped the department plan the 1893 International Naval Rendezvous and Review. In the end, the needs of the Navy, specifically for his talents and experience, required Chadwick to become the Bureau of Equipment chief in June 1893. It did not help that Tracy and Soley probably thought Chadwick's abilities were wasted on a flagging ONI.

By the mid-1890s, ONI leaders had accepted war planning and promoting the Navy as missions of necessity, with the hope ONI would be an important part of a future Navy general staff. Although the office dutifully followed through with information collection and reporting, the department looked for more from naval intelligence so that the secretary could both promote the Navy and justify funding ONI. The new CIO, Lieutenant Frederic Singer, past office leaders, and his current staff slowly realized that the organization must get better at preparing for future wars through prepping contingency campaign plans. Future funding and fame depended on war planning duties and public relations.

In the fall of 1885, as ONI was branching out, MID barely existed. There was no staff and little organization. MID's first action was to mirror ONI's card filing system, which Adjutant General Richard C. Drum had observed in the Navy's intelligence office. Building a database to answer any senior Army leader's questions was a priority for Major William J. Volkmar. MID leadership also emphasized topography as an important mission. Since colonial times the northern frontier was fraught with disputes over fishing rights, conflicts over boundary lines, and the occasional British intrigue. The southern border had a history of war, banditry, and chaos. Volkmar was a solid officer, but he had little authority, no guidance, and only one clerk. It was as if Drum forgot he had created MID and did not man it, a situation compounded as the department slowly pushed Volkmar out as head of MID.

On April 3, 1886, Drum detailed Captain Daniel M. Taylor for duty to the Adjutant General's Office, and he became the de facto division chief of MID.[16] Taylor had a topography skillset and an extensive background with the northern frontier.[17] Together, Drum and Taylor established centralization and efficiency as MID's focus if it wanted to meet the Department of War's demands for intelligence, especially with such little manpower. Taylor continued the card catalogue system brought to MID from ONI the previous fall. But his next task was to streamline the information flow as data came to the office.

For three years the division only had an officer-in-charge, a civilian chief, two civilian assistants, and a messenger. It occupied one room within the State, War, and Navy Building, which was not nearly enough room for even MID's miniscule staff and file cabinets. Eventually, General Drum realized that to accommodate MID's management of future military attaché corps and the data they could produce, he had to expand the office physically and with more personnel. He launched MID's transformation by promoting the division within the department so that it was not buried beneath other branches or divisions, assigning more personnel to it, and redefining its office space.[18] This order was more of a reaffirmation of MID's value rather than the creation of the organization, since Drum had hidden MID within layers of bureaucracy. He let other parts of the department know it existed and was meant to take on the information collection role in step with the new attachés.

As ONI's influence declined within the Department of the Navy, MID's influence was on the rise in the Department of War between 1889 and 1892. The division set about its mission to collect data, index it, and answer requests for information from its customers. By 1892, officers and clerks had carded four thousand items of military interest even when as the office was still barely known outside of the department.[19] Within the State, War, and Navy Building its status swelled, so much so that control of MID became the subject of a bureaucratic battle.

Brigadier General Adolphus W. Greely, chief signal officer of the Army, tried to have the division moved from the Adjutant General's Office, headed by Brigadier General J. C. Kelton, to his own. The subsequent debate turned bitter. Greely argued that the Signal Corps mission stated in 1890 called for collecting and transmitting data by Army communications networks, a somewhat dubious claim for nabbing MID. He also wondered why if MID was so important, it only had one unskilled, assigned officer; surely, his own organization would make better use of that individual. In response, MID prepared a report on what it considered its mission—data management and topography. Major General John M. Schofield, the commanding general, weighed in with the secretary of war in support of the Adjutant General's retention of MID. He reasoned that the Adjutant General's Office was the nearest equivalent to a General Staff and required intelligence to perform its duties. If successful in it claim, the Signal Corps would have compartmentalized MID. When advising Secretary of War Stephen B. Elkins, Schofield gave Kelton his full support.

That was all Elkins needed to make his decision. In a January 1892 memo to the Department of War, he spoke of the adjutant general's significance as the communications hub of the Army.[20] In his view, the Adjutant General's Office was more essential to the Army than the Signal Corps; the adjutant general was "the necessary custodian of all the military information" of importance to the Army therefore MID had to reside in his office.[21] Elkins reported on March 8 to the chairman of the Committee on Military Affairs that the law of October 1, 1890, did not allow the Signal Corps to perform duties of the information division. He said that appropriations for clerks should be kept separate between the Signal Corps and Adjutant General's Office to keep straight in appropriations one clerk in the latter belongs to MID.[22] Two weeks later, Representatives Joseph H. Outhwaite (Ohio) and William S. Holman (Indiana) debated the Army appropriations bill. They quickly agreed to MID's place in the Department of War and merely tussled about whether the House should allow money for a clerk in the Adjutant General's Office or force Elkins to detail an officer.[23] Greely had failed in his attempt to seize MID.

Just as the Navy put a more senior rank at the head of ONI in 1889, the Army wanted experience in the lead at MID. Elkins placed Colonel Robert Williams in charge of the office, assisted by Major Arthur MacArthur (who later rose to general rank in the Philippines portion of the Spanish-American War). Williams immediately went to work reorganizing MID by creating five sections: militia, military progress, frontier, map, and Latin American. He placed officers in charge of the sections who were carefully selected from different arms of the service and had skill sets for the work required of them.[24]

Despite ONI's forays into public relations and war planning, both strategic military intelligence organizations remained central reference facilities at their core. In late 1892, MID adhered more to this function than its counterpart. Renewed by a sense of purpose and mission and the backing of the secretary of war, the division grew rapidly in size. Williams had his staff concentrate on basic missions of data collection and mapmaking, with only a few refinements in 1893. In the age of "progress" both in society and within the Army, MID officers dreamed about a much more ambitious Hamiltonian vision: competing on an equal footing with overseas powers required effective strategic intelligence through data collection and analysis.

In 1893, Williams consolidated gains afforded by well-defined general orders and supportive leaders. Furthermore, although reformists in MID knew that a clash with Europe was possible in the long term, they discounted the likelihood of this happening within the next year. Instead, they collected data on European advancements in techniques, tactics, and procedures. The immediate concentration of staff effort was in the frontier and Latin American sections. Analysis of Canada, Cuba, and Mexico occupied the most time. Williams's team also launched a program to publish annual or semiannual reports of military advancements for all Army personnel. Then, Williams rotated to another position: his responsibility was to get MID moving, and once accomplished, the Army needed him elsewhere.

MID followed ONI's lead by downgrading the chief's rank. The Army decided to reduce the billet's rank because the position did not require a colonel to reinvigorate and protect MID's prestige anymore. MID staffer Major John B. Babcock succeeded Williams as chief. By all accounts, he did not deviate from the missions of data collection and mapmaking. He produced a report in September concerning what he felt the responsibilities of his office should be. Babcock noted that recent General Order no. 23 listed responsibilities that were comparable to "a large share of the duties of the 'Great General Staffs' of European armies," making his duties monumental.[25] He believed that his main customers were the secretary of war (Daniel S. Lamont in 1893) and the commanding general of the Army, as they were advisors to the president on military matters. He argued, like Williams, that "it is almost impossible to conceive of any contingency arising which would necessitate the transportation of an army from our shores to wage war in the interior of Europe, and almost equally impossible to believe that any European force will ever penetrate into our own territory." Therefore, in Europe, he believed, the military attachés' focus should be on data regarding military material, future continental war preparations, and changes in tactics and training.[26] Babcock concluded that no foreign army immediately threatened America, but America's borders still "warranted scrutiny," for that was where the next war would come.[27]

In the mid-1890s, as ONI began to take on its war planning missions in order to remain a viable institution, MID bested ONI in attention from Americans, Congress, and the military establishment. MID's success seemed to be due to its focus on core missions and less pressure by superiors to promote the Army's reform efforts. By 1894, MID had amassed thirty thousand index cards in its files. Annual and semiannual publications had enough circulation to be noticed and reported by media around the country. And an attaché corps that did not exist five years previously was now larger than ONI's corps. The succession of chiefs of the division revealed solid officers of character. Major Babcock transitioned duties seamlessly with Colonel Thomas M. Vincent in October 1895. Historian Marc B. Powe remarked on a key component of MID's success: the agency largely directed itself.[28] Even when the experienced Vincent rotated out, the respected Captain Arthur L. Wagner filled the slot effortlessly.

ONI and MID's foreign representatives, the attaché corps, blossomed between 1885 and 1895. Attaché Chadwick set the example and proved that naval and military attachés were imperative for information gathering. Therefore, with Congress and the Departments of the Navy's and of War's approval, America's military representation grew exponentially overseas.

ONI's foundational mission was information gathering, storage, and reporting. Since 1882, naval intelligence mainly achieved the data collection portion of this mandate through the naval attaché in London. Chadwick had acted alone, with enormous amounts of sources to tap. ONI's collection capabilities across the Atlantic doubled when Commodore Walker sent Lieutenant Buckingham as a naval attaché to Paris in November 1885, with future jurisdiction expected in St. Petersburg and Berlin. Buckingham sailed to London, where he spent a month overlapping duties with Chadwick. They visited three shipyards near London and toured the city, and Chadwick introduced him to foreign naval and military attachés to help Buckingham establish a social network. Buckingham accompanied Chadwick to France and continued the task of establishing a network of contacts.[29] Throughout, Chadwick mentored Buckingham as to European etiquette and taboos, and tutored him on administrative matters, such as how to get authorization from the Bureau of Navigation to obtain materials and settle accounts with the US Treasury.[30]

The new naval attaché corps proved to be vital in the expansion of ONI's chartered mission. Chadwick and Buckingham supplied the overseas technical information and material to help build a new Navy, as they were both competent men and perceptive observers, well positioned to report on naval progress in Europe. It helped Chadwick and Buckingham that they represented a nonthreatening North American country. They were welcomed into the exclusive attaché circles because their client was weak and willing to pay lavishly for technologies and information. The United States was an economic rival but no threat militarily to European powers.

The year 1888 saw continued growth in naval overseas representation with an additional attaché for ONI. As Congress acknowledged the information collection role in naval appropriations, for the first time ONI had dedicated funding for the attachés just as the Navy prepared a third attaché for duty in Europe.[31] In November, Secretary of the Navy William C. Whitney delegated Lieutenant Nathan Sargent as naval attaché to Rome and Vienna, a result of the sophistication of his published articles on war planning and strategy.[32]

Between 1882 and 1889, the Navy's first attachés sent hundreds of technical reports back to Washington. Historian Jeffrey Dorwart argues that these officers did not have training in intelligence or international law and were only equipped with perceptive minds and the social etiquette and education provided by the Naval Academy. Therefore, their reports were simple, direct, and technical.[33] The reports contained information on equipment, ideas, and doctrine; the attachés also sent back to ONI purchased materials, such as blueprints and drawings. Slowly, even skeptical officers started finding some benefit in ONI's hard work. And in February 1889, for the first time Congress used strategic intelligence supplied by ONI on the House floor—another sign of ONI's growing competence and influence.[34]

In the early 1890s, the corps experienced some hiccups. The naval attaché corps suffered under CIO Chadwick's watch due to attaché disagreements with the CIO, changes in information sharing with the Europeans, and squabbles with foreign manufacturing firms. In terms of the first circumstance, the precipitating factor was the Department of the Navy decreasing funds to the attachés. Feeling the crunch, Chadwick told Lieutenant Commander Rodgers (now attaché to Paris and St. Petersburg) not to travel to Russia from Paris to establish his credentials. Rodgers angrily told Chadwick that under his watch as CIO, he would have been able to secure funds for intelligence trips in Europe.[35] Rodgers probably was a little harsh in his assessment.

Meanwhile, the European political atmosphere had changed for the worse over the past five years because of great power tensions. Overt collection of information became more difficult as nations created restrictive laws about sharing intelligence. For instance, biographer and naval flag officer Albert Gleaves notes that Emory was having trouble extracting information in the London of the early 1890s: "The Admiralty was loath to give out anything, and often refused point blank. In the House of Commons, a member did not hesitate to accuse the First Lord of giving the secrets of the English to Commander Chadwick, our former attaché, although the statement was afterward retracted."[36] Another issue was reciprocity: European governments began asking attachés for information in return, but agents such as Emory had nothing to offer.[37] Adding to attaché hardship, other nations' attachés were reckless in covert information gathering in Europe. As a result, would-be sources tightened their lips. Overseas weapons and technology manufacturers were hesitant to sell goods and services to Americans who "bought little and demanded much."[38] To add injury to insult, the department did not increase the attachés' allowance.[39] Nevertheless, the Navy needed the corps for data collection. In the context of the Spanish-American War just a few years later, the department's overseas representative would be an invaluable source for information collection targeting Spain.

Meanwhile, the Army took notice of the Navy's attaché program. The first indication that the Army wanted to build a military attaché corps came on June 16, 1888, when Congressmen Samuel J. Randall (Kansas) and Richard W. Townshend (Illinois) debated providing $1,500 to the Department of War "for the pay of a clerk attendant on the collection and classification of military information from abroad."[40] Congress approved the bill on September 22, 1888, establishing the Army's attaché system.[41]

It was not until early 1889 that the Army sent its first attachés to Berlin, London, Paris, Vienna, and St. Petersburg, the same places where the Navy had attachés. The military establishments of those countries reciprocated by sending attachés to Washington. Secretary of War William C. Endicott instructed the attachés to "examine into, and report upon, all matters of a military or technical character that may be of interest and value to any branch of the War Department and to the service at large." Endicott went into specific resources they should explore in their host country, noting that they will "perform such special duties as the

Secretary of War may, from time to time, assign to them" and "make stated reports to the Secretary of War, at least once every month, and as much oftener as circumstances may require."[42] Secretary Endicott's personal interest in the new attaché corps signaled MID's rising influence within the Army.

In its first thirty years, the military attaché corps grew tremendously, drawing on many rotating line officers who displayed extraordinary talent.[43] Some went on to achieve distinction beyond intelligence collection, such as John J. Pershing, Peyton C. March, and Tasker H. Bliss. The recruitment of qualified officers marked the Department of War's commitment to the development of intelligence, and MID could now conduct its Hamiltonian overseas data collection mission in earnest.

The core mission of ONI and MID between 1885 and 1895—agreed upon by the departments, Congress, and intelligence professionals—was data management, that is, collecting, organizing, analyzing, and storing information that mostly came from attachés overseas. At the same time, ONI eagerly sought to conduct war planning and promotion of the Navy. For its part, although the Army's strategic intelligence organization also took on topography responsibilities, it stuck to the main mission. Both organizations performed these duties looking outward toward the American geographic boundaries and beyond.

ONI initially did a much better job at its information-gathering duties than did MID. It had a three-year head start on the newer division. Ensign Ellicott arrived at ONI in 1886 to join a strategic intelligence organization that was just hitting its stride. Ellicott described the Office when he arrived: "I found Lieutenant Rodgers in a roomy office with a permanent stenographer, and beyond it a long, wide room, its walls lined high with filing cases."[44] Employees filled the cabinets with information accrued over four years. Ellicott marveled at the fine-tuned data collection machine ONI was becoming: "I soon found that a complete hookup had been established between the Office and our naval attachés abroad and that even our foreign consulates were being integrated."[45]

In Army intelligence matters, Volkmar started MID's data collection processes but efforts did not really begin until Taylor took the reins. Drum protected Taylor, whom the adjutant general respected, just as Walker helped Mason navigate the political waters of the Department of the Navy. Notably, Drum initially helped Taylor with his regular Army and militia tracking duties. He wrote letters in November 1886 to national guard and militia adjutant generals and to the Department of War bureau chiefs requesting information be furnished to MID.⁴⁶ To the adjutant general, every officer was an information officer. Drum even requested information from officers on hunting and fishing trips because of its potential for topographical and natural resources data.

But MID did not start running effectively until Drum had the full backing of the Secretary of War Redfield Proctor and the attaché corps was in place. On April 19, 1889, the secretary informed his subordinates of the process by which information would filter from attachés to consumers in the Department of War, through MID.⁴⁷ The secretary reiterated MID's mission and its responsibilities to the attachés. MID's official historian, Colonel Bruce W. Bidwell, claims that Drum and Proctor's pronouncement constituted the first mission given to the strategic military intelligence organization.⁴⁸ Yet, MID had been a repository of information since the fall of 1885, even as most Americans and Department of War personnel had not known it existed.

The division spent the early 1890s consolidating its gains of personnel and legitimacy and establishing productive routines. The secretary of war and adjutant general expected MID to conduct information management; the division set about daily routines in concert with attachés to achieve their directives. The staff created data banks with the cabinets in their office and proved efficient at delivering information on request. In response to an inspector general request in 1891, MID was able to provide numbers and types of weapons in the arsenal of eleven European countries.⁴⁹

The 1892 battle to decide MID's place in the Department of War highlighted that data collection was not yet an officially sanctioned mission. All previous orders and circulars established that there should be an attaché corps and generally that MID needed to collect and disperse information, but the details were vague. Therefore, in mid-March 1892, Kelton proposed making the assistant adjutant general the division chief and formalizing MID's missions. The issuance of General Order no. 23 three days later indicated that the secretary was already in agreement with this plan. The adjutant general issued orders on March 18 with follow-on guidance.⁵⁰ The general order reflected an Army at the crossroads of understanding its purpose—protecting the frontiers as traditionally done or looking in Hamiltonian fashion toward overseas threats. The order tasked MID both with monitoring the US militia and collecting foreign intelligence. Secretary Elkins restated this contrast of missions later in the year in his report to Congress: "The scheme [of MID] now includes not only the collection of foreign intelligence but is intended to accomplish the compilation and scientific arrangement of information relating to the military resources of the nation."[51] In the next decade, MID spent less time looking inward as the frontiers closed and expending more effort on international military affairs.

This general order also marked a milestone in MID's history. For the first time, Army leaders unambiguously defined MID's missions of data management—collect and classify information—and publishing intelligence in the form of maps and monographs. The guidance clearly hints that the secretary and adjutant general foresaw MID as a building block to a future Army general staff akin to organizations in Europe. The mandate to gather information such as army strength, lines of communication, war material, and logistics suggests the secretary wanted MID to help with war planning, too. To solidify the adjutant general's control of the division, General Order no. 23 noted that the chief of MID would be chosen from within the Adjutant General's Office by the secretary. Under this definitive guidance, the division made considerable advancement in internal processes and overall reputation between 1892 and 1902.

MID chief Williams continued foreign and militia intelligence collection, preparation for emergency mobilization, and developing contingency plans for war with Mexico and Canada.[52] MID was particularly interested in gathering information on Canada and Cuba. Army reformers, such as Lieutenant Arthur L. Wagner, saw Canada as the prime target of foreign data collection. As Great Britain had always been a foreign power threat to American sovereignty and there had been a long history of Americans fighting the British in their own dominion, they reasoned that Canada would be the battleground for any future wars with Great Britain. Robert Angevine has argued that it was not the Spanish that preoccupied military intelligence's attention prior to the Spanish-American War; it was Canada.[53] According to Bidwell, MID was aware of an early responsibility to track Cuban affairs and collect data as early as 1892.[54] MID collected, collated, and produced intelligence on both countries with vigor throughout the 1890s.

At the same time, naval professionals wanted to do more than just collect data. The first serious efforts at war planning by ONI took place in early 1885, by which point ONI staffers could supply the rest of the department with intelligence and maneuver schemes against future foes. The office possessed all the information not only on foreign navies but on the US Navy. In some capacity, ONI held war planning responsibilities until 1915, when a separate division of the Chief of Naval Operation's staff took over these duties. But in 1885, war planning was embryonic, and ONI was learning from scratch how to accomplish this mission.

Rodgers's staff experimented with reporting information and building war scenarios and campaigns with Naval War College students in Newport, Rhode Island. The first class convened in September 1885, and they were the perfect test subjects. Since the NWC faculty and staff understood world progress in naval sciences, they could appreciate the information and scenarios that reflected real-world conditions ONI supplied. And the impressionable students were eager to take on the scenarios. ONI and NWC personnel were kindred spirits. They found their support from the same navalist clique of the Navy and similar opposition from officers of the traditional establishment. Mutual assistance between ONI and NWC would help educate naval officers, test out war plans, and ensure bureaucratic survival. But war planning still took less of a priority than data collection in the late 1880s.

In late 1891 into 1892, a crisis demonstrated that ONI had started shifting focus from old missions of information management to war planning. Navalists were realizing their dreams of a warship fleet made of steel. Ten years of elevated naval appropriations and construction yielded new vessels. This windfall of hardware for the US Navy meant that ONI's mission to keep informed on foreign naval science was no longer as imperative. However, ONI would experience the discomfort of losing technologically savvy officers and funds for naval attachés overseas. Tensions with Chile in late 1891 exemplified this switch of mission priorities.

A Chilean civil war ended in September 1891, but not without dragging the United States into the internal conflict. The USS *Baltimore* crisis marked a dramatic turn in U.S.-Chile relations as America demonstrated a navy superior to Chile's, a reversal from ten years previous. Specifically, a Chilean mob killed two US sailors from the USS *Baltimore* in Valparaíso in October in response to a perceived insult. When the Chilean government rebuffed American protests, President Harrison urged a strong military response in Congress. Chile got the message, apologized, and paid $75,000.

The incident from October 1891 into 1892 showed how ONI was evolving. Secretary of the Navy Tracy began war planning in Washington in late October. He asked Captain Mahan to come to the State, War, and Navy Building to join a team comprising Soley, Commodore William M. Folger, and possibly the CIO. The group sought intelligence on Chile, a logical first step in planning a war against a competitor of close to equal power. The department had asked the Pacific Squadron for information from its shipboard intelligence officers for months. ONI embarrassingly confessed that it had little operational intelligence regarding Chilean warship locations or even general strategic information on Chile itself.⁵⁵ Still, with the help of shipboard intelligence officers and the naval attachés in Europe, the office was able to generate and distribute intelligence packets to commanders at sea off Chile. The intelligence packet was the first plan of campaign produced by naval intelligence. It provided assessments of Chile's war capabilities and suggested areas where their Navy would operate. ONI assessed that the US Navy would rout Chile.⁵⁶ On January 15, 1892, the *New York Times* reported ONI's role in "a definite plan of operations in the South Pacific" under discussion in Washington.⁵⁷ It is the first time that media noted naval intelligence's war planning mission.

For all this, even Davis realized that ONI had played a minor role in department deliberations during the Chilean affair. The CIO understood that ONI's limited operational intelligence capabilities prompted the secretary of the Navy to confer only in a limited way with his office during the months of tension. ONI no longer had the influence in the department it had in the ten years previous.

In contrast, ONI's collaboration with the NWC broadened as war planning became more prominent in Navy circles. Secretary Hilary Abner Herbert widened the NWC curriculum to coastal defense, naval strategy, and international law. The Newport school began to perform general staff duties such as war planning and studying strategic and tactical problems. Their solutions were filed at ONI or in their college archives.⁵⁸ And like ONI, NWC founders advocated for a general staff for years. As Luce said in 1888, "There was no one to administer the affairs of the Navy as a military arm of the Government—and therein lies the secret of the decadence of the Navy."⁵⁹ In the early 1890s, ONI and NWC worked together well as naval intelligence put together plans of campaign and the war college tested them in wargames. From 1895 to the end of the Spanish-American War, events would test how well both organizations had progressed in planning.

Change was in the air at Navy shipyards, in the squadrons, and on the desks of some of the Navy's most prominent theorists at the NWC and the US Naval Institute. ONI officers noticed how times were changing in the Navy through their numerous publications concerning innovations in foreign and US navies. But the Navy developed with exasperating drudgery. Design problems and matériel shortages delayed the launch of experimental squadrons to test tactical steam evolutions.⁶⁰ Secretary of the Navy Tracy's 1889 report included a table illustrating eleven navies (Japan excluded) with greater combat power than the US Navy.⁶¹ The Navy's growing pains reflected the angst of an adolescent nation industrializing at a lethargic speed. In the reformers' mind, perhaps what the Navy needed—and the public who funded it required—was reminders of just how well construction was progressing. Could ONI fulfill this role?

On October 3, 1890, Secretary Tracy told the Bureau of Navigation he was transferring ONI to the secretary of the Navy's office. Henceforth, Soley screened ONI's access to Tracy. All attaché reports had to go through his office first, and Soley bypassed the CIO when sending guidance to attachés and shipboard intelligence officers. In effect, navalist Soley acted as the CIO who politicized ONI's work. Historian Mark R. Shulman has argued that ONI developed "a policy-driven methodology" to help promote a blue-water navy, discouraging go-getter officers.[62] Davis's diminutive role stunted the strategic military intelligence organization's growth and validated a questionable public relations mission.

By 1893, ONI had settled into a role akin to that of a public relations manager. It still dutifully conducted the intelligence repository mission, but that was not the reason it garnered praise from superiors and the public. Naval reformers in the department needed a promotor of their evolving internationalist agenda, a program independent of the traditional Pax Britannica umbrella that had dominated the globe for decades.[63] "Fleet strengths" dominated the discourse of navalists, the NWC, and naval intelligence. "How well could the U.S. Navy stack up to the European powers?" was the question ONI's bosses wanted answered. ONI appeased them with tables of data for war games and press articles and Congressional hearings for public consumption, becoming a propaganda instrument for government navalists.

ONI had little choice in the matter. Even if it did not want to perform the mission of promoting "fleet strength," it had little standing within the naval establishment. The office's departmental devaluation was exemplified in the selection of Lieutenant Singer as CIO in mid-1893, to a position occupied by a commander for the previous six years. The German-born officer began his tenure operating in accepted realities: a miniscule budget, meager handouts to naval attachés, and low morale. He was not expecting much improvement in ONI's position but tried, nonetheless. Singer kept ONI at the ready in case his superiors would need his organization to conduct missions, such as promotion of naval interests. When Secretary of the Navy Herbert, a navalist and old ally of ONI, took office, he immediately asked ONI to boost his shipbuilding program by providing him ideas and information to improve the hulls and weapons systems. ONI organized its card catalogue system by vessel and weapons system, which allowed staffers to supply customers, such as the secretary, intelligence based along functional lines. Singer excitedly took on Herbert's patronage because it could mean more resources, funding, and personnel. With Herbert's interest in ONI and an influx of new personnel, Singer's office could show that it could be useful in the marketing of the new Navy.

On the other side of the building, MID faithfully performed its topography responsibilities. It was only logical since the Department of War had units in the Army making maps for decades, which often suited commanders intelligence needs. New and old threats such as Great Britain, Mexico, Canada, and Cuba made maps a hot commodity. The tension with Great Britain kept the Army attuned to possible conflicts along the Canadian border throughout this entire time. The Adjutant General's Office and MID's forays into Canadian topography comprised an important task for Army intelligence, but it was a sideshow of MID's fundamental mandate for data collection, storage, and reporting. Early in 1891, for the first time in Army intelligence history, they delivered to the department authentic maps of Canada and Mexico. The maps came with intelligence of the strengths—personnel and equipment—of these armies. Later that year, MID prepared maps of Spanish-held Cuba, Puerto Rico, and the Philippines. This step is important, for it marked Hamiltonian efforts to collect intelligence of overseas powers, not a Jeffersonian mission to explore the continental frontiers. MID's effective topography tasks made the organization more visible throughout the Department of War.

ONI's and MID's effectiveness as organizations in a Hamiltonian era can be observed in the intelligence doctrines that sprouted and the praise heaped upon the organizations by their respective departments, Congress, and the American public. ONI's popularity and influenced waned between 1885 and 1895 as MID's grew. These varying fortunes were indicative of the talent these offices could attract and the support the secretaries could or wanted to provide.

After over a decade of ONI and MID operations, theorists could reflect upon the successes and failures of strategic intelligence and what these boded for the future of the naval and war departments. Chief of the Bureau of Equipment and former CIO Chadwick had time to contemplate the future of the Navy. He wrote an article for the *Proceedings* called "Naval Department Organization," in which he advocated for a naval general staff and an important place for ONI within it. In the article, he traces the evolution of naval administration from the American Revolution to July 1894, arguing, "But while its [US Navy] record has been so honorable in respect to action, it has made a signal failure in the development of any administrative system which has not been more or less a makeshift."[64] Chadwick venerated the admiralty boards and general staffs in Europe and wished the US Navy would replicate them. He noted that in other countries, naval intelligence was vital to a general staff, but that ONI, although established, did not exist by mandate of law.[65] Chadwick's article demonstrates that navalists had by this point changed their focus from building a navy to administering it in an efficient manner.

With a healthy foundation, MID's staff reflected on what their missions were and, more deeply, how to hone their craft. Although Captain Wagner did not report to MID until 1896, he was keenly aware of the value of intelligence from his instructor seat at the United States Infantry and Cavalry School in Leavenworth, Kansas. The cerebral tactician of the military arts wrote several books on his profession, including *The Security of Service and Information*, the first pivotal publication on strategic intelligence since Charles Rogers's "Naval Intelligence" ten years previous. In his introduction, he bluntly stated, "Information in regard to the enemy is the indispensable basis of all military plans, and nothing but faulty dispositions for the security of an army can be expected if such information is lacking."[66] Wagner believed in the importance of intelligence in peacetime war planning, specifically information relating to geography, topography, and resources in potential theaters of operation; in his view, this is what MID was charged with and beginning to explore in 1893.[67] He also wrote that obtaining information on the composition of enemy forces, especially in war, may be done through spies, deserters, prisoners, newspapers, and reconnaissance.[68] These were techniques rarely used by Americans up to this point, but MID would use them in the Spanish-American War and World War I. Wagner's thoughts previewed MID's expansion from its central mission to war planning and espionage over the next thirty years.

ONI received commendations from its superiors often, especially under Rodgers's tenure in the late 1880s. ONI had political protection from not only Commodore John G. Walker but from Secretary of the Navy William C. Whitney and President Grover Cleveland. ONI respected Whitney, who could be a reformist at times and relied on naval intelligence for warship construction programs. Whitney asked ONI for European shipbuilding firm blueprints and weekly ONI reports. In return, he defended ONI and used his friendship with Secretary of State Thomas F. Bayard to help supply diplomatic data to ONI. Whitney may have had some influence in Cleveland's favorable spin on intelligence operations in an address to Congress. In general, Walker encouraged ONI to have contacts with congressmen to promote itself and naval construction. Rodgers complied and had a working relationship with Chairman of the House Committee on Naval Affairs Herbert. Other Navy bureau chiefs began to crave ONI's technical reports on foreign navies to assist their own warship designs.

Walker looked upon the creation he helped make with pride. He frequently referred requests for information regarding the Navy from the public to ONI, and he included the office's staff on his professional trips. For instance, in 1887 Walker asked Rear Admiral Stephen B. Luce, commander of the North Atlantic Squadron, to try some different fuel and report the benefits to ONI.[69] Like Drum and Taylor, Walker had concerns with Canada, especially about fishing rights.[70] In general, by this stage ONI had gained the full confidence of the Bureau of Navigation.

Tracy's support was one of the high points in ONI's history, as for the first time ONI was lauded by a senior member of government.[71] It marked an agreement between high level leadership and ONI officers on the office's missions. There was nothing to indicate that trouble was on the horizon. ONI still attracted young, energetic officers such as Ellicott and Lieutenants William H. H. Southerland and Charles E. Fox. After the passage of the Naval Act of 1890, ONI hoped that with new ships and hardware coming to the fleet that the secretary would turn to Davis's staff for advice. And he did so. For instance, Tracy asked naval intelligence to investigate overseas warship manufacturing techniques of nickel steel to harden armor plating and the office happily obliged. In January 1890, ONI also supplied memoranda on other equipment and weapons installed on foreign warships.[72] The secretary continued to lavish praise upon ONI in return. In his report to Congress in 1890, he said, "The work of the Office of Naval Intelligence is constantly increasing; with the increase in constitution and the growing work of arming and equipping the new ships, the importance of this office is felt by every bureau and officer of the Department and in the service at large."[73] But ONI's influence on the department dwindled with ineffective leadership and mediocre officers at ONI in the early 1890s.

The downward spiral roughly coincided with increased effectiveness of the MID in the Department of War. The secretary of war produced several paragraphs in support of the division in his 1892 report to Congress. Elkins had quelled a bureaucratic tussle about MID's place, reorganized the office, and wrote to Congress on its behalf in March of that year. He gave Congress a rundown as to its mission, production thus far, and prospects for war planning, while also praising its value.[74] In the same report, the adjutant general used Elkins's support as an opportunity to beg

Congress for office space for MID.⁷⁵ The lack of physical space to work was a difficulty, but it also meant MID was expanding.

The secretary of war and adjutant general were pleased with MID's performance, as they noted in the secretary's report to Congress in 1893.⁷⁶ The adjutant general invited members of Congress and fellow Army officers to find out what this office was reporting, as he considered them "extremely valuable."⁷⁷ Kelton boasted about the some four thousand index cards MID produced in 1893, the reports sent by attachés abroad, and the division's new annual or semiannual reports on military advancements at home and overseas. Some of the superiors' praise was intended to prop up the organization and accredit it for the congressional audience, but Lamont and Kelton probably honestly believed in MID's potential. Secretary Lamont wanted the rest of the department to grasp that he still considered the division the central depository for information. He reemphasized, in a circular published in 1889, the processes by which attachés and bureau chiefs must send reports to MID and how department requests for information must filter through MID to reach attachés.⁷⁸ In the annual report to Congress, the secretary of war and adjutant general spoke highly of the division and the expansion of the military attaché corps into Mexico City and Tokyo, the first non-European attaché destinations.⁷⁹ Through department lobbying and MID production efforts, Congress recognized military intelligence financial needs. The legislature allocated money for the agency in 1894, its first specific mention of either MID or ONI in legislation.⁸⁰ Lawmakers repeated the congressional allocation in the following years, but it soon became insufficient for the growing organization.

America newspapers noticed the efforts of ONI and MID to collect military data for the government. The *Saint Louis Daily Globe-Democrat* reported one of the first known media uses of ONI's publications *Information from Abroad—War Series*.⁸¹ Media continued to cite ONI's informational releases through World War I. In 1885, the *Indianapolis Journal* described how the State Department required consuls abroad "to secure all information appertaining to the ship-building of the governments to which they were accredited, and in obedience to these instructions there has been forwarded to the intelligence office of the Navy Department very comprehensive statements from these consuls."⁸² When Rodgers reached the end of his first tour at ONI in 1889, even Americans outside Navy circles observed that he was leaving and that ONI was "flourishing." The *New York Times* wrote an editorial on the secretive organization that was becoming more public. It claimed:

> The office of Naval Intelligence was started upon an excellent foundation by the predecessor of Lieut. R. P. Rodgers, the present incumbent, but it was left to Lieut. Rodgers to perfect the plans and to arrange a system of thoroughly classifying the immense mass of information that had been accumulating from every quarter of the globe, and to improve on the methods for such collections in addition to the regular work of arranging information concerning navies and the resources for war of all powers, which has been regularly advanced.[83]

The article further noted that ONI marked the beginnings of a general staff because the "office has now established itself so firmly as a power and necessary feature of the Navy Department" and that the office should progress to its inevitable conclusion: an agency for war planning.[84]

Media across the country took note of the new Division. The small-town newspaper *North Platte Tribune* commented that "the secret archives of the intelligence office the public will know little of their contents."[85] MID acquired the public reputation as mysterious, a trait that the public would place upon military intelligence organizations through to the present day. Public recognition demonstrates that MID had grown considerably since late 1885. Part of MID's delayed coming out party is what an 1894 *New York Times* editorial believed was intentional secrecy on the division's part: "The rooms which are occupied by the bureau now bears placards, warning of intruders, and those connected with the miniature department take on an air of impenetrable mystery."[86] The paper advocated more MID publications be made public and at the same time ensuring that sources of the information remain secure. The editorial compared MID to ONI as both splendid ideas with services of value but continued that the "features of secrecy and mystery must be abated."[87] The American public's frustration in keeping tabs on ONI and MID is noted, but secrecy will always remain a trait of military intelligence organizations. Other media outlets zeroed in on the Division's activities through its publications. The *North American* newspaper from Philadelphia praised MID staffer Major Theodore Schwan's volume on *The Organization of the German Army*, calling it "one of the most valuable results of the establishment of the military information division of the War Department."[88] A newspaper in Goodland, Kansas, reported that MID published a helpful volume of notes "of organization, armaments and military progress in American, and European armies."[89] MID gave rural America a worldly view of the military beyond their county line, a definitely un-Jeffersonian concept.

Between 1885 and 1895, ONI and MID were two strategic military intelligence organizations going in opposite directions. In the late 1880s, ONI frequently had far better intelligence than that provided by the State Department or even produced by foreign governments.[90] By 1895, the office became more focused on war planning and public relations to justify the existence of a Hamiltonian Navy for power projection. The Army's intelligence bureau swelled from nothing in the fall of 1885 to arguably the best American intelligence organization ten years later. MID from the start imitated ONI's processes but had nothing new to learn from its older sibling in the 1890s.

ONI and MID demonstrated growing pains as they struggled to define their missions and interpret what their superiors wanted them to accomplish. Hamiltonian navalists and Army reformers pressed intelligence officers to look outward—beyond American borders and even overseas. Even everyday Americans, through the media, took notice that the Navy and Army were not nearly as focused on the coast and internal frontiers as in years past and that ONI and MID collected intelligence beyond America's boundaries. ONI took on new mission sets, while MID worked on redefining the missions it had. Their growing pains occurred while appeasing the country's leaders and citizenry interested in exploring economic possibilities beyond the nation's boundaries and across the protective oceans. The Spanish-American War, the first foreign war in fifty years, would reveal how strategic military intelligence organizations adjusted to war planning when Americans turned to empire-building beyond their borders.

Chapter Three

1895–1900: Operational Tests for ONI and MID

William McKinley's presidential election victory over William Jennings Bryan in 1896 confirmed a thirty-year trend of transformation: the United States had transitioned from an agrarian, frontier-oriented young country to an industrial, interventionist, rising world power. The Republican president represented the elite, capitalist protectionists' gaze toward overseas markets. Hamiltonian visions of development paralleled America's economic growth beyond its border. The Republicans' expansive 1890's foreign policy reflected a belief that the United States' "unique and beneficent frontier no longer existed."[1] America's limitless bounty of riches now had boundaries; to get past them and thrive economically, it appeared necessary to look overseas. Imperialist elites saw the industrial revolution in America as resulting in surplus goods, economic turbulence, and radicalism that could only be solved by intrusion into overseas affairs. In *The New Empire: An Interpretation of American Expansion 1860–1898*, Walter LeFeber argued that the expansionist path on the 1890s was not a "spur-of-the-moment" policy and that the United States deliberately chose to acquire an empire.[2] In contrast, Ernest R. May proposed that political isolation was the historical norm and that 1897 to 1898 was just a blip of imperialism.[3] Of the two, LaFeber more accurately assessed the economic and political trends—including the growing complexity of government institutions—building since the Civil War.

Since the early 1880s, the Navy and Army had demonstrated through service-building and reform that new naval ships and Army institutions served larger purposes than coastal patrolling and constabulary duties on the frontier in a supposedly isolated America. As the military services continued to develop, navalists and Army reformers shaped the Office of Naval Intelligence (ONI) and Military Information Division (MID) to aid in national expansion. In the mid-1890s, when the Cuban crisis erupted, the reformist departments tasked the strategic military intelligence organizations with overseas-centric missions: information gathering and war planning. When tensions escalated to war, the Navy and Army adjusted their intelligence requirements to reflect operational and tactical realities.

Secretaries and senior military leaders drove ONI's and MID's missions from 1895 to 1900, as the president and Congress were content with these small offices conducting their traditional data management duties. But, if they wanted to publish a war series report, the president and legislators were not averse to reading them.

McKinley's America looked at ONI and MID, if at all, with curiosity. Broadly speaking, the public could observe the increase in Navy ships and the Army's rising professionalism. In the late 1890s, newspapers became more jingoistic in large part because the public knew that the United States had more military might to back up international claims. ONI and MID helped foster Americans' knowledge of the military's power through annual publications and press releases. The intelligence services gained the reputation of federal almanacs that could churn out data, such as sizes of fleets and armies or European technological trends. But ONI and MID deliberately wore the cloak of mysterious information gatherers in the public eye. Strategic military intelligence organizations reasoned that, even in a democratic republic, officers had to keep secrets.

In the years before the Spanish-American War, ONI and MID took on war planning as their main mission. True, both organizations filled their file cabinets with information as usual; ONI still promoted the Navy in newspapers, while the MID still made maps. But the naval aristocrats and Army elitists manning these offices saw themselves as empire enablers, and planning was the best method for economic and land expansion. When hostilities broke out between Spain and the United States in April 1898, ONI and MID took on operational intelligence duties, such as enemy tracking and reporting battlespace obstacles. The war gave ONI and MID their first chance to operate in conflict. But it did not substantially increase their missions, it just altered the offices' purpose. For the intelligence organizations could not do much in the summer months of conflict. The departments gutted ONI and MID in Washington to deploy officers to ships and army units. Intelligence was not career enhancing; the officers were first and foremost warriors in an expanding America. The US foray into empire building between 1895 and 1900 tested the federal government's ability to fulfill America's Hamiltonian urges to compete with great powers overseas. In the process, ONI's and MID's superiors abruptly switched what was required of them between the events leading to the Spanish-American War and the war itself. But the crisis demonstrated strategic military intelligence organizations' inability and disinterest in trading the strategic missions of war planning and foreign intelligence collection for the enemy movement tracking involved in operational intelligence. This wartime trend would continue through World War II.

Halfway through the 1890s, ONI and MID were two organizations going in opposite directions in terms of respectability. Overall, military intelligence professionals continued the trend of managerial innovations and reorganization. ONI had branched out to new missions of war planning and public relations. Data collection did not seem as important as these activities to a Navy that was growing bigger than a coastal force and needed other support from ONI. The office had duties that exceeded the officer talent available and needed to find ways to improve both leadership and staff production. MID, on the other hand, continued to be a data collection and mapmaking organization and steadily increased in size and capability. During the three years before the Spanish-American War, the two organizations acquired better leadership and patronage, leading them to be well-prepared for their first test as strategic military intelligence organizations in a time of war.

Ever since its birth, ONI had readily attached its name to the navalist and reformer movement. Supporting the Naval War College, the US Naval Institute, and politicians seeking to build a new navy, ONI wanted the public to recognize the naval circles it associated itself with. When Frederic Singer's tour at ONI ended in 1896, the department leadership publicly sought to fill the CIO job with a famous name. They even reached out to the Mahan family in their effort to ensure the position's prestige. Captain Frederick A. Mahan, brother of the renowned naval theorist, met with Secretary of the Navy Hilary Herbert to discuss his next shore job on April 10, 1895. Subsequently, the *Evening Star* reported, "He was offered the place of chief intelligence officer at the Navy Department but is not disposed to accept it under existing conditions."[4] The phrase "existing conditions" may have referred to the negative reputation ONI had acquired from both lackluster leadership and fluid missions. Frederick Mahan did not accept Herbert's offer. Instead, the department settled for a newly minted lieutenant commander, Richard Wainwright, classmate of ONI founder Theodorus B. M. Mason, and charged him to change the mindset of the office from Mason's emphasis on information gathering to strategic planning.

Wainwright arrived in April 1896 to an ONI staff of ten, including his former shipmate Lieutenant William W. Kimball (the senior officer) and three other officers. Kimball was the only gifted and prolific officer of the bunch. The five staff members in 1897 were ONI's smallest crew since the office's inception. As the Navy's number of active ships increased, the department had to assign more commissioned officers to sea duty, leaving shore commands struggling to man the offices. Wainwright's solution to the shortages was to borrow clerks from other parts of the building to fill gaps. The department did not expect much brain power and improvement from ONI even with the change from Singer to Wainwright.

Despite this pessimism, Wainwright immediately implemented alterations to the office processes. Seeking to get his staff out of past routines and to think about innovation, while dealing with the lack of manning, he inaugurated the production of a pamphlet designed to push out intelligence faster and get readers' attention. Furthermore, Wainwright reorganized the office space and overhauled the index card system, removing obsolete data and updating the classification system.[5] By streamlining the daily efforts of his staff, Wainwright was able to reorient ONI on production and war planning. His reforms began to make ONI relevant again, but the office did not have powerful champions such as Commodore John G. Walker back in the 1880s. This changed with the inauguration of President McKinley and his naming of John D. Long as secretary of the Navy and, more importantly, Theodore Roosevelt as assistant secretary of the Navy. The navalist Roosevelt had the qualifications for his position; he had written a manuscript on the War of 1812 and was a keen student of history. He had interests in international affairs, realpolitik, and Alfred T. Mahan's theory of sea power—key concepts for a navalist. Roosevelt naturally attracted talented men and led with a swagger not seen in the naval establishment in some time, if ever. He and Wainwright understood each other right away and worked well together for the eighteen months their tenures overlapped.

Wainwright made a deep impact on naval intelligence, creating an improved filing system, instituting a renewed partnership with the Naval War College (NWC), and implementing and a robust reporting system to his superiors and the fleet. It is quite remarkable that he reestablished ONI's credibility with a reduced and undistinguished staff—attachés not included. It certainly helped that the CIO had the complete backing of Secretary Long and the real mover in the department, Roosevelt. Notably, one of Wainwright's lasting accomplishments was to set up ONI as a player in military planning.

After Wainwright's departure in the winter of 1897 to 1898, the office had to adjust to a new CIO and a demanding assistant secretary of the Navy, all the while not knowing that a war was on the horizon. As

Roosevelt told ONI alumnus Kimball in late 1897, "the Chief of the Office of Naval Intelligence has got to be the man on whom we rely most for initiating strategic work."[6] Complicating matters, the new CIO had to backfill a naval intelligence superstar. Roosevelt assigned navalist Commander Richardson Clover to ONI as CIO and expected his compliance with the assistant secretary in running intelligence throughout the department. For instance, Roosevelt often corresponded with naval attaché William S. Sims in Paris.[7] Clover knew at once who he had to answer to in the department, embarking on an uneasy relationship with Roosevelt for the first few months of 1898 before the beginning of the war.

As ONI flourished between 1896 and early 1898, MID maintained a high level of effectiveness. The division also gained talent in the spring and summer of 1897 as two giants in Army intelligence history, Major Arthur L. Wagner and Second Lieutenant Ralph H. Van Deman, arrived for duty. These expansionist-minded reformers ensured that MID's reputation for planning and data collection would grow as the Caribbean crisis deepened.

In December 1896, the Army promoted Lieutenant Colonel Wagner and made him the next chief of MID. Wagner brought obvious qualifications to the division: he was an author of a book on military intelligence and famous lecturer of military and foreign affairs and enjoyed a reputation as a strategic thinker. As he was the most competent intelligence professional in the service, the department chose him because of MID's growing status. On April 7, 1897, Wagner took charge of an office with double ONI's officer corps and with sixteen attachés, which Wagner wanted to expand to twenty-five.

Under Wagner's supervision, MID stretched beyond what funds and physical space would allow. The four rooms on the ground floor were inadequate and the MID budget (established three years previously) of $3,640 a year, including attaché expenses, was insufficient. By comparison, the Signal Services received $18,000 a year. Wagner took up the pen to air his grievances and to inform his superiors of the state of the division. He wrote the adjutant general that the division had eleven duty officers and that he wanted more attachés abroad. Wagner asked for more officers in the Military Progress, Militia, and Map Sections, because the current officers were "overworked" and suffered "fatiguing mental labor."[8] He also called MID's budget "totally inadequate"; in his view, $6,000 would better suit the office.[9] The division, Wagner felt, was overflowing its four workspaces.[10] He advocated for four more offices and if the department could not get the space from the State, War, and Navy Building, its leadership should ask Congress's help to get it elsewhere.

Wagner demonstrated proficiency in action and devotion to reform. His staff perfected maps and showed a willingness to lead the department with war planning. His focus on training and efficiency put him squarely in one of the leading American social trends of the late 1890s. He desired tactical modernization, education, and responsible command of not only Army intelligence but the entire Army. Historian Todd R. Brereton argued that he was a reforming professional typical of the Progressive Era, "albeit not an actual Progressive."[11] Ultimately, Wagner was a pioneer in the administrative reforms that would sweep the Navy and Army institutions, including ONI and MID, in the high tide of the Progressive Era of the next decade.

ONI's attaché corps was much more important than MID's representatives overseas in the lead-up and execution of military duties in the Spanish-American War. After all, American military forces were not fighting in Europe under the Army's military attachés' watchful eyes, allowing them to collect data. Naval attachés in Madrid and Paris were better situated, near Spanish ports and shipyards, to collect information on naval matters than their Army counterparts thousands of miles away from potential fronts. In addition, around this time ONI acquired the services of the future admiral Sims, who proved to be a fount of information during his tenure in Paris.

Sims's biographer Elting E. Morison related a probably apocryphal tale of the commanding officer of the USS *Charleston* appointing Sims as the shipboard intelligence officer on a cruise to the Far East: "Sims at first protested that he knew nothing of such work, to which his commanding officer replied, 'Neither do any of us.'"[12] True or not, Sims's reports provided valuable and voluminous information on the Sino-Japanese War.[13] The war tested Sims and the naval attaché corps, both those attachés in Europe and ONI's first permanent representative to a non-European country, as Commander Francis M. Barber took his post in Tokyo and Beijing in January 1895. Besides monitoring events in eastern Asia, naval intelligence continued promoting the Navy and itself in newspapers, temporarily lifting the veil of secrecy for all Americans to see.

As Singer's tenure as CIO wound down, he made ONI's first attempt at gaining Sims's services in early 1896. On April 4, Singer asked Sims to fill the attaché billet in Paris.[14] Sims's reputation had grown, as he took his intelligence duties on the *Charleston* more seriously than other shipboard intelligence officers. ONI senior officer Lieutenant Kimball wrote to Sims expressing Wainwright's offer for a position at ONI.[15] His petition to Sims had a pleading tone, but Sims turned down the offer multiple times because of ONI's poor reputation.[16]

Meanwhile, the naval attaché corps also received an infusion of talent. Lieutenant Commander Alfred P. Niblack continued his long association with ONI, first as a shipboard intelligence officer in the early 1890s and then as an attaché in Berlin beginning in 1896.[17] Niblack did not stray from naval intelligence after this tour, accepting assignments as naval attaché in Buenos Aires in 1910 and director of naval intelligence in 1919.

Meanwhile, ONI finally cornered Sims. In early 1897, Wainwright again asked Sims for his services at ONI, specifically as naval attaché to Paris, Madrid, and St. Petersburg. In the end, the CIO ordered Sims to ONI before the younger officer made up his mind.[18] Sims may have decided anyway to take up Wainwright's offer, as he wanted to hone his French.[19] He replaced Lieutenant Commander Raymond P. Rodgers on March 5, 1897. The Department of the Navy additionally accredited Rodgers to Madrid in 1895 when tensions with Spain ratcheted up, and Lieutenant George L. Dyer took over Sims's Madrid responsibilities in August. Sims did not disappoint his superiors. By the time Dyers arrived, Sims had set up contacts and links from his Spanish connections to his Paris post. This network was particularly useful when the Spanish-American War forced Dyer to leave Madrid. Sims's services would be instrumental in the American victory, as he helped set up a primitive spy network the next year.

The USS *Maine* disaster mobilized naval intelligence. Between February and April 1898, ONI's attachés took on pseudo-espionage roles, coordinated by Roosevelt, to gain information and to purchase ships and weaponry. Through a slew of agents, naval attachés developed a surveillance network to track down the movements of Spanish squadrons headed by Admirals Pascual Cervera y Topete and Manuel de la Cámara. Attachés arranged for secret deliveries of arms American forces under foreign flags. Roosevelt asked ONI to provide informational papers not only on Spanish naval assets but also on US warships for comparison purposes.

As they dealt with these new responsibilities, naval attachés attempted to cover for a glaring ONI weakness: ship tracking. With war looming, the Spaniards moved their ships often, making initial reports useless. ONI did not have an accurate system for sustaining a running plot on enemy assets, and it could not answer its superiors easily when asked operational questions. Clover relied on the attachés who had built makeshift covert espionage rings to supply locational data. Sims sent information on Spanish cruiser flotillas dispatched to intercept US ships. He also included details in reports of Cartagena defenses, Spanish coal supplies (in such places as the Canary Islands), and Spanish vessel construction.[20] Sims even picked up information on the morale of the Spanish Navy; one report indicated the Spanish thought they would crush US naval assets.[21]

Some of Sims's reporting seemed too outlandish. He passed on erroneous information regarding Spanish plans to disable US naval ships with secret magnetized automobile torpedoes.[22] Attachés sent information overestimating Spanish capabilities and planning. But without other intelligence to dispute ONI, the Navy erred on the side of caution in planning for the most dangerous courses of action the Spanish could take. Guided by military advice from bodies such as a new Naval Board and spurred by public opinion, President McKinley and Congress took up a harsher prewar tone with Spain.

Strategic military intelligence organizations still conducted their core mission of data collection and management between 1895 and early 1898, but their superiors were asking ONI and MID to do more, especially as war planners and (in ONI's case) as naval promoters. The division also performed topography responsibilities with ease. Intelligence professionals were happy to oblige if it meant more prestige, money, and personnel.

ONI had neglected information management duties in the early 1890s. This mindset was changing in light of global events. Just as its Army counterpart, ONI had had its eye on Cuban events for the past three years. The Cuban Revolution of 1895 put more naval intelligence emphasis on the island colony. CIO Singer directed the staff to gather data on Spanish naval assets and coastal fortifications in the Old and New Worlds. Monroe Doctrine protection duties required US Navy policing in the Western Hemisphere. Also, by this point ONI was able to advise the department on whether the United States had enough warships to protect the Atlantic Seaboard from an arguably first-rate world navy threat. Admiral Richard Wainwright's biographer Captain Damon E. Cummings later wrote that after the outbreak of the Cuban revolution in 1895, the Cuban situation became ONI's sole focus; indeed, gathering data on Spain's defenses in late 1895 would be one of ONI's first forays into more serious war planning.[23]

Still, when Clover arrived at ONI in November 1897, the prospects of war with Spain still seemed a distant possibility. Naval intelligence continued war planning for overseas ventures against Spanish holdings, but other events consumed ONI staffers' time. For instance, Commodore George

Dewey visited ONI late 1897 before taking command of the Asiatic Squadron. He wanted the most recent materials on the Spanish-held Philippine Islands. He found that ONI's latest information on the colony dated from 1876, as no US Navy ships had visited the islands in many years and naval attachés did not cover it.[24] Meanwhile, the office worried about Germany. Niblack sent disturbing reports of German designs for colonial aspirations in Latin America. The naval attaché to Berlin insisted German imperialists were the next US enemy.[25] Nonetheless, the ONI was reminded of the immediate threat when Wainwright's ship blew up in Havana Harbor on February 15, 1898. Data collection became all that much more important.

For its part, since the late 1880s MID had focused heavily on Canada's military and geography. Information management and mapmaking assumed equal priority within the division in the three years before the war. Army leaders and the public had concerns about a great power military machine, such as Great Britain's Army on the northern border. Also, expansion advocates urged striking at Canada first to neutralize the northern neighbors and perhaps take some territory. During the Anglo-Venezuela Dispute of 1895 and subsequent tensions with England, American newspapers heightened the public's interest in Canada. The *New York Times* discussed MID's role as data managers in aiding the Army if the South American crisis spilled into North America, in an article demonstrating how the popular media viewed MID as an encyclopedic organization.[26]

At the same time, despite this focus on Canada, Army intelligence also diligently planned for conflict with Spain. MID had collected data on Cuba since 1892 and doubled its efforts in the last half of the decade.[27] Division chief Colonel Thomas M. Vincent and his predecessors impressively had the foresight to realize Spain was America's next military opponent. The organization gathered information meticulously from sources such as travelers, attachés, publications, and newspaper articles. By 1895, the Army possessed adequate maps and intelligence on Spain's military locations in the Caribbean. With this information they also advised department leadership on how best to exploit Spain's weaknesses.

MID's tempo of data collection increased considerably under Wagner. As usual, MID published semiannual and annual reports. But Wagner continued and enlarged MID's traditional task of making accurate and up-to-date maps of key countries and the United States, some of which the American public could access.[28] Before Cuba consumed all his attention, Wagner attempted to improve open-source collection, such as studies of periodicals and magazines to reduce dependency on attachés. The division chief also placed Van Deman in the Mapping Section when he came aboard in July 1897, an important first assignment as maps would be in high demand during the war's lead-up.[29] Wagner and intelligence work probably made an impression on the young Van Deman, enough for him to remain in the intelligence profession after he retired from the Army in 1929 until his death in 1952.

Spain and Cuba soon drove every activity in MID in 1897. The office had collection assets zeroed in on the island since the spring of 1892, but with the possibility of war looming, these intensified. The principal source of military information in early 1898 on Spanish deployments and preparations was Captain Tasker H. Bliss, the attaché in Madrid. He noted Spanish dispatches of troops and material to Cuba, and MID officers computed the strength of the Spanish Army in Cuba from his data. His troop numbers were later confirmed by Spanish sources to be within 2,000 men of the actual figure of 130,000.[30] Cuban insurgents also supplied data from safe havens in New York. And the MID Map Section strictly and frantically prepared maps on island defenses.[31] Despite these intense efforts, in the postwar years there persisted an impression that MID was not prepared. As military attaché Captain T. Bentley Mott wrote in a 1903 essay for the *Journal of the Military Service Institution*, the Army believed that MID did not have maps and detailed information at the outbreak of hostilities. But Mott accurately countered these charges by noting that the nature of intelligence was discreet and that truly the only Army officers who knew the extent of MID's contributions were the secretary of war and the adjutant general.[32]

After the *Maine* explosion, Wagner reorganized the division to emphasize overseas events and de-emphasize internal and militia duties.[33] Army intelligence leaders set up MID well to provide intelligence to the few officers in the Department of War who were essential customers. Staff officers also demonstrated the dynamism of MID between February and April. Van Deman debriefed Frederick Funston, an American who had served with Cuban guerrillas fighting the Spanish, gaining valuable information.[34] MID also investigated the probable impact of yellow fever if operations in Cuba were conducted in the summer; its officers reported past the chain of command that such operations would be inadvisable. Later, Van Deman claimed the president decided not to carry out a late-summer invasion after reading Wagner's report. Wagner's bypassing the chain of command rankled Secretary Russel A. Alger so much that he reportedly promised not to promote Wagner in the future.[35] Insubordination aside, Wagner and Van Deman took other helpful measures, such as making a map of Cuba that was printed on cloth to be used in the field.

Wagner also yearned to get operational intelligence from Cuba either by going there himself or sending representatives. He sent Lieutenants Andrew S. Rowan and H. H. Whitney to meet with insurgent Cuban leaders in late February. Wagner did so under his own volition, and the officers came back with much material.[36] With General Nelson A. Miles's approval, Wagner also attempted to create a tactical intelligence staff for Major General William R. Shafter, whose forces were preparing to invade Cuba, but Shafter rejected Wagner, believing he did not need intelligence.[37] Shafter's snub reflected a larger Army-wide prejudice, that is, the belief among senior officers that military information was of questionable value for Army operations, especially in terms of its relevance in field work. Shafter may have also believed that Wagner's proposal was an attempt by the Department of War to spy on how the war was being conducted in the field.[38]

All in all, both ONI and MID attempted to improve their war planning capabilities in the three years before the war as tensions increased in the Caribbean. There were many growing pains. The Anglo-Venezuelan border dispute of 1895 and Chilean-US tensions in 1891 highlighted ONI's initial inadequacies and apathy toward real-world war planning under Singer's watch. ONI did not contribute noteworthy intelligence to decisionmakers in either circumstance. In the later incident there may have been even apathy in the face of the British threat to US naval forces in the Western Hemisphere, unlike the attitude of the NWC. College president Henry C. Taylor led Department of the Navy efforts in war planning; he and Secretary Herbert did not enlist ONI's help. ONI had dabbled in war planning responsibilities as a secondary mission. The Department of the Navy gave the office two separate general orders in 1885 and in 1892 telling staffers that it was okay to engage in war planning. But under CIO Singer it did not totally embrace the mission. At the same time, the two latest secretaries of the Navy firmly grounded NWC as a permanent institution. NWC had learned exponentially from the primitive war scenarios ONI had provided the Newport school in the past decade, becoming a rival with ONI for valued responsibilities under Taylor's watch.[39] Herbert wanted warfare strategists to be more than just information providers—the cognitive step above data collection—in planning for future conflict. It was not clear in late 1895 if ONI could evolve to keep up with the NWC in this respect.

In these circumstances, in late spring 1896, CIO Wainwright dedicated his crew to daily intelligence reports and on planning. He set about renewing collaboration with the NWC to create contingency papers suggesting courses of action for commanders afloat in case of conflict. On June 1, this relationship with the NWC bore fruit as Kimball wrote the first full-scale war plan produced in the Navy. Kimball, assigned as a liaison staff intelligence officer to Newport, wrote the document "War with Spain, 1896, General Considerations of the War, the Results desired, and the Consequent Kind of Operations to be Undertaken." Wainwright proudly sent the piece to the chiefs of the Bureaus of Ordnance and Navigation, the president of NWC, and the commander of the North Atlantic Squadron—a rudimentary war board.[40] With this document, ONI proved that not only could it collect information but could attach plans to it as well.

Wagner took notice of the ONI-NWC collaboration in war-gaming, as MID and ONI shared the same building. MID did not have a formal planning unit, but Wagner soon adopted ONI's example.[41] MID wholeheartedly took on war planning duties, partly because it had already been collecting information on England and Spain for mapmaking purposes for three years. The Army did not have a board like the Navy and therefore could not easily approve campaign plans drawn up by MID or other bureaus. However, Secretary Alger did collaborate with Secretary Long to convene an informal joint Army-Navy board. Alger appointed Wagner to the panel, whose main mission was to draw up joint plans for war with Spain. He also attended a Navy board meeting on April 2, 1898, to help define the duties of the joint board. Wagner found the Navy was well ahead of the Army on war plans production. Although his division had conducted informal war planning for a couple of years, the rest of the Army had no contingency plans. What is more, the Army did not have a general staff to coordinate such matters.[42] Wagner alone represented the Army on the board and had the luxury of knowing he had the freedom to draft Army strategy. Before the war, he was the link in coordinating Army and Navy operations.[43] Ultimately, though, without much oversight from the Department of War leadership, the joint board was unsuccessful in coordinating Army mobilization plans with the Navy.[44] MID was just too far behind in the war planning business to be much help to its sister service.

Both ONI and MID were diligent in conducting their missions, such as war planning. Their industrious efforts were confirmed by the support they received from their superiors, the increased attention of Congress, and the credibility national media attributed to strategic military intelligence.

The Department of the Navy leaned on ONI for intelligence support, especially as senior department officials propped ONI up as a viable and needed institution. Secretary of the Navy Herbert noted the positive changes in the office by the end of 1896. His annual report discussed publications of interest, the new filing system, the energetic attaché corps, and Wainwright's strengthened relationship with the NWC. For example, Wainwright attended a portion of a college session to help understand his customers, after which both the CIO and the department pledged to have one to two ONI officers attend sessions annually in the future.[45]

Roosevelt officially took on assistant secretary responsibilities in April 1897 and quickly let it be known that his supervisory role of ONI was more than superfluous. Wainwright's boss wanted all the intelligence on foreign navies that ONI could provide, from battleships to naval stations. He also respected Wainwright enough as to confide with the CIO on matters not related to intelligence. In turn the assistant secretary rerouted warranted ONI reports straight to Secretary Long. While Roosevelt's use and commentary on intelligence bordered on security infractions, it signaled definitively that during this administration, ONI would no longer be ignored.[46]

Most notably, Roosevelt wanted the office to continue honing war plans as an integral part of war planning writ large. Future expansion of the overseas markets and perhaps a territorial empire required intelligence and a plan to use it. And ONI did not disappoint: Dorwart has argued that Wainwright led the most thorough efforts in war planning in coordination with the NWC before the formation of the Navy General Board in 1900.[47] The focus was Spain, but Japan (which had recently routed China) was also under consideration. Roosevelt appreciated Wainwright's assertiveness and only requested updates from the CIO on his planning endeavors.

Roosevelt also paid close attention to naval attaché reports from Europe. He instantly noticed Sims's hard work and often sent cables to Paris requesting more information from the attaché or even to simply praise his work. For example, he wrote Sims on August 16, 1897, "expressing . . . appreciation of the quality and quantity of the [furnished] information."[48] After visiting principal naval bases in Europe, Sims reported on their methods of ship construction and target practice. He was especially alarmed that American gunnery was far less effective than that of the European powers.[49] Roosevelt channeled his statements to the secretary, advocating gunnery reform in the Navy. When in late 1897 news came that his friend Wainwright was to leave Washington for operational duties as the executive officer on the USS *Maine*, Roosevelt was distraught. He forwarded to Wainwright a letter of commendation he had written to Long on the CIO's performance.[50] In the same correspondence, Roosevelt told Wainwright confidentially that the assistant secretary was sad to see him leave and hoped the outgoing CIO would be promoted rapidly.[51] Under Roosevelt's watchful eye, ONI had the potential to play a big part in America's naval expansion overseas. Not since Rodgers's tenure had the office had this much attention from naval leaders in aiding naval foreign policy.

On the other side of the building, between 1895 and the start of the war MID produced general intelligence and answered questions at a remarkable clip. The division's superiors took notice. The adjutant general boasted to Congress in the secretary of war's annual report in 1895 that MID's materials, "information communicated covered over 100 typewritten pages," were in high demand from Army officers, congressmen, and civil servants in the executive branch.[52] The following year MID could take credit for five special reports, the distribution of six thousand publications to customers, and the start of the first complete military map in US history.[53]

In 1897, the recently installed Secretary of War Russell A. Alger and Adjutant General Samuel Breck praised Wagner's "devotion" and told the legislative body that MID's "progress and usefulness" was "hindered by scant accommodations." The secretary requested more capable junior officers and better facilities.[54] The adjutant general was more effusive in his report on the needs of MID, often parroting the secretary's requests. He also wrote on additions to the military attaché corps and the need for more funds. On the workspaces, Breck argued for more rooms through appropriations from Congress.[55] Alger's and Breck's reports demonstrated their trust in Wagner and support for a successful division. They saw the value of this strategic military intelligence organization for American economic and territorial expansion, particularly through its production of plans and maps.

Media outlets began to understand ONI's and MID's missions more and to appreciate their potential usefulness (as promoted by the agencies themselves), but there was still an air of mystery to them. Americans, as seen through the press reports, probably comprehended that the development of the military's intelligence component was part of US society's adaptation to industrialization: ONI and MID documented supposed "progress" in not only foreign militaries but their own. Strategic military intelligence organizations seemed to tell Americans that the United States was getting "better"; although that too was ill-defined in the era. The *Washington Times* printed a public relations piece about the ONI on June 23, 1895, the most thorough public description of the organization in the press since 1882. The article explained to the layman that the secretary of the Navy must know all about the movements of foreign navies and that through "alert officers in a busy little workshop of the Navy Department . . . may at any moment know the disposition of the forces for any given day."[56] Interestingly, the *Times* described the task of operational intelligence, which ONI was not equipped to perform. The piece portrayed the office on the fourth floor of the State, Navy, and Army Building as a small force with an important mission: "Within its portals are kept, and from it have been communicated, as occasion demanded, weighty secrets that called for the issuance of orders upon the prompt execution of which depended the accomplishment of victory or the prevention of disaster."[57] The phrase "weighty secrets" may refer to the ONI's data management mission but only served to make the office appear more mysterious. Certainly, the public and press noted ONI's continued ability to provide information on the great naval powers. For instance, the *Saint Paul Globe* reported "an interesting item" published by ONI on Spanish naval construction.[58]

In the yellow journalism frenzy of early 1898, the press and the public's panic amplified the pressure for information. Articles on the creation of the new naval board and ONI's place within it immediately picked up. On March 14, the *Kansas City Journal* discussed the naval intelligence office's "careful work" in describing how ship construction of all types could be utilized in the event of hostilities and its data on "forty ships of all sizes and classes which will be inspected and examined if their owners desire to part with them."[59] The paper did not understand ONI's core mission of data collection, but the office leaders were probably pleased with the publicity. On March 28, the New York City *Sun* positively spun naval and military intelligence's information and planning roles in the prewar efforts. As press and the public beat the war drums, this article made ONI and MID seem like heroes.[60] Newspapers also expressed relief when the naval attachés provided locational data on Spanish warships.[61] They reported naval board strategic planning meetings to signify perhaps to their readers that the Department of the Navy was on top of the military situation.[62] Thus, ONI received much desired publicity from the media, even as the department started to second-guess ONI's utility for accurate intelligence as tensions mounted.

The insatiable press showed the same interest in MID's prewar activities. On April 1, 1898, the *Herald*, a Los Angeles based paper, eagerly printed MID's tables describing the strength of the American militia in 1897.[63] Like most Americans, the newspaper's editors wanted comprehensive knowledge of what the US military could bring to bear on Spanish holdings. The public also confused the MID's responsibilities with those of ONI. Both the *New York Times* and *Sun* published on April 3 that MID provided a pamphlet of information on Spanish *naval* assets. Most likely, ONI published the information and gave it to the press.[64] The confusion likely arose because, to the 1898 public, both MID and ONI seemed indistinguishable. And indeed, they served the same purpose: when the United States declared war on Spain April 25, Wagner's and Clover's staffs were prepared—with maps, information collection processes, and the capability for strategic war planning.

But what ONI and, to a lesser extent, MID's superiors wanted from intelligence professionals during the Spanish-American War was not as much planning and data gathering as operational intelligence, specifically, locational data on Spain's military assets. Wartime realities flipped the script on intelligence professionals, and they were unable, or often unwilling, to adjust to the departments' requirements.

Once war broke out, events in the Department of the Navy occurred in rapid succession. Almost immediately, Long formally established the Naval War Board, which became ONI's primary customer over the course of five months. Furthermore, the day the United States declared war on Spain, the department shifted ONI back to the Bureau of Navigation. Roosevelt left Washington to take a lieutenant colonel's commission in the First US Volunteer Cavalry Regiment. Naval intelligence lost the most powerful ally it ever had. Similarly to Roosevelt, ONI officers demonstrated in the months after the United States declared war that they wished to do their part in American expansion, just not at ONI. The record of the office's performance in Washington during the Spanish-American War was somewhat empty, just like its office spaces.

In 1898, naval officers—just as in past and future generations—believed a sailor's place is at sea, not behind a desk. ONI may have been a crucial part of the managerial revolution and the rise of a new navy, but it was not important to this war effort. Officers took their cue from CIO Clover who, as the New York *Sun* reported on April 8, requested and was granted sea duty as commander of the USS *Bancroft*.[65] The younger ONI cadre followed his lead and received sea duty orders as well. ONI cleared out. The department, realizing the drastically reduced value of ONI in war, replaced Clover with retired Captain John R. Bartlett. Bartlett had just one assistant officer, Edward E. Hayden (a retired ensign), during the entire period of the conflict. Lieutenant Humes H. Whittlesey staffed the cipher room, but he served as Navigation Bureau Chief Arent S. Crowninshield's personal aide, spending the bulk of his time with the Naval War Board.[66] To his credit, Bartlett was competent and knew both the office's limits and what was needed from the minimal staff. It helped that he was retired; he could criticize superiors with fewer consequences.

Bartlett described the work he did as strenuous and wide-ranging.[67] But when ONI had just two officers and seven clerks, this could be expected. Cables streamed into his cipher room continually from sources abroad. Naval attachés encrypted most of the cables and it was ONI's job to tend to this message traffic. They processed approximately three hundred outgoing and eight hundred incoming cable messages over the course of the war. Bartlett received daily requests for information and intelligence summaries from the Naval War Board, recalling later that he constantly had sea charts standing by for the board, which resided next door to ONI.[68] Throughout the conflict, ONI scrutinized newspapers for foreign naval opinion. He also instituted a "Memorandum of Information" for squadron officers and updated it daily. And as an example of what the department thought of ONI's value in a time of conflict, the Navy assigned Bartlett supervision responsibilities of the Coast Signal Service and Auxiliary Naval Force as well. At the same time, while ONI was busy, this was due to the lack of manpower, not to its workload. The war ended quickly without ONI playing an essential role in the outcome.

For two months after the war, no one in the department clamored for ONI's services. Naval intelligence spent August into December regenerating the office, self-evaluating intelligence officers' performance, and pushing for official recognition from superiors and Congress, after attesting satisfaction with the way the office had carried out duties during the war. ONI had dismantled its wartime infrastructure and started welcoming back the scattered intelligence officers. The Navy phased out the makeshift spy system in Europe: some agents continued to report on the peace process through September, but the department stopped paying most sources for lack of need. Clover returned to ONI in early October to relieve Bartlett, and three officers from the staff were back in the State, War, and Navy Building by the end of December. Not everyone returned from overseas immediately, however. Because the Navy had a scarcity of officers and only a few officers on duty, ONI could not fill four department-head billets through the rest of the year.[69] Still, the office had a better manpower situation than in the summer months.

Late 1898 through early 1900 were transitional months for Clover and ONI, with changes occurring that would alter the nature of naval intelligence. Officers streamed back into the space, played catch-up with piles of information yet to be filed, and virtually ignored the war that persisted in the Philippines. In March 1898, the board reorganized the office into six branches, each representing a specific functional area: ship card indexing, personnel, ordnance, steam engineering, communications, and attaché correspondence. An intelligence officer headed each branch with an allotment of clerks, with the board scheduled to meet monthly to revise processes and policy if needed. Clover revised the card catalogue system so that staffers created cards with new items, filed by topics vice where the information came from, which could be cross-referenced in a complicated but efficient system. Clover altered the previous system, as he realized he could not keep up with both data management and filing backlogs caused by wartime personnel shortfalls. Once all the officers had returned to ONI from the fleet, Clover had all his subordinates work on cutting down the backlog. In June, this working party consisted of seven officers and about ten civilians.

The conclusion of the nineteenth century marked an end of an era for some missions and for naval intelligence leadership. On October 16, 1899, former CIO Lieutenant Commander Theodorus B. M. Mason died, at sixty years of age.[70]

ONI leaders, past and present, reported war stories through official publication and humorous speeches. The Kansas-based *Atchison Globe* reprinted a wire story circulating around the country's media demonstrating how little Americans and government officials still knew of ONI. The newspaper reported that Bartlett regaled the Society of the Colonial Wars in New York in early February 1899 with two anecdotes. First, he shared that it worried him after taking charge of ONI to hear a woman he knew "explain that the naval intelligence office was a place where sailors applied for places in the navy, just as cooks, waitresses and the like applied to civilian 'intelligence offices.'"[71] In his second tale, Bartlett pointed out Americans still used "intelligence" with the term "information" interchangeably in 1899. Bartlett said the Army made the same mistake.[72]

Like their ONI counterparts, MID officers rotated out of the State, War, and Navy Building offices upon America's declaration of war. They too followed their chief's example. Wagner wrote to Adjutant General Henry C. Corbin on May 7 saying it would be "humiliating" if a military affairs theorist like himself was stuck behind a desk while colleagues and former students got to carry out what he lectured.[73] Corbin concurred, and Wagner was in the field two weeks later. As was the case with naval intelligence, the Department of War thought military intelligence was nonessential in a war to expand American influence overseas, and thus MID let its officers scatter to more operational and tactical duties.

On April 25, there were eleven officers on duty at MID and sixteen attachés. By June, MID had two officers manning the office spaces and five of sixteen attachés on station. It was natural for officers to clamor for field service; volunteer units needed regular officers to lead them. The Department of War did not even name a temporary chief of the division back in Washington. Captain Lloyd C. Scherer and Van Deman remained at the office with about ten clerks.

MID returned to routine much quicker than ONI in late 1898 and into 1899 only because the department expected little intelligence production from the division while officers slowly returned to Washington. Those officers manning the shop carried on their information collection and mapmaking duties after the Cuban theater closed. MID's war responsibilities carried on into 1899 as the Philippine portion of the conflict continued.

In 1899, MID slowly stood down from its wartime duties, especially since the Philippine conflict took longer to manage. Unlike the situation faced by the Navy, the ground portion of the war and occupation was more time consuming, and the intelligence service experienced difficulties as MID could not adapt to the demands of the Philippine campaign as easily as to Cuba. No one had anticipated major conflict in the islands; therefore, it took months before the division could send enough maps, terrain studies, and general intelligence to the theater.[74] Detailed operational intelligence, such as current enemy locations, was out of the question. MID's late-arriving intelligence was too much for General Wesley Merritt, American military governor of the Philippines, to bear. In early 1899, he created the Bureau of Insurgent Records in Manila to deliver intelligence on Filipino insurgents and the mood of the general population. The bureau, later renamed the Military Information Division, became the first theater operational intelligence organization in American history. Washington's Military Intelligence Division was relieved, in more ways than one, of its duty in Asia and could focus on returning to a normal routine.

During the war, the skeleton ONI and MID staffs faced significantly altered duties. The Navy expected more from Bartlett, his meager staff, and their attachés than they could provide. They were barely able to conduct their data management missions and floundered in providing operational intelligence. The Army's leadership was much more realistic in what they could expect from two intelligence officers in Washington, DC; as such, MID only aided the war effort with data collection and reporting.

The USS *Maine* disaster was a surprise to naval intelligence. At the beginning of the war, the questions remained for the Department of the Navy: Where was the Spanish Fleet and what was its intentions? Because of how the organization had developed to this point, ONI could only conduct war planning and collect information of a strategic nature and was unable to provide ship locations and tactical warnings.

The lack of locational information created a panic about protecting the fleet within the department leadership. They desperately needed news of the Spanish armada. This hunger was only partially satiated by ONI. The Navy also needed a plan as to how to proceed. Therefore, in mid-March Long and Roosevelt assembled the commander-in-chief of the North Atlantic Fleet, the chiefs of the Bureaus of Navigation and Ordnance, the president of the Naval War College, and the CIO of the ONI as an ad hoc war board. Long lacked professional military experience and had no general staff, which made such an informal board essential. Also, ONI and the NWC had war plans already on the shelf, which they presented to the board, which approved them. Assistant Secretary Roosevelt, Rear Admiral Montgomery Sicard, Captain A. S. Barker, Captain Crowninshield, and Commander Clover manned the first iteration of the board. ONI was integrated into strategy sessions. The first formal meeting occurred sometime in late March, with weekly meetings thereafter.[75]

The Navy War Board, desperate for intelligence, dispatched two agents, Ensigns Henry H. Ward and William H. Buck, disguised as tourists to Europe to gather intelligence on the Spanish Navy. The secretary of the Navy hounded attachés for information. Long cabled Sims and naval attaché to Berlin, Rome, and St. Petersburg William H. Beehler on May 5 demanding information on where the Spanish squadrons were.[76] Sims, never one to disappoint superiors, provided the information two days later, underscoring how essential American naval representatives abroad were if only for the scant locational information they could collect.[77] The Spanish-American War thus changed attachés from not mere technical information collectors to agents who clandestinely acquired restricted intelligence.

The attachés also served as geopolitical analysts and procurers of naval weapons and equipment. The CIO pleaded for attachés to buy information and material, telling them that money was no object.[78] And so, they did, using the "Secret Service Emergency Fund" to hire spies and buy data. In France, Sims employed a retired military officer and an impoverished nobleman with intimate contacts in the Spanish government. Niblack's replacement in Berlin, retired Captain Barber, recruited a former naval officer and an American fencing champion for missions in Cairo.[79] These spy rings were rudimentary, but under the circumstances this was to be expected. The naval attachés may have lacked professionalism during the five months of the war, but they were the best asset available to a hollowed-out ONI.

Operational intelligence deficiencies continued to plague ONI through the summer months. The situation was excruciating for the Navy Board, which worried that the Spanish Fleet could launch surprise attacks along the eastern seaboard. In the face of these scant operational intelligence capabilities, the board had to consign ONI to answering requests for information, issuing daily publications, and tending to the naval attachés. It was mundane work for a skeleton staff.

In 1899, ONI's support to commanders of the Western Pacific fleet was almost nonexistent. Aside from generic Spanish naval intelligence material that the office had forwarded in its daily ship message traffic during the last few years, Dewey received no intelligence help, even in such a significant engagement as the Battle of Manila Bay.[80] Naval attachés did provide purchased supplies, including the Australian refrigerator ship *Culgoa*, and watched arms shipments from European ports potentially bound for the Philippine rebels.[81] But other than minor tactical intelligence provisions, there was nothing truly noteworthy in naval intelligence's assistance to the Navy.

On June 1, 1900, the Navy detached Sims from his post in Paris after three years of service. In his stint as attaché, Sims compiled an amazing eleven thousand pages of reports and filled twenty-two letterpress books. Such voluminous diligence set records for naval attachés probably not equaled in the corps' history.

For their part, MID caretakers Scherer and Van Deman did not offer lower-echelon intelligence to units in the field in the Caribbean, and indeed Secretary Alger did not expect this of them. They continued information collection, mapmaking, and analysis tasks limited to predicting the strength of the Spanish Army, publishing intelligence pamphlets on Cuba, Puerto Rico, and the Philippines for use by all Army officers. They also produced maps of Spanish holdings and a strategic war map for the White House, no doubt helpful to McKinley but in no way real-time information. Wagner had molded an efficient organization capable of carrying out data management and topography even when war planning tasks evaporated.[82] Thus, MID generally stayed ahead of the department's requirements for intelligence.

In the war's immediate aftermath, ONI and MID's military and congressional superiors ignored the fact that these intelligence agencies were virtually useless during the war. Perhaps they too believed that a soldier or sailor's place was in battle, not on a staff far from the frontlines. Intelligence leadership had convinced senior department leaders and congressmen of the merits of ONI and MID based not on data provided during the war but on the preparations the two organizations accomplished before the early months of 1898. In short, intelligence agencies were the military's embodiment of the Progressive era's trends toward professionalism and managerial/bureaucratic efficiency when planning for the next war, but when major conflict arose intelligence semiprofessionals abandoned those principles to join the fight. Unlike the end of US wars in the twentieth century, ONI and MID did not have to worry about demobilization after hostilities ceased. The offices had mostly disbanded when the Spanish-American War began.

It is a credit to Bartlett's devotion to duty and work ethic that with only five full months in the post, he offered a lengthy report to Congress on October 1, 1898, detailing ONI's achievements and needs. His statement, carried in the Bureau of Navigation's section of the department's annual report to Congress, may be considered the first annual report of the CIO in the ONI's sixteen years of existence.[83] But his main purpose for addressing Congress was to make the case for separate appropriations and legislative recognition, which he said would correct the confusing clerk payroll.[84] He claimed ONI needed a permanent civil clerical staff, including a permanent registrar.[85] He bolstered his case by pointing out that ONI had performed its duties such as publications well and had demonstrated its capacity for intelligence work with its service to the newly created Naval Board. He ended his report with a plea "that every effort be made to place [ONI] on the plane of highest efficiency."[86] Clover, for his part, submitted a supplementary report to Congress a few weeks later outlining the wartime efficacy of ONI and the importance of naval attachés but noting the limitations imposed by the insufficient workforce.[87] He played to Hamiltonian, expansionist sensibilities: "All foreign naval powers have offices corresponding to our Office of Naval Intelligence, established on a permanent and liberal basis."[88] Both Navy Secretary Long and Crowninshield endorsed Bartlett and Clover's recommendations.[89] Crowninshield also advocated for incorporation of ONI into his bureau by congressional action.

ONI continued to serve Secretary Long faithfully. In return, Long gave Clover's office the responsibility of acting as the clearinghouse for all information from attachés and other foreign officials to the United States, necessitated by foreign governments' further tightening of information released to US naval attachés overseas.[90] Long helped naval attachés gain more bargaining power with foreign governments in an atmosphere of secrecy. Long and Crowninshield also attempted to raise expense allotments for attachés, but funding shortfalls plagued ONI for years to come.[91]

ONI received more publicity after naval intelligence offered recent war narratives. Clover instinctively knew that the public and Congress wished to understand more about the Spanish perspective on the clashes of the recent war. Therefore, he reprinted Spanish newspaper and journal articles in "ONI Notes on the Spanish-American War" in late 1898 and early 1899. The series had quite a following not only in Navy circles but among public libraries, congressional legislators, and foreign attachés in Washington. The Printing Law of 1895 initially limited the "Notes" to one thousand copies, but it was so popular that in 1900 the Senate reissued it under the banner of a congressional document, allowing for four thousand more copies. This was the public relations windfall that ONI leaders had always sought.

After months of lobbying, Long, Crowninshield, and Clover convinced Congress of the merits of ONI's services. Giddy over naval successes, Americans seemed responsive to advancements in the naval establishment; after all, an informed navy was necessary to protect the new empire.[92] In February 1899, Congress authorized an office of naval intelligence and approved funds to increase ONI's General Information Series from one thousand to five thousand copies. Congress permitted the office to employ five clerks, a translator, a draftsman, and a laborer. The new job openings brought the first women employees to ONI.[93] Congress also allocated money for naval attachés, of which there were at this point a modest four—three in Europe and one at Tokyo and Peking. Official congressional recognition, demonstrating the value of the organization (as confusing as its mission was at times), was an important ONI milestone seventeen years in the making.

Like ONI, MID used its perceived successes to press Congress for more funds. Adjutant General Corbin spoke for the division in the Department of War's annual message.[94] Corbin thus asked that Congress allow for higher rank and pay for military attachés to allow them to stand on equal social and military footing with their counterparts from other nations. MID emerged from the war with an enhanced reputation, receiving praise in 1899 from President McKinley himself.[95] The "Dodge Commission," which investigated the Army's conduct of the war, had nothing negative to report on the division. Thus, after the conflict, the department gave MID the freedom to direct its own action and patterns of operation.

It would be easy to gloss over the failures of the strategic military intelligence organizations in the Spanish-American War by stating they were bound to make mistakes in their first international conflict. But ONI and MID displayed faults needing to be addressed.

The Navy's definitive victory over the Spanish fleet determined American triumph. The naval battles at Manila Bay and Santiago de Cuba allowed for American dominance of the seas, isolating Spanish strongholds and guaranteeing their defeat. How much did naval intelligence play into this triumph? Probably a little credit can be given for war planning, but none for operational help. Basic information for a war with Spain was on hand, and with Naval War College collaboration, the CIO had war plans at the ready. But naval intelligence proved unwilling and unable, once the bullets started flying, to provide intelligence on Spanish fleet movements required for commanders at sea to be at their most effective. Technology advancements, such as real-time reporting radios, and a departmental revision of ONI's mission would help eventually solve operational intelligence weaknesses. That is, of course, if the public, ONI's superiors, and the CIOs themselves agreed that this was an office mission.

For the Army, intelligence was not a fundamental reason for the US victory. MID too failed to give real-time data on the enemy in both the Cuban and Philippine theaters. But, unlike their naval brethren, there was little interest from the parent department in acquiring locational information. Those officers left in the division after hostilities commenced were content with information consolidation and reporting and mapmaking. Because of Wagner's foresightedness, the organization could afford to scale down strategic intelligence efforts. He and his staff made attempts at war planning in 1897 and had been gathering information on Cuba for maps and intelligence reports since 1892. Thus, MID accomplished its mission to prepare the Army for war with an accurate picture of Spanish defenses.

In 1900, the United States had an empire. Now what would Americans do with it? Historian Robert H. Wiebe has argued that although proponents for empire talked about how expansion reflected maturity, an ability to bring humanity to savages, and commercial opportunities, there was no policy for administering the new territories.[96] From their small office spaces tucked away in the State, War, and Navy Building, ONI and MID leaders would have to decide how, if at all, they would monitor these new territories for their superiors. Surely, they would continue to be called upon to report events and advancements overseas, probably with even higher fidelity. After all, as historian David F. Trask notes, the largest consequence of victory was its acceleration of Americans' acceptance of global responsibilities with their newfound power.[97] Strategic military intelligence organizations needed to expand to help the military meet those international responsibilities. Yet, this is not what occurred at the pinnacle of the Progressive Era from 1900 to 1915. Instead, ONI struggled and MID arguably ceased to exist.

Chapter Four
1900–1915:
The Nadir of ONI and MID

Hamiltonian ideals continued to win out over Jeffersonian thought in the United States, as evidenced by the rise of Progressivism in the industrial age. Progressivism was a political philosophy that supported social reform between 1890 and 1920. But it was so much more. Historian Michael McGerr called Progressivism "an explosion, a burst of energy that fired in many directions across America."[1] The era of dynamic reform "was a moment in which the entire structure of American institution—from the government to the economy—seemed to be up for grabs, poised to be reshaped by new movements and ideas," wrote historian Beverly Gage in her book *The Day Wall Street Exploded: A Story of America in Its First Age of Terror*.[2] Progressives, largely middle class in background and tired of being caught in the crossfire between a disgruntled lower class and an apathetic industrialist class, desired to make the world safe for themselves and future generations through reform of social problems.[3] In so doing, they sought to harness the untapped potential of government regulation to push their wide-ranging agenda.

The new system that Progressives embraced was "impersonal sanctions" and regulation, imposed by governmental levers, to centralize authority.[4] The executive and legislative branches, Progressives argued, must establish a dependable bureaucratic order through laws and their enforcement to manage the social chaos spurred by industrialization. The new bureaucracy needed conservation and efficiency to control both the pace and direction of change.[5] "Efficiency" is a key term, emerging from Frederick W. Taylor's theories on industrial management. Taylor's *Gospel of Efficiency* preached that a "factory was to be one big machine, with all the tasks organized and distributed accordingly, and with men of special training placed to see that gears meshed."[6] Progressives loved Taylorism because the theory explained how to control and manage turmoil, allowing for reform. Progressivism and Taylorism thus pervaded not just businesses but the increasingly complex government institutions and the military.

Military progressivism was an extension of both social Progressivism and the managerial revolution that started with reformers such as Emory

Upton and Theodorus B. M. Mason. They shared the spirit social reformers and wanted to improve their services. In turn, the military benefited a society coming to terms with industrialization and America's enhanced place in the world. Military progressives recognized that national and international developments had brought the United States and the armed forces to a decision point: to hold onto the past or strike out in new directions. They claimed victory over the traditional establishment with aggressive measures—such as the creation of a general staff—strikingly akin to bureaucratic processes advocated by private sector reformers.[7] Progressive leaders sought to create a more disciplined and ordered military through the application of American business management structures.[8] Military progressives emphasized Taylorism, organization, war planning, and professionalism to best protect America and its empire. All the while, the military continued to grow in personnel and complexity.

Early twentieth-century Americans, especially the progressive middle class, had a benign view of the military. They recognized that the progressives of the civilian sector and their military counterparts had the same social goals—the downtrodden could only benefit from reformer legislation and professionalized peacekeeping. Of all publications, surprisingly the *Ladies Home Journal* described how the modern military had made the world a better place through strength, reform and the protection of commerce.[9] The *Ladies Home Journal* and other media outlets accentuated strategic military intelligence organizations' role as informants to a peacekeeping, reforming, and powerful US military.[10] Throughout the Progressive period, American cultural references continued to perceive the Office of Naval Intelligence (ONI) and Military Information Division (MID) through the lens of its publications, reports to Congress, and trivia quoted in papers.

As mysterious as the Navy and Army intelligence was to the public, the services increasingly became irrelevant and misunderstood by superiors in the US government between 1900 and 1915. Their ineffectiveness can be attributed to the constant reforms, reorganization, and redefinition of mission that slowly pushed ONI and MID into forgotten corners of their respective departments. National leaders instinctively identified military intelligence as something that needed to reside at more operational levels instead of remaining in the realm of strategy. For the first eight years of the century, President Theodore Roosevelt protected the strategic military intelligence organizations, especially his old friends at ONI; he was a reformer who wanted to safeguard the new empire. But Presidents William H. Taft and Woodrow Wilson had less interest in their services. The secretaries of the Navy and War allowed military leaders in the departments to control ONI and MID through emerging general staffs. In the division's case, the department traditionally gave little guidance on what information to collect overseas and how to publish the material; MID's superiors figured they knew what they were doing and let them go their own way.[11] For their part, admirals and generals tightened the reins on intelligence as they demanded more support to planning. By 1908, the Army chief of staff just let Army War College planners consume MID in war-planning responsibilities.

The decade started out promising for ONI and MID leaders, as their bosses believed they performed well in the Spanish-American War in the pre-planning and postwar publication phases. ONI Chief Intelligence Officers (CIOs) judged that their first mission was to work with the Naval War College (NWC) to prepare for the next wars to protect America's maritime holdings and to continue collecting and storing naval intelligence. There was a strong military progressive vein in the naval staff, which ONI exemplified. But naval intelligence officers soon found themselves engulfed in bureaucracy. MID fared much worse.

The early years of the twentieth century overwhelmed both ONI and MID.[12] The high tide of Progressive era and military progressivism between 1900 and 1915 had a damaging effect on strategic military intelligence organizations because of the period's overemphasis on reorganization and management—the very trends that spawned them. ONI weakened throughout the period as staff officers struggled to interpret society and government needs. The Department of War submerged MID through indifference. The division, once respected as an organization for its planning and information collection expertise, melded into the general staff bureaucracy until only traces of Army intelligence existed in 1915.

The new century started with much potential for ONI and MID as organizations. They had earned the respect of their bosses, Congress, and the American public through their performance in the latest war and planned to cash in on the newfound prestige with growth in personnel, money, and more sought-after missions. The leaders of Army intelligence in particular had secured the service's autonomy and hoped that a future general staff would prominently place MID at the top of military leadership. Still, although strategic military intelligence organizations had the backing of Roosevelt and powerful secretaries, reorganizations took a toll on both ONI and MID.

In 1900 ONI displayed a healthy vitality, boosted by personnel and a positive reputation. The whole staff returned to ONI after the officers, who had scattered to sea duty for the Spanish-American War, came home. Office space became an issue in the State, War, and Navy Building. ONI received money from Congress in 1899 for more clerks and was busting at the seams. The Bureau of Navigation requested from the department an additional room for the CIO so that he could provide confidential material to those who needed to know. Eventually, the Navy allotted a storeroom for clerks to use, while CIO Commander Richardson Clover commandeered a larger space. The lack of room was a welcome problem for the CIO; it meant ONI was growing, as it still enjoyed the organizational high that Lieutenant Richard Wainwright achieved in 1897.

However, unlike previous chiefs, incoming CIO Captain Charles D. Sigsbee did not view ONI as a first-rate organization within the department. Sigsbee became the first permanent captain to head up ONI; his posting signified the trust that the Navy leadership placed in naval intelligence. At the same time, Sigsbee had been in command of the USS *Maine* when it exploded in the Havana harbor in February 1898. The catastrophe haunted Sigsbee and explains how he directed ONI between 1900 and 1903. He thought that the shop should have provided better intelligence to him and the fleet concerning Cuban events, possibly preventing the explosion. It was from this context that Sigsbee made it a personal crusade to fix ONI's perceived deficiencies.[13]

Upon arrival, Sigsbee wrote to the Bureau of Navigation chief about problems he had identified within the office spaces. In his view, there were security violations with handling classified information and storing secret documents. Sigsbee claimed that files were chaotic and that materials lay strewn about the rooms. He also highlighted the lack of general space that Clover complained about. ONI needed more tables to continue campaign planning for a Navy war board. He chafed at the department's policy to substitute clerks into officer billets to compensate for officer shortages. Sigsbee set about instituting reforms that streamlined office processes. He pushed a new economy-sized Navy Codebook to attachés that replaced a fifteen-year-old multivolume edition. His staff received improved Kodak cameras. He ordered naval attachés to improve general business practices by numbering all their reports, typing their correspondence, and keeping their letters strictly professional. Sigsbee was determined to right a ship he felt was sinking.

In 1900, Sigsbee detailed his major changes in to superiors. He reported that the office complement was usually seven officers, but there were currently only six on duty "hardly adequate for the regular division work of the office throughout the whole year."[14] Sigsbee planned to have his clerks review and get rid of files of no currency to free up more space for more important information. He reiterated ONI's office space issues in the annual report to Congress. But he was pleased to mention that because the "Notes on the Spanish-American War" was so popular, the office supply was exhausted, and Congress authorized more copies under the name "Senate Document No. 388." The Navy received an additional five hundred copies.[15]

In 1902, the office experienced an officer reduction from seven to four officers. Perhaps the Bureau of Navigation believed ONI's importance had diminished in the department. ONI had to rely more on the civilians in the shop for analysis. Consequently, Sigsbee decided to discontinue the General Information Series after twenty years of publications. The last edition was five hundred pages with 105 sketches of foreign naval advancements, written by Lieutenant Commander John H. Gibbon, Lieutenant Charles L. Poor, and Lieutenant Louis M. Nulton. It was the only unclassified publication series produced by ONI at the time. The office also kept busy translating foreign documents for the Office of the Secretary and the Bureaus of the Department. Also, Sigsbee sent Lieutenant Commander Marbury Johnston to Venezuela, the first naval attaché to Latin America. The CIO was particularly concerned with the German threat and ordered Johnston to monitor German efforts to collect debts from a struggling Venezuelan government.[16]

ONI had occupied the State, War, and Navy Building for over twenty years. It started as a one room outfit on the first floor with a few desks and some filing cabinets. But even with the downsizing of recent years in terms of officers, the number of clerks Congress allowed the office to possess forced a reevaluation of the allocation of rooms to ONI. In one of Sigsbee's last acts as CIO, he successfully lobbied new space for the organization. In April 1903, ONI staffers moved across the street to the Mills Building. The move shifted ONI away from leaders in the Department of the Navy and the president, causing it to lose some influence with its superiors in naval affairs. Sigsbee left ONI with a mixed record. He successfully lobbied for an intelligence role in planning campaigns, but he could not maintain a full complement of officers. In June, ONI had only five officers assigned to it, with one of them serving on temporary duty at the NWC.

As the US government grew larger to meet the demands of middle-class progressives, naval reformers continued their assault on the traditional establishment. ONI felt the effects of change with new leadership. Sigsbee's successor and ONI alumnus Captain Seaton Schroeder inherited a small and overburdened office. Schroeder arrived at an ONI much different from the cadre of idealistic, reformist-minded officers he experienced in the 1880s. Many of his staff, like himself, probably thought of this shore tour as a chance to recharge the batteries before going back to sea. Schroeder would later recall that he did have some ideas of how to expand naval intelligence with new activities, but his Navy superiors shut him down.[17] The Department of the Navy charged other bureaus and the NWC with the very responsibilities that he envisioned for ONI. Consequently, he put his energies "to the perfection of internal matters and methods."[18] As a consolation, the department reiterated that ONI was still the authority on centralizing information from the fleet and disbursing information and intelligence to department leaders and bureau chiefs.[19]

Schroeder, forced to tend to his own internal matters, experienced a rocky start in his relationship with the NWC. Captain Caspar F. Goodrich, commandant of the Portsmouth Navy Yard and friend of the college, advocated that fleet intelligence officers report directly to the NWC and his command and not ONI. The CIO's fighting spirit revived; he became adamant that ONI retain its centralization authority. The very autonomy of ONI was at stake as the CIO fended off predators during his 1903 to 1906 tenure, protecting its planning and information-gathering responsibilities.

In April 1906, Schroeder's rotation ended, and he assumed command of the USS *Virginia*. The Department of the Navy tapped a familiar face, Captain Raymond P. Rodgers, as his replacement. Secretary Charles J. Bonaparte probably selected Rodgers, a second-time CIO, because he knew the job and was a navalist like the president. His main responsibility was to feed the General Board (the successor to the Naval Board) and the NWC with information on Japanese naval assets, material, and general geopolitical conditions. Although Rodgers worked administratively under the Bureau of Navigation, the office's effective operational chain-of-command was to those who really influenced policy and planning: the board and NWC. Rodgers employed nine permanent civilians in his office, slightly more than during his 1886 to 1889 tenure. Rodgers's agenda for this tour was Japan, establishing more secrecy procedures in the office, information gathering, and public relations. Stagnant organizational growth and a lack of more prestigious responsibilities characterized Rodgers's second tour.

For its part, MID started the 1900s as an organization in a comfortable position: fully in charge of its own destiny with the promise of a major seat in a future general staff. It faced a promising bureaucratic context, as well. Russell A. Alger resigned as secretary of war at President William McKinley's behest on August 1, 1899, yielding to his critics' claims that the Navy had been more prepared than the Army for the war and that he ran the department inefficiently. Progressive and distinguished lawyer Elihu Root quickly made everyone forget the previous secretary, as he led the Army into an era of reform. Root had a clever, investigative mind and critics and supporters alike admired his ability to impartially solve problems. He was a Taylorist and enjoyed reshaping a disorderly environment with strong, executive leadership through centralization. Root admired Upton's philosophies and used his roadmap from the 1870s to help reform the Army in the Progressive Age. When Root took office, MID could expect to be an indispensable element of future reorganization because intelligence was prominent in the armies of Europe that Upton had observed so many years ago. After the war, MID came away with a solid reputation for information gathering and war planning; there was no indication the next few years would not be just as successful as the preceding ones.

The Insurgent Records Office in the Philippines became the Military Information Division on December 13, 1900. Lieutenant Colonel Joseph T. Dickman, who led the agency, answered to the Adjutant General's Office, Headquarters, Division of the Philippines, but also had a close liaison with MID in Washington. The agency became a branch of MID in Washington in 1903. The close partnership evolved partly due to Captain Ralph H. Van Deman's efforts. After Van Deman left MID for the Philippine theater, he became an assistant to Dickman. He would deploy to the islands three more times in his career; that may be where Van Deman discovered a passion for counterintelligence.[20] When Van Deman became the chief of a revitalized MID sixteen years later, counterintelligence would become a major mission of Army intelligence.

MID adjusted to reforms in 1902 as it felt the effects of perceived Army-wide failures of the last war. Secretary of State Root sought to find ways to reform the Army as it had, in his view, displayed weaknesses in 1898 and continued his plans to overhaul staff organization and procedures. It would be only a matter of time before Root's reforms would impact MID's traditional semi-autonomy. Division officers found themselves answering more questions related to war planning from the adjutant general and the war college. To help it take on the responsibilities of information collection of additional overseas territories, Congress authorized MID's budget increase from $6,640 to $10,000. It helped defray costs for a new military attaché in Havana.[21] In these circumstances, MID eagerly welcomed the addition of the Military Information Division to its portfolio. The Manila-based office delivered useful intelligence on nearby countries. Strategic military intelligence organizations expanded their networks around the world, thanks to a rapidly increasing attaché corps and a nascent operational intelligence apparatus.

Other improvements appeared on the horizon as well. MID and ONI found their intelligence officers gradually intruding into each other's collection and analysis territories. They had been rivals since 1885, but it was counterproductive for the two organizations to keep information from each other. In 1902, ONI and MID established a liaison for the full exchange of information. The spirit of cooperation also extended to attachés. If a naval or military attaché left a station before the relief arrived, it became common for the sister service attaché to fill in as acting attaché until the relief appeared. These courtesies were part of a new understanding of interservice cooperation in the Progressive Era.[22] In a broader sense, the centralization of government and regulative authority brought ONI and MID in orbit with each other amid government bureaucracy.

The monumental General Staff Act suggested that MID could have a larger part in Root's reforms. The act passed on February 14, 1903, establishing a general staff corps.[23] There was no mention of a specific structure to the new organization. This would be hashed out by Army leaders, specifically the War College Board, once the act became effective August 15. The bill created a chief of staff position to replace the commanding general as head of the new General Staff Corps. It also gave the staff the responsibilities of planning for national defense, mobilization, and supervising the functioning of the Army. Surprisingly, the act limited the staff to just forty-five officers because of congressional distaste of a German-style staff. Only time would tell how MID would fit in and how many officers the staff would allocate to Army intelligence.

Secretary Root fought the orthodoxy in the Army—the established alliance of congressional Democrats, state governors, and many militia officers—for the General Staff's creation.[24] The greatest opponent of the initiative was the last commanding general of the United States Army, Nelson A. Miles. The "brave peacock" (as he was called by Roosevelt) represented the old Army of the Civil War and Indian Wars, which was resistant to change. But Root had the backing of Roosevelt, Assistant Adjutant General William H. Carter, and several distinguished Civil War soldiers, including former commanding general John M. Schofield. As he reached the mandatory retirement age of sixty-four, Army regulations forced Miles to step down, making it easier for Root to lobby with Congress.[25] The general staff's creation was a major victory for military progressivism, setting the stage for more reforms and reorganizations through World War I and beyond.

MID chief Lieutenant Colonel W. A. Simpson confronted the possibilities of the next iteration of Army intelligence. The secretary of war and Adjutant General's Office no doubt asked Simpson for his recommendations but also queried him for the current state of the division. He reported that the division had six sections: military progress, map, militia, frontier, Latin American, and photographic. Simpson then defined each section's responsibilities.[26] This report was fact-based, but not yet revealing the direction of Army intelligence.

A few months later Root issued a set of orders to put the general staff in motion before the August 15 congressional effective date. He was determined to provide the Army with a centralized organizational system similar to that which existed with large businesses.[27] On August 8, he issued General Order no. 120, mandating that Military Information Division headquarters, with its records, files, property, and personnel, be transferred to the office of the chief of staff, to take effect in seven days.[28] The MID became the Second Division in a three-division general staff, thus ending an eighteen-year period where Army intelligence operated directly under the adjutant general.[29] The division still held responsibility for information collection, managing military attachés, maintaining files, and topography. But it did not have war planning duties.[30]

The new division launched operations in the new general staff. Like ONI, the Second Division needed space; the four rooms in the State, War, and Navy Building were simply insufficient. Therefore, the organization moved to the third floor of the nearby Lemon Building. This was close enough to conduct routine business with the Office of the Chief of Staff and the First Division but perhaps too close to the Third Division, which was situated temporarily at Jackson Place on Lafayette Square. The first chief, Major W. D. Beach, only received a complement of six officers, along with several experienced clerks left over from MID. The department detailed future deputy chief of staff for intelligence, G-2, Captain Dennis E. Nolan for staff work October 26, which began a decades-long career with Army intelligence. He met senior Captain John J. Pershing at the Second Division and would begin a successful collaboration that lasted into the 1920s. Root's architect for the general staff, Carter, endeavored to keep the Second Division on equal footing with its counterparts.[31] For example, he forced other organizations to keep Second Division and its attachés in the communications loop. Newly appointed Army Chief of Staff Lieutenant General Samuel B. M. Young also had high hopes for the new division, reporting in 1903 that the Second Division's personnel had increased and its duties reorganized and extended.[32] The department revitalized Army intelligence and it seemed nothing could deter the service from performing intelligence at the highest echelons.

Yet, the events of 1903 were a double-edged sword for Army intelligence. The Second Division had a coequal function with other duties within the general staff. But an unnoticed shop within the department now received more attention from advocates and more notably, bureaucratic predators. Root and other military progressives assumed that MID would naturally fit into the general staff because of its fine reputation from the Spanish-American War. After all, the great general staffs of Europe had military intelligence organizations and they seemed to fit in nicely. Why couldn't the Second Division? This was an era of regulation, Taylorism, and reorganization; functionality had to be a large consideration of general staff structure. Intelligence was a major function. But the Second Division was only a military information service. It did not possess any authority to influence policy, conduct planning, or to regulate itself.[33] Without the ability to express views on military affairs or to protect itself, the Second Division was vulnerable.

The winter after the Second Division's formation the entire general staff adjusted to new office spaces and duties. Terminology and titles changed so much that it was hard for Congress to keep up with the reforms. Army appropriations bills consistently named the "Second Division" the "military information division" until 1917. The 1904 appropriations bill was also the first time Congress authorized "contingent expenses" to the military information division on the general staff, a loophole the War College Division later used to draw more funds when the Second Division ceased operating.[34] In 1904, though, military intelligence had adequate funding and support from the Department of War.

In May of that year, the Third Division made its first move to take over Army intelligence. Beach heard of a proposed modification to General Order no. 115, which would entail the merging and subordination of the Second Division under the Army War College. He took up the pen and wrote the chief of staff to show Army intelligence's frustration.[35] Apparently, advocates of the proposed merger contended that war college students were collating military information that the Second Division should have been dealing with but had delayed because of lack of facilities.[36] For his part, in defense of his division, Beach contended that intelligence had to be a major function of the general staff, just as it was in every other world power. The Department of War issued the general order in June 1904 without the proposed modification. But the Third Division yearned for intelligence in-house.[37] This uneasy relationship between the two organizations would continue for the next three years.

Intelligence professionals were often involved with war planning in the first eight years of the century. ONI and MID still performed their traditional missions (information management, topography, and public relations), but organizational challenges (internal and external) kept straining their ability to support customers.

ONI had more protection from bureaucratic maneuvering than its Army counterparts, because of the organization's old friend President Roosevelt. His administration was aggressive in foreign affairs and provided CIOs many opportunities to increase ONI's reputation within the department. To help acquire international respectability, Roosevelt needed intelligence. Roosevelt's and Secretary of the Navy Charles H. Darling's support assured ONI officers of naval intelligence's value. In 1904, Darling gave the CIO a list of danger spots across the globe that the department wanted ONI to further scrutinize. ONI focused on the core mission of accumulating data, especially on both the Pacific and Caribbean approaches to Roosevelt's planned Panama Canal. The presidential administration specifically required intelligence on harbors, foreign navies, and the geopolitical atmosphere in Central America. But the situation was never stagnant: the information-gathering focus quickly shifted when on February 8, 1904, naval attaché Lieutenant Commander C. C. Marsh told Washington that Japan and Russia were at war.

Whereas Sigsbee was obsessed with Germany's intentions in the New World, CIO Schroeder was more interested in eastern Asia because of the rising power Japan. The United States had recently acquired overseas colonial possessions that were desirable to other nations. In the Pacific, the Japanese had a sphere of influence that bumped up against US strategic interests, such as the Philippines and Marianas Islands. Would Japan's Navy be interested in these territories? Schroeder ordered his naval attachés to find out. So, in addition to technical information, the CIO welcomed news on political and economic atmospherics from his agents overseas. Also, the possibility of war between two great powers in the maritime environment piqued ONI's interest; modern fleets had not fought each other in decades. Battles between Russia and Japan would answer theorists' curiosity as to the effectiveness of artillery against armor, newer fleet tactics, and the torpedo against battleships.[38] And so ONI had renewed purpose when war did break out.

Schroeder's chief hope for information were assistant naval attachés dispatched to the war zone: Lieutenants Irvin van Gorder Gillis, Newton A. McCully, and Lloyd H. Chandler. And while he anticipated that this roving band of lieutenants could gather the most information, he also utilized other sources, such as Marsh in Tokyo, news correspondents, and the State Department. McCully was assigned to the Russian side. Although he was not an intelligence officer by trade, he did know Russian and was meticulous in his reporting.[39] Initially, the issue for McCully was getting to the front; he had to go through Russia first.

The CIO told McCully to travel to St. Petersburg to serve as the assistant naval attaché and accompany the Russian forces in the theater of war.[40] Schroeder's tone was nurturing rather than exacting; he mentored McCully on how to make himself persona grata with the Russians—even to the point of appearing sympathetic to their cause.[41] On March 15, the State Department granted permission for McCully to perform his duties. Two days later Schroeder gave him further instruction to go to the front and check in from time to time.[42] To avoid confusion, Schroeder cabled Marsh in Tokyo and told him that Newton was not Marsh's assistant as originally planned; rather, Lieutenant Gillis was his assistant instead.[43] McCully reached Moscow and Russia's foreign office gave him permission to join the Far Eastern forces. In getting to his post, McCully made an unprecedented journey for an American naval attaché, across Eurasia from St. Petersburg to Beijing utilizing exotic modes of travel, such as camels across the Gobi Desert.

In this war, however, naval attaché access and reporting was not as valuable to the president and the department as Schroeder expected. Gillis could not receive Japanese permission to embed himself with forces or visit naval bases. Chandler told ONI that he was having difficulties obtaining information. There is conflicting information as to how useful McCully's observations were in Manchuria. Dorwart notes that McCully spent most of his time in Port Arthur (modern day Lüshun), from whence he could send a few reports on wounded Russians, minor military matters, and personal observations on people and places.[44] In contrast, historian Mark R. Shulman called McCully's reporting "insightful" because his intelligence, especially on torpedo boats, had the potential to enlighten strategic thought.[45] Of the two, Shulman is more correct; any observation, even if personal, had some value to Washington customers.

Roosevelt made regular demands for detailed reports on the conflict from ONI. The long-time navalist was curious about the advancements of naval technology and sought information to help assist his own thoughts on increasing the US Navy's size. Roosevelt also pondered the strategic implications of the Russo-Japanese War for world powers and Open Door trade. In addition to supplying the president with information, ONI also copied the General Board on every cable from the Far East. Furthermore, the office complied with superiors' requests for information with weekly war bulletins, special papers on battleship technologies, and memoranda for Friday cabinet meetings. One ONI memorandum, for example, described how well Japan conducted landing operations at Chemulpo.[46] ONI staffer H. W. Whittlesey reported to Roosevelt how confident the Japanese appeared to be.[47] Whittlesey was Roosevelt's personal briefer and conduit to ONI. He supplied the president with a report titled "Battleships in the Russo-Japanese War" on October 27 and drew a war room map for showing the positions of Russian and Japanese forces.[48] ONI's prompt intelligence reporting to leadership was helpful in forming opinions of Japan's naval war-fighting potential.

After the Russo-Japanese War, ONI's collection assets remained boresighted on the east Asian potential adversary; the naval attachés reported rumors regarding Japanese war preparations again between 1906 and 1908. Rodgers monitored attachés' reporting directly because Roosevelt, the General Board, and the NWC were exceedingly interested. Commander John A. Dougherty was a voice of reason in Tokyo, reporting that the Japanese Navy had ceased naval construction and did not have the budget to conduct another war. ONI advised superiors to monitor but not be too concerned about Japan yet. The General Board agreed and requested that Rodgers and his staff maintain a plan of campaign of Japan for war planners to use.[49] Reporting on Japan was especially crucial, as Roosevelt's "Great White Fleet" visited Japan in 1908. Roosevelt tasked ONI with analyzing Japanese public opinions of the goodwill cruise and naval intelligence indicated that Japan had no ill will toward the endeavor.

Other aspects of Roosevelt's cruise and office routines in general indicated the rising levels of security required in intelligence affairs of the early 1900s. As rumors of sabotage directed at the Great White Fleet abounded near harbors and chokepoints around the globe, Rodgers directed attachés to find out any pertinent information. At home, the Department of the Navy issued orders in April 1907 to all officers to restrict foreigners' access to US naval assets and to practice operational security when speaking to foreigners. The order mandated that officers direct inquiries and permission to tour ships to ONI.⁵⁰ Rodgers also tinkered with the Navy Codebook, finding it inadequate in the new security environment and creating an updated cipher with new codewords. In general, ONI officers dabbled more in security administration as they were being squeezed out of war planning and senior government officials lost interest in ONI's data collection capabilities once Roosevelt left office.

For its part, with Department of War support for Army intelligence's semi-autonomy, the division kept performing data collection. Intelligence experts sensed the opportunity for their tradecraft to have a leading position in the new general staff. The staff was a blank slate and experts wondered whether and how MID would fit, or if it would morph into something else. First Lieutenant Edwin R. Stuart wrote that indeed the general staff must have a "perfectly organized and equipped Bureau of Military Intelligence."⁵¹ Stuart advocated that this new bureau be an information provider to the general staff on possible foreign antagonists and future theaters of war, specifically foreign army organizations and topographical data.⁵² Stuart was a strong supporter of the division's core missions of data management and mapmaking, with no mention of the analysis of strategy as a war planning function. From another point of view, Captain T. Bentley Mott wrote an essay stating that the Bureau of Military Intelligence should have three responsibilities: information collection and intelligence preparation on potential enemies, systems analysis of hostile forces, and publication of material to enrich Army officer professionalization.⁵³ Mott viewed this bureau as a war planning body. And from yet another, former MID officer Brigadier General Theodore Schwan spoke disparagingly of MID's past, calling it a history of a "bureau weighted down with records and routine work."⁵⁴ Schwan believed that a future bureau should strictly conduct data management and distribution.⁵⁵ Whereas theorists Stuart and Schwan advocated a bureau that would stick to its traditional core mission, Mott wanted military intelligence to do planning as well. However, all three represented the military progressivism widespread in Root's Army.

The intelligence service continued its information-gathering and mapmaking missions, honed now for almost twenty years. In June 1904, the Office of the Chief of Staff ordered the division to recommence work on the map of the United States that MID had suspended in April 1898. It also launched new topography studies on Latin America and the Far East. On September 14, Beach told Chief of Staff Lieutenant General Adna R. Chaffee about the division's activities since August 1903. He boasted of eight assistant attachés embedded within the Russian and Japanese armies since the start of conflict and the work the military attaché corps had accomplished. The chief also stated that the liaison with ONI for information was strong.[56] In 1905, the division had six officers with the self-described mission of data management and reporting. Army intelligence duties had not varied much in the organization over the years, at least as its own leaders described them. The division had six sections: the military attachés, the Branch Office at Manila, two libraries, a map section, a photograph section, an historical section, a translation section, and a publication section. According to Beach there was still a healthy contingent of fifteen observers, including twelve military attachés, monitoring the war in the Far East.[57]

In 1906, the division sent officers on secret reconnaissance trips to foreign countries to supplement attaché reporting. The program provided the Department of War more information, allowed Army officers an insight into intelligence work, and gave access to countries that did not necessarily like Americans within their borders. Army intelligence rekindled its tradition of aggressive intelligence collection in foreign countries as well.[58] The Second Division also provided support to the US intervention in Cuba in 1906 in response to the resignation of the Cuban president and his cabinet. It delivered analysis of the potential enemies, maps, geopolitical studies from the office files. Intelligence officers deployed with the expedition to Cuba to offer operational intelligence on the island. In September, the division had ten officers to cover five in-house sections; a month later, the chief halved his manpower because of deployments. One MID captain complained about manpower and office space to his superiors.[59] The Department of War still understaffed Army intelligence in small workspaces, even with its recent move. In 1907, the Army solved this problem in a way most Second Division personnel would not approve.

Van Deman returned to Washington in early 1907 and joined the Second Division staff. He quickly went to work helping the staff produce intelligence reports. Van Deman said that Roosevelt tasked his office with weekly memoranda on the activities and intentions of the Japanese. The Second Division often furnished reports to the president and the secretaries of war and Navy.[60] Second Division's reports helped warn of possible Japanese intentions to attack and supplemented ONI's pre-cruise intelligence for the Great White Fleet. This was Van Deman's first experience with the general staff structure. He probably learned new bureaucratic approaches from the give-and-take, questions and answers processes that occurred throughout the chain of command, which he applied almost a decade later as head of Army intelligence.

ONI eagerly jumped into war planning duties during Roosevelt's presidency. As soon as CIO Sigsbee took the post, he made planning a priority. Sigsbee felt his staffers lacked specific intelligence skills and that it was desirable to resurrect a defunct NWC officer exchange program to provide them gaming and strategic training opportunities. He created a new section designed to help ONI with planning; it would calculate strategic weaknesses in foreign navies. He also ordered his officers to concentrate their publication efforts on potential adversaries' naval doctrine and strategies.

The CIO's intent was to embed ONI comfortably in a relationship of the NWC and the next iteration of the Naval War Board. Akin to Lieutenant Raymond P. Rodgers in the 1880s, Sigsbee was generous with the information he gave to the Newport institution. And when the General Board formed in 1900, he made his staff prepare intelligence documents to distribute for him when he attended meetings. Sigsbee believed ONI's mission included not only traditional information collection and reporting but also how to use that intelligence against adversaries. The CIO was determined to have a primary role in war planning in the department. Specifically, Sigsbee believed the primary enemy in a future war would be Germany, basing his assessment in part on the fact that in 1900, the European country was tied for fourth place worldwide with the United States in terms of the construction of new ships. He let congressmen know his fears of Germany through memoranda and statistical data.[61] He believed America had stakes in two maritime regions of the world and that the military could not stand by for a foreign power (like Germany) or alliance to rise before initiating planning.[62]

Despite Sigsbee's gestures of goodwill, ONI had an uneasy relationship with NWC from 1900 to 1915 when it came to deciding who controlled planning and naval strategy and how the processes of analysis would work. But they needed each other: ONI provided the intelligence and the NWC had the brain power and time to develop strategy and policy. When opinions in the Department of the Navy coalesced in a spirit of reform to make the Naval War Board more permanent, ONI and the NWC took prominent positions.

For decades Rear Admiral Stephen B. Luce advocated something resembling a naval general staff. A navalist and military progressive, he had been instrumental in the success of the US Naval Institute and the establishment of the NWC; at the turn of the decade, he renewed his reformist crusade. In March 1900, he declared that the "need for a General Staff in our Navy is not unnatural"; rather, it was a necessity that the service shared with "large business enterprises in civil life."⁶³ He argued that the Navy had already instinctively formed elements of a general staff by creating ONI and the NWC, and that it would just need further elements—such as having the assistant secretary or the chief of navigation to head the organization—to be complete.⁶⁴ Luce recognized the Navy was not considering a staff in a vacuum; he observed the Army wrestling with the same concept. In the end, when Luce recommended a Navy board to Secretary John D. Long, Sigsbee concurred with his suggestions.⁶⁵ ONI and NWC plans met with bitter opposition from Senator Eugene Hale and many naval bureau chiefs who were traditionalists resistant to change. Still, current NWC president Captain Henry C. Taylor took ONI and the college's proposals to Long as he too saw the opportunity of creating a naval general staff considering the maritime protection demands of a new empire.

Secretary Long endorsed Luce and Taylor's recommendations, issuing General Order no. 544 on March 13, 1900. It created the General Board composed of the admiral of the Navy, the chief of the Bureau of Navigation, the ONI CIO and his principal assistant, the president of the Naval War College and his principal assistant, and three other officers of lieutenant commander grade and above. The purpose of the board was to "insure efficient preparation of the fleet in case of war and for the naval defense of the coast."⁶⁶ The head of the NWC and CIO had the responsibility of providing the information required from them by the General Board. The general order avoided the term "general staff" because it reeked of Old World bureaucracy. Admiral of the Navy George Dewey became the senior member. The General Board also had an advisory role on such matters as naval strategy, war planning, and coastal defense. It lacked executive, administrative, and command authority responsibilities. Because Long and not Congress created the board, there was no special relationship with the constitutional commander in chief and therefore no real authority.⁶⁷ The board was a step in the right direction, but it did not solve the absence of an authoritative body.⁶⁸ The department tinkered with the Navy's general staff for years to come. Nonetheless, Luce achieved a significant milestone in his distinguished career, which did not go unnoticed by newspapers, such as the New York *Sun*.⁶⁹

The Russo-Japanese War and President Roosevelt's intense interest in Western Pacific affairs made war planning for Japan an ONI priority between 1906 and 1908. The East Asian country's victory over a great power piqued people's interest. At the same time, Japan took a more unfriendly policy toward the American government because of US segregation of Japanese Americans, perceived racism toward Japanese people, poor mediation of the recent war, and growing power in the Pacific.[70] Government leaders ordered ONI to provide as much intelligence on the rising power as possible. However, ONI staff found that their bosses and colleagues increasingly left them out of policy discussions and war planning meetings. ONI's reduced mission sets started to resemble the Second Division's dwindling responsibilities.

Root launched his reforms and continued to pursue his goal of an Army general staff with military education, a prerequisite for war planning. In February 1900, he directed Brigadier General William Ludlow, with the support of a board, to form a war college. Congressmen early in Root's tenure knew of his plans for a general staff and a war college's place within it; to achieve them, Root required legislative approval and sowed the seeds of support.[71] The Ludlow Board took on Root's suggestions that the new war college would be a temporary substitute for a future general staff until Congress created such a body through legislation.[72] From the start the Department of War sowed confusion as to whether the Army War College was an educational institution or a staff organization and the accumulation of its prospective duties overburdened the fledgling establishment.[73] Ludlow muddled the situation further when he said that while the college would have military information duties MID needed to be a permanent part of the general staff as soon as it came into being.[74] Root and Ludlow had high regard for MID. But the foundational beginning of the Army War College and the formation of a war planning juggernaut had disastrous effects on Army intelligence.

On November 27, 1903, a general order prescribed a detailed program for accomplishing military education for officers and established the Army War College as the main element of the Third Division. The War College was supposed to be an institution for advanced courses of professional education. It was intended as only a portion of the Third Division, which was charged with preparation of war plans, combined Army-Navy operations, technical manuals, military education, permanent fortifications, harbor defense, and new developments. But the War College housed a War College Board that habitually received tasks associated with military plans and assessments from the department. This linking of the Army War College to strategy made the institution a much larger part of the service's reforms and planning efforts. Brigadier General Tasker H. Bliss, the first president of the college, attempted to keep the educational function from the general staff but was unsuccessful.[75] Efficient war plans required detailed Army intelligence that made the Second Division a close partner. The library, the catalogue system, and the attaché corps tied them together. It was just a matter of time before the Third Division's planning vacuum would suck in the Second Division.

ONI and MID/Second Division became less effective as organizations as the Roosevelt administration ended and the departmental structures were reworked to the detriment of intelligence professionals. The decreasing kudos from Congress, department leaders, and the media testify to the diminishing power the office and division had within the military establishments.

As had been ONI's practice since the early 1890s, it continued to promote itself and the Navy in all possible venues to its superiors and American people. In 1903, ONI attempted to curry congressional favor by supplying tables and charts of the size of foreign naval powers compared with the US Navy.[76] ONI also received attention from the media interested in this same issue.[77] ONI's open access publications received curiosity from papers like the *New York Times*.[78] Representatives from naval intelligence lectured at NWC as part of efforts to impart information to naval officers. Captain Goodrich, former president of the NWC and an advocate for shipboard intelligence, gave a lecture on the subject to students on July 28, 1902. He told them that ONI was the "eyes and ears of the commander-in-chief" and "without it he would be as one blind and deaf."[79] Goodrich was more familiar with what the fleet intelligence officer provided in tactical intelligence and focused most of his lecture on such topics. But he commented how "complete and fresh" the materials were in its archives for the Navy's use.[80] ONI and its advocates displayed, through articles and speeches, how valuable the office wanted to be to its customers.

ONI impressed Congress and the American public by how well it covered the Russo-Japanese War and the state of great powers competition in the maritime realm. Schroeder provided Representative George E. Foss with foreign naval powers tables and charts in a memorandum of information.[81] The House Naval Committee used ONI's intelligence for naval appropriations discussions. Also, Schroeder had the ears of the president on events and strengths and qualities of the two fleets leading to the Battle of the Tsushima Strait.[82] A week later, after the battle, Americans relied on ONI's reporting to decipher how Japan defeated Russia. Admiral George Dewey studied the maps and charts of the theater of war and followed the news of the battle as it came to him from ONI.[83] The Russo-Japanese War showed that some customers still demanded ONI's information-gathering skills even if they were losing influence in war planning responsibilities.

Naval intelligence proved the capability to provide quality intelligence. The public and press remained fascinated by the US Navy's relative naval power compared to that of other great powers and ONI enthusiastically obliged to inform them. ONI provided the *Washington Post* the "relative totals of the war ships' tonnage of the principal naval powers."[84] The Department of the Navy also submitted similar tables of the programs of principal naval powers to Representative Foss, chairman of Committee on Naval Affairs, on February 4, 1908.[85] Representative Lemuel Padgett (Tennessee) used ONI's data to crow about the US Navy on the House floor. Padgett exclaimed, "What is the condition of our Navy? I say that we have a magnificent navy."[86] ONI appreciated citations from representatives. Not only was naval intelligence attempting to show its viability, but name recognition would perhaps assist in obtaining proper amounts of funding in next year's naval appropriations bill.

Army intelligence's attention from Congress and the American public thrived up until the end of Root's tenure. Then, as the Third Division began to smother the Second Division's voice, people began to forget that such an organization as the Military Information Division existed. But in 1900, the department's military leaders praised MID on a regular basis and stepped in occasionally to get funding for the division from Congress.[87] Adjutant General Henry C. Corbin once more mentioned to the House and Senate a chronic issue that plagued both Navy and Army attachés for years: expenses. Corbin requested that the military affairs committees revisit increasing allowances for attachés overseas to pay for exorbitant expenses in European cities, otherwise "the choice of military attachés must be restricted to the few officers who have incomes in addition to their pay and are willing to spend their private means in the performance of this public duty."[88]

Meanwhile, many Americans held MID in high regard for its ability to collect information and relate data to the public. American media outlets picked up on Root's reforms in Washington. One article reported that Root might even recommend that the war college be placed under the supervision of MID because Army officers would benefit from the "army knowledge of the advanced type" kept at the division.[89] Americans saw the mysterious, but benevolent, strategic military intelligence organization as a fount of information. One journalist wrote about the preparation of a pictorial history of the Spanish-American War produced by MID's Captain Edwin A. Root, calling it "one of the most interesting picture-books ever published."[90] Unfortunately, the attention MID received from the media for its open-source publications evaporated once after Root's era of reforms ended in 1904.

The year 1907 opened the worst stretch of organizational strife in the history of the two strategic military intelligence organizations. The Army overregulated its intelligence capabilities almost out of existence, to the point that military attachés had no organization to turn their information over to in Washington before the Great War. ONI lost its powerful political patrons, leaving its leaders struggling to find meaning in an evolving pseudo-general staff.

In May 1907, a bureaucratic coup interrupted the division's work. The Third Division or War College Division (WCD) moved into its new building at the Washington Barracks five miles away from the Lemon Building. The WCD was accustomed to daily information material dumps on its doorstep, but distance now made this virtually impossible.[91] Brigadier General William Wotherspoon of the WCD suggested that the Department of War move the Second Division to the barracks to best serve the needs of the planners. Second Division officers strenuously objected to the proposal, stating that Army intelligence would be cut off from the rest of its customers in Washington and more importantly, the Second Division would lose autonomy.

But the division had no mentors, much less senior officers who really understood Army intelligence. The chief of staff, Major General J. Franklin Bell, in his portion of the 1907 Secretary of War annual message to Congress, repeated almost verbatim Major Beach's memorandum to the chief of staff October 12, 1905, regarding the missions of the Second Division.[92] He and other Army leaders had lost interest in Army intelligence, a cadre that kept to themselves. Bell approved the transfer over Second Division protests, ordering the division's personnel to transfer to the Army War College building on May 24. Department of War General Order no. 116 established Army intelligence's relationship with the WCD and marked the beginning of its loss of independence. Unwittingly, the apathetic chief of staff soon found himself without an effective strategic military intelligence organization. Overregulation and reforms that marked the era trapped Army intelligence in bureaucracy.

The situation worsened for Van Deman and his colleagues in October. The Department of War ordered that all official correspondence for or from Army officers must pass through the Adjutant General's Office. This meant a possible disruption of direct communications to military attachés overseas, the only way the Second Division could supervise collections abroad. The assistant chief of staff backed Adjutant General Major

General Fred C. Ainsworth's order, but the division skirted this directive until 1909 when it no longer had the power to resist. Ainsworth represented one of the last efforts to oppose the general staff modernization program, reasserting the old bureau system by using his political influence with Congress. Some historians even argue that Ainsworth unofficially ran the Department of War.[93] Not only was the progressive initiative hampering military intelligence but nineteenth-century thinking also hurt the beleaguered officers.

The final blow to the old MID came on June 27, 1908. Bell ordered the chief of the Second Division to form a Military Information Committee (MIC) under War College control.[94] Why was Bell so eager to approve Wotherspoon's proposal for a merger?[95] Bell, like other senior officers, did not understand military intelligence's value to a general staff. They reasoned intelligence officers were secretive men behind closed doors who could not possibly inform policy. He wondered what intelligence really could do for him and the staff. Army intelligence lost the public relations battle in the department. Bell's simple acceptance of the disintegration of the Second Division represented the willingness of a military progressive to use Taylorism to centralize authority and fine-tune his general staff as he saw fit. In this crucial decision, he overregulated the general staff.[96] Army intelligence fell victim to the Progressive Era.

Intelligence officers such as Beach and Van Deman protested to the merger, pleading with Bell and Wotherspoon as to the importance of Army intelligence for the service. But senior officers outgunned them in rank with no patron politician to come to their aid. Former MID officials followed through with orders. Van Deman indignantly served the new organization for two more years, filing numerous maps in some random office of the college. The Second and Third Divisions merged into the new Second Section (or WCD). The existing First Division became the First Section. Wotherspoon subdivided the Second Section into the MIC and War College Committee. Lieutenant Colonel Thaddeus W. Jones, former chief of the Second Division, became chairman of the MIC. Wotherspoon had department approval to effectively dismantle the old MID apparatus. He dispersed all the MID files and officers throughout the Second Section. Former military intelligence officers had other duties assigned, such as teaching. According to Van Deman, the MIC "consisted of practically every officer on the War College staff."[97]

The chief of staff brought up key issues about the state of Army intelligence in the fall of 1908. First, he reiterated the recommendation that military attachés receive rank increases commensurate to those foreign attachés receive from their governments—the equivalent of lieutenant colonels and majors.[98] He intimated that the attachés needed more pay from Congress to do their jobs. Also, Bell held up his reorganization as a great move for the General Staff. He stated, "I am convinced that time is bringing a better understanding of the usefulness of this new body, and, being familiar with its work, I am able to testify that its usefulness at present is very great and prospectively promises to be in more so."[99] By emphasizing "understanding" in his remarks, Bell was unintentionally indicting himself: he could not come to an accurate understanding of the value of Army intelligence. And so the Army's intelligence structure slowly degenerated.

The MIC, a much weaker intelligence organization then the old MID and ONI, entered a period of hardship. One reform by the Department of War prohibited the Second Section from direct contacts with the State Department and the Department of the Navy. Under the new regulations, the MIC's military attachés could not confer quickly with their naval counterparts at the embassies overseas, effectively stopping the liaison between ONI and Army intelligence in Washington. The committee probably disregarded these regulations until World War I out of necessity. The chief of the Second Section resumed disassembling the intelligence structure early in the year as he took over the clerks from the Second Division. Wotherspoon also assumed the communication functions for the entire section.

More reorganizations rocked the general staff in 1910, making it harder for Army intelligence to recover. For the first time since the Second Division (effectively MID) dissolved, Congress downgraded the organization's title for contingency funding to the "military information section."[100] It was a misnomer: the organization really did not exist. The Second Section—and later the WCD—had to justify to Congress that the Army still conducted military information business for funding purposes. It became harder for the War College to convince them of this throughout the next ten years. In the middle of the year, Lieutenant General Leonard Wood assumed the chief of staff post. Like his predecessor, he was indifferent to Army intelligence. Instead, Wood directed his staff to find measures to aid the Army in the field. He believed that organizational conflicts, such as Ainsworth's feud with his staff, hurt Army work inside and outside of Washington. To help solve his problems, Wood restructured the general staff by discarding the First and Second Section concept. The functionally designed structure he imposed consisted of four divisions: Mobile Army, War College, Coast Artillery, and Militia Affairs. Wood confirmed

Army intelligence's submergence into the WCD with his reforms. In the same month, Wotherspoon transferred most of the MIC work to other parts of the division. Army intelligence officer Lieutenant Colonel Walter C. Sweeney would note that by the end of 1910 only two members of the MIC did anything remotely related to Army intelligence, as the WCD officer corps drifted between the committees in the building.[101]

Army intelligence's fortunes continued to plummet between 1910 and 1915. One could not decipher if officers conducted intelligence work within the MIC and the larger WCD. In 1915 Congress debated appropriating funds to the WCD based on "Contingencies, Military Information Section, General Staff Corps." The War College felt the pressure from the legislative body to prove that officers still performed a semblance of the Army information functions. To ensure they received the funds on an annual basis, the WCD reorganized again. The chief split the college into a "Military Information Section" (MIS) and an "Army War College Section" in May; however, he made clear that the officers' main duty was general staff work.[102] Only one in ten functional areas assigned to MIS were related to intelligence. The War College buried the remnants of MID within the Military Information and Monographs Committee. Even as the WCD convinced Congress to increase the funds to $15,000 for the next fiscal year, Army intelligence reached the bottom, the lowest point of strategic military intelligence in thirty years. Near the end of the Progressive era, Army intelligence almost ceased to exist.[103]

Perhaps the only reason ONI did not succumb to MID's fate was that the Naval War College was geographically separated by states, not miles. Otherwise, the college, which succeeded in taking planning functions away from ONI, may have engulfed naval intelligence as well. ONI was in transition in 1909 as the organization had three different CIOs amid a major US Navy reorganization and the loss of its mentor Roosevelt.

For the previous nine years, ONI had leadership stability, with only three CIOs. However, Rodgers was an aging intelligence professional. He had served with distinction in naval intelligence for over twenty-five years, but his tour was over. In May 1909, he departed the Mills building offices to assume presidency of the NWC after a brief tour of European naval yards. Captain Charles E. Vreeland, a former Rodgers staffer, took over. Vreeland was not CIO for long, as his imminent promotion to rear admiral allowed him to go to sea. By moving Vreeland along, the department indicated ONI was not yet ready for a flag officer. Vreeland handed over the post to Captain Templin M. Potts, a pioneer of ONI from 1882. Potts was a reasonable choice for CIO, as he had served both in the office and as a naval attaché. He held the post for three years and the organization regained some stability.

Steadiness was important amid another major naval reorganization so characteristic of the era. Secretary of the Navy George von L. Meyer shuffled the department as Potts arrived in December 1909. He placed ONI under the aide for operations of the fleet, directed by former CIO and Spanish-American war hero Rear Admiral Richard Wainwright. Wainwright chose Potts for the intelligence slot not for his pedigree but as a shipmate from a previous sea tour.[104] His division was one of four aids created to advise Meyer with the four other divisions designated for administrative matters. Meyer's system reflected the tinkering of an inadequate general staff system that failed to live up to naval progressives' desires for centralization of fleet movements, warship construction, and policy reforms. But it was a step in the right direction. Since Congress did not create the aid system—unlike the Army's General Staff—the divisions remained just advisory organizations. For ONI, the reorganization had the potential for more planning duties. The Office of Aid for Operations also included the NWC and the General Board. By virtue of sharing the same division, perhaps naval intelligence could share some of the analytical workload. Two years later, Meyers changed the title of the chief intelligence officer to director of naval intelligence (DNI) in November 1911. He probably felt that the previous title was too generic and that the post demanded a qualifier to show the chief of intelligence worked for the Department of the Navy. It was the first change to the title since 1882; with one disruption in the late 1940s, the job still uses the moniker "Director of Naval Intelligence" today.

Meyer asked Potts to be the aid for personnel in 1912. Captain Thomas S. Rodgers, younger brother of naval intelligence pioneer Raymond, became the new DNI. The younger Rodgers was not an intelligence officer by either trade or experience; Meyer may have selected him to nominally fill a senior shore billet. The secretary of the Navy indicated with the Rodgers's selection how lowly valued ONI had become since the days of President Roosevelt's mentorship. Unsurprisingly, Rodgers displayed mediocre management in his tenure that straddled the Taft and Wilson administrations. He seemed content with ONI's old public relations and data management missions, engaging in neither innovation nor transformational initiatives.[105]

The Navy still did not have a general staff in 1913. The General Board and the Aids were advisory staffs and could not stand in as markers for the centralization of authority Progressives had preached for over twenty years. Yet the confusion of reforms and reorganizations instituted by secretaries of the Navy over the years took a toll on ONI. It had physically been moved, given new titles, shifted on organizational charts, and received conflicting guidance on responsibilities since 1900. Naval progressives such as Commander W. S. Crosley continued to advocate the necessity of a true general staff with ONI as a prominent member.[106] In his proposal, ONI would be elevated to an assistant to the chief of staff. ONI was cash-strapped, Crosley said, but reparable through reorganization.[107] He argued for Congress to establish a general staff through law just as it had ten years previously in the Department of War. Otherwise, ONI would maintain its slow decline.

Captain James H. Oliver took the DNI reins from Rodgers in January 1914. He inherited an ONI at its lowest point of morale and effectiveness in twenty years.[108] The office seemed to retreat to its core mission of gathering technical information; intelligence leaders still organized the office spaces along functional lines. In April 1914, ONI made a second move to the Navy Building, just a block from the Mills building and still near the White House. Navy legend Lieutenant Commander Dudley W. Knox came to ONI after finding no billets open at the Torpedo Station or General Board. Captain William S. Sims suggested he try naval intelligence as it was suited for his analytical talents and interest in history. Knox was a Taylorist and military progressive and wrote an article in *Proceedings* about scientific management.[109]

ONI restructured as part of Navy-wide major reorganization in early 1915. Specifically, Oliver allowed eager reformist Knox and Marine Major John H. Russell to plan an overhaul of the office. The staff officers proposed to divide ONI into three major sections: Section A, general administration; Section B, incoming information; and Section C, collating and disseminating information. The Department of the Navy made its last major reorganization of the era that, typical of its Taylorist tendencies toward overmanagement, curtailed ONI's missions. On March 3, 1915, Secretary of the Navy Josephus Daniels created the office of chief of naval operations as head of the Office of Naval Operations (OPNAV). He labeled ONI the "Division of Naval Intelligence" or "OP-16," one of nine divisions. ONI's main task was a familiar one: obtain information from foreign sources, collate it, and file it. War Plans was a new OPNAV division with the power to create strategy and draft campaigns. ONI was only expected to feed intelligence to this division as required. ONI would be War Plans' inferior, with the DNI often restricted from making strategic, analytical assessments. The latest reorganization confirmed the department's relative disinterest in ONI.

During the William H. Taft and the early years of the Woodrow Wilson administrations, government officials expected ONI and what was left of Army intelligence to continue their information gathering mission. ONI lobbied hard for more war planning responsibilities but generally was shut out from making policy. Department of the Navy leaders were also eager to give naval intelligence professionals unwanted security administration duties. This move portended the domestic security missions with which ONI would be saddled for the next few decades.

The outbreak of the European war in August 1914 immediately increased ONI's workload in information gathering as tasked by the department. The secretary of the Navy asked Oliver for personnel strengths of the European armies. Oliver complied with tables "Peace Strength" and "War Strength" on August 12.[110] Congressional debates referenced ONI's 1914 world navies warship tonnage tables for naval appropriations discussions and general war information from Europe.[111] Data management and reporting was a skill ONI had honed for decades and it would not fail its superiors.

Oliver's main provider of information, as had been from ONI's charter, were naval attachés. The department recognized the importance of attaché reporting in international crises; the Spanish-American War and the Russo-Japanese War drove this lesson home. Information collection expanded when the Navy ended the practice of double accreditation to France and Russia by placing attachés in both Paris and Petrograd. The department did the same for Tokyo and Beijing. The naval representatives overseas were still the most reliable data collector the DNI had at his disposal.

In September 1911, Chief of the WCD Colonel John Biddle provided the yearly report of the division to the chief of staff. It demonstrated how blended the missions of military intelligence with the rest of the college had become. According to Biddle, there were 1,430 calls for military information from government customers.[112] Military information became defined as general staff work of the division and much more than just old intelligence missions. He grumbled that because the division could not communicate directly with its military attachés as imposed by the adjutant general, the staff could not keep an accurate record of exchanges of information.[113] No one in the division either gave collection guidance or processed attaché material, so Army representatives overseas operated virtually on their own. There were no signs of relief for Army intelligence as it was picked apart by overmanagement.

Lieutenant General Leonard Wood reminded the WCD of its information duties in early 1912. The chief of staff described the MIC's responsibilities, few of which were apropos for Army intelligence and others that reflected the committee's purpose as a catch-all for miscellaneous WCD tasks. He charged the MIC with the maintenance of military monographs with no specificity as to foreign or domestic subjects. The MIC had to coordinate and direct military education, a non–intelligence related mission. But it could continue mapmaking functions. The chief of staff assigned MIC with preparing histories of military events, a duty the old MID did not have. The committee further had to compile and edit articles on all subjects for publication and provide officers monthly lists of books kept in the War College library. The only duty traditionally related to Army intelligence was seventh on the chief of staff's list: data management of information coming from attachés abroad.[114] Military leaders defined Army intelligence missions in 1912; they were categorically unrelated to strategic military intelligence.

Foreign intelligence seeped out of the office to customers. Wood noticed that he was not getting a satisfactory amount of intelligence and wrote a memorandum to the WCD chief in January 1913 inquiring as to why military information work had ceased. Brigadier General Albert L. Mills made excuses for the inertia. Woods let the issue go and took no corrective action.[115] Reforms and reorganizations had practically snuffed out intelligence gathering and subsequent publication. The only intelligence work conducted by the Department of War came from military attachés and officers on scouting trips as observers or special operatives. Ironically, as tensions increased in Europe, this was especially the time an intelligence organization needed to observe and report overseas military developments and events. Much closer to home, the WCD monitored actions on the Mexican border in mid-1913 but had no mechanisms for collecting and reporting information to field commanders or Department of War or general staff leaders.

In early 1914 the Army had an acute deficiency of available officers. Their leaders' solution was to minimize the total number of officers in detached status. Then President of the War College Brigadier General Hunter Liggett suggested in a memorandum to the general staff removal of attaché billets to Spain, Italy, Austria-Hungary, and Belgium and the designation as temporary the positions situated in Russia, Switzerland, the Balkan states, and Turkey. Further, if the Army had a major exercise, then all European attachés and students in France and Germany would be recalled.¹¹⁶ Liggett's incredibly illogical proposal disregarded the worth of military information in the time of increased tension. Unsettling developments in Europe may have rescued the attaché corps as department leaders ignored Liggett's suggestions. New WCD chief Brigadier General Montgomery M. Macomb told the chief of staff Wotherspoon that attachés should stay put. He agreed and added more observers to help relieve some of the burden attachés felt in collecting information during major war.¹¹⁷ The military attaché corps remained healthy with at least thirteen attaché posts overseas and numerous observers embedded in the French, German, and Austrian armies by November.

At home, the MIC was an unsurprising failure in intelligence work, but its superiors did not care. It had neglected to give the expeditionary forces in Mexico any operational information, much less general intelligence. War broke out in Europe in August 1914 and the American public changed their focus from Mexican affairs to events in France. There were only a few signs of MIC intelligence work, as America observed the Great War from afar. Captain Nolan returned to what was left of military intelligence at the MIC that year. Secretary of War Lindley M. Garrison tasked the WCD to revise the Army's mobilization plan. Nolan provided an exaggerated threat estimate: the possibility of a large armada descending on the United States with lightning speed and landing huge masses of troops on the East Coast. No one in the department questioned it. Nolan exaggerated manpower, equipment, and timelines because he had no threat analyses or background data to reference.¹¹⁸ Future military intelligence pioneer Captain Marlborough Churchill (a distant relative to Winston Churchill) took a post as an observer to the French Army. He and other American representatives found the French unfriendly as they initially denied non-Allied personnel access to the French lines in war zones.¹¹⁹ True change was at least two or three years away. Meanwhile, only traces of Army intelligence existed on the eve of world war.

Yet the agency representing it carried on as best it could. ONI tried to inject itself more in war planning starting in 1910. The Aid for Operations of the Fleet drafted plans in earnest at the beginning of that year. The department even activated a Naval War Plan for government unrest in Nicaragua; ONI became involved when it collated reports made by naval intelligence observers for strategic analysis. But Japan remained the prime target of ONI.

The office participated in the famous War Plan Orange, an evolving plan targeting Japan that started off as an exercise in 1906. The division asked Potts and his staff to gather data and provide information country defenses, port studies, weather conditions, lines of communications, and warship specifications for everything pertaining to Japan and where its Navy may operate. Potts sent three junior officers to Japan for language training but also to collect information. All ONI East Asian collectors had their eyes on the rising power.

Acting Secretary of the General Board Beekman Winthrop issued order no. 425 on October 1 clarifying the planning process. He explained that ONI existed mainly to complement the NWC and his board in war planning. ONI's duty was to provide intelligence on every aspect of a potential enemy, which the board designated for plans of military operations. After the board approved ONI's material, the NWC prepared the war plan. Once the board signed off on the plan, ONI stored the plan of campaign allowing for periodic updates.[120] Five days after Winthrop's order and his designation of Japan as a potential enemy, Winthrop ordered Potts to furnish the General Board with the information on Japan in accordance with the instructions.[121] The acting secretary authorized Potts to "direct any recommendations or suggestions which may aid in perfecting the formulation of campaign plans," Implying that ONI still had input into strategy and policy-making aspects of planning.[122]

ONI explored other target countries as well in 1911. The department sent Lieutenant Commander Samuel I. M. Major and Commander McCully to Vera Cruz, Tampico, and the Gulf of Mexico on secret scouting trips in March. They determined strength of port defenses in case the US Navy had to act against the southern neighbor. Germany was also a potential strategic adversary in the Atlantic Ocean. In March, Winthrop ordered Potts to gather information on the European country for War Plan Black. ONI began preliminary work such as charts and tables but did not really get involved until they completed the latest research for War Plan Orange.[123] As ONI concentrated on war planning tasks, Meyers reiterated the processes between the Board, ONI, and NWC on October 26 and changed the name of "plan of campaign" to "naval war portfolio." But Meyers did not clarify if and how ONI could provide recommendations for strategy to the Board and NWC.[124]

ONI had an uneasy agreement with the General Board and the NWC in war planning in 1912. Intelligence officers had some influence on strategy and policy within the department, but they were on the outside looking in. They provided intelligence to war plans, such the portfolio for Mexico in case the president tasked the Navy to aid involvement in Mexican affairs. They advised the board as to the merits of a blockade on both sides of

Mexico. Intelligence work had changed in complexity from thirty years ago when information was generally obtained in the open and government senior leaders only expected ONI and MID to perform information collection, storage, and publication duties.

Personalities also hindered ONI's planning growth. ONI and the broader Department of the Navy worried about how the new president Wilson would use their services when he came into office in 1913. Government officials knew him to be a pacifist and feared he could oppose war planning.[125] A Japanese war scare occurred that year and the board asked ONI to help revise War Plan Orange. News of renewed war planning seeped to the press and Wilson immediately ordered meetings to stop. With Wilson concerned with perceived bellicose thought in his executive branch, war planning ceased temporarily in the department. ONI, by no fault of its immediate superiors, took a hiatus from the planning mission.

Meanwhile, ONI hung onto other missions it had accrued over three decades—data management and public relations. The staffers desired planning responsibilities to influence strategy and policy in the Navy, but they found that prospect elusive. Department leaders wanted something different from intelligence, but they could not express it in words and orders. Secretary of the Navy Meyers finally did; he burdened ONI with nontraditional missions that hardly could be considered strategic intelligence. If he dumped these unpleasant duties that no bureau wanted on some departmental organization, it might have well been on the struggling ONI. In December 1911, the secretary ordered ONI to censor articles written by naval officers. ONI had recently become the lead on the classification and control of information given to foreign naval attachés. But this order put naval intelligence in the security administration business. There is no indication that Potts and later Rodgers protested to such an unusual mission. The Navy wanted operational security to increase within the officer corps. ONI first took on censorship of text and then took on the responsibility of censoring photographs in 1913. This trend of nontraditional assignments increased up to and beyond World War I. Shut out as the office was from the most prestigious aspects of war planning and given menial tasks, ONI's poor reputation was a far cry from the glory years after the Spanish-American War.

ONI and Army intelligence found themselves at the nadir of their fortune at the precipice of America's involvement in World War I. For ONI, a feeble reputation and lack of funds hampered its growth during the Progressive Era.[126] Professional officers would have rather gone to sea than sit behind a desk collecting information. The Department of the Navy pushed ONI out of planning and strategy at higher levels of government. Army intelligence fared much worse; it arguably did not exist. The Army leadership failed to appreciate, in contrast to great powers in Europe, how intelligence was indispensable to the general staff concept in preparing for future wars and then fighting them.[127] Military leadership placed those who knew the importance of strategic military intelligence organization in subordinated positions with no senior mentor to speak for their views.[128]

World War I hastened the end of the Progressive Era. It did not put an end to the constant churn of reforms and reorganizations afflicting the Navy and Army nascent general staffs. But war often stimulates the need for intelligence. The events of the next three years revitalized ONI and Army intelligence. Surprisingly, though, society and government ordered strategic military intelligence organizations to turn to entirely new missions . . . in domestic security.

Rear Admiral John G. Walker, 1989, after leaving his tour at the Bureau of Navigation. As chief, Walker was instrumental in the creation of the Office of Naval Intelligence in 1882 and nurturing the fledgling institution from bureaucratic predators within the Department of the Navy. (Photograph courtesy of the Naval History and Heritage Command: Photo Section, Photo # NH 119385)

A group of Korean and American officials, including Minister Plenipotentiary Prince Min Yong Ik in 1883 at the University of Wisconsin–Milwaukee. Lieutenant Theodorus B. M. Mason (on the far left) was a pioneer of US naval intelligence who helped found ONI and create the naval attaché system. Lieutenant Junior Grade George C. Foulk (on the far right) served as a US diplomat (chargé d'affaires) in Korea in the 1880s. (Photograph courtesy of the Library of Congress)

An undated photo of Brigadier General Richard C. Drum, adjutant general of the US Army. As a matter of bureaucratic expediency, he created the Military Information Division in 1885, which mirrored the Navy's ONI. (Photograph courtesy of the Library of Congress)

Captain French E. Chadwick on the USS *New York* in the late 1890s. Chadwick was the first US naval attaché. He also served as chief intelligence officer from 1892 to 1893. (Photograph courtesy of the Library of Congress)

Assistant Secretary of the Navy Theodore Roosevelt in early 1898. Navalist Roosevelt was a huge proponent of strategic military intelligence organizations, especially the Office of Naval Intelligence. He leaned heavily on the advice of naval intelligence professionals Richard C. Wainwright, William S. Sims, and Seaton Schroeder. (Photograph courtesy of the Library of Congress)

Major General William R. Shafter in 1898. Shafter refused Major Authur L. Wagner's offer for tactical intelligence in Cuba during the Spanish-American War. (Print courtesy of the Library of Congress)

Lieutenant Commander N. A. McCully (standing at left) crossing Lake Baikal April 11, 1904. He was en route to the far eastern war zone during the Russo-Japanese War via the Trans-Siberian railway. (Photograph courtesy of the Naval History and Heritage Command: Photo Section, Photo # NH 101298)

An undated photograph of the Lemon Building. The Second Division (Military Information Division, or MID) moved into this building in 1903. The relocation was one of many moves for both MID and ONI into nondescript buildings in Washington, DC, between 1903 and 1943 as the organizations grew bigger. (Photograph courtesy of the Library of Congress)

Assistant Secretary of the Navy Franklin D. Roosevelt in the 1910s in Washington, DC. Like his distant cousin Theodore, Franklin was an advocate of strategic military intelligence organizations. He was a friend of naval intelligence officers until World War II, when he seemed to favor other intelligence avenues like the Office of Strategic Services. (Photograph courtesy of the Library of Congress)

Vice Admiral William S. Sims, commander, US Naval Forces Operating in European Waters in London, England, with members of his staff, circa mid-1918. Seated in the second row are, from left to right: Captain Dudley W. Knox, Captain Frank H. Schofield, Captain Nathan C. Twining, Sims, and Captain Harry E. Yarnell. Standing behind and between Sims and Yarnell, with arms folded are, left to right: Commander William Ancrum and Commander John V. Babcock. (Photograph courtesy of the Naval History and Heritage Command: Photo Section, Photo # NH 50114)

Brigadier General Marlborough Churchill in the late 1910s. He became the first director of military intelligence in August 1918 after the Army promoted him two ranks. His tenure is controversial due to his enthusiastic support of Attorney General A. Mitchell Palmer during the Red Scare of 1919 to 1920. (Photograph courtesy of the Library of Congress)

An undated photo of Brigadier General Dennis E. Nolan. Nolan was part of a prominent military intelligence triumvirate together with Brigadier General Marlborough Churchill and Colonel Ralph Van Deman in the late 1910s and early 1920s. He served as American Expeditionary Forces G-2 from 1917 to 1918 and deputy chief of staff for intelligence, G-2 from 1920 to 1921. (Photograph courtesy of the Library of Congress)

ONI staff officers, March 1920. Rear Admiral Albert P. Niblack is seated in the center of the photograph. Director of Naval Intelligence Niblack was a throwback navalist of the nineteenth century. Bureaucratic fights with the Department of the Navy and misunderstandings regarding the missions of domestic security punctuated his short tenure as naval intelligence head. (Photograph courtesy of the Naval History and Heritage Command: Photo Section, Photo # NH 120013)

Lieutenant Commander Ellis Zacharias in 1928. Zacharias was a careerist naval intelligence officer, a rarity before the creation of an intelligence designator in the late 1940s. Because he was seen as too ambitious by his superiors in the Department of the Navy, Fleet Admiral Ernest J. King denied Zacharias his dream post as director of naval intelligence in 1942 and dismissed him from his staff in 1943. (Photograph courtesy of the Naval History and Heritage Command: Photo Section, Photo # NH 50963)

Brigadier General Logan Feland in the early 1920s. Feland was the first director of the Division of Operations and Training that housed the first Marine Corps' strategic military intelligence organization, the Military Intelligence Section. (Photography courtesy of the Library of Congress)

Captain Arthur H. McCollum in 1943. The Office of Naval Intelligence's Far East Section head tangled with the War Plans Division Chief Admiral Richmond K. Turner in the fall of 1941 over which organization made assessments of Japanese intentions in the Western Pacific. (Photograph courtesy of the Naval History and Heritage Command: Photo Section, Photo # NH 68797)

The duke of Windsor (formerly King Edward VIII of England) leaving the Main Navy Building during a visit to the Department of the Navy, Washington, DC, September 26, 1941. Walking beside him, just to the right, is Captain Alan G. Kirk, USN, director of the Office of Naval Intelligence. Kirk was the naval attaché in London during the fall of France and the Battle of Britain in 1940. He also served an unsuccessful six months as director of naval intelligence in 1941. (Photograph courtesy of the National Archives and Records Administration)

Captain Harold C. Train in 1939. The director of naval intelligence was in the post from 1942 to 1943. The Department of the Navy selected Train over Captain Ellis Zacharias for the position because his excellent managerial skills suggested he would be able to handle the infusion of personnel and money brought on by war. (Photograph courtesy of the Naval History and Heritage Command: Photo Section, Photo # NH 119280)

Rear Admiral Sidney W. Souers awarded the Legion of Merit for exceptionally meritorious services as intelligence officer of the Sixth and Tenth Naval Districts, and as head of the Planning Branch of the Office of Naval Intelligence, from the outbreak of the war until December 1945. Assistant Secretary of the Navy John L. Sullivan (left) made the presentation March 2, 1946. Souers became the first director of central intelligence, leading the ineffectual Central Intelligence Group (CIG) earlier in 1946. (Photograph courtesy of the National Archives and Records)

Chapter Five
1915–1919:
The Resuscitation of ONI and MID

President Woodrow Wilson desired to keep the United States out of the European war. But many of Wilson's critics—including Progressives, national security leagues, and military leaders—construed his neutrality stance as neglecting the military and showing weakness. Out of the opponents' angst was born the Preparedness Movement, whose leaders argued the United States needed to build up the military for defensive purposes because clearly the country would fight in Europe sooner or later. This movement was an extension of the internationalist, Hamiltonian, and managerial revolution currents circulating through government offices since the 1870s. Heavy political hitters, familiar navalists, and military progressives comprised the opposition, which included Theodore Roosevelt, former chief of staff General Leonard Wood, and former secretaries of war Elihu Root and Henry Stimson. Even current administration officials (Secretary of War Lindley Garrison and Assistant Secretaries Henry S. Breckinridge and Franklin D. Roosevelt) were vocal about increasing defenses. According to historian Manuel Franz, a once limited campaign against US military weaknesses became a mass movement that dominated the public discourse and left its mark on American thought.[1]

With this resurgence of a defense reform mindset, a rebirth of military intelligence was sure to follow. Once again, when the nation needed its protectors, military intelligence was sure to benefit. On the Army side, a debate continues among military intelligence historians as to whether the Military Intelligence Division (MID) was established in 1885 or 1917. The question is whether Army intelligence existed as a coherent, useful organization prior to American entry into the Great War. In the view of historian James L. Gilbert, there was no permanent intelligence element in the Army before World War I.[2] Marc B. Powe argues in contrast that such an assessment ignores that the Military Information Service did perform some functions such as attaché collection and filing within the War College Division in the years between 1912 and 1917. Furthermore, MID was a sound, permanent organization praised for its planning and information gathering for over twenty years.[3] Powe's assessment is more accurate.

Army intelligence may have been barely breathing prior to the war, but its heart was still beating. Elements existed—institutional memory, intelligence needs, and personnel—that made possible MID's renaissance.

One of those intelligence needs was domestic security. Both the Office of Naval Intelligence (ONI) and Army intelligence performed domestic security missions during World War I, such as counterintelligence, plant protection, censorship, security background checks, and port and base security. Whether by choice or by order, these organizations had to take on these roles, as both society and the military pushed military intelligence out of more traditional roles and into more immediate concerns. Americans' perception of the war and the spy mania that accompanied it required ONI and MID to look inward to identify threats, particularly since there was a dearth of intelligence agencies that could do so.[4] At the same time, the Departments of the Navy and of War did not want their intelligence services conducting war planning because other agencies fulfilled that job. And they did not ask for operational intelligence because military leaders knew ONI and MID were not equipped for such a mission; besides, America's new allies had established intelligence organizations overseas that the United States could rely upon.[5] As a result of these factors, ONI and MID still handled the traditional mission of information gathering in concert with the attachés, but domestic security was where the glory and funding resided.

Prior to World War I, American society identified ONI and MID as providers of encyclopedic information on how the Army and Navy stacked up to other world powers. But American understanding of intelligence changed drastically as fear proliferated of reported spies and saboteurs seemingly seeded throughout society. ONI and MID became spy-catchers and worked alongside the federal government to identify perceived bad guys and protect vital wartime industries. Newspapers and the media helped identify military intelligence as counterespionage agencies to the public through articles, editorials, and movies. They also stoked the spy mania: at the beginning of the war, editorialists advocated more anti-espionage measures.[6] As ONI and MID leadership eagerly took on more of these responsibilities, the American public took positive notice, because spying had more intrigue and excitement than data recording. The average citizen read about intelligence in European spy novels much more avidly than "just-the-facts" information sharing on tables and graphs. And because intrusion into civil liberties had not yet reached national consciousness, ONI and MID had freedom from oversight and the esteem of the public as good guys catching evildoers.[7]

The agencies' superiors, many of whom had little appreciation for the potential benefits of strategic military intelligence, were fine with intelligence professionals conducting domestic security if they did not interfere with the Navy and Army's war effort. Generally, the departments sent mostly desk officers, not rising stars of the Navy and Army, to these offices. Military intelligence was not one of Wilson's concerns; he had other more pressing interests during the war. For its part, Congress thought of ONI and MID as information providers and opened the purse considerably as emergencies of war required in 1917 and 1918. Congressional oversight of MID and ONI spending was negligible; ONI and MID were free to spend liberally on all sorts of missions. They reaped the benefits of the government infusion of money, a precursor to when money really flowed within the departments in World War II. The Offices of the Secretaries of the Navy and of War were agreeable to their intelligence bureaus catching spies. In fact, Assistant Secretary Franklin Roosevelt, who had the same intense interest in ONI as his distant cousin Theodore, encouraged naval intelligence to find the enemy within. But the average senior officer lacked interest in intelligence, especially in planning processes or enemy locational data. Intelligence veteran Lieutenant Colonel Walter C. Sweeney would later recall of Army intelligence's superiors in World War I, "Nor was there a general appreciation of the need for the Army and higher commanders to have at all times prompt and complete information of the enemy from the combat troops in contact with him. Rather it was the idea that commanders of troops in contact should seek information of the enemy for their own use."[8] The Army General Staff and the Office of the Chief of Naval Operation were fine with military intelligence self-policing the departments and monitoring America's internal security if MID and ONI stayed out of planning and operations.

Before the war, ONI and Army intelligence took on domestic security roles reluctantly. After all, missions such as counterintelligence, censorship, and security classification and control can barely be considered strategic and are loosely related to the military depending on context. They were catch-all functions that no agency in the departments could manage or even want. Even in the wider federal government, not many agencies had these duties. As a result, once naval intelligence professionals latched onto other domestic duties, ONI paid less attention to strategic foreign intelligence.[9] Likewise, Army intelligence acquired several functions that had little to do with intelligence gathering and reporting, but MID leadership agreed to take them on.[10] Why? MID officers (as well as ONI officers) wanted to have a role in the war effort, but more significantly, they yearned for greater prestige and funding. The US entry into World War I in April 1917 breathed new life into an oft-ignored ONI and a near flatline MID not because Americans expected military intelligence in Washington to track enemy movements, plan campaigns, or collect foreign intelligence. The resuscitation of strategic military intelligence organizations occurred because ONI and MID accepted societal, governmental, and military expectations that they primarily conduct domestic security duties—marginally strategic and military intelligence missions at best—and avoid operational intelligence functions and strategic planning.

Between 1915 and American entry into the war, ONI and Army intelligence professionals struggled to maintain cohesive organization. ONI officers discovered that because they did not have a major role in war planning leaders took their data collection mission for granted. Their reputation and funding suffered, and the office remained small.

In 1915, ONI was reduced to only eight officers and eight clerks. Captain James H. Oliver, the agency's DNI, labored to revive ONI's reputation in the generally anti-intelligence atmosphere of Wilson's administration. But how? He reasoned there had to be a need for ONI's expertise so that the office could get more recognition and perhaps more funding.

The German sinking of the *Lusitania* on May 7, 1915, with the loss of 128 America lives, greatly factored into the US shift away from neutrality. Moreover, Wilson was coming around to the Preparedness Movement's way of thinking. Secretary of the Navy Josephus Daniels, although generally a pacifist, also converted to war readiness principles considering the dangers Americans faced overseas and at home in 1915 and 1916. He ordered the General Board and Naval War College to complete general mobilization plans for the Atlantic Ocean. In Washington, the department fretted about protection of state secrets within the State, War, and Navy Building.[11] Here lay an opportunity for ONI to interject itself into department security affairs.

On June 26, 2015, Oliver informed the General Board that the reorganization of ONI, orchestrated by Lieutenant Commander Dudley W. Knox and Major John H. Russell, was still "under detailed consideration."[12] By the fall, the three senior ONI officers considered making counterintelligence a mission of ONI, given a perceived German threat to domestic naval interests. Oliver reviewed Knox and Russell's blueprint and expanded it to include a War Information Service to the Naval Defense Districts. The General Board reviewed and approved it in October

1915. Under Oliver's plan, a district information officer or aide for information would arrive at his assigned district and set up an intelligence service. This officer would circulate information throughout district offices and create secret war portfolios for the district's informants.[13] The War Information Service staff also operated abroad as civilian assistants to the naval attachés. As part of Oliver's reforms, ONI issued a periodic *Information Bulletin* series beginning in 1915, which continued in some form until 1942.

US Marine Corps intelligence, meanwhile, made strides during these years toward an organizational structure. In 1893, ONI welcomed its first United States Marine Corps officer, First Lieutenant Lincoln Karmany. This began an informal relationship between the Department of the Navy and the subordinate Marine Corps in which marines learned the tradecraft of intelligence at ONI. By 1915, authorities attached marine officers to several naval attaché missions throughout the world. Russell was the latest, and most productive, marine officer in this pipeline. As he was steeped in scientific management philosophies, Oliver encouraged him to use these theories to improve ONI and military intelligence in general. Yet, marines did not have a military intelligence apparatus until 1920 and relied heavily on naval intelligence for information on threats overseas.[14] For example, in 1915 when the United States landed 330 US Marines at Port-au-Prince, Haiti, and insurgents murdered dictator President Vilbrun Guillaume Sam, the Marine Corps turned to the ONI for information. Russell and his colleagues were enthusiastic to help. For his part, Russell took what he learned about military intelligence and brought it back to the Corps.

As the Department of the Navy intelligence apparatus restructured, the Department of War scarcely had any component features representing intelligence in 1915. The secretary of war, chief of staff, and War College president were content without a functioning strategic military intelligence organization. The Military Information Section had only one mission related to intelligence, an obligation to the attaché corps. The ever-worsening international situation surely would necessitate the Army to think more deeply about how to prepare for a future conflict. This required information from an intelligence agency to plan and strategize. Throughout the preceding seven years a few experienced intelligence officers assigned to the WCD pleaded with Army senior leaders for the return of traditional military intelligence missions and they did so on a regular basis. If not for the Preparedness Movement and more importantly, the arrival of an experienced intelligence officer in May, the Army would have begun World War I without strategic intelligence.

Major Ralph H. Van Deman, a veteran of the MID when it resided in the Adjutant General's Office, arrived to a WCD that ignored its information service responsibilities. This did not surprise him as he had left a withering intelligence component in the War College in 1910. Van Deman would later note that he found after he returned to the building that he was the only officer with any intelligence training or experience.[15] Officers filed the military attaché reports streaming in from the European fronts but did not distribute those reports to a wider department audience. Also, they left information from the Punitive Expedition in Mexico on tables unread. Alarming and indicative of the state of Army intelligence, there was no information about northern Mexico available in the Department of War in 1916.[16] Army officers from the expedition telegraphed reports to the War College, which the Military Information Section filed, but there is no evidence that any senior officers acted on the intelligence. A frustrated Van Deman began implementing reforms. At first, he made it a priority to develop a filing system requiring reading, summarizing, and cataloguing. By the end of the year, he petitioned heavily with his superiors for a revival of Army intelligence. He was well on his way to becoming the man whom historians called the "Father of Military Intelligence."[17]

An energized Van Deman took to the pen, writing numerous memoranda to the Chief of Staff of the Army Major General Hugh L. Scott through President of the War College Brigadier General Montgomery M. Macomb, advocating the resurrection of Army intelligence. He submitted probably the most important memorandum, "Historical Sketch," on March 2, 1916. He opened his report by stating he felt also compelled to give causes and remedies to the dismal situation.[18] Van Deman argued that the WCD did not collect information; reports just came in and officers were derelict in their duties to collate information, digest it, and publish it to the rest of the Army. He praised the endeavors of the attachés who collected information as requested but had no supervision or coordination of their work. Van Deman made a bold recommendation that the Army could not cure the present conditions until the chief of staff authorized a separate division reporting directly to him on military information.[19]

The report was remarkable in its length, boldness, and honesty. Intelligence historian Nathan Miller accurately notes that it was the most significant single document in the history of American military intelligence, comparable to Martin Luther's indictment of the Catholic Church.[20] Macomb promptly approved Van Deman's ideas as he believed the time was ripe to rejuvenate not only Army intelligence but the entire General Staff. Noting that the General Staff was disorganized., Congress passed the

National Defense Act of 1916 and abolished two of the four staff divisions and reduced the number of officers on the staff. This was the era of the military progressive, where efficiency and centralization ruled through reorganization and reform. Conservative Scott, a veteran of the wars of the nineteenth century and a traditionalist, resisted the tide. The chief of staff ignored Van Deman's recommendations.

But with Macomb's encouragement, some form of organized intelligence activity took shape in the WCD and the larger Army. Incrementally, the department issued orders and established procedures that made Army intelligence more relevant. In April 1916, Acting Chief of Staff Major General Tasker H. Bliss gave instructions to establish departmental headquarters intelligence offices with assigned intelligence officers. For the first time in the Army's history, the six geographic departments within the continental United States had an intelligence agent.[21] While Van Deman was frustrated by such a small step towards a new MID. Early in 1916, he made military attaché information from Europe accessible to the Command and General Staff College at Fort Leavenworth. And in July, Macomb made formal recommendations to the chief of staff to revamp the general staff, including the creation of a separate Army intelligence division, complaining that it was impossible for him to oversee the functions of both WCD and intelligence work. But Scott snubbed Macomb again.[22] No major steps toward Army intelligence's independence occurred until early next year.

Real momentum for a military intelligence organization within the Department of War occurred in late 1916 to early 1917. Macomb's successor, Brigadier General Joseph E. Kuhn, was also a Military Preparedness advocate and appreciated the value of intelligence during times of crisis. He allowed Van Deman a long leash to continue structuring an intelligence outfit. Because of the recent National Defense Act, the General Staff Corps had a shortage of personnel. The WCD only had nine officers at a time when the flow of military information coming from overseas intensified. Finding his staff inundated with vast amounts of material to digest, Kuhn made the decision at the beginning of the 1917 to cancel War College classes and use all personnel to sort, analyze, and report intelligence to the rest of the Department of War and field troops. Kuhn also requested permission from Scott to reorganize the WCD into three sections: Military Information, Military Operations, and Military Preparedness.[23] The chief of staff reluctantly agreed.

In these circumstances, Van Deman learned how to work around Scott to reform Army intelligence. The chief of staff was not a visionary;

President William H. Taft once described Scott's mental capacity as "wooden to the middle of the head."[24] He represented a clique of Army generals that preferred to be aggressive in operations, often acting in disregard for intelligence. Who needs knowledge of the enemy when US soldiers could just bludgeon them to submission with overwhelming firepower and manpower? It is this American way of war that historian Russell F. Weigley described as "annihilation," which General Ulysses S. Grant perfected and Scott practiced.[25] Van Deman had dealt with this type of conservative, traditional officer his entire career. To overcome the obvious obstacle, he schemed together with Kuhn to organize a new MID without Scott's permission. The two asked Colonel Stephen L. Slocum, the military attaché in London, to approach British military intelligence for recommendations on how to start up a military intelligence organization. Slocum reported that the British divided intelligence into collection and denial of information. The British further subdivided these categories into subsections and numbered them.[26] Still, despite Van Deman and Kuhn's plotting, some tipping point needed to occur to either convince Scott of the need for a new MID or make it a reality without the chief of staff's permission.

Before the US entry into World War I, the only use Department of the Navy and of War leaders had for intelligence professionals was in the new niche of domestic security. Oliver often complained that Assistant Secretary Roosevelt tried to take over intelligence work from ONI.[27] Still, despite Roosevelt's overbearing tendencies in the naval department, he was a major driver in ONI participating in domestic investigations. As 1916 unfolded, ONI found itself more involved in domestic security, despite the DNI's reluctance to take on these missions. He only had eight officers, had just become the supervisor to aides for information, and likely found himself overwhelmed. For example, in February, Chief of Naval Operations Admiral William S. Benson asked Oliver about the feasibility of collecting industrial information within the United States with ONI taking the lead. The purpose of such measures was to enable plans for the mobilization of industrial resources in the event of war.[28] The DNI recommended that the plan be tabled because ONI did not have the manpower and other departments had a stake in the outcome; furthermore, he believed that the prosecution of detached plans for parts of such work would be premature and might lead to serious confusion later on.[29] Oliver's reticence to take on too much in the name of military preparedness may have caused consternation among some of his go-getter subordinates. For instance, Knox wrote to his mentor Captain William S. Sims, "Have been trying to build a fire under O.N.I. but so far have found it incombustible!"[30]

But with the approach of a possible war, the office perceived the necessity to surveil immigrant activity within the United States in naval matters. To recall, ONI's reorganization of 1915 and 1916 resulted in four divisions, one of which, Division A, Organization & Control of Agencies for the Collection of Information, encompassed subsections concerned with domestic security. These sections collected files on German espionage, compiling dossiers on possible German agents. Specifically, ONI kept name lists on index cards of prospective and hired agents and informants arranged by foreign country. Oliver believed that the department must act on his files' accounts of spies within American borders. He thought that Secretary Josephus Daniels was too cautious when it came to acting against perceived German agents discovered by naval intelligence. Daniels was not fully on board with military preparedness; his boss Wilson also hedged between readiness and neutrality. Nor did Daniels wish his authority circumvented by a general staff or intelligence cabal. In November, Oliver requested more money for hiring informants and more authority to determine where the funding went. Daniels agreed to increased funding but reserved his and Benson's right to clear financial destinations. While Oliver resented his superior's micromanagement and assumption Oliver lacked competency to make fiscal decisions based on available information, he complied, if under protest.[31]

Meanwhile, the district intelligence office system developed rapidly throughout the year. On July 27, the DNI sent comprehensive plans to formalize the War Information Service, which had been formed the previous year, to senior leaders in the department. The chain of command approved the plans at various levels until Daniels signed off. In the fall, ONI used congressional appropriations to establish a key branch intelligence office in New York, the first of many. Its first mission was to inspect and guard manufacturing plants having naval contracts. Notably, at this stage ONI became the first intelligence agency authorized to have undercover agents.[32] The department established the district intelligence office system in 1916 to deal with Oliver's expected increase in mission requirements. The city offices were comparable to theater military intelligence branches that conduct operational intelligence missions today. Branches such as the one in New York thus functioned in the operational counterintelligence realm, as ONI and its subordinate organization took on duties that ONI's founder Theodorus B. M. Mason never envisioned for naval intelligence.

In the first few months of 1917, anxiety grew within the American public regarding a coming war, as did excitement about possible spies within the country's borders. The media and congressional debates signaled to the public that the US government had to act in the face of perceived foreign agents monitoring American vital interests. Newspapers from around the country reported spies were in the United States; one outlet stated there were one hundred thousand of them.[33] There was a need, the country's general mood indicated, for organizations such as ONI to catch spies, and thus ONI became further involved with domestic security missions, such as censorship and naval asset protection.

ONI had been in the censorship business since the early 1910s, but this was an internal department mandate to monitor what officers published in the media. In 1916, the Joint Army and Navy Board made recommendations for censorship following a presidential proclamation prohibiting news reporting of information that was valuable to the enemy in a time of crisis. Specifically, the Department of the Navy was concerned with cable and radio censorship. In February 1917, Secretary Daniels appointed former naval attaché and intelligence officer Lieutenant Commander Reginald R. Belknap as official censor for the Navy as the German crisis worsened. ONI worked with Belknap closely on censorship policies throughout the war. As hostilities loomed in March following the sinking of three American vessels, Daniels looked to Oliver to discover solutions to protecting US vessels both in and out of port.

Once the United States declared war on Germany April 6, 1917, strategic military intelligence changed dramatically, as did the Departments of Navy and of War. ONI structurally ballooned into a complex apparatus with thousands of personnel. At the same time, once the secretary of war permitted Army intelligence to create an organization, it grew exponentially, even surpassing ONI in size by the end of 1917. ONI and a revived MID's intelligence operation supported various types of missions, but the main responsibility was protecting the home front.

By early April, Kuhn and Van Deman had created a small organization with a healthy attaché corps, a system of special observers overseas, intelligence officers in the Army's regional departments and National Guard divisions, and officers in the War College committed to analyzing information. The entry of the United States convinced them that they had to intensify efforts even further.

Kuhn tried first to persuade the chief of staff to create an Army intelligence organization in earnest. He sent a memorandum on April 11 describing the unsatisfactory state of intelligence operations at the WCD and asking to form a separate section for intelligence with four mission areas: military information collection, espionage, counterespionage, and tactical intelligence. He also requested permission for the WCD to conduct clandestine operations, have direct correspondence privileges, and receive more personnel. The reply did not reach the college until May 3. Both the secretary of war, Newton D. Baker, and Scott said that he could reorganize his division the way he saw fit but would not be given carte blanche on the other requests.[34] Apparently Scott acted as a screen for Baker and the decisions came from the Office of the Chief of Staff.

Van Deman next attempted to sway Scott, receiving permission from Kuhn to approach the chief of staff directly. But even after two or three meetings, the veteran intelligence officer could not convince the stubborn Scott.[35] Scott, at best, understood intelligence through a tactical lens. Van Deman called the chief of staff a "fine officer" who knew nothing either about the business of collecting foreign information or protecting the nation from enemy spies domestically.[36] In short, Van Deman believed the chief did not get the value of intelligence at higher echelons. Van Deman revealed his fascination with domestic security duties, which are arguably not strategic intelligence missions. The two officers would not compromise: Scott told Van Deman to cease his efforts and gave him strict orders not to approach the secretary of war on the subject.[37]

That same month, in a sneaky and somewhat insubordinate fashion, Van Deman and Kuhn did manage to circumvent the chief of staff. Specifically, Van Deman knew that Baker had breakfast with Raymond W. Pullman, chief of police of Washington DC, an acquaintance of Van Deman, at a club every morning. The major asked Pullman to talk with Baker about the military information situation within the Department of War.[38] Subsequently, Kuhn received a curious communiqué directive from the Office of the Chief of Staff on April 28 to organize a Military Intelligence Section.[39] Scott had apparently changed his mind. Perhaps Baker had said something to him after his breakfast with Pullman. Be that as it may, Van Deman received a phone call on April 30 to report to the secretary of war immediately. Baker asked Scott's question: If the French and British armies provided adequate military intelligence in Europe and the AEF had its own G-2, why would the US Army need an intelligence outfit in the States? Van Deman's answer must have been satisfactory because Baker told him that the Office of the Secretary of War would send an order to the War College within forty-eight hours that an intelligence organization "be set up at once."[40]

With changes to the "War College Department Manual" by Kuhn on May 3, 1917, the Military Intelligence Section came into existence.[41] Its new functions resembled more what a strategic military intelligence organization should have than any of the previous directives handed down by WCD in the past ten years. The Department of War had assigned most of these roles in some form between 1885 and 1908; they were nothing revolutionary, although the insistence on coordination with allies and government agencies to insure against failure and duplication was a new emphasis.[42] Though this was not obvious at the time, the War College's lead on creating MIS would hurt the organization in the future. MIS did not have direct access to the chief of staff or the ability to deal with other senior leaders on the General Staff. Nonetheless, this WCD directive was a monumental reboot for Army intelligence. Van Deman probably ghostwrote these functions similarly to how the father of naval intelligence Mason wrote ONI's charter directives in 1882.

The changes to the manual coincided with a memorandum by the chief of staff and were approved by the secretary of war on the same day. Kuhn put Van Deman in charge of the section as the only experienced intelligence officer in the Army.[43] The designation "Military Intelligence" rather than "Military Information" reflected British influences, demonstrating a broader understanding that intelligence did not just mean information in the nineteenth-century context: the term "information" was too generic. The MIS had three branches: Administrative, Information, and Censorship. The Information and Censorship branches roughly resembled the British intelligence concept of positive intelligence (or collecting foreign intelligence on the adversary) and negative intelligence (or protecting secret information from the adversary).

Yet, immediately after the formation of MIS, Van Deman was forced to deal with problems like those he had encountered much of his intelligence career. Army intelligence was still tied to the War College and Baker and Scott were still averse to an organizational divorce. Van Deman took to the pen again on May 11, recommending the immediate creation of a Military Intelligence Division so that MID could have better access to the chief of staff, improve speed of operations, gain more personnel, and secure more funds. Scott again denied Van Deman's request on May 15, failing again to realize the potential value of intelligence to the chief of staff in making important military decisions. He thought, as his predecessors did, that military intelligence should remain submerged under the WCD.

The chief of MIS obeyed and built his organization. Major A. P. Ahern and Captain Alexander B. Coxe, whom Van Deman had worked with in east Asia, became his principal assistants. Because the War College allocated two civilian clerks—a modest work pool for such grand ambitions—MIS followed the same path as ONI by finding civilians with certain skills and commissioning them as reservists to help build the staff. Shortages of trained and qualified personnel in the field of intelligence plagued Van Deman throughout the war. Initially, MIS's one-room office overlooked the library. Kuhn placed the map room and photographs under Van Deman's supervision. Congress originally appropriated $11,000 to the "Contingencies, Military Information Section, General Staff Corps" fund for fiscal year 1918 plus an additional $15,000 for military observers abroad. This fund had been a money source for WCD for almost ten years and used for everything but military information. Now MIS applied it correctly. But the section needed more for the demands placed upon it in the war context. The secretary of war also requested $1,000,000 for military intelligence from Congress, a shared endeavor with the Department of the Navy and ONI for emergency funding.[44] This was too much in retrospect; the organization's finance officer reported an expended balance of only $1,862.13 in the direct appropriation account as of June 30, 1918.[45] Meanwhile, Department of War comptrollers quietly pushed money to MIS from other divisions without the hassle of seeking legislative approval.

Out of MIS grew a primitive cryptologic capability. Van Deman recruited Herbert O. Yardley, a former State Department code clerk, to receive a reserve commission as first lieutenant and head the MIS's Code and Cipher Bureau, or MI-8. It would prepare codes and cryptanalysis duties.[46] During the war, Yardley's MI-8 became the principal cryptologic agency in the government.

The chief of MIS spent the early winter of 1917 and 1918 tweaking the empire he created within the WCD. He reorganized MIS along the lines of British-styled positive and negative intelligence and copied their numbering scheme. Specifically, Van Deman designated a Positive Branch and a Negative Branch, with each branch having five to six sections. The Positive Branch included: M.I 2-Collection, Collation, and Dissemination of Foreign Intelligence; M.I. 5-Military Attachés; M.I. 6-Translation; M.I. 7-Graphic; M.I. 8-Cable and Telegraph; and M.I. 9-Field Intelligence. The Negative Branch had the following sections: M.I. 3-Counter-Espionage in the Military Service; M.I. 4-Counter-Espionage among Civilian Population; M.I. 10-Censorship; M.I. 11-Passports and Port Control; M.I. 12-Graft and Fraud; and the Military Morale Section. Van Deman designed this reorganization so that MIS had room to grow to adjust to the ever-expanding intelligence requirements.

Army intelligence morphed again in early 1918, suggesting its increasing status in how key military leaders perceived intelligence. On February 9, the secretary of war reorganized the General Staff and placed strategic Army intelligence under the Executive Division.[47] General Order no. 14 renamed the section the "Military Intelligence Branch" (MIB).[48] According to a manual published for MIB in the spring, its main duty was to supply the Department of War with all types of information foreign intelligence and to conduct counterespionage, essentially leaving Army intelligence's positive and negative missions unchanged.[49] Meanwhile, Van Deman cut down his sections from eleven to eight to include: Administration, Information, and three Contra-espionage offices (Translation, Graphics, and Codes and Ciphers).

MIB leadership reemphasized old missions from MID's past. The Graphics and Maps section was a holdover responsibility from WCD, which it inherited from the core MID missions in 1885.[50] The section also had to copy, process, and distribute photographs. The military attaché corps, an integral part of MID since 1889, expanded to one hundred officers at twenty-six posts. Van Deman created a separate section in the spring specifically to support attachés. On paper, positive and negative intelligence had equal weight, but realistically domestic security was more important. The change to branch status was an improvement to Army intelligence; it supported Van Deman's escape from WCD's purview, but MIB was still not a division as the chief desired.

The Department of War authorized more space for MIB and its separation from the War College, which had trapped Army intelligence within its walls in 1907. In March, it moved all but the Translation and Graphics Sections to the Monroe Courts "seven-story apartment house," much closer to the agencies MIB coordinated with and about a half mile from the White House.[51] This move away from bureaucratic predators was another sign of MIB's increased independence.

Another positive development for Army intelligence was Major General Peyton C. March's arrival March 4 as chief of staff. March was a decisive man with plans in hand for the General Staff even before he left his previous tour in France. He intended to reestablish the old Military Information Division, referring to the MIS and MIB as "a minor appendage of the War Plans Division . . . wholly inadequate" to cover wartime duties.[52] March had a high respect for Army intelligence professionals.[53]

Van Deman, recently promoted to colonel, hoped to oversee more changes to MIB in May. The chief outlined his plans for the future of Army intelligence to the *Washington Post*. The newspaper reported to

Americans what the Army spy-catchers did for the war on the home front. Van Deman told the *Post* he wanted intelligence officers at all division camps and more secret agents at home and abroad.[54] But Van Deman did not lead the organization to becoming a division: his endgame. Van Deman's nemesis, Scott, had retired recently, and the intelligence chief anticipated that the new chief of staff would look favorably upon MIB. March did, but not upon Van Deman's leadership. The intelligence chief played too much bureaucratic politics and was overeager in his use of domestic security tactics. But historians truly do not know the exact reasons for Van Deman's reassignment.[55] It may simply have been his turn to rotate jobs after three years on the General Staff. On June 1, the department ordered Van Deman to service overseas. Lieutenant Colonel Marlborough Churchill, for whom Van Deman had nothing but praise, relieved him.[56]

Under March, transformation was afoot for MIB and the rest of the General Staff.[57] Churchill elatedly telegrammed Van Deman on August 26: "FOR VAN DEMAN: REVISION GENERAL STAFF ORGANIZATION MAKES MILITARY INTELLIGENCE DIVISION. Churchill."[58] Indeed, as part of a major reorganization of the General Staff (and not the last one), Secretary of War Baker and Chief of Staff March released General Order no. 80, in which they ordered the creation of the Military Intelligence Division on par with other General Staff Divisions (Operations, Purchase, Storage, Traffic, and War Plans).[59] According to March, the division titles were intended to indicate to the customers the nature of the business the General Staff conducted.[60] It was a major victory for Army intelligence advocates, a struggle this small band of agitators had waged since the War College swallowed up MID in 1908.

The general order designated a director of military intelligence. It would not be Van Deman. A few days before the announcement, the military intelligence pioneer unceremoniously shipped off to France. The director and assistant chief of staff post became a brigadier general billet, probably another wound to Van Deman's ego. The Army promoted Lieutenant Colonel Churchill two ranks to assume command of the division, at which point he became the first general officer in strategic Army intelligence history. Churchill was surprised and embarrassed by the double promotion. But he benefited from having a friendship with March, a bond that his predecessor never had.[61] For the time being, Army intelligence had a seat at the "big kids' table" with general officer representation.

Two days after the department released General Order no. 80, MID executive assistant Colonel Coxe issued Memorandum no. 64 detailing the new division's responsibilities.[62] None of these duties surprised Churchill, as MIS and MIB had been carrying out similar responsibilities since May 1918. However, the director had an increased supervisory role over Army intelligence: the power to organize, train, direct, and coordinate the intelligence service. The order and memorandum also reaffirmed the concepts of positive and negative intelligence. MID split into two branches, with Colonel John W. Dunn assigned to duty as chief of the Positive Branch and Colonel Kenneth C. Masteller named as chief of the Negative Branch.[63] The branches grew into incredibly large organizations; the Negative Branch alone had approximately 140 officers and 300 civilians in Washington by the end of the war. The August reorganization, which lifted Army intelligence's Washington office to division status, was the last shake-up MID would experience before the end of the war.

Churchill moved into the State, War, and Navy Building so that he could spend a few hours a day in his assistant chief of staff role, conferring with department leaders. He also had an office at MID headquarters for his intelligence responsibilities. Churchill recognized that Army intelligence had improved greatly in a few years and that future historians would have questions. Therefore, he authorized the publication in October of a piece titled "Work and Activities of the Military Intelligence Division, General Staff"—part report to March, part historical document for posterity.[64] Staff officers documented MID's history and its missions to help justify the division's existence. In October, March relieved Churchill of military morale duties by creating a separate branch for it in the General Staff. Protective of MID's brand, Churchill monitored press reports for errors.[65] With a strategic military intelligence organization reestablished in Washington and senior leader's support to the MID's missions, Army intelligence was the healthiest it had been since 1885.

After the Armistice was signed on November 11, the demobilization of a gigantic Army was a Department of War priority. Eventually demobilization would impede MID's ability to conduct operations, but in the first postwar months Army intelligence leadership thought they could keep most of the progress they had made in personnel and responsibilities intact. On November 30, Churchill told Van Deman who General Pershing had recommended for promotion the previous day.[66] Namely, "It is planned to continue the functions of Military Intelligence Division with as nearly full personnel as necessary as long as we can, with the ultimate view of perpetuating the organization in the peacetime establishment of the army."[67] MID held off the tide of demobilization as long as it could, but the inevitable came.

Meanwhile, the chief of staff sent Churchill and twenty members of his staff with President Wilson to the peace conference in France.⁶⁸ The Department of War made Churchill the general military liaison coordinating officer for the Peace Commission. In Paris, Churchill and his staff provided secure and accurate information of every conceivable nature until March 18, 1919, when MID personnel returned to Washington.⁶⁹ Van Deman was also at the Paris Peace Conference and headed the Contre-Espionage Service for the American Commission to Negotiate Peace for the next ten months. He departed Europe August 12 for temporary reassignment as deputy director of MID before commanding the Thirty-First Infantry in the Philippines in March 1920. MID directors continued to hear from Van Deman for another three decades (whether they wished to or not), especially on counterintelligence matters.

On the naval side, ONI started the war in transition. Oliver served a three-year tenure and rotated to another job. Captain Roger Welles Jr. took over as DNI on April 16, 2017. His superiors promoted Welles to rear admiral, ONI's first flag officer, later in his tour—a signal to naval intelligence professionals how important domestic security missions were to the war effort. Welles brought a renewed excitement to the office as the duties of the post appealed to him. He wanted to become the next Sir William Reginald Hall, the brilliant director of the NID, and make ONI the next great naval intelligence organization.⁷⁰

Welles turned to volunteers and reservists to man an expanding wartime ONI office. The DNI was not afraid to consult with Assistant Secretary Roosevelt, who was eager to provide reservist officer recommendations from elitist contacts he had in New York: the assistant secretary held a fascination for the potential of ONI. Welles lured veteran intelligence officer Humes H. Whittlesey from retirement. The fifty-six-year-old, who had been an ONI headquarters staffer during the Spanish-American War, took charge of a section collating domestic and overseas intelligence. Despite these moves, the DNI had difficulties with manpower throughout the war as ONI needed to expand in space and personnel to meet the wartime challenges.

In May and June 1917, ONI was on a war footing. Welles consolidated his growing bureaucratic empire and increasingly concentrated on domestic security. New York socialite Roosevelt liked the DNI because Welles enjoyed fraternizing with the rich and powerful from New York and New England. His rich reservist employees manned his branch offices in New York and elsewhere and became amateur naval officers and detectives. Concerns over spying within the United States and the patriotism of some Americans allowed for more aggressive domestic security practices, which many of the new officers assumed was part and parcel of naval intelligence. This elite group of reservist intelligence officers stayed close to Welles like a clique.[71] Welles also strengthened ONI and branch offices with volunteers, enlisted personnel, and agents who carried out the drudgery of bureaucratic life in the organization. The DNI assigned these employees with passenger ship searches, report dictations, filing suspect index cards, and providing security for naval properties and interests. ONI officers and clerks also carried out surveillance duties, such as wiretapping, mail opening, and censorship. Much of this work occurred in the naval districts at the operational level, but some sections in the main office engaged in domestic security.

Unsurprisingly, the sudden demand for domestic security, intelligence gathering, and administrative work not only required new employees but more money. Congress recognized that war demands made the Departments of the Navy and of War financially strapped. Senators and representatives passed emergency appropriations on June 15, 1917. As part of the monetary relief, ONI received $5,634.[72]

Throughout, ONI observed Army intelligence's progress. ONI had always been the big brother to MID by virtue of age and reputation but Welles noted how Van Deman's efforts resurrected Army intelligence and in July admitted that little brother was catching up. That month, when Roosevelt asked him to find a position in the office for a friend, Welles said that he had no slots but referred Roosevelt to the MIS, which had a large pot of money and billets open.[73] Welles wanted to air his grievances about the shortage of billets. As responsibilities increased and foreign intelligence requirements shrank, Welles aired his grievances, writing to the secretary of the Navy on July 7, 1917, regarding the poor conditions at ONI and attaché offices because of department restrictions placed upon officer allotments for naval intelligence.[74] Welles also wanted to provide strategic warning "notice to mariners" reports but lacked the manpower to do it. The naval attachés in Europe asked for more officers to help with information gathering, but according to Welles received no reservist help. It pained Welles to report to Daniels, but the Army was signing up more men in MIS than ONI had altogether because of Department of the Navy enrollment restrictions.[75]

For all that, Welles tried to balance traditional concerns of information gathering abroad and new missions at home.[76] Some naval attaché stations had adequate manpower and funding, but many did not. At home, the aid for information systems grew quite large, with close to three thousand personnel in the Naval Defense Districts, each district having its own staff. Welles's staff established eight Branch Intelligence Offices in 1917 that directed over five hundred personnel. The DNI tried to ensure that he had full control over his branch personnel rather than a split administrative chain of command with the district commanders. By choice and obligation, ONI's efforts increasingly turned to less traditional roles neither necessarily strategic nor military in nature.

The Great War ended on November 11, 1918. On Armistice Day, ONI had reached its peak efficiency as well. The office expanded from eight officers and eight civilians in 1916 to three hundred and six officers and eighteen civilians by early November. ONI's distribution list for intelligence to bureaus and naval assets afloat reached four hundred and fifty names.[77] Welles employed hundreds of officers and civilians to investigate foreign-born people within the United States. Because of its domestic security duties, ONI (like MID) was the most powerful it would ever be in its history.

But the Armistice was the signal for an immediate demobilization on personnel and duties. The total of 1,462 people attached in the Office of the Chief of Naval Operations, with at least a fourth belonging to the intelligence arm, surely would be reduced. Censorship responsibilities almost ceased by November 16.[78] Moreover, ONI and the naval districts deactivated their plant protection sections in November. The demobilization process had begun.

To be sure, military intelligence did conduct its core information-gathering mission in the Great War, but this assignment was not a source of recognition, money, and personnel. Prewar preparations had set the two agencies up well for homeland security duties. And almost immediately after hostilities started, the realities of distance shut strategic military intelligence organizations out of operational intelligence just as had happened in the Spanish-American War. Not coincidentally, events unfolded similarly between ONI and MID, where strong personalities at the European front combined with pragmatism to block Washington intelligence leaders from lower echelon intelligence operations.

It had been over three decades since William S. Sims first reported to ONI. The once young navalist lieutenant was now a rear admiral and designated Commander, US Naval Forces Operating in European Waters (COMUSNAVFOREUR) in March. He selected London as his headquarters so that he could establish a liaison with the British in naval matters. Sims would also tap into information the British made available from their Naval Intelligence Division (NID). By virtue of using British intelligence, he did not need ONI; instead his aide, Commander John W. Babcock, and a small staff collected intelligence. This intelligence section, akin to today's theater intelligence centers, handled operational intelligence matters. Babcock even detailed an American officer to the NID. Over time Sims's intelligence section published summaries, compiled statistics, and provided operational intelligence not only to the other sections but to the Departments of Navy and of War and to the American Expeditionary Force. Without some form of coordination, Sims's arrival to Europe with his staff promised to cause clashes between the strategic military intelligence organization in Washington and an operational intelligence center closer to the conflict.

Sims's intelligence section, the experienced Allied intelligence apparatus, and domestic intelligence duties took ONI out of strategic and operational intelligence collections business in Europe when the war started. Babcock built a solid liaison with the NID, and his section had intelligence covered. The British had the best naval intelligence organization in the world by 1917, tempered in three years of war. NID did not want an amateur naval intelligence organization from America to intrude in their business, and indeed, provided all the operational intelligence American forces required. Besides, ONI—by Department of the Navy pressure and by its own volition—had plenty of work on the intelligence home front. Like ONI in 1898, the staff found itself an ineffective operational intelligence and strategic planning organization.

Unsurprisingly, then, the intelligence section in London and the British NID ignored ONI in Washington. The NID was not anxious to share secrets with amateur and chatty Americans an ocean away who might be a postwar great power rival.[79] Sims had early frustrations when he sought more freedom from the Department of the Navy to make decisions on policy in Europe. In his view, ONI was just another layer of control from Washington. The DNI wrongly believed that Sims and his staff served as a naval attaché for the office; rather, he was COMUSNAVFOREUR, who probably worked an echelon level higher than the naval intelligence command. For his part, Sims saw his intelligence section staff as another ONI. Although Sims and Welles were on good terms, the admiral handled his own intelligence affairs. While not possessing the naval attaché corps, Sims owned naval intelligence in Europe; they were closer to the problems of war and had better connections to Allied intelligence. By comparison, the naval attachés sent information to Washington to be processed by ONI and back to Europe as operational intelligence too late to be of much use.

Sims's intelligence section was efficient, useful, and expanding. He made it an integral part of the Naval Planning Section, a role ONI had been pushed out of in 1915. A few months into the war, the section was already larger than ONI had been in 1916. It had some talented officers as well, including Knox, Babcock, Knox, Surgeon Edgar Thompson, and Lieutenant Junior Grade Tracy B. Kittredge, among other active duty and reservist officers and enlisted and volunteer agents. ONI had scant input in the section's policies, methodologies, or goals. In short, Welles turned to domestic security within the United States because Sims already had operational and foreign intelligence requirements covered.

Army intelligence's operational situation was similar to that of ONI. President Wilson put General Pershing in charge of the American Expeditionary Forces (AEF). Unencumbered by Department of War bureaucracy and with the president's backing, the general had the freedom to create his own organizational structure, spending a month planning and creating liaison networks with British and French allies. Pershing, an MID alumnus, knew the value of intelligence and did not hesitate to make it the focus of one of his sections. The intelligence section, or G-2, had four divisions: Military Information; Secret Service for clandestine work and counterintelligence; Topographical, Map Supply, Sound and Flash Ranging; and Press and Censorship. The heavy emphasis on security missions reflected the broader concerns regarding spies within the AEF. The Military Information division concentrated on operational and tactical intelligence. In this arrangement, the G-2 had many characteristics of Sims's intelligence section, such as not needing Washington-based intelligence.

From the beginning, the AEF G-2 shut MIS out of most foreign intelligence operations in Europe. The G-2 acted like a theater operational intelligence center; from today's vantage point this seems quite logical. The MIS charter put the section at the strategic level. Pershing picked an old friend from MID, Major Dennis E. Nolan, as the G-2 head, selecting him because of his tact and administrative, organizational, and leadership skills.[80] Pershing's trust in Nolan surprised the latter, as he had not asked for the post. When Nolan arrived in France, he embraced the philosophy that the AEF G-2 would focus on operational intelligence not only in France but other European fronts that might affect Western operations. In this belief he eventually infringed upon the MIS's perceived turf. There were no initial coordination efforts between Van Deman and Nolan. Van Deman did not have the resources (except for military attachés) for operational and foreign intelligence in Europe—at least early in America's participation in the war. While Van Deman became wrapped up in domestic security and setting up MIS as a viable general staff organization, Nolan's G-2 was three thousand miles closer to the enemy and in much better position to gather operational intelligence.[81] Furthermore, MIS had no voice in AEF G-2's internal operations. The department expected Van Deman's section, though, to train intelligence personnel heading to Europe. In May, based on necessities, practicalities of distance, and perceived threats, Nolan took the lead on positive intelligence, especially at the operational level, whereas Van Deman oriented MIS to security against the enemy within US borders. Although this seems a somewhat odd arrangement, Van Deman and Nolan took comfort in knowing that just a month ago Army intelligence was barely existent.

In August 1918, not many of the busy AEF staff read MID's reports. Churchill realized that there needed for greater contact between MID and the AEF G-2, a long-standing weakness.[82] Van Deman's transfer to Europe facilitated a renewed spirit of cooperation between Churchill and newly promoted Brigadier General Nolan. The trifecta of Nolan, Churchill, and Van Deman began the process of deconflicting the animosities unresolved because of distance.

On September 16, Churchill sent a series of memoranda to Nolan and Van Deman on subjects ranging from personnel to censorship to military attachés. He argued that they must form a partnership of mutual understanding and create a "homogeneous American Intelligence Service." Churchill wrote, "With the exception of our contre-espionage [sic] work in the U.S., we exist only to help you. Don't leave us in the dark. . . . It isn't easy to stay over here with the A.E.F. in its stride 'over there.' The least you can do is send us the news."[83] Churchill's memoranda slowly made it across the Atlantic by courier and by mid-October Nolan and Van Deman had responses for the director. Van Deman wrote that he had a two-hour conference with Nolan and Coxe to discuss the issues brought up by Churchill and how to better coordinate AEF G-2 and MID. Among other coordination decisions, Van Deman noted they agreed upon the interchange of personnel because it would improve efficiency and morale.[84]

At ONI, Welles found his staff bogged down in domestic security duties; patriotic, concerned Americans and informants, who feared foreign people within the United States, expected intelligence agencies to investigate every allegation of espionage in their midst. ONI was the logical choice not only within the Navy but within all of government to be on the front lines of counterintelligence work. The department also expected ONI to take the lead in protecting Navy property and subcontractors from espionage. The office also had to increase efforts to collect and distribute intelligence to all naval bureaus, stations, districts, and the fleet. Welles found himself in charge of an office with many tasks, traditional and nontraditional.

ONI's participation in censorship grew considerably in just a few months after America's participation in the war started. These duties were imperative to the Department of the Navy, which expected ONI to prevent leaks, find spies, and uncover illicit business practices. Accordingly, ONI helped investigate suspicious firms and individuals and monitored censorship materials from stations around the country. It also assisted the chief cable censor in determining the reliability of recipients of sensitive message traffic, relying on their card catalogue of suspects and investigations built up through years of due diligence.

Traditional naval intelligence work did occur at ONI in the first few months of the conflict. But Americans did not hear about ONI's information-gathering duties from either the press or Congress. The media were more interested in publicizing domestic security and civilian protection activities because they knew their readers were nervous about spies operating in the United States. Congress held similar war espionage anxieties. On June 15 it passed the "Act to Punish Acts of Interference with the Foreign relations, the Neutrality, and the Foreign Commerce of the United States, to Punish Espionage, and Better to Enforce the Criminal Laws of the United States, and for Other Purposes." The legislation envisioned a huge role to naval and Army intelligence.[85] By mid-1917, the American and congressional perception of ONI was that of a homeland protector, replacing its older image as a fount of trivial knowledge.

The strains of war affected Welles's well-being as he directed an office with tentacles in many major America cities and abroad. As information poured in, Welles's staff ballooned to seventy. The DNI was in poor health before the war, but his physical state declined even more over the months at the post and became an impediment to his promotion to rear admiral. Still, the Department of Navy stuck with him.[86] Daniels expected Welles to continue the course that ONI had set for domestic security, informing the department, "It is the duty of the Office of Naval Intelligence to collect and investigate information upon all subjects connected with a naval war on which can have a bearing upon naval action or plans of action."[87] As a statement of ONI's mission, this could not have been more generic. But Daniels did specify that department personnel must report suspicious activity to ONI, indicating ONI's main business was in the domestic realm.[88]

As part of these efforts, the DNI directed his branch offices to focus on plant protection. ONI persuaded naval contractors to take recommended steps to protect their plants and pick loyal employees. By the spring of 1918, ONI and its branches had grown large enough to emphasize not only security but intelligence collection related to US naval plants. Washington headquarters created a whole section dedicated to this endeavor.

In 1918, ONI staff became indispensable as domestic intelligence experts, taking on more duties like plant protection and fine-tuning reports and operations within the US. Hundreds of naval intelligence personnel worked in New York and in Washington to gather information on labor unrest, radicals, the spread of subversive thought, and the potential for sabotage. Between March and October, ONI produced a weekly confidential bulletin reporting suspicious individuals, firms, and general information on subversion.[89] ONI demonstrated, in the summer months of 1918, that its officers were eager to take whatever measures possible to root out spies and subversives.

Daily mail to ONI grew so large that by August clerks were swamped with seventeen thousand letters per day, requiring hundreds of new personnel to handle the inundation. Some letters were from citizens who observed suspicious individuals allegedly acting like Germans. Dorwart notes that ONI investigated American Jews with particular zeal, revealing the underlying anti-Semitism among the white, Ivy League, Anglo-Saxon, Protestant officer corps.[90] ONI branch offices and aides for information also took a special interest in pacifists, radicals, and labor unrest: ONI's suspect list reached 105,000 individuals. Its overexuberance in rooting out spies at the expense of civil liberties raised some eyebrows among Department of the Navy senior leaders, such as Rear Admiral Leigh C. Palmer, and at the Justice Department. Welles and his staff were admonished to curb their enthusiasm in dismissing and interning naval personnel before they could defend themselves, a practice the office apparently engaged in.[91]

One could defend ONI's conduct in World War I in the domestic arena as a necessity of war. The office and its subordinate units were the only agency in the department equipped to conduct security missions. Secretary Roosevelt and DNI Oliver had the foresight to recognize in 1915 that ONI needed to fill this void. Defenders may argue ONI agents did not have the power to arrest; they could only make recommendations to local police jurisdictions, Justice Department agents, and naval commanding officers. Yet, ONI's zeal in pursuing spies and subversives must have not been too detrimental to the Office's reputation: Welles received his delayed promotion to rear admiral in August 1918.[92] Naval intelligence's perhaps nefarious deeds did not seem to have affected other promotions and moves to bigger office spaces, either.[93]

Strategic Army intelligence also was heavily involved in domestic security. Van Deman stated later that almost immediately after MIS went into business, customers asked for services that "really have nothing to do with military intelligence matters."[94] The chief established contacts with various investigatory government agencies such as the Bureau of Investigation (forerunner to the FBI) and a secret service section at the State Department. MIS also found its growing body of personnel in ONI's claimed jurisdictions.

In Van Deman's view, the biggest domestic concern was espionage. Indeed, some German Americans, pacifists, and isolationists comprised a vocal minority against the US entry into the war. Although it is still debated among historians how serious the enemy agent infiltration was in 1917, there are documented incidences of sabotage before and during America's participation in the conflict. Still, it is likely the anti-German sentiment and concerns over domestic spies were exaggerated. No matter to Van Deman; he feared that the war industries and perhaps even the Army's new combat divisions might be infested with agents and sympathizers.[95] Secretary of War Baker concurred with the MIS chief and allowed Army intelligence to play a larger role in domestic security than it had previously.

Van Deman first built up the home front intelligence apparatus to mirror ONI's operational counterintelligence system. The department could not handle domestic security in Washington; MIS had to decentralize this authority. New York City had become a hub of Army activity, especially war material exports, which made the harbor a target of espionage by German agents. Therefore, in July 1917, MIS opened a branch office in Manhattan. Army intelligence eventually established offices in Philadelphia, St. Louis, Seattle, Pittsburgh, and New Orleans. Van Deman provided fifty trained men to the AEF G-2 in August that helped form the Corps of Intelligence Police, an operational level counterintelligence branch. Van Deman's domestic security network swelled to a much bigger size than that of the Secret Service and ONI, nearly matching the size of the Bureau of Investigation.

Fearing subversive civilian groups, Van Deman accepted the aid of the controversial American Protection League (APL), an organization of close to two hundred thousand members. The APL, formed in 1917 from several vigilante groups, monitored civilians at the street level for seditious activity. Van Deman allowed APL leadership to report such activity to his office and even conduct background investigations. During the war APL located as many as three hundred thousand military deserters, gathered military information, and provided US troops with orientation materials about French geography and culture.[96] This paramilitary organization was similar to organizations within Great Britain and France, manifesting the extreme nationalism of the period. One could argue that Van Deman's willingness to turn to civilian watchdogs stemmed out of necessity, but the chief himself identified with the ultrapatriotic citizenry and the work APL performed was beyond the scope of MIS responsibilities.

As Army intelligence sought to perfect and surpass the missions their superiors required of them, Van Deman had many projects in home front matters. The MIS set up Army-wide security measures, including identification cards, personnel investigations systems, and undercover counter-espionage procedures within each Army unit. Van Deman was concerned about the politics of each soldier, especially the foreign-born, whose loyalty to America was a section priority. Seeing threats from all parts of American society, including labor agitators, black activists, and the Industrial Workers of the World (IWW), Van Deman directed his Section to counter all of them.

Was Van Deman a little obsessive and excessive? Intelligence historians debate this topic.[97] Every other government agency with investigative powers for domestic security—ONI, the Secret Service, the Bureau of Investigations—committed excesses in World War I.[98] Army Intelligence and ONI could have limited their endeavors to domestic security spies and sympathizers deemed a direct threat to the war effort, but their crusade attacked fundamental civil liberties in excess of what was required for the mission.[99] They were forced into the domestic security business, but by 1918 MID and ONI may have liked it too much.

MID and ONI expansion guaranteed turf battles between them and with other government agencies. The two strategic military intelligence organizations traditionally had accommodated each other despite a certain rivalry, but the foray into domestic security fundamentally changed that relationship. In this context, the organizations' respective chiefs realized the need for better coordination. On March 6 and 13, MID, ONI, and other offices in the security business held conferences to improve synchronization between intelligence services. The attendees reaffirmed ONI's control of maritime investigative cases related to illegal immigrants, sabotage in shipyards or Department of the Navy plants, shipping, crews, vessels, and generally the work of the naval department.[100] Army intelligence would handle similar cases as related to war information. Van

Deman noted in particular that he instructed his intelligence officers to cooperate with the other agencies as they agreed to in the recent conferences.[101] The representatives agreed to meet more often but were against the pooling of their resources.[102]

Despite these efforts at cooperation, the relationship remained far from cloudless. MID's domestic intelligence apparatus, almost by virtue of Van Deman's counterintelligence zeal alone, grew to surpass ONI's capacity in 1918. And the DNI knew it. The Navy depended on the Army for security-related intelligence on American maritime territories: the Philippines, Hawaii, and the Panama Canal Zone. Van Deman sent daily intelligence nuggets to Welles on spies and subversives related to naval matters.[103] MID's growing power in domestic security also meant Army intelligence agents often interfered with ONI's operatives and vice versa in investigations. The two intelligence agencies continued to engage in turf battles into the early 1940s.

Meanwhile, MID's domestic security footprint continued to expand. The Department of War assigned Army intelligence a military morale mission in June 1918, another decidedly nonstrategic military intelligence–related mission. The General Staff named Churchill as the chief censor.[104] Because MID specialized in negative intelligence, leaders considered it a natural home for censorship efforts. Army censorship duties entailed surveillance of postal and telegraph communications, press, and propaganda. MID also assumed responsibility for anti-graft and fraud measures in the department with the creation of M.I. 12. The section conducted 1,128 cases resulting in 206 convictions in the courts. While Van Deman began the war with two officers and two clerks, Churchill ended the war with 282 officers, 250 enlisted personnel, and 1,157 clerks. More than half of these personnel concentrated on finding the enemy within. According to March, Army intelligence investigated as many as five hundred thousand cases during the conflict.[105] Churchill told Americans to remain alert even until the Armistice and beyond, calling on them to be vigilant for "anarchists, plotters, and aliens" who would be "more active because of their suppression during the war."[106] Indeed, the next few years would see Churchill attempting to maintain the wartime domestic security missions.

The public, Congress and department leaders all agreed: strategic military intelligence organizations were highly effective within American borders.

Unsurprisingly, ONI and MID enjoyed enhanced reputations within the United States as spy-catcher agencies.

Naval intelligence appeared in numerous newspapers in 1917 and 1918 and received equal print share with MIS and the Bureau of Investigation. On September 27, 1917, New York City detectives arrested ninety-one Germans suspected of spying for the Kaiser. The *New York Times* credited ONI with the "big haul of enemy aliens."[107] With front-page publicity why would ONI want to stop performing domestic security duties during the war and beyond, especially as the secretary of the Navy often told Welles and his staff that threats to America were their main concern?

The media and silver screen of the war period reflected American worries of German agents infiltrating everyday life, often referencing ONI in the fight to combat espionage. Some cultural references suggest media efforts to both allay American's fears and aggrandize their concerns. A *New York Tribune* editorial from January 23, 1918, bemoaned the fact that the government had not yet caught a German spy, treating naval intelligence as a salve for American fears while calling upon citizens to be vigilant.[108] Over a month later, the *New York Tribune* reported on a spy arrested with the help of naval intelligence officers. In the spy's room, the officers seized three cameras, binoculars, and "a vast lot of correspondence." He had an excellent view of warships and transports on the Hudson River.[109] The *Washington Post*, for its part, described a raid by ONI officers at a New York City restaurant that nabbed seventeen people on the technical charge of failing to register as immigrants from hostile nations. No doubt the editors sought to get the readers' attention with sensational text in this case.[110] The *Post*'s report echoes a Stan Laurel and Oliver Hardy vaudevillian film, *Huns and Hyphens*, from the same year. The plot centers on Larry, a man who romances a woman whose father invents a new kind of gas mask. He works at a restaurant secretly run by a German spymaster. The owner tries to use an oblivious Larry to get the plans for the gas mask to the restaurant where the spies can steal them. Stereotypical images of beer-toting, mustache-wearing Germans populate the movie. Director Lawrence Semon portrays the spies as treacherous and bumbling. Although naval intelligence was not featured in the movie, the restaurant scenes resonated with the real-life restaurants where naval investigative officers operated, as depicted in the *Post*.[111] In the public eye, naval intelligence became synonymous with counterintelligence.

As at the end of the Spanish-American War, after the Great War Congress and the Navy leaders asked ONI's help to document the history of its involvement in the recent conflict. The office provided Congress with intelligence on all US naval losses from April 6, 1917, to November 11, 1918.[112] The House of Representatives used statistics to determine if and how to appropriate money to the Navy to compensate for its losses.

Van Deman's MIS gained some power in administrative policy. When Pershing asked Washington to allow division intelligence officers to forward deploy to the front lines to train before their units arrived, Van Deman thought this an excellent idea but added that they should then return to the home divisions to train their subordinates. The department agreed with the intelligence chief over the general.[113] Chief of Staff Tasker H. Bliss, a former military attaché in the Spanish-American War, showed how a new wave of generals valued MIS and field intelligence during war. He noted in a December 31, 1917, bulletin that the General Staff did not appreciate intelligence professionals and his hope was to change this mindset.[114] Bliss said instead that Army intelligence offices dealt almost exclusively with information on the enemy to help operators prepare plans.[115] In his view, Army intelligence should be in direct support of the operators for war, particularly at the lower echelon. He called all Army officers to look at appendix A of the 1917 Staff Manual and understand intelligence's role. In subtle ways, Van Deman had succeeded in changing some opinions in the General Staff about the military intelligence profession.

During the Great War, ONI swelled from just a few rooms to occupying a whole office building in nineteen months. In the same period, MID transitioned from near nonexistence to equal standing as a division on the General Staff. What accounts for this tremendous expansion of the strategic military intelligence organizations? For MID, support from seniors and obstinate intelligence veterans led to the division being reorganized for efficiency.[116] Still, the biggest reason for growth was the impact of the domestic security missions, which required more personnel and funds for both ONI and MID. The question in the coming years would be whether demobilization and the deflation of resources would interfere with this growth trajectory.

The resuscitation and success of ONI and MID during the Great War came at a price. As American citizens and military leaders granted these organizations more support to perform domestic security missions, ONI and MID directors sacrificed most of their operational and foreign intelligence pursuits, the more so because they were excluded from the European front. Perhaps they also became too thirsty for domestic security missions. ONI "slipped across nebulous guidelines into affairs devoid of naval interests" to resurrect its reputation within the department.[117] MID did the same with its widespread investigative powers in nonstrategic intelligence matters. With the Red Scare looming in 1919, ONI and MID coveted their new role as primary investigative agents within the United States. The question, on the eve of the era of disillusionment and isolationism, was how long Americans would allow the agencies to exert broad influence in their affairs.

Chapter Six
1919–1929:
ONI and MID Navigate the Rapids

Three converging streams of American thought and experience—the Red Scare, the isolationist movement, and demobilization—churned up already tempestuous rapids after the Great War. These three factors defined how the Roaring Twenties reverberated in the American consciousness.

The Red Scare of 1919 and 1920 marked a widespread American fear of extremism—more specifically, Bolshevism and anarchism—due to real and imagined events. According to historian Beverly Gage, the federal government's reaction to these fears in 1919 and early 1920, led by Attorney General A. Mitchell Palmer, allowed for the deportation of hundreds of immigrant radicals based on mere suspicions of advocating "force and violence" against the United States.[1] There was real social tension in the United States exacerbated by the recent war and the waning of the Progressive Era, which had realigned and reoriented American thought toward finding a new order.[2] In military culture, this translated into a changing of the "old guard" from the military progressives and navalists of the past four decades to something that the Navy and Army had not yet defined.

Closely related ideas of disillusionment, isolationism, and pacifism filtered through society in the immediate postwar years. Historians William L. Langer and S. Everett Gleason have noted that disillusionment after victory caused a "confusion of mind," as some Americans wondered if the war effort had just been engineered by "munitions makers, international bankers and foreign propagandists."[3] Disillusionment also helped reseed isolationist sentiment in some parts of American society. This movement preached the rejection of the League of Nations, disentanglement from European and Asian affairs, nonintervention and neutrality in foreign wars, and a defensive posture for the US military.[4] Meanwhile, Republican administrations stalled the increase in the complexity of government growth as they preached a "return to normalcy" wherein the federal system stayed out of economic matters and the average citizen's affairs. In this way Jeffersonian ideals briefly made a comeback. Even as, pacifism was still an extreme idea in American society, advocates of peace demanded comprehensive international disarmament. In broader terms, most Americans sought pleasure and prosperity in the 1920s. A strong military did not fit into the equation.

Finally, demobilization befell the US military after the Great War. The sequence of events fit a frustrated General Emory Upton's posited pattern of an American way of war: early battlefield defeats, panicked response, acceptance of military leadership and training, a hard-won victory, immediate demobilization, and return to peacetime complacency.[5] The year 1919 seemed to follow this pattern: Americans, traditionally averse to a large standing Army, encouraged their elected representatives to reduce funding for Navy and Army personnel and equipment. In response, Congress forced the armed services to demobilize over a five-year period after the war. The government's infusion of money and resources brought on by conflict came to an end. After all, why did the country need the swords of the republic when the Great War was the war to end all wars? In these circumstances, disarming mechanisms trickled down to the Office of Naval Intelligence (ONI) and the Military Intelligence Division (MID), which began to suffer again from the lack of funding and inadequate personnel numbers.

As shown in the previous chapter, the Great War had solidified ONI and MID's public image as spy-catchers. Now, however, things would change. The strategic military intelligence organizations' relationship with society went through three phases during this decade. Initially, Americans were grateful that the agencies had caught subversives and radicals within their midst and ONI and MID appreciated citizens' assistance. For example, naval intelligence officer Ellis M. Zacharias praised Americans for providing their observations to intelligence agencies, demonstrating restraint, and exhibiting intelligent and enlightened patriotism.[6] But during the Red Scare pockets of the population tired of military intelligence activity that could be interpreted as intrusions into their affairs. Left-wing, pacifist, and immigrant-sponsored news agencies railed against excessive investigation agencies.[7] Once the Red Scare abated, the public retained a weariness of ONI and MID even when these organizations cut back on domestic security as the decade progressed. The damage was done; for better or worse, Americans in the 1920s viewed ONI and MID primarily as spy agencies.

Federal government officials struggled with what their military intelligence services had become and what they wanted them to be. Except for the four American presidents of the period, who often ignored the smaller offices and wished for normalcy without an expansive military, most government officials came to be wary of the expansive powers of ONI and

MID in 1919. Congress approved of Navy and Army appropriations bills granting funds to ONI and MID for information gathering and reporting, not necessarily domestic security. Even then, ONI and MID chiefs had to justify their existence to senators and representatives who threatened to cut funding every year. Secretaries of the Navy and of war had to defend and often curtail the intelligence agencies' apparent excessive practices. Intelligence historian Rhodri Jeffreys-Jones has written that after the Great War and the Red Scare, there was a strong reaction from politicians and the American people against intrusive practices and thus "counterintelligence suffered a particular bloodletting."[8] By late 1920, the secretaries of the Navy and of war tried to push the DNI and director of military intelligence away from security matters and toward traditional data management roles and public relations. Senior military leaders like the chief of naval operations and the chief of staff became less interested in domestic security, with its messy intrusion into Americans' lives, and more accepting of the idea they still needed a peacetime flow of foreign information to make decisions.[9] More so, military intelligence had learned no lessons about the lack of operational intelligence from the Great War; even at this stage, ONI and MID still tried to satisfy strategic customers. The degree to which senior officers respected the two organizations varied widely, from some being a champion of military intelligence to others wondering why they existed at all.

Meanwhile, ONI and MID leadership desperately sought to remain relevant by holding onto their domestic security missions. To be a vibrant agency with more funding, they needed to retain the war's investigative duties.[10] The alternative was to fall back on library duties of collating, storing, and reporting intelligence in Taylorist fashion in secret rooms beyond most senior officers' understanding or interest. Unsurprisingly, therefore, Attorney General Palmer had eager accomplices—especially in MID—in the raids he oversaw in 1919 and 1920.

To be sure, later in the decade, ONI and MID's aggressiveness in domestic affairs steadily retreated, as the three converging streams of the Red Scare, the isolationist movement, and demobilization had a detrimental effect on the agencies between 1919 and 1929. The booming missions of domestic security declined in concert with the rise in Americans' concerns over civil rights infringements and a general apathy to foreign affairs. While a strategic military intelligence organization formed in the Marine Corps, the older agencies again struggled to define their mission, focusing on more traditional duties as the turbulent waters subsided later in the decade.

The decrease in the organizational sophistication of the military intelligence agencies stemmed from demobilization, lack of utility, and departments' forced cuts in their missions. By the beginning of the Great Depression both ONI and MID resembled the meager organizations of 1916. True, the intelligence profession received a boost in 1920 when the Marine Corps installed an intelligence section in the commandant's headquarters. But demobilization was the prevailing trend for strategic military intelligence in the 1920s.

ONI's demobilization began in late 1918 and proceeded at a rapid pace the next year. The DNI released reservists, including Rear Admiral Roger Welles's old lawyer, banker, and businessmen friends from the Northeast. War records went into storage rooms unorganized, unused, and forgotten, and some ONI offices closed throughout the country. The DNI shuttered all branch offices on December 1. Welles asked that their files be turned over to the aid for information in the naval districts if possible. ONI withdrew or merged many of the naval attaché positions so that by the mid-1920s there were no more than ten officers abroad. It was difficult for the military to justify attachés to Congress when the perception of many legislators was that the departments of the Navy and war sent officers on luxurious vacations at the expense of the American taxpayer.[11] Thus, Secretary of the Navy Josephus Daniels put ONI in peacetime status and authorized cuts to their appropriations.

The transition to a peacetime intelligence agency continued in early 1919. On March 24, Acting Secretary of the Navy Franklin D. Roosevelt changed the title of "Aid for Information" to "District Intelligence Officer." When Zacharias arrived for intelligence duty he was at once impressed with his colleagues.[12] Welles assumed command of the First Division of the Atlantic Fleet, and naval intelligence veteran Rear Admiral Albert P. Niblack stepped into the post May 1. Niblack was a holdover naval intelligence officer from the nineteenth century. He believed that ONI's main mission was data management, with naval attachés as the central collectors; he was neither familiar with domestic security nor comfortable managing that mission.

Niblack determined to control the glide path of his organization away from his unwanted domestic duties and toward foreign intelligence collections while demobilizing ONI according to his own preferences. But ONI played the role of naval Cinderella, still waiting for Navy leaders to turn up with the glass slipper, namely, more responsibility it thought it fully deserved.[13] Instead, in the early 1920s the DNI found himself involved in departmental bureaucratic battles and facing the repercussions of ONI's participation (albeit more limited than MID's) in domestic affairs.

The biggest quarrel pitted Admiral William S. Sims and Daniels against each other, with ONI caught in the crossfire. Specifically, Sims wrote Daniels in January expressing his frustrations, analysis, and criticisms of the Navy's performance in the Great War. First, he noted that the Navy was unprepared to enter the fray even with two and half years warning. Second, once the United States declared war, naval leaders had no plans or policies. Finally, he argued that it took many months of mobilization to get the naval fleet on a war footing. Sims made his grievances public in a congressional hearing.[14] As part of his evidence, he asserted that naval intelligence was unprepared for the German U-boat menace. Sims was correct: ONI was much more concerned about the domestic situation between 1915 and 1918. Ironically, Sims also was partly responsible for this situation, given that his own Intelligence Section pushed ONI out of operational intelligence matters, such as submarine tracking and fleet movements.

Niblack could not evade the department bureaucratic shots fired around or directed at him. Some of his own actions were to blame. He fought demobilization harder than Marlborough Churchill did at MID. He continually told his superiors that ONI was underfunded. Niblack found $450,000 unexpended from a wartime secret fund, channeling some of it to ONI personnel.[15] In July 1920, he also testified before senators about the Sims–Daniels rift. Until as late as July 1919, Sims and Niblack had been friends, a long relationship going back to Naval Academy days. But their friendship soured and Niblack sided with Daniels to discredit Sims.[16] Niblack's testimony came across to senators as ruffled, vindictive, and abrupt.

The Department of the Navy removed a tired Niblack from the DNI post and replaced him with Captain Andrew Long in September 1920. Chief of Naval Operations Robert E. Coontz sent Niblack overseas as naval attaché to London and then commander of US naval forces in Europe. Coontz and the naval establishment just wanted him out of Washington. On his way out the door, Niblack performed two noteworthy acts for strategic military intelligence. First, he asked Major Earl "Pete" Ellis to showcase his Latin American expertise by looking over two monographs and to "familiarize himself with the information methods of ONI."[17] Ellis soon would help set up the Marine Corps' own intelligence organization and no doubt carried back ideas from these monographs to Marine Corps Headquarters later that fall. Second, Niblack published a manuscript titled *The Office of Naval Intelligence: Its History and Aims*. This was the first history of ONI and, perhaps, the naval intelligence officer's most lasting contribution to the organization.[18] It provides an excellent snapshot in time of where naval intelligence professionals felt ONI's reputation stood in the Department of the Navy. Niblack's comments reveal his legacy as a DNI reared in nineteenth-century intelligence philosophies.[19] Specifically, Niblack detested domestic security missions and thought this was more MID's domain.[20] The office's focus in peacetime should be strategic foreign intelligence, he wrote.[21] Furthermore, Niblack complained that naval attachés did not receive nearly enough allowances from Congress to do their jobs, an argument repeated by ONI's chiefs for decades.[22] Finally, he advocated that the old ONI and MID rivalries be put to rest. With Niblack's departure, the age of navalists and managerial information gatherers came to an end.

ONI needed a youthful, energetic DNI to rejuvenate a demobilizing and restructuring organization. Long fit the bill. On the one hand, he was a Captain and technically by rank a departmental downgrade of ONI's standing. But, on the other, the new DNI was even-keeled and uninterested in bureaucratic infighting. He worked well with the CNO and understood cutbacks were a necessity in an increasingly disillusioned America. Long did not mind domestic security missions and would carry on smartly when ordered. He could also switch tasks and direct ONI to collect foreign information from attachés. In his first month as DNI, his staff dispatched twenty-eight ONI reports to the fleet.[23] In short, ONI truly began the transition from the turbulent waters of the Red Scare and demobilization into the more halcyon years of the twenties under Long's tenure.

In 1921, the office continued to evolve. The Department of the Navy lifted censorship of naval officers' magazine articles, but ONI remained responsible for reviewing photographs. The Office of Naval Records and Library and the Historical Section, a section of ONI formed in 1918, received a new head. Captain Dudley N. Knox took up this position in July and retired from active duty in the fall. He held this post until 1946. Another ONI legend, future World War II admiral William "Bull" F. Halsey Jr., took his post as naval attaché in September. When he arrived at ONI, he overheard a discussion of superior officers about who would take the attaché job in Berlin. He approached them and suggested himself, and to his surprise, they agreed.[24] Captain Luke McNamee assumed the DNI billet in September. Unlike Niblack, McNamee took the view of strategic intelligence as a broad tent to include planning and domestic security. He believed that a healthy ONI should use all sources of information, whether it came from attaché reporting or more clandestine measures such as spying, domestic investigations, aerial photography, and undercover reporting. Of course, in public, he denied that ONI's personnel delved into non-naval, covert matters. But during his tenure he thrust the office back into surveillance and secret operations despite poor funding and lack of support from Congress and the public.[25]

McNamee rotated to naval attaché duties in London November 1923, just when some of his reforms took root. His demotion to an attaché job perhaps indicated the department disapproved of his promotion of covert activities. On the other hand, he was due to move to another position as was customary with naval personnel rotations and the post was a prestigious job. The Navy had once again removed an effective director from ONI when naval intelligence needed stable leadership the most. Captain Henry H. Hough stepped in after governing the United States Virgin Islands for a year. Zacharias was melancholy about the state of the office, battered as it was by funding and personnel reduction, when he visited it in December.[26] Thus, ONI settled into a pattern of dormancy and uselessness after a few turbulent years following the war.

The next six years of ONI operations were unexciting, as a parade of captains filled the DNI post. On June 24, 1924, Hough provided a laundry list to his superiors of completed projects almost devoid either of true accomplishments or references to failure.[27] Since the information he described was meant for public consumption, there was no mention of domestic security work in headquarters or at the District Intelligence Offices. In October 1925, Captain William W. Galbraith assumed the DNI position. An approving junior lieutenant Zacharias observed Captain Galbraith was energetic about his duties and contributed several innovations and organizational changes.[28] Not for long, however: Captain Arthur J. Hepburn relieved Galbraith in July 1926. His staff prepared quantitative intelligence for the Geneva Naval Conference in 1927 as directed by the department. Soon enough, Hepburn went to sea and Captain Alfred W. Johnson, a former naval attaché to Chile, became the new director on New Year's Day 1928. The new DNI performed all positional duties—traditional and of questionable repute—with vigor. Johnson's administration skills were above average for DNIs, and he would keep ONI steady given the financially constrictive environment of the 1920s.

In early 1929, John A. Gade, a New York businessman and former naval attaché to Denmark, made an interesting proposal to ONI, calling for the centralization of all United States intelligence efforts. He addressed the same initiative to MID, which conferred briefly with naval intelligence; both agencies, however, dropped the proposal. The idea was ahead of its time: it would take another eighteen years before the Central Intelligence Agency came into being.[29] Meanwhile, ONI stood on the precipice of a new decade in the context of the Great Depression with a small, underfunded office restricted to intelligence gathering meant to be of use in a possible future, far-off war.

Meanwhile, Army intelligence head Churchill realized that he would have to rein in many of his division's activities as peacetime routine descended upon Washington. He knew that as the Army cut back on personnel, manning, and equipment, so would it also reduce his staff. Intelligence officials planned, as early as 1919, to cut the agency down to a fraction of the wartime MID but developed mechanisms to expand rapidly in case of a national emergency.

Churchill and other intelligence leaders saw signs of diminishing capability and status. On February 1, the Department of War forced MID to move from the Hooe Building to a temporary structure on the National Mall. Officers complained it was a firetrap for the staff and the vulnerable secret files.[30] Colonel Ralph H. Van Deman urged Churchill to create a tracking system for personnel who worked for Army intelligence during the Great War but then scattered to civilian life.[31] MID seemed to be shrinking considerably and the questions remained for Churchill: How much would MID diminish? What duties could it fulfill to remain relevant in a peacetime America?

The general staff, and thus MID, reorganized yet again in the late summer of 1920. General Peyton C. March ordered the War Plans Division to create a postwar general staff. The department recommended the changes to Congress, which in turn passed the National Defense Act of 1920 on June 4. March staff preserved the organizational structure he had ordered in August 1918:the four divisions of Operations, Military Intelligence, War Plans, and Supply. The act revalidated the general staff system and set the groundwork for growth of the staff for decades. Crucially, in the list of duties assigned to the general staff, Congress did not mention military intelligence. Demobilization took its toll. Nineteen months after the Armistice, MID had lost 203 officers, 25 noncommissioned officers and enlisted soldiers, and 789 civilians. It was now less than a quarter of the size of the MID of November 1918.

On August 20, 1920, the Department of War Information Section announced that Brigadier General Dennis E. Nolan would succeed Churchill on September 1 as Churchill was due to rotate.[32] Department of War leaders were likely weary of Churchill's excessive enthusiasm in the domestic arena. After returning from Europe, Nolan had spent a year on the Army War College faculty. The new director had the tough task of maintaining a military intelligence capability in the Department of War despite personnel and budget cuts.[33] After he took up the post, Nolan ordered a reorganization of MID to mirror the recent general order. The Positive Branch now included M.I. 2 (Information), 3 (Publication), 5 (Military Attaché), 6 (Translation), and 11 (Planning). The Negative Branch contained M.I. 4 (Foreign Influence), 8 (Communications and Geographic Branch): 7 (Map and Photo), 9 (Monograph), and 10 (Training). While his new setup had a much-reduced domestic emphasis, the division still retained a security section.

March signed off on the first doctrinal publication on intelligence, called *Intelligence Regulations, 1920*. The original draft came from the general staff, AEF, during the war. The drafters, probably with Nolan's consent, based the regulations on lessons learned from operations in Europe. March and Nolan intended the publication to be a guide for conducting peacetime intelligence.[34] The document covered such topics as organizational structures, missions, definitions, and training. Significantly, the regulations included one of the earliest modern definitions of military intelligence, according to which MID still had a counterespionage function.[35]

After the turmoil of the Red Scare and reorganization calmed, MID took stock of how much it had accomplished during the war and the gains it maintained two years later. Former director Churchill held an MID conference in Washington to which speakers, many of whom were intelligence officers, came to discuss lessons learned from the war. They sought to retain the knowledge of doctrine hard-earned during war for peacetime.[36] At the end of 1920, although demobilization had reduced the staff and the Red Scare had diminished its wholesome reputation, MID still had a solid foundation with superiors who championed it, financial support, and a healthy attaché corps. So far, MID had not repeated the disastrous events of 1907 to 1908.

Still, MID suffered two setbacks in 1921: severe funding cuts and another reorganization. Both problems, related to the shrinking peacetime Army, would haunt the division through the interwar years. General Nolan ordered his intelligence officers to prepare monographs on foreign countries, both adversarial and allied. He was especially interested in new tactics and high-tech advancements, but funding was not available. Nolan also closed the Negative Branch because of money and probable ethical concerns. In general, Congress and the Department of War made it much harder for MID to function.

General John J. Pershing became chief of staff on July 1, and with his arrival came another reorganization. He revised the general staff along the lines of his AEF structure in the Great War, establishing five divisions with functional duties labeled G-1, Personnel; G-2, MID; G-3, Operations and Training; G-4, Supply; and War Plans Division. The reorganization hurt MID's standing. The National Defense Act only authorized a general officer for four divisions. But with a fifth division, the general staff had no congressional authority to authorize a fifth general officer. Pershing chose MID as the division with a lower-ranked commanding officer, showing military intelligence was still misunderstood and underappreciated.[37]

Consequently, Colonel Stuart Heintzelman replaced General Nolan as the newly titled assistant chief of staff for intelligence (ACSI), G-2, on August 23.[38] Heintzelman decided to reorganize MID because of limited funds and personnel. He created a new press relations element under the executive officer's authority. This was a non–intelligence related mission, yet the G-2 had no choice but to accept this responsibility from superiors. The headings Positive and Negative branches disappeared as ten sections nestled under Heintzelman's leadership. MID still dabbled in domestic security missions on a restricted basis.[39] The G-2 division reorganized under necessity, not as a proactive change to improve the organization. Forced restructuring was a reoccurring theme until the start of World War II.

The assistant chief of staff G-2 sensed that the next year's appropriations bill would be another battle. He wrote to Pershing on December 7 to provide a statement for an upcoming congressional hearing on the budget.[40] Both Pershing and Heintzelman stressed the importance of the valuable military information MID coordinated, compiled, and sifted through from other federal departments. At the same time, the G-2 revealed his philosophy of Army intelligence, hinting how imperative funding was for MID, as an essential element of national defense.[41] The head of MID continued his appeals for more money throughout the winter.

The G-2s of the early 1920s, reeling from scandals and budget cuts, realized that the present MID could not handle an international crisis in its current organizational state. Therefore, intelligence leaders planned for contingencies, in which skeleton crews could swell to a robust division in war. This mindset reflected the larger general staff's stance on expansion. The division devised procedures for enlargement of Army intelligence within the structure of a thorough Department of War mobilization plan.

The National Defense Act required the larger department to conduct manpower studies, and General Pershing took a personal interest. Following guidance, the G-2 prepared an appendix to the "War Plan Mobilization Plan, 1923" and then expanded the text with a more detailed "Plan for Expansion and Operation of MID, G-2, Under War Department Mobilization Plan."[42]

Pershing moved Heintzelman to the Supply Division at the end of 1922. He was destined for more respected duties as a general officer, being named the War Plans Division chief in 1924. Colonel William K. Naylor, a cerebral man who wrote *Principles of Strategy* as director of the General Staff School at Fort Leavenworth, stepped in as G-2. He contended the G-2 was more than just a collecting agency of information; in his view, smart analysts also have the intellect and ability to evaluate and draw conclusions.[43] Naylor's insistence on an analytical assessment role in policy and war plans represented a battle MID and ONI leaders fought throughout the interwar period. Lawmakers weakened their department standing by underfunding them. The remaining years of the 1920s were subdued for strategic military intelligence as their superiors limited MID and ONI missions and funding in an environment of an inward-looking America.

The pace of requirements and activities in Army intelligence slowed between 1924 and 1929. With little expected from MID by superiors except monitoring the international situation, MID intelligence professionals had time to give lectures and theorize through books and articles about the state of the division and military intelligence in general. The writings reflected professionals taking stock of the gains Army intelligence made in the past decade. Colonel Walter C. Sweeney published an influential book titled *Military Intelligence: A New Weapon in War*, a landmark Army intelligence publication. He regarded Army intelligence as a "new weapon whose value to the country in peace as well as in war can scarcely be estimated."[44] He believed that most Army officers misunderstood this function of the general staff. In his view, in contrast, intelligence was vital to soldiers to help penetrate the fog of war.[45] He also thought that Army intelligence had to be a permanent function of the general staff because modern conditions made keeping track of the potential enemy an essential duty.[46] The book created a stir in the public and intelligence professional community. One magazine review called it "clear and informative" and of "keen interest."[47]

MID continued to retreat into quiet routines in the late 1920s. By 1927, G-2 James H. Reeves had been in his post for two years and reshaped MID to his own views of Army intelligence. He found that the division had become too inefficient and reduced it on August 4 to five branches: Administration, Intelligence, Press, War Plans and Training, and Reserve. When bureaucratic procedure is the engaging task of the MID, the organization's relevance could be questioned.

Peacetime attitudes toward a standing army in the cynical, isolated America of the 1920s whittled away at the Army. The service that had once been 280,000 personnel in 1920 comprised a meager 130,000 at the end of the decade, and Army intelligence deteriorated along with it. The converging streams that shaped the intelligence bureau in 1920 had calmed, leaving a severely shrunken MID relegated to basic information-gathering missions.

Despite these limitations, ONI and MID dominated the strategic military intelligence landscape between 1882 and 1945. It is easy, in these circumstances, to ignore the fact that the Marine Corps had its own organization starting in 1920. Moreover, the Navy's subordinate service had been involved with organized intelligence almost since the beginning: the corps had a long-standing relationship with ONI. As mentioned earlier, the Marine Corps assigned Lieutenant Lincoln Karmany to the office as far back as January 1893. Marine Brigadier General Dion Williams served in ONI from November 1909 to March 1913. Major John H. Russell was an influential staffer at ONI in 1915 and 1916. Lieutenant General William L. Reddles worked as assistant naval attaché in Tokyo from 1915 to 1918 and then in ONI from 1920 to 1921. Through their billets at ONI, the Marine Corps officers gained an appreciation of strategic intelligence. The time was ripe for an intelligence staff of their own. And so one was launched, thanks to the efforts of three men in the fall and winter of 1920: Major General John A. Lejeune, Brigadier General Logan Feland, and Ellis.[48]

Congressional acts of July 1919 and June 1920 set the size of the Corps at 27,400 marines. To administer this demobilized postwar corps, Commandant Lejeune reorganized the headquarters staff in November and December, seeking an organization akin to the General Staff of the Army and the Office of the Chief of Naval Operations. Lejeune divided his staff into three divisions, including the Division of Operations and Training, which was to have cognizance over military intelligence.[49] Feland, Lejeune's trusted friend and longtime lieutenant, became the division's first director, assigned to develop and organize it.[50] Feland arranged his division by function, with military intelligence designated as one of five sections. The section's only initial guidance from above was to collect and compile "intelligence useful to the Marine Corps, in carrying out its mission."[51] Be that as it may, the new Military Intelligence Section represented the first permanent Marine Corps intelligence organization.

Feland asked Lejeune if he could have his former brigade chief of staff and intelligence officers from his time in Haiti join the organization. Lieutenant Colonel Ellis had served him well in Port-au-Prince and Feland could not think of a better marine to lead the new section. Lejeune consented and Ellis became the Military Intelligence Section head. Ellis built the section with the intention of imitating the most successful aspects of ONI and MID's organizational structure and functions. Why start from scratch, he figured, when blueprints were available?

Much of the Marine Corps Intelligence Section's duties, manning, and activities are lost to history as the archives are mostly empty. This dearth of information can be attributed to the section being quite small—perhaps only five officers and clerks attached to it at any given time. The Marine Corps likely loaded the personnel with information-gathering tasks but burdened them with more time-consuming, nonintelligence, general staff work. The section probably relied heavily on ONI intelligence; it acted as a pipeline between other strategic military intelligence organizations and their superiors. Nonetheless, albeit extremely limited, the section existed and served a purpose.

Domestic security dominated the responsibilities of ONI and MID during the first half of the 1920s. This was where the money and prestige lay for intelligence organizations needing missions in the face of downsizing and reduced funding. Department of the Navy and War senior leaders, sensing discontent from Congress and the public, redirected the agencies to duties elsewhere by the mid-1920s. ONI refocused on traditional data collection and public relations missions to aid efforts in arms reduction conferences and the development of plans against potential adversaries such as Japan. MID returned to information-gathering duties as well. The Marine Corps Intelligence Corps, trying to find its footing, collected information and performed general staff work.

The Red Scare, characterized by an atmosphere of bombings, labor unrest, and panic, ramped up in 1919, and many Americans expected ONI to take part in suppression methods. Although Niblack had decades of intelligence expertise, domestic security was foreign to him and would tax the ageing admiral. After naval attaché duties, Niblack had been away from naval intelligence for five years; meanwhile, the work and ONI had changed drastically. After a month on the job, he shared his concerns with his old friend and naval intelligence legend Admiral William S. Sims.[52] Niblack clearly wished to return ONI back to the days of Chief Intelligence Officer Richard Wainwright. Domestic security tasks, including investigating subversives, radicals, undesirable immigrants (as well as the alleged homosexual tendencies of naval personnel) worried the new DNI.[53] Sims sympathized with Niblack in a letter two days later.[54] The two ONI legends did not understand that traditional naval intelligence (and the America they knew) did not exist anymore.

Niblack finally comprehended the situation that summer. Attorney General Palmer asked his organization to search out undesirable and dangerous subversives using such tactics as breaking into offices without warrants, seizing materials, tapping phone lines, and arresting and deporting suspects. His targets were perceived radicals such as members of the Socialist Party, Communist Party of America, International Workers of the World (IWW), and the American Jewish Congress. The State and war departments followed Palmer's lead. The DNI reluctantly allowed his operational subordinate organizations to join Palmer's efforts: these raids were where the action was if ONI was to remain relevant. Accordingly, ONI sent daily intelligence to department officials regarding Bolshevism at home and abroad. In December, Niblack prepared a summary regarding an alleged nationwide plot of anarchists based on data sent by MID.[55] Although he was not fond of the missions, he still ordered his counterintelligence branch and DIOs to conduct domestic security duties all over the country.

In another department political controversy, Niblack's own men created a firestorm in Congress over questionable methods that his bosses asked him to investigate. Specifically, journalist and *Providence Journal* editor John R. Rathom covered naval affairs and focused on the local base, Naval Station Newport. In January 1920, the *Journal* reported that Rhode Island's episcopal bishop James DeWolf Perry railed against the Navy's inability to close perceived immoral establishments that allegedly sold sex and liquor to Navy sailors. In response to these allegations, Assistant Secretary of the Navy Roosevelt reportedly authorized naval intelligence to infiltrate the gathering places of Newport's homosexual community, resulting in the arrests of sailors and civilians. Rathom, a political enemy of Daniels and Roosevelt, alleged that ONI personnel authorized fellow sailors to entrap innocent men.[56] The secretary of the Navy and his assistant ordered the DNI to investigate the matter. A disgruntled Niblack probably felt this was not his idea of intelligence work, but his subordinates' potential missteps forced him to deal with domestic security concerns. By

March, the Senate subcommittee authorized a full investigation into the charges "of gross immorality, and reprehensible practices in connection with the activities of a naval intelligence vice squad at the Naval Training Station at Newport."[57] Niblack could not escape the fallout from military intelligence's participation in the Red Scare.

Demobilization, Niblack's hesitancy, and shifting of political winds against military intelligence use in domestic affairs reined in ONI's security program in early 1920. The DNI discontinued the B, or Counterintelligence Branch. He approved of a reorganization of four sections: Section A, Administrative; Section B, Intelligence; Section C, Compiling; Section D, Historical Section. Cases such as the Rhode Island scandal demonstrated that there was some latent hostility in Congress and among the public to the Navy's use of secret tactics.[58] Many Americans, especially in peacetime, began to consider it inappropriate for military intelligence to conduct domestic snooping tactics in a respectable democracy. Secretary Daniels, unlike his counterpart in the Department of War, was less inclined to give Niblack more autonomy (even if he wanted it) to perform domestic surveillance as he saw fit.

In early 1923, DNI McNamee denied that his office performed domestic security duties as it had during the war. If personnel found domestic information detrimental to the government, they immediately passed it to the Department of Justice.[59] This reflected McNamee's belief that domestic security belonged more to that department and MID. Nonetheless, after McNamee left the post, Hough continued covert work that his predecessor had pursued. In early 1924, his West Coast offices and fleet intelligence offices increased efforts to intercept Japanese radio traffic to agents within the US and overseas. Later in his tour he asked the commercial telephone and telegraph companies in the United States to gather information about the Japanese even though federal law forbade release of such information.[60] Thus, Hough and McNamee let it be subtly known that surveillance in the United States should be pursued even if it pushed the envelope of legality.

DNI Galbraith continued his predecessors' interest in eavesdropping by creating an in-house desk for monitoring communications intercepts. Security-minded Galbraith also advocated tighter restrictions pertaining to the release of sensitive materials to the public. The Navy had not performed adequate operational security for decades and the DNI worried the department leaked and released too much information. Still, Galbraith's efforts to curb classified information disclosures during his tenure proved unsuccessful.[61] Subsequently, during his stint as DNI, Hepburn allowed

ONI assets to surveil American businessmen, immigrants, and criminal elements within the United States.[62]

MID was not as hesitant to conduct domestic security duties as ONI, especially during the Red Scare. Army intelligence, reflecting the inclinations of its founder Van Deman, had an obsession with fighting Bolshevism. Churchill enthusiastically joined Palmer against the internal threat and any other subversive menace. Americans could discern in the newspapers how involved the division was in domestic security investigations. As the *New York Times* reported in a January 26, 1919, article, MID's Colonel Archibald E. Stevenson helped create a "Who's Who in Pacifism and Radicalism" list for a Senate committee investigating pro-German propaganda in the United States.[63] The division became an authority on finding bad guys, according to a *New York Tribune* piece on February 5 of the same year. The paper reported that MID believed "the great menace" of Bolshevism was spreading rapidly.[64] For its part, the *New York Tribune* reported on a Senate committee meeting in which congressmen admonished Secretary Newton D. Baker for ordering MID to withhold information on investigations from them. Both political parties condemned this action.[65] Baker had done so out of concern that revealing MID's methods of domestic security would show Churchill's staff in a bad light.

Behind the scenes, Baker softly encouraged Churchill to restrain his division from engaging in illegal investigative measures. At the same time, Baker trusted Churchill and let him run MID with a long leash, whereas "a stern word or a well-chosen dismissal" could have restrained the agency in 1919 and 1920.[66] Instead Americans heard of MID's deep involvement in domestic affairs through Churchill's own statements, as he told Congress that his officers were surveilling communists and other radicals all over the country. He showed the legislators New York City maps marking the hideouts of these allegedly nefarious individuals. At the same meeting, Churchill asked for more money for MID to continue this investigation.[67] He warned senators that, "even after the war ended, the German secret service had tried to place agents in every large unit of the Army, but the system was uprooted and driven out."[68] In short, Churchill showed no signs of restricting MID. His organization's offices, especially those in the negative branch, contained huge maps of hotspots in the United States with pins symbolizing Bolshevism, labor unrest, racial tensions, and other domestic concerns. MID helped draft the department's War Plan White for dealing with extensive domestic disorder. Baker and his chief of staff Peyton C. March had concerns about Van Deman's zeal for pursuing American radicals and sent him to Europe rather than promoting him by assigning him the director post. Perhaps they should have worried about Churchill's conduct as well.[69]

MID was deeply embroiled in domestic affairs in the late summer and fall of 1919. Media recounted Army intelligence officers' activities throughout the country. Lieutenant Donald C. Van Buren, in charge of MID's investigation offices for northeast Illinois and northwest Indiana, spoke in front of the Senate Committee on Labor and Education about radical activities in the Gary, Indiana, steel district.[70] Cases such as this filled MID headquarters with paranoia. Churchill's situation officer, Colonel C. H. Mason, wrote a frenzied memorandum to the director on Halloween sharing his concerns about the future of the country, which he saw as being in a situation "verging on revolution in which all persons will have to take sides."[71] According to Mason, MID was "fundamentally vital" to protecting the Constitution and the United States government.[72] The situation officer recommended that Churchill ask Baker for more personnel, money, and full war status and powers "during this emergency."[73] Mason's sense of urgency reflected the mindset of many Americans and government officials at the height of the Red Scare.

Yet, the Department of War tried to decrease its support of Palmer's Red hunt in early 1920. The Army had been at the forefront of the American government's battle against radicalism since the end of the war. It was difficult for MID to extricate itself from events of the Red Scare. Churchill's officers often exaggerated reports from around the United States and served to enhance his obsession against spies and subversives. Secretary of War Baker ineffectually attempted to control Churchill and end the Army's domestic spying in 1919. He finally succeeded in March 1920 when he put more restrictions on MID, telling agents that they could only investigate allegations of misconduct involving disloyalty, graft, or fraud, by military officers, enlisted men, or Army civilians. From now on, MID could not investigate any leads outside of the Army's jurisdiction. Churchill followed these orders and the division scaled back its domestic security programs.[74] Still, domestic spying did not entirely cease, nor did MID's officers drop their suspicions about radicals and suspicious foreigners.

Churchill's ready acceptance of Baker's orders may be attributed to the director second-guessing his own methodology. In an article explaining the philosophy of military intelligence as it related to MID, Churchill noted sadly that most Army officers "think of Military Intelligence only as a bureau of investigation, or sort of military secret police."[75] He defended MID's forays into investigation as a wartime necessity, adding that the investigation of soldiers may be repugnant to most Army men. But, he argued, it had to be conducted by military officers, not a unempathetic civilian bureau.[76] He claimed incongruously that MID had not conducted secret service methods, except in cases of graft and fraud, since the Armistice.[77] Evidence proves otherwise. MID, he wrote, concentrated on collecting foreign army intelligence, maintaining foreign maps, evaluating information, and disseminating intelligence. Churchill considered it was the division's job to educate Army officers on foreign languages, countries, and historical events to understand world situations.[78] The director tried to press a reset button, as if MID had not partaken in the Red Scare. He said of MID, "It is imperfect. No one knows that better than the officers who control it. We want only a chance to perfect our service, to be used and to be criticized in a constructive way."[79]

Nevertheless, MID's domestic security missions did persist and the agency remained in the public eye as a result. The *Washington Herald* reported on July 27, 1920, that MID agreed to join a dragnet made up of the Bureau of Investigation of the Department of Justice, local police, and members of Washington, DC, patriotic organizations. They sought to locate and "punish" 572 DC draft slackers and over 100,000 nationwide.[80] As already mentioned, MID provided estimates for War Plan White and had not stopped censorship operations. But the division's domestic operations did decline out of necessity; demobilization had a dramatic effect on Army funding and personnel. Future directors found they had to depend heavily on the Bureau of Investigation if they wished to track radicals and subversives in the country.

March reordered MID's duties in August 1920. There was no mention of domestic security in the new general order. He merely emphasized duties revolving around "the collection, evaluation and dissemination of military information."[81] The secretary of war and chief of staff tried to steer MID away from investigative matters that could be considered illegitimate. Instead, Army leadership tasked MID with responsibilities traditional to data management jobs MID was accustomed to carrying out.

The submersion of domestic security missions continued through the rest of the decade. G–2 Reeves gave a lecture to the Army War College in January 1927, the third in over two years, to convey his thoughts on his craft.[82] In it, he stated Army officers just do not understand Army intelligence or what MID can do for them. He recalled that one general officer told Reeves his definition of intelligence: "That by which a commanding general plans and fights. That is all there is to it."[83] This is a satisfactory definition of tactical intelligence, but not the broad subject of strategic intelligence. In Reeves's view, the function of MID was to keep the Department of War aware of the military thought and technological advancements elsewhere in the world.[84] The G-2 claimed that MID did not conduct domestic security duties, especially in peacetime. Such duties had occurred out of necessity during the Great War, as MID helped the civilian investigative bureaus by assuming some of the burden in counterintelligence responsibilities at Army bases and even among the civilian population. He regretted the repercussions of the wartime decision.[85] Reeves honestly asserted that the missions MID had performed enthusiastically seven years previously within the country's borders during the Red Scare were no longer functions of Army intelligence. And his self-awareness of MID's reputation is enlightening.

The ghosts of MID's domestic security past kept haunting G-2s during the interwar period. Proponent of counterintelligence Brigadier General Van Deman wrote to G-2 Colonel Stanley H. Ford on December 15, 1928, regarding the rumored decision by the Department of War and MID to end negative intelligence activities and to entrust counterintelligence to the Department of Justice in case of war.[86] The former director wrote that, if true, such a policy would be erroneous.[87] Van Deman still had an intense interest in the activities—from the mundane to the controversial—of the organization he created. Ford replied to the general in a tone of a petulant son irritated with a prying father. He wrote that the subject has been a great concern of the Department of War and MID since 1920, when the military committees of the House and Senate and Secretary Baker directed the G-2 to stop civilian investigations.[88] After 1924, Ford said, the MID kept abreast of radicals through the Department of Justice, the radical press, and patriotic society and individual tips. As to Department of War domestic security policy in time of war, Ford said his bosses had not decided yet, but he knew that G-2 would be called upon to investigate cases of disloyalty within the Army and that investigations might necessarily occur within the civilian population.[89] Ford assumed a patronizing tone with Van Deman, stating he would be "very glad" to hear his continued views of the subject in future proposed Army regulations later in the year and for Van Deman to send a list of radicals he kept tabs on "as soon as practicable."[90] Ford did not want the political headaches of this type of mission for MID.

At ONI, the information-gathering mission made a comeback after the Great War as well. In reorganizing the War Plans Section of the Chief of Naval Operations in April 1919, a trio of captains led by Harry E. Yarnell proposed ONI be the authority over all information for war plans.[91] ONI, excluded from the strategy and policy of war planning since 1915, settled for supplying intelligence to this section; it may have been flattering to Welles and other intelligence leaders to still be of service. But in future years, the office's duty to provide analysis to the information they provided would be jeopardized.

Niblack attempted to ignore the events of the Red Scare and ONI's limited participation in it in 1919. Yet, the specter of domestic security responsibilities remained as Niblack tried to refocus ONI on more traditional missions. Secretary Daniels's orders and other pressing matters allowed Niblack to overlook some of the less appealing collateral duties thrust upon him and focus on such areas as the breakup of the Ottoman Empire, Chinese nationalism, and Japan's threats to the Open Door policy. The language training program also revived under Niblack. Bureaucratic tasks took much of the DNI's time. On July 31, 1919, Daniels asked Niblack to prepare a publication accounting for all the phases of ONI's activities throughout the war. His intention was to show the American people "the very important work accomplished by the Office of Naval Intelligence."[92] The press duly noted that the office performed other duties beyond domestic security. The *Pensacola Journal* used ONI's tables demonstrating the sea strength of the various world powers, in an August 18, 1919, article proudly reporting that the United States was second only to Great Britain as a sea power based on building programs.[93] In the same vein, Niblack's office provided strategic intelligence to the director of War Plans in the form of a product called "Estimates of the Situation and Base Development Plans." The reports contained a political situation section that War Plans used for annual reports to the chief of naval operations. The estimates could also help determine budget requirements and inform basic war plans. Through these and other projects, the DNI was determined to reorient ONI away from domestic concerns.

In October 1919, Niblack addressed the Army War College on the history, missions, and philosophy of ONI. He pointed out similarities and differences between ONI and MID but also showed how older ONI functions should take precedence. A naval overseas representative veteran himself, Niblack argued for the importance of the naval attaché.[94] His statement acknowledged and supported ONI's roots as an information-gathering organization first and foremost. Niblack abhorred "trickery and double-dealing" and preferred that his employees "play a gentlemen's game" of sportsmanship.[95] It is as if these words were spoken by an 1880s chief intelligence officer. He also reiterated his belief that the MID had more complex duties than ONI, especially "in keeping track of enemy activities within our own borders and foiling them."⁹⁶ By acknowledging MID's mission in the United States, he was conveniently ignoring the fact that his own office had similar duties at home.

The DNI tried to shift the shrinking organization back into collecting foreign intelligence on maritime countries. By July 1920, ONI had forty-two personnel, whom Niblack reoriented toward data collection and reporting in an effort to remake ONI into the center of valuable information collection Navy-wide. He instituted a monograph system of filing data on foreign countries, similar to the card catalogue days at ONI in the late nineteenth century.⁹⁷ Niblack tasked the Foreign Branch with being the intelligence production shop for all foreign navies. In the coming decades, the branch also reported secondary objectives, including military, political, economic, and sociological intelligence. The branch would sometimes lose focus on maritime affairs information that Department of the Navy customers required. When the geographically organized branch and larger office were on task, however, they concentrated on threats mainly from East Asia. The DNI warned the department of Japanese interests in Siberia, Manchuria, and the Western Pacific. Specifically, Niblack worried about the island country's acquisition of former German islands as it could be part of a Japanese long-term strategy to create a defense parameter.

In 1921, ONI swam against the current of newly inaugurated president Warren G. Harding's policies and focused much of its attention on foreign intelligence, especially information pertaining to the Washington Naval Conference. Harding advocated a return to normalcy in America, encouraging the populace to think pleasant, unpolitical thoughts rather than engaging in Progressive crusades and entangling international alliances. The new politics worked against the Navy; the public did not have the appetite to increase the Navy's size to rival Great Britain. Harding's administration took its cue from disillusioned Americans and worked to decommission naval assets and encourage foreign powers, through arms reduction and naval limitations, to do the same.

Even before Harding's staff began setting up the conference, ONI informed officials in the administration and in Congress about foreign navy sizes. ONI had perfected this task, with the help of naval attachés, since the late 1880s and was now able to provide a pamphlet titled "Information concerning the United States Navy and Other Navies" to inform a House of Representatives debate.⁹⁸ In January and February 1921, Long asked naval attachés to take the pulse of the local populations' opinions regarding disarmament and naval limitations. When the United States sent invitations in earnest to foreign powers, ONI transmitted reports to naval leaders on foreign naval expenditures, construction programs, and the current fleets.[99]

ONI's staff and naval attachés stayed ahead of requirements, demonstrating that after five years of focusing on domestic missions, ONI could still collect and report on foreign intelligence at the strategic level. Attachés combed through open sources and conducted local interviews with foreign authorities to pass to the home office. Staff officers compiled the information and analyzed it before passing the intelligence to the State Department. As they often did for congressional appropriations debates, ONI supplied quantitative data on tonnage of warships and strengths of navies. ONI also eavesdropped, through advancements in breaking codes and ciphers, on foreign delegations and attachés communicating in secret with their home countries. Long's office passed this intercepted mail to American delegates. Both Secretary of State Charles E. Hughes and Assistant Secretary of the Navy Theodore Roosevelt Jr. were appreciative consumers of naval intelligence during the conference. From the DNI's point of view, the Washington Naval Conference was a successful undertaking, because ONI could still shine as a strategic intelligence provider separate from its more questionable activities within the United States.

At the same time, DNI McNamee and his staff pressed forward with less savory methods in 1922. Namely, Japan and its territories in the Pacific were still mysteries to naval intelligence, even though the island nation had a reputation as a military power. McNamee was one of the first DNIs to conduct surveillance and secret operations in Japan and Micronesia. He would even approve of surveillance of Japanese diplomats in the United States, in the belief that old-fashioned intelligence missions and techniques were no longer adequate.[100] The DNI also sought to apply similar covert methods abroad: in Europe, McNamee considered secretive methods with the assistance of Niblack. The former DNI argued that the US intelligence network in Europe was weak, with only naval attachés providing information to the home office. A man once disgusted by undercover methods apparently had an epiphany: Niblack now wished to organize a secret network of agents in Paris, London, and Berlin. He asked McNamee for money to finance the venture, and the DNI concurred. Acting Secretary of the Navy Theodore Roosevelt Jr. disagreed and put a stop to Niblack's plan.

The agreements that emerged from the Washington Naval Conference were weak, confusing, and unenforceable. It was not helpful for the Navy that the American public was apathetic to international issues and unconcerned with arms reduction matters. ONI officers worried that treaty violations would inevitably occur. They were determined to warn the populace that the treaties were not enough to stem new foreign naval construction and that the US Navy had to continue to bolster naval defenses. In the spirit of 1880s navalists, they lectured and wrote articles to promote the Navy. Knox penned essays and corresponded with politicians to enlighten them on the conference's agreements. One highlight of his efforts was the book *The Eclipse of American Sea Power*, written in the tenor of naval theorist Alfred T. Mahan. Knox and ONI personnel also published pamphlets to educate Americans on the treaty and the importance of the Navy.[101]

McNamee often complained that he had little money to spend to maintain the office and perform basic missions. With his budget the lowest it had been in seven years, in 1921 he cut back on intelligence product lengths and simplified analytical methodology. At the same time, McNamee also ensured the naval attachés stayed on task by holding conferences with them. The DNI increasingly became concerned with Japanese activity in the Western Pacific. It was unknown what fortifications existed on the Pacific Islands or if the Japanese obeyed treaty agreements. Naval attachés also did not have adequate access to information on new weapons advancements or submarine construction in the island nation. McNamee constantly pressed US representatives for more data and often received little. Much of the information the attachés did send during this period was false, misleading, or reinforced racial and psychological stereotypes; it did not present an accurate picture of the Japanese Navy.[102]

In the late 1920s, DNI Johnson's staff supplied the tables and charts to Congress for debates involving naval appropriations.[103] Johnson believed that naval intelligence's missions should be "the collection, summation and evaluation of information" and "protection against foreign espionage and propaganda."[104] Being a former naval representative abroad, Johnson eagerly updated a 1919 ONI publication "The Duties of Naval Attachés." In it, the DNI directed new attachés on how to prepare for their new posts, to include making the most out of visits to ONI, learning extensively on their accredited country before arriving there, and talking with experts at the State and Commerce Departments as well as MID. Following his tour, Johnson said, the veteran attaché should return to the office to brief the director and settle his accounts.[105]

Johnson had to protect the evaluation or analytical assessment phase of data management duties because many in the department did not consider it a function of ONI. To recall, in the 1910s, the office lost the responsibility to actively participate in war planning as policy and strategy makers. In

1928, senior officers such as Captain D. M. LeBreton, a former assistant director of naval intelligence, openly disagreed with ONI on who should even evaluate collected information. At a lecture to the Army War College, LeBreton said that evaluation of data should belong to the War Plans Division and the Naval War College; technical information evaluation belonged to the technical bureaus.[106] In a statement on April 15, 1929, the chief of naval operations settled the dispute (at least temporarily), specifying it was ONI's duty. The Navy also recognized for the first time that information must be evaluated to become intelligence.[107]

For its part, MID tried to shed its spy persona after the Red Scare and focus on collecting and analyzing data. In a 1924 lecture to the incoming class at the Army War College, Reeves called Walter C. Sweeney's *Military Intelligence: A New Weapon in War* a "valuable" book.[108] He used Sweeney's text, past lectures, and department pamphlets to explain the functions of MID, stating that the main mission of MID was "the collection, evaluation and dissemination of military information," reflecting the nineteenth-century view of MID's purpose.[109] Reeves told the students that MID had shrunk to twenty-four regular officers, one reservist, and fifty-two research and clerical personnel after demobilization. But he declared that G-2 would expand if Army leaders activated the Department of War General Mobilization Plan. He barely mentioned domestic security missions and only in passing as wartime functions. It was a sensitive subject Reeves would not advertise in an open forum. By 1925, MID was not active in counterintelligence activities; hostile public opinions to past MID actions tempered G-2's pursuit in performing such duties. US Army intelligence had reverted to traditional missions; that was all the budget would allow. Both the Department of War and Congress showed little appetite for domestic intelligence activities given the legal headaches related to civil rights infringements. The Red Scare was over and MID downsized to a state where superiors and G-2s themselves expected the bare minimum performance of duties.

Advancements in technologies changed the nature of MID's unproductivity compared to a decade earlier. For instance, military attachés were now required to collect air information and thus, the division published more intelligence on aerial innovations. The Army formed a separate Army Air Corps in 1926, adding a wrinkle to the customers MID supported. The new corps started detailing officers to MID that year. Air Corps Major Joseph T. McNarney came to MID August 2 to head the new Air Section. Army intelligence officials took a great interest in the new arm because airplanes became a fundamental source—separate from attachés, secret operatives, and open-source publications—of military information. Crucially, air intelligence held the potential for overhead photography and new mapping techniques. The G-2 charged McNarney's section with answering operational intelligence policy questions, photographs and mapping, air codes and communications questions, and helping the parent intelligence branch with aviation studies.[110]

The Marine Intelligence Section also performed information-gathering duties in Marine Corps Headquarters. The section sent out the document "List of Intelligence Regulations, etc. Transmitted to Certain Marine Corps Units" to the field, including the Army's "Intelligence Regulations. 1920," military orders, articles, and reports.[111] The Army's new publication was so thorough that Ellis and his staff decided to use it as a model. In April 1921, Section staff officer G. A. Johnson began a folder explaining activities at his office. Johnson organized it like a military standard operating procedure (SOP) for the section and future staff officers to follow. One of the immediate tasks the section worked on was compiling data and maps on China, Cuba, Nicaragua, Honduras, Mexico, and Guatemala—"those places the Marine Corps is liable to be called on for a sudden expedition."[112] The SOP explained how staffers should catalogue files in the safes called "case files." And because the section's communications network was not that robust, Johnson explained personnel should use ONI to send copies of Marine Corps intelligence reports to the other intelligence agencies.[113] Ellis's section initially had two reports for the review of the commandant: the monthly preparedness report of expeditionary strength and the quarterly preparedness report. Johnson felt confident that the section was successful in putting Marine Corps Headquarters on all appropriate mailing lists for current intelligence reports of value to the Marine Corps.[114] This SOP and available evidence suggest the section mainly collected and compiled information as its main mission.

However, Brigadier General Logan Feland had another task for Major Pete Ellis: war planning. The section head eagerly accepted. The Navy and Marine Corps intended to update War Plan Orange (Japan-focused), specifically for the Micronesian Islands. The Department of the Navy ordered Feland to create a war plan for advanced base operations in this region. Ellis apparently went into monastic seclusion, surrounded by maps and intelligence reports, and ignored his section head duties.[115] He drew heavily from information available at ONI to draft tactics for reducing Japanese island defenses and employing amphibious operations. In early 1921, Ellis produced several versions of Operation Plan 712, "Advanced Base Force Operations in Micronesia." Commandant Lejeune approved of the war plan, which became Ellis's signature document.[116] He died in early 1923 in the course of an undercover mission in the Caroline Islands to determine Japanese fortifications in the South Pacific.

Meanwhile, ONI officially acquired a public relations duty. Secretary of the Navy Edwin Denby recognized that his department was the subject of negative publicity from the media as his increasingly antiquated fleet sat in American ports undervalued and underfunded. He determined that the Navy needed a way to counter possible distortions of its operations and programs. The director of the War Plans Division suggested that ONI house a press relations office. McNamee reluctantly concurred with his colleague two days later. On February 21, Denby issued a directive to the department that established ONI's Information Section. A week later, the secretary directed bureaus and offices to assign personnel to help the new section and also told fleet commander, commandants, and station commanders to pass information of open sources publicity value to ONI.[117] Although ONI had performed public relations duties mainly to influence Congress and the press regarding fleet sizes, this was an unofficial duty that DNIs only employed to improve ONI's reputation. This type of information management pitted opposites—public relations versus security. The Navy expected the DNI and his staff to push out general positive information to the public but to restrict information of a sensitive nature. It was a difficult task and one not necessarily intelligence related.

Events came full circle for strategic military intelligence in the late 1920s. Data collection and reporting became once again the Departments of Navy and of War intelligence agencies' main mission. Their interest in homeland security duties temporarily subsided. Demobilization and fiscal constraints ensured that ONI and MID did the bare minimum to stay relevant.

In 1919 strategic military intelligence received positive attention from Congress, department leadership, and the American public. The DNI and MID chiefs got publicity for their part in the Red Scare. But over time that recognition soured as the intelligence agencies seemed too intrusive and strayed away from core intelligence responsibilities and into the domestic arena. Congressmen often wondered why ONI and MID needed more funds. If strategic intelligence coveted domestic security missions, why were they asking for more money for attachés? Difficult questions like this made it harder for ONI and MID to receive healthier budgets.

ONI's recent acquisition of missions in domestic security created a public reputation for it as mainly an investigatory agency. The *Tonopah Daily*, for example, reported that a naval intelligence officer investigated the construction of a bomb sent through the mail that showed a resemblance to a type of German sea mine.[118] In this environment of intrigue, the story demonstrated even a small-town media outlet's interest in naval intelligence as spy-catchers. Senator Kenneth McKellar (Tennessee) brought up on the Senate floor a New York newspaper article regarding $1 million worth of material stolen from a Navy yard on December 22, 1922. He wondered why ONI knew nothing about the theft while the Department of Justice made arrests in the case. He asked why the Senate should allow a $30,000 appropriation to naval intelligence if it did not do its job and "seems absolutely unable to cope with the situation."[119] Senator Miles Poindexter (Washington) corrected McKellar by stating that the purpose of the Office of Naval Intelligence was not domestic security: the latter, in his view was the duty of the Bureau of Investigation of the Department of Justice.[120] McKellar persisted that any kind of naval intelligence that could not keep up with thefts of this sort should be abolished. The Washington senator questioned McKellar's ignorance of ONI and its missions and defended naval intelligence.[121] Poindexter then criticized the Tennessee lawmaker's basic knowledge of government institutions in condemning an organization he knew nothing about. Misperceptions abounded in Congress as to ONI's purpose, but the office was partly to blame, as it welcomed missions outside its chartered duties.

Congress audited and threatened MID with cuts in funding in the postwar period. It occurred every year when lawmakers debated the Army appropriations bill. On February 13, confusion reigned on the House floor as to why military attachés needed more funding, and the broader issue of why MID requested so much money.[122] Proponents, such as Ashton C. Shallenberger (Nebraska), won a victory as Congress granted MID $400,000 for the contingent expenses fund on July 11, 1919.[123] But in the later 1920s, MID leaders would not be so fortunate. Debates in the House in the early months of 1921 show how difficult it was for MID and its attachés to obtain funding in the turbulent environment of the early 1920s. In a repeat question in 1920, congressmen questioned why military intelligence should receive $125,000 when Congress funded it with $26,000 before the war. They questioned why the Army asked for housing allowances for attachés when the State Department provided quarters. This question showed the ignorance of representatives concerning expenses attachés incurred in their normal duties.[124] The House agreed again that the amounts allocated to MID, and its attaché corps, were adequate. MID may not have been enthusiastic with the allocated money in the next fiscal year, but it could have been worse. In March 1922, G-2 Heintzelman told the military attaché in London, O. N. Solbert, of the fight he was expecting to have in Congress for appropriations.[125] He feared that the committees on military affairs would reduce his request for the $225,000 for "contingencies, M.I.D."[126] Heintzelman asserted if MID funds were reduced, he would have to release data collection clerks in the division and close nine military attaché offices.[127] Secretary of War John W. Weeks championed the G-2's concerns. He leaned on Secretary of State Charles E. Hughes to come to MID's defense and assist funding military attachés.[128] With congressional funding being so limited, Weeks said that he might be forced to reduce attaché representation.[129] Five days later, Hughes asked the military affairs committee for more funding for MID.

Thus, MID experienced a steady decline in personnel and funding fueled by a penny-pitching Congress and disillusioned public. In the Department of War, leaders neglected or ceased many functional activities by necessity. MID fell into that neglected category. Like the unproductive years of 1908 to 1916, the division failed to process much of information received in a timely fashion due to the lack of manpower. Because of cuts, the division reduced its Positive Branch to a much smaller Intelligence Branch, with just a few officers for managing foreign information coming to MID.

MID occasionally was in political trouble with Congress as well, usually regarding domestic security. Weeks had to come to its defense. An intelligence officer at Vancouver Barracks in Washington State wrote to local law enforcement that the Army's intelligence service viewed the American Federation of Labor as potentially hostile to the US government. This officer's letter was then printed in the *Nation* on January 31, 1923. Naturally, W. G. Lee, president of the Brotherhood of Railway Trainmen and Samuel Gompers, of the American Federation of Labor, lobbied against this action in Congress. On February 5, the House discussed the ethics of the intelligence officer's actions and possible Department of War remedies for the situation.[130] Weeks defended MID to Congress, but not the individual officer, stating that the division did not conduct peacetime investigations of this nature.[131] Weeks's words seemed to satisfy congressional impatience with MID, but the incident suggests the extent to which Congress tired of reports of MID and ONI overstepping their bounds in domestic affairs.

Two trends hindered ONI, MID, and to a much lesser extent, the Marine Corps' Intelligence section during the interwar period. But in many ways, the patterns were an extension of strategic military intelligence organizations' struggles from their inception. First, even though they survived as separate agencies within the Departments of the Navy and of War, ONI and MID's superiors did not quite understand what military intelligence was, its importance, and what it could do for them. This problem stemmed from the core difficulty in defining these organizations' missions. The military establishment debated whether intelligence work should continue in peacetime. Consequently, military officers generally regarded strategic military intelligence organizations as clearinghouses for all types of information unrelated to intelligence.[132] Only nine of twenty-three directors of ONI of MID between 1919 and 1939 were flag officers, demonstrating how military intelligence professionals languished as second-class personnel in divisional positions of lesser importance because of the lack of senior officers' understanding of their value.[133]

The other trend was directly related to the first. Since officers did not quite understand military intelligence and the department function did not seem related to perceived Army or Navy business, these billets were oddities at best. Job placement officers assumed any breathing officer could fill the intelligence positions. Therefore, attracting talented officers proved hard for ONI and MID, especially if the prospective recruit wanted promotion. In the interwar period, MID became a "dumping ground" for unfit regular command officers and the Navy, which encouraged sea duty for general line officers, discouraged intelligence desk jobs if and officer wanted to advance.[134] Army and Navy officers such as Van Deman or Zacharias, who wanted to pursue military intelligence careers, were a rarity. Who would want to risk his career for a misunderstood, little-known function in the Departments of the Navy and of War?

The 1920s started tumultuously but ended quietly for strategic military intelligence. Budget cuts and the larger developments in American society forced ONI, MID, and the Marine Corps Intelligence Section to retreat from more controversial missions and return to basic strategic information-gathering duties. This pattern would continue well into the 1930s.

Chapter Seven
1929-1939:
Storm on ONI and MID's Horizon

The stock market crashed in 1929, ending a decade of American prosperity and plunging the United States into the Great Depression. Two other developments shared the spotlight in domestic politics: the New Deal and the Jeffersonian-style movement toward isolation of Americans from international affairs. The New Deal was President Franklin D. Roosevelt's policy to counteract the great economic downturn with government programs to stimulate and organize capitalism. According to historian Richard Hofstadter, the New Deal "was itself a product of that overorganized world," conforming to the trend of "management, toward bureaucracy, toward bigness everywhere."[1] Key to this all-consuming focus on the economy was America's inward-looking turn. Although Roosevelt was an internationalist, he knew the success of the New Deal and the increased growth of government hinged on fixing the American economy first while staving off involvement in overseas matters. True, when international tensions increased in the latter half of the 1930s, Roosevelt suggested on a few occasions turning away from isolationist sentiments and toward the crises in Asia and Europe. He was hampered, however, by the fact that—as historians William L. Langer and S. Everett Gleason write—many Americans considered any degree of involvement in preventing the spread of the conflict unwanted and unproductive.[2] These challenges in a disillusioned American society and government worked against the military and its intelligence agencies. For the second straight decade there was little growth in the Navy and Army; the cutting edges of the swords of the republic were quite dull.

Naval and war department administrators measured the damage of the Great Depression and isolationism to the Navy and Army in dollars and cents. For the maritime service, the pattern that began with demobilization after the war intensified after 1929 into general naval reductions and funding cuts. The fiscal cutbacks trickled down to the Office of Naval Intelligence (ONI) in appropriations bills each year. A director of naval intelligence in the late 1930s could only receive more funding by justifying domestic security missions through publicized spy convictions. The

Military Intelligence Division (MID) and its directors faced the same issues, as the Army felt the effects of fiscal constraints and public apathy. MID's general health would not make a resurgence until at least 1939. ONI and MID's version of recovery, a theme of the New Deal in an ailing capitalistic America, was organizational planning for a future war when the money and manpower flowed in again. In short, American society's response to the troubled the post-industrialized economy drove the evolution of the military intelligence agencies.

As should be abundantly clear from the preceding chapters, Americans had mixed feelings regarding ONI and MID. Before the Great War, the public only knew these strategic military intelligence organizations as information brokers that would provide data about the US Navy or Army compared to the rest of the world. After substantial reports surfaced over the years of military and naval agents spying on Americans and infringing on civil liberties, public opinions of ONI and MID generally changed in a negative direction. Dwight D. Eisenhower once wrote, "The American public has always viewed with repugnance everything that smacks of the spy."[3] Yet, ONI and MID held an air of mystery about them, which portended some positive emotional connections. The American public generally liked mysteries, as evidenced by the popularity of the spy novel and film in American culture of the 1930s.[4] In this medium, writers and film producers depicted military intelligence officers as protagonist spies or spy-catchers, in part to the agencies' reputations during this era as being solely involved in espionage. Ironically, ONI and MID often downplayed their domestic security programs, especially in the early 1930s as they recognized limits of manpower and funding imposed by the same society and congressional representatives who viewed them as all-powerful investigative agencies.

On some level, the DNI and G-2's superiors accepted that ONI and MID conducted activities other than strategic military intelligence. This relative tolerance intensified when international tensions escalated in the late 1930s. On the one hand, President Herbert Hoover generally ignored military intelligence unless it suited his personal political interests. On the other, FDR, always an ally of intelligence (especially ONI), expected the agencies to collect foreign information but also encouraged their counterintelligence activities. In the legislative branch, Congress sparsely funded ONI and MID to conduct information gathering through Taylorist methodology but was still reluctant—even in 1939—to approve of their domestic security inclinations. The secretaries of the Navy and their senior subordinates supported ONI's data management duties and tasked DNIs to provide intelligence to assist with war plans. They were even willing to overlook

ONI's interest in intelligence activities within the United States. But there was a growing opposition, especially within the senior naval officer cadre, to naval intelligence officers analyzing raw information. For its part, in the Department of War, the secretaries and chiefs of staff wanted their small, underfunded intelligence agency to gather information and report it. They too overlooked MID's increased domestic security efforts from 1936 onward. More broadly, within government circles, many officials thought of ONI and MID as useless: real military officers fought wars; they did not idle behind desks collecting data. Within this overall context, budget cuts forced by the Great Depression and peacetime attitudes, notably isolationist sentiment, downgraded the agencies' effectiveness.

The entire period of the 1930s was a frustrating era for ONI and MID. The organizations' staff discerned that momentous events were happening around the world, but they were too small to meet the associated strategic intelligence challenges.[5] The military intelligence officer viewed himself as above the bureaucracy, a breed apart from the normal citizen and a protector of the American way of life. But he had a short leash. ONI's senior officers often chose domestic security operations and preferred conducting surveillance on spies and radicals over traditional missions. The DNIs of the New Deal era longed for more than just providing information to the War Plans division; they tried to protect their assessment obligations from others in the department even as their seniors shut them out of strategy and policy discussions. G-2s recognized their limits of manpower and funding imposed by the Great Depression and stuck to information-gathering duties, but new government efficiency programs offered hope for future years. As the turbulent decade marched on, MID became more involved in counterintelligence.

Just as demobilization, the Red Scare, and disillusionment stunted ONI and MID's growth in the 1920s, the Great Depression and isolation from world affairs continued to dampen their influence within the US government throughout the 1930s. Government officials expected ONI and MID to simply gather and report strategic information—not evaluate it—and on occasion, support planning for future conflicts. As tensions increased overseas and at home, Congress and the departments overlooked these enthusiastic organizations' increased efforts to conduct domestic security missions, military intelligence's response to New Deal initiatives.

The organizational structures of ONI and MID during this period were bare-boned, built for the future, not for the 1930s. Both strategic military intelligence organizations had no choice but to deal with the realities of poor funding, under-manning, and lack of prestige. The Departments of the Navy and of War had more pressing challenges than trying to prop up two agencies of seemingly little use in an isolationist, peacetime America. The size and scope of ONI and MID little resembled the fiction of American literature and film.

The early years of the Great Depression forced DNI Captain Alfred W. Johnson to contend with limited personnel and funding, more so than in the previous decade. The DNI left certain ONI branches, sections, and units vacant. ONI leaders hoped that if crises arose, they could rapidly fill the ranks with personnel. The DNI established the first intelligence mobilization quotas in the document "War Plans—Division of Naval Intelligence" in 1930 to prepare for potential conflicts. Johnson rotated from his post in June to Nicaragua as part of a national board to monitor elections on behalf of the United States.

His replacement, Captain Harry A. Baldridge, had a quiet, unremarkable, and short tour of eleven months, and was followed in the post by Captain Hayne Ellis in June 1931. Ellis was pleased with the election results in 1932. Old friend and ONI mentor FDR moved into the White House in 1933. Ellis and other ONI officers could anticipate that the new president would share their anxieties about international affairs and concepts of preparedness. To naval intelligence officers, anything would be better than the cautious and demoralizing Hoover policies after the economic collapse and failed arms limitation discussions of his last years in office. Morale soared at ONI as Roosevelt immediately asked the small office for information on treaty data, security of naval facilities, and Japanese island defenses. It was the most attention a president had given ONI since Theodore Roosevelt in 1908.[6] Both Roosevelts had served as assistant secretaries of the Navy and knew ONI's potential. But ONI's growth under Roosevelt did not occur immediately; funding continued to diminish. Ellis closed naval attaché posts in Rio de Janeiro, Tegucigalpa, and The Hague.

The Department of the Navy replaced the competent DNI in Ellis in June 1934 with an even better intelligence officer in Captain William D. Puleston. Ellis warned Puleston about the problems he would face in domestic security. The outgoing DNI believed that ONI was more attuned to serious domestic threats than anyone else in the naval establishment but thought the office would be forced to attend to other matters. He was correct; his superiors were more concerned that ONI conduct its more traditional duties. The new DNI was aggressive and well-educated; he had published a major biography on Alfred T. Mahan and brought some of the theorist's philosophies, as well as his other war college ideas, to the position. He believed intelligence's value lay in war plan exercises and estimates. It was immediately apparent that Puleston treated the post as not just some useless shore billet between coveted sea tours. Lieutenant Commander Ellis M. Zacharias was impressed and praised Puleston as an ideal planner and an inspirational, motivated, energetic, and capable leader.[7]

Puleston began his command with twenty-two talented officers at ONI's headquarters, including Zacharias and Arthur H. McCollum. He also had on his staff future DNI Leo H. Thebaud, the future first director of central intelligence Roscoe H. Hillenkoetter, and Edwin T. Layton. In more good news, ONI received $121,000 from Congress (much more than in previous years under Republican administrations) for information collection. ONI dove into routine work with much vigor as the staffers followed their enthusiastic leader's example, updating old monographs and revamping filing and record keeping.[8]

Yet, the government still undermanned ONI. ONI's "OP" code in the Office of the Chief of Naval Operations was OP-16-B, with seventeen subcodes: B-1, dissemination; B-2 through B-7, the Domestic Intelligence Section; and B-10 through B-17, the Foreign Intelligence Section. The Department of the Navy restricted the organization to sixteen active officers, two retired officers, twenty civilians, and three marines. Despite Puleston's strong leadership, the division had trouble carrying out all the office's missions considering ongoing international tensions, which likely required at least ten more officers. ONI did convince Congress that it needed to appropriate money in 1936 for nine more clerks. The agency's Naval Records and Library Branch began the systematic collection and filing of photographs in 1936. The branch and its War Records Section received, recorded, and distributed photos under the watchful eye of retired Captain Dudley W. Knox. Before the department instituted the War Plan for Photographs that year, ONI did not have a central photo section. Puleston was one of the most aggressive DNIs in ONI's history.

The winter of 1936 to 1937 marked the passing of a naval intelligence icon, Admiral William S. Sims. The praises celebrating his service came in from all parts of the naval establishment.[9] The former naval attaché Sims had made a career in an era of Hamiltonian progress, imperialism, and military progressivism. His command philosophies centered on change and improvement. In his youthful prime, ONI had a sort of innocence: obtaining and reporting intelligence was good enough for DNIs and their superiors. In 1937, when Puleston handed over his position to

Rear Admiral Ralston S. Holmes, naval intelligence was much more complicated and hectic.

Holmes took over May 1 and duties quickly overwhelmed him. It took time for him to adjust to the different culture of ONI. In department matters, Holmes needed to get a grip on ONI's priorities to inform his superiors. He gathered himself and informed Chief of Naval Operations William D. Leahy of four points of concern. First, government leaders forced ONI (as had always been the case) to conduct strategic political intelligence by default, given that there was no centralized intelligence agency. Next, ONI had to be proactive on information gathering in non-military matters. Related to this, his third point was that domestic security was getting hard to manage unless (fourth) ONI expanded personnel to meet the workload.[10] Leahy agreed to enlarge the office but limited ONI in domestic security issues to cases that had a definitive connection to naval security, such as base, personnel, and equipment protections. Holmes was not the aggressive anti-communist his predecessor had been and was more cautious about taking on domestic security missions.

Under Leahy's mentorship, Holmes and ONI were more prepared to conduct their duties than MID. Leahy encouraged ONI's growth and the DNI, a former naval attaché, knew that ONI's traditional duties were at the core of his strategic responsibilities. Holmes also understood, because of precedent in past two decades, that he could not ignore domestic security missions. In early 1938, he established a Planning and Training Section to find vulnerabilities in ONI's mobilization plans and ways to correct them. The section created training manuals for domestic security missions.[11] Holmes also developed a working relationship with Assistant Secretary of State George Messersmith to ensure naval attachés and their host embassies agreed on administration, security, and information-gathering. Leahy helped the DNI by backing Holmes's authority as the Navy's classification control officer, giving him important seats on the department's various boards, and reminding the War Plans Division to continually check with ONI for intelligence on European belligerent mobilization activities. Through these shows of support, Leahy helped ONI regain some of its prestige.

Holmes concentrated on funding issues and had his staff update him on mobilization plans. In working on the 1940 budget, Holmes requested a modest $375,000 from Congress. Because this was an increase from fiscal year 1939, he had to justify it as preparations for possible hostilities with Japan and support to naval attachés in gathering information. Captain Walter K. Kilpatrick, head of the Planning and Training Section, gave the

DNI a detailed report on the office's mobilization plans, state of readiness, and weaknesses ONI should address.[12] In terms of the latter, the ONI was in a partial state of readiness in most of its sections, but Censorship (OP-16-D), Commerce and Travel (OP-16-B-5), and Plant Protection (OP-16-B-6) were inactive during peacetime.[13] Holmes was sure that a war was coming; funding requests and concerns for mobilization reflected his outlook.

But ONI still was comparatively small. On the eve of Roosevelt's order for a Limited Emergency on September 8, 1939, made in response to the outbreak of a general war in Europe, ONI only had thirty-five officers and twenty-five civilians at headquarters. In 1939, hopes of peace in the world faded. Holmes knew the Department of the Navy would expand ONI. But the question was by how much? More importantly, as the possibility increased of Americans being pulled into another world war, what roles did Americans, Congress, and Department of the Navy foresee for ONI?

Turning now to MID, G-2s came and went during this period, and the division withered in size. Colonel Alfred T. Smith became the latest G-2 in January 1931, at a time when ONI and MID found themselves working closer together than they had before. They had to: the meager Depression-era budgets forced cooperation. Smith reported to Adjutant General Major General Charles H. Bridges on September 15, 1932, that MID and ONI discussed how to avoid duplication of effort in data collection.[14] By mid-decade, MID was a tiny division in the Department of War, and Brigadier General Harry E. Knight inherited a skeleton crew from Smith on February 1, 1935. While American pop culture crowed about a crackerjack counterintelligence unit in the department, the real division struggled for survival as an intelligence-gathering outfit preparing for potential war.

Even in these circumstances, Army intelligence tried to retain some influence within the Department of War. G-2 Colonel Francis H. Lincoln advertised his division's usefulness and need for parity on the general staff in 1937. The G-2 delivered a lecture to the Army War College and used this opportunity to enlighten Army officers on MID's worth.[15] He informed them that MID's mission charged by the general staff was "collection, evaluation and dissemination of military information" and "preparation of plans and policies."[16] Lincoln denied that MID conducted domestic security missions in 1937, but acknowledged that mobilization plans required the creation of a secret service section for counterintelligence in time of conflict.[17] Lincoln was not entirely truthful with the students; Army intelligence officers had rebooted counterintelligence efforts at headquarters by this time.

The G-2 reopened an old MID problem in June, related to the rank structure of the general staff: Lincoln was the only colonel among the staff's division chiefs.[18] Lincoln urged Chief of Staff General Malin Craig to ask Congress to amend the early 1920s act that restructured the general staff because "intelligence has had the table scraps."[19] Lincoln believed G-2 should discuss matters with other division chiefs at equal rank.[20] But the Army ignored Lincoln's request until 1939, an indication of MID's low reputation.

MID had just twenty officers, three enlisted men, and fifty-six civilians before Roosevelt's emergency order in 1939. Compared to wartime peaks, this is not even a company-sized unit. MID had undergone fifteen reorganizations since the Great War, each based on peacetime necessities rather than functional practicality.[21] G-2s allowed for rapid wartime expansion of the organization by creating empty billets and vacant sections. It is fair to state that MID's physical condition in 1938 and 1939 was the lowest it had been since the beginning of the Great War.

During the 1930s, the Departments of the Navy and of War assigned ONI and MID missions familiar to them and ingrained in the institutions: gather and report information and support planning for future conflicts. But the intelligence agencies also performed domestic duties, not because their bosses ordered them to do so but because their leaders were so inclined. ONI secretly monitored threats at home throughout the interwar period, while MID slowly reacquired these responsibilities in the mid-1930s. As tensions increased overseas and at home, superiors overlooked these eager organizations' increased forays into domestic security.

President Hoover sometimes relied on ONI's services for legitimate intelligence collection purposes, but used them also for questionable pursuits. DNIs and their officers happily obliged in either case. Hoover, like his Republican predecessors, continued the policy of arms limitations and reductions in the effort to keep Americans blissfully in their prosperous, isolationist cocoon in mid-1929. As such, he ordered ONI to prepare the customary tables and charts of warship tonnages, weapons, and ages for the London Naval Conference in 1930. ONI officers created the most thorough products yet for government officials.[22] With the help of naval attachés' prepared studies, DNI Johnson provided the data to the General Board. The department's senior naval officers then evaluated the relative naval powers of adversarial nations and presented the results to Hoover. In this case, the department forbid ONI to provide analyzed information to policymakers, an increasingly common occurrence.

Johnson wanted to improve the traditional data management mission in the office space by getting better typewriters and copy machines and teaching his staff to be economical in their writing. The DNI cautioned naval attachés to be clear and concise on reports and judicious on what to report. Johnson still worried about a data-swamped ONI. He showed his frustrations to his attachés as he commented on the mass of information sitting on his desk unread. He had to choose between reading these dispatches and other constructive work. And he had little clerical help due to budgetary shortfalls. Therefore, he asked his naval representatives overseas to cut back reporting.[23]

Shorthanded as ONI was, this did not stop the office from pursuing surveillance missions foreign and domestic in 1930. After convincing some senior American officials to use such methods at the London Naval Conference, Johnson's staff eavesdropped on communications from foreign governments. Some intercepts came from the Japanese delegation, which pleased politicians such as Secretary of State Henry L. Stimson.[24] The DNI also relied on district intelligence officers to recruit volunteer agents, reserve intelligence officers, and regular civilians to perform investigations, deploying all the outside resources he could acquire to mitigate the personnel shortfalls in domestic security.

ONI's emphasis increasingly tilted toward Japan between 1931 and 1933. Information on Japan's perceived aggression and violations of arms reduction treaties taxed the limited manpower of ONI to produce intelligence and support war planning. In 1931, ONI's production and updates of intelligence monographs proved arduous for such a small staff; the DNI had to limit the workload to sections involving essential naval, political, and economic information needed by the War Plans Division and commanders afloat.[25] ONI tried to put emphasis on all classes of information, especially naval and maritime matters, but officers could not cope with the large amount of material. Insufficient personnel were a constant handicap. For instance, the Foreign Branch had eleven employees. Compare that with the equivalent section in the Imperial Japanese Navy, which reported only on US naval affairs: it had a captain, eleven other officers, and numerous clerical assistants. The Japanese Navy seemed to be much more interested in the American Navy than vice versa.[26]

Nonetheless, ONI improved its collection capabilities on Japan, as the empire took momentous steps in Eastern Asia. Naval intelligence foresaw danger in the Far East through its naval attachés in Tokyo as well as Far East Division head and Japan expert Zacharias. ONI broadened its information network in China and increased its naval attaché staffs in Beijing and Tokyo. Naval intelligence warned policymakers that a weakened China would allow Japan to infiltrate the Chinese social, political, and economic base.[27] Then Japan invaded Manchuria on September 18, 1931. Disarmament seemed like wishful thinking for Hoover's administration after Japanese aggression and the Great Depression hastened militarism and distrust in international affairs. ONI correctly assessed tensions would only worsen in Eastern Asia and across the globe.

Opportunities for analytical work abounded in Europe and Asia in the mid-1930s. Italy's invasion of Ethiopia, Spain's civil war, and the potential for a Sino-Japanese all-out war all required the DNI to step up information-gathering by the naval attaché corps. And indeed, ONI was productive under Puleston's leadership. In 1935, major efforts revolved around the London Naval Conference. ONI collected data for the American delegation with the understanding the department would give the office free rein to collect information on foreign participants both openly and covertly. Most in government knew the Japanese would opt out of the Washington Treaty in 1936 by pressing for total equivalency with other naval powers; the London Conference would not see any arms reduction breakthroughs.[28]

Still, ONI was not all-knowing. Puleston had an anti-communist bias and underestimated the Nazi threat. His tenure coincided with Hitler's rise and consolidation of power, violations of the Versailles treaty, territorial grabs, and German involvement in Spanish affairs. But ONI's reporting on these matters showed little anxiety. At the same time, even though the DNI feared the Soviet Union's intentions, information gathering on the USSR was difficult due to budget shortfalls and the lack of a naval attaché in Russia. In short, ONI's intelligence efforts on potential adversaries in Europe were weak and inadequate.[29]

Puleston's assessment that Japan would leave China alone cracked and then fell apart in June 1937 when Japan attacked China proper from Manchuria. Fortunately for ONI, this was an excellent opportunity for American naval attachés to observe the Japanese warfighting machine close up. The assistant naval attaché in Tokyo frequently reported information back to the Far East Section headed by Arthur H. McCollum. McCollum would often send guidance back to Tokyo as to intelligence collection priorities. The new DNI, Holmes, also determined promptly that he must add more attachés to the system, especially in the Far East. He figured the more information he and his staff could find out about Japan the better prepared ONI would be to give assessments to the rest of the department.

DNI Holmes also attempted to manage foreign intelligence, military-related subjects, and topics associated with politics and the economy of foreign nations. The challenge to ONI in late 1937 was the Sino-Japanese conflict. Seven staffers from the Far East Section compiled, analyzed, and dispersed information to the department and the fleet in the form of weekly summaries that included both strategic and limited operational intelligence. Considering the intense workload, it is unlikely the section put that much analytical rigor into their reports. Meanwhile, Holmes bolstered the Latin American Section with more personnel, simultaneously adding more naval attaché posts to neighbors south of the American border—such as Argentina, Colombia, and Ecuador—to monitor European threats to the Monroe Doctrine and the US Navy's freedom of movement through the Panama Canal Zone. The DNI also continued his expansion of the naval attaché network, finding extra money to help offset attaché extra expenses and to provide maintenance funds for overseas office spaces. In South America alone, Holmes increased attaché representation to five missions and seventy-nine personnel by the end of 1938. Holmes's office supplied the White House with volumes of naval attaché reports from various European capitals. Furthermore, during Holmes's two-year tenure, ONI published twenty-nine strategic intelligence bulletins to the rest of the department.[30] Although he was inundated with potential threats to monitor, the DNI performed well under pressure.

Throughout the 1930s, MID performed much of the same data management duties as ONI, if less well. The division assigned military representatives around the globe and reported intelligence up the chain to department leaders uninterested in information and more preoccupied with training and peacetime maneuvers. MID had little staff to stay on top of the information coming into the agency. ONI had a better reputation providing military intelligence and government sought its services more often than MID.

As the decade progressed, ONI increasingly became involved in war planning duties once more. DNI Ellis's small staff of fifty-six officers and civilians provided a major update to the intelligence annex of War Plan Orange in January 1932. The plan revised the empty billets—in terms of how many and which sections they would man—for mobilization in case of war with Japan. ONI supported the annual Fleet Problem in 1932, which involved a hostile carrier force attacking US possessions in the Pacific Ocean. Eager to get ONI involved in planning, Ellis created a planning section (OP-16-x) by April 1933, but its duties were narrow. The section head prepared and revised plans and manuals for in-house issues and the district intelligence officers. It would be years before OP-16-x would support department-wide planning. Ellis genuinely believed that Japan had a long-term plan to dominate the Pacific. He swam against the isolationist, pacifistic tide of public opinion and administration policies by advocating increased alertness and preparedness.[31] He thought that war could come soon and that there were potential enemies anywhere. For example, the naval attaché in Berlin and staff at ONI analyzed secret data suggesting Germany violated rearmament agreements in the Versailles treaty.[32] In light of these violations and failed reductions in world fleets, Ellis expressed his philosophy about the use of the Navy to a colleague, Captain J. V. Babcock, then a faculty member at Yale University. He argued the US Navy was an instrument of national policy and should not be reduced in size lesser than that of other powers, risking disregard by other nations.[33] Ellis also expressed to Babcock his confidence that naval attachés were making every effort to learn how foreign naval powers were developing, whether legitimately or in defiance of treaties.[34] Ellis was intent on keeping ONI ahead of threats and hoped the larger naval establishment and Congress felt the same way.[35]

In the same vein, DNI Puleston, an avid follower of Mahan's theories, sought a closer relationship with the Naval War College and its president, Admiral Edward C. Kalbfus. While ONI had not worked in an extensive partnership with the war college since the 1890s, the DNI pushed the office to go beyond data collection and into strategic analysis, an understanding of what potential enemies were going to do next. He convinced the General Board and war planners to expect that ONI provided not just information but analysis to projects, like the Color plans.

Puleston's interest in war planning tempered by the end of his tour as he became more interested in domestic security. The department concentrated on updating War Plan Orange, which was quite a successful planning effort.[36] But ONI's staff did not seem too interested in it by 1936. ONI officers provided basic information to planners such as naval assets and geopolitical context in their Japanese monograph in the mid-1930s, but the engaged in no extensive strategic analysis. In fact, Puleston seemed disinterested in the prospects of the possible invasion of China from puppet state Manchukuo at the end of 1936 and told the War Plans division not to worry about Japan attacking China.[37]

On the Army side of intelligence, in the early 1930s MID earned some respect by helping the Department of War create mobilization and war plans. The War Plans Division allowed MID to contribute to the Color plans. Senior leaders charged the division with preparing current estimates of the situation and annexes for War Plan Orange (for Japan) and War Plan Green (for Mexico). Although MID's involvement was limited, the G-2 furnished expert evaluations on adversarial situations to the department.[38]

Both organizations still were haunted by its other past missions whether wanted or not. During the 1920s and 1930, most ONI chiefs ordered their staffs to conduct domestic security missions, At the start of the Great Depression DNI Johnson allowed surveillance on domestic targets. He gave his district intelligence officers (DIOs) direction to observe foreign nationals, especially consular and business offices, within each US naval district. Lieutenant Commander Glenn F. Howell was the 3rd Naval District DIO in New York City in 1929 and 1930. He heartily took on Johnson's orders to spy on the Japanese. In his personal and voluminous logbooks, he wrote about how he physically broke into the Japanese Consulate in Metropolitan Tower Building at Number One Madison Square five times in May 1929.[39] Howell's team of seven men copied secret codes, Japanese airplane characteristics, and photographs of gun shells with muzzle velocities.[40] This was just one of the many secret raids Howell pulled off.

Left-leaning Americans also were a favorite target of the New York DIO. On August 25, 1929, Howell and his operatives, including four off-duty police detectives, raided the headquarters of the Communist Party of America.[41] They ransacked the place to create confusion and stole files; the Communist Party never suspected that ONI was to blame.[42] Historian Jeffrey M. Dorwart, who was the first to write on this incident in *Conflict of Duty: The U.S. Navy's Intelligence Dilemma, 1919–1945*, argued Howell's operation showed naval intelligence's domestic security methods at peak efficiency.[43] Although his operations shows only one such incident, there is enough evidence to suggest ONI's subordinate offices often conducted and relished domestic security missions.

One of the most extraordinary instances of ONI's willingness to perform domestic missions also involved Howell. Hoover, through his personal contacts, discreetly asked ONI to spy on the Democrat Party. A millionaire and a naval intelligence reserve officer, Lewis Strauss, was a close friend of the president and asked Howell to meet with him on May 21. Apparently, a Democratic Party hired hand named "O'Brien," employed by Tammany Hall, may have had some "documentary dope" on Hoover.[44] Strauss relayed to Howell that Hoover was "anxious to know what the contents of the mysterious documents" were, in order to be able to rebut any accusation.[45] Authorized by Hoover to use any of the secret services, Strauss asked the naval intelligence officer to break into O'Brien's office, find the documents, copy them, and make them appear undisturbed. Howell knew the danger: "I am going to tackle it, of course, but it's a devilish awkward job, and I may very readily find myself in a hell's brew of trouble."[46] Interestingly, he called it his duty as a lieutenant commander to serve his commander in chief by stealing the documents.[47] This mission had nothing to do with either national security or the military; therefore, it should have been his privilege to disobey an unlawful order of a superior—in this case, President Hoover. The episode had tones of the Watergate scandal more than forty years later.

Together with a private detective named Peter Kin, and with the help of a manager and president of the firm where O'Brien worked, Howell broke into the office June 16, 1930.[48] The investigation turned up nothing substantial.[49] Howell concluded "that no President of the United States need be afraid of a ham and egger like this O'Brien."[50] He reported to Strauss and eventually Hoover relayed through the covert chain to call off the investigation and close the case. It remained a secret for over fifty years. Documented and untold incidents like this occurred throughout the 1930s under ONI purview, even as domestic security still took a backseat to more aboveboard missions such as information gathering and support for war planning.

DNI Ellis increased counterintelligence and security activities. In the domestic arena, Ellis was troubled by perceived radical groups, such as Bonus Marchers and the Communist Party of America, and continued his predecessors' policies of pressing informants, ultra-patriotic groups, businessmen, and campus faculty for information. The DNI also desired to classify more sensitive information to tighten security. Furthermore, Ellis wanted to safeguard the Navy's codes and code-breaking ability.[51]

Certainly, the Depression, New Deal, and tensions overseas intensified radical and extremist activity in America in the mid-1930s. But funds and manpower limited DIO investigations because the public had no interest in further spy-catching and unrest after the Red Scare. DNI Puleston had asked for money to combat communists and made domestic security a priority when he arrived at ONI. He mobilized reservists, detectives, patriot groups, and other volunteers to investigate leads on domestic leftist activity.[52] Targets of ONI-supported agents included labor strikes, civil rights gatherings, entertainers, historians (such as Charles Beard), and well-known isolationists and pacifists. Puleston had no reservations about having his strategic military intelligence organization perform missions that were not necessarily related to the military and intelligence.[53]

The DNI sought tighter controls on security investigations and reporting. He solidified a more rigid chain between himself and the DIOs, telling his underlings in the naval districts to run their operations by him before launching them. But he did not restrain the DIOs from targeting the various actors that threatened the US government.[54] He ordered ONI to produce an "Estimate of the Situation for 1937," which advocated for naval intelligence funding and personnel increases to evaluate and disseminate information for both foreign and domestic intelligence. He also sought to improve efforts to locate Japanese spies within the country. Puleston's reinvigoration of the domestic program in the United States, especially targeting Japan, naturally meant that he often would be in the FBI's business. The DNI developed a working relationship with J. Edgar Hoover and the FBI, cooperating in such areas as tracking suspected radicals and spies in naval yards and bases, exchanging information, and training naval officers as investigators at FBI facilities.[55] Notably, Puleston sought a close relationship with not only the FBI but with MID: perhaps he envisioned the creation of a centralized intelligence agency focused on domestic security.

Roosevelt and others occasionally constrained Puleston's boldness on the domestic front. ONI criticized the Federal Council of Churches and other civilian organizations for giving "aid and comfort to the Communist movement and party." Obviously, the civilian organization objected. Roosevelt met with representatives of the National Conference of Jews and Christians and following the meeting ordered the Army and Navy not to make comments on any civilian organizations without his consent.[56] In 1935 ONI had increased funding and stature by virtue of President Roosevelt's support, but this incident demonstrated there were boundaries, set at the highest level.

In January 1936, Puleston learned that his superiors had passed him over for flag rank. The news probably soured his outlook on both his future and current post. He spent many hours in the next few months recalibrating his thinking on the important aspects of his job and leaned more aggressively on domestic issues.[57] ONI's reputation as a civilian surveillance organization swelled. American Civil Liberties Union chairman Harry F. Ward complained to Roosevelt in March that naval intelligence was injuring civilian civil liberties. With the constant noise ONI made in American cities in counterintelligence matters, media confused the purpose of Puleston's organization. In July, the *New York Times* claimed the Navy maintained an intelligence agency was to deny foreign powers information on US naval matters.[58] The newspaper failed to mention any of

ONI's other responsibilities., noting that Department of the Navy officials felt naval intelligence engaged in close cooperation with other agencies "in tracking down suspects."[59] Indeed, in September Roosevelt asked J. Edgar Hoover to work together with ONI, MID, and the State Department to step up efforts to track down subversives and spies, especially fascists and communists.[60] In this environment, it was hard for Puleston and his subordinates not to be distracted by domestic concerns.

The international environment changed rapidly, with unstable politics and military events making more espionage inevitable. The Department of the Navy realized that if the United States became entangled again in a foreign war, they would need to protect naval assets and bases and the contractors who supplied their equipment. And one could not discount enemy activities within US borders.. Therefore, ONI's "Estimate of the Situation for 1939" (produced in April) put more emphasis on ONI's ability to conduct counterintelligence. The DNI opposed isolationist and pacifist thinking in Congress and among the public. They faced active opposition, as congressmen such as Senator Gerald P. Nye (North Dakota) crusaded against a big navy by continuing to advocate restrictions in American ship building. Puleston, like most DNIs and naval officers, advocated naval preparedness. They could not understand why Americans would conspire to limit naval growth. And the DNI's own department, he felt, displayed the stereotypical contempt for domestic security; spying was not honorable in a traditionally open society. Secretary of the Navy Claude A. Swanson's unwillingness to allow ONI to enforce domestic security policies fed Puleston's frustrations in counterintelligence duties.[61] At the same time, American society still experienced a fascination with naval domestic intelligence work. George F. Eliot's new 1937 novel, *The Navy Spy Murders*, demonstrated how naval intelligence was doing its part to catch Japanese spies.[62] When Admiral William D. Leahy arrived as chief of naval operations in Washington early in the year, the DNI gained some traction in persuading seniors of the dangers from the fifth column. Leahy ordered the fleet and naval bases to forward all counterintelligence information to ONI.[63] At the onset of the European war, ONI was more focused on domestic security than any of its other missions.

The Department of War had tried to shed most of MID's domestic responsibilities after the Red Scare. But voices from MID's past kept reminding G-2s of their other more dubious duties. Even in retirement, Major General Ralph H. Van Deman remained fixated on counterintelligence and tracking down radicals within the United States. From his San Diego home, he opened a semiofficial spy shop in 1932. Van Deman still had his patriotic group and investigator contacts, and he had the backing of private and official agencies at every level as he indulged his obsession with national security, even while keeping up his reputation as an upright citizen in his community.

Significantly, Van Deman still had clout to influence MID's G-2s. In December 1933, he wrote to recently promoted Brigadier General Smith, just as he had five years previously to Colonel Stanley H. Ford, asking if there was any change in the Department of War's policy on counterintelligence. Van Deman argued the G-2 must be more active and aggressive in countering subversive activities.[64] The retired general said he would write a personal letter (copying Smith) to Chief of Staff General Douglas MacArthur on what he believed should be done. In doing so, Van Deman claimed he was not trying to criticize MID but felt the Department of War was not fulfilling counterespionage obligations.[65] Smith wrote back to Van Deman in January 1934 in an irritated tone, just as Ford had in the 1920s, reiterating the department's policy.[66] Smith assured the intelligence veteran that MID was "kept well informed of subversive and pacifist activities" and expressed his belief that they had a "sound estimate of the subversive situation."[67] The G-2 probably did not appreciate the "Father of Military Intelligence" getting into his business, especially with chief of staff involvement. But Smith did tell Van Deman he showed the December correspondence and the current letter to MacArthur in a sign of good faith.

Smith's annoyance aside, Van Deman remained involved in counterintelligence during the rest of the interwar period. His private intelligence network operating in the Army's Ninth Corps area aimed at rooting out communist subversion. He even developed a card file of over one hundred thousand entries that included photographs and communist literature.[68] In fact, he continued his private intelligence organization until he died in 1952. By writing to Ford and Smith, Van Deman tried to stir up a dormant mission not ready to be awakened in the early 1930s. It would take a couple more years, when tensions rose dramatically in Europe, for Army intelligence to return fully to these missions.

Two military intelligence legends, one past and one present, met at the "Father of Military Intelligence's" home in San Diego in 1938. Van Deman welcomed Zacharias for a chat about the nature of their business.[69] Zacharias wrote later that he and Van Deman believed there were subversives threatening national security within the United States.[70] But despite enthusiastic intelligence veterans' wishes to spark MID interest in domestic security (and a culture that already believed that this was the division's purpose), Army intelligence in this area ramped up slowly.

Ironically, while ONI and MID remained unimportant organizations in federal government during the 1930s, undermanned and underfunded, American culture depicted strategic military intelligence organizations as vibrant and omnipresent.

Naval intelligence appeared often in movies and books of the thirties. Most media outlets did not specifically name ONI as the intelligence agency to which the protagonist reported, but there was no need. The American audience generally was not sophisticated enough to name actual government agencies. The *Mr. Moto* book series—which subsequently evolved into a set of movies—emerged in 1935, depicting the espionage world of the 1930s. It rose to the status of the most popular counterintelligence series that decade. Author John P. Marquand created the titular leading role as first, a Japanese secret agent and then an international detective in *Your Turn, Mr. Moto*, originally serialized in the *Saturday Evening Post*. One of his main characters is Commander James Driscoll, "attached to the intelligence branch of the United States Navy." When Driscoll discussed an ethical dilemma about his profession with another character, he said, "We're not talking about honor, Casey. . . . There's no honor in this business. This isn't Lady Vere de Vere's drawing room. We're dealing with realities and not with any code of chivalry. That belongs in another incarnation, but not in the Intelligence Service; that's a fact which is recognized by everyone in the game."[71] Unlike ONI's mix of information-gathering analysis and domestic security investigations under Puleston, Marquand's naval intelligence business was all spy work. The DNI received free publicity yet still retained the cloak of mystery.

MID gladly received any table scraps of money, authority, and publicity it could get from Congress, the Department of War, and the American people. Its domestic security programs had gone largely dormant, as MID concentrated on information gathering, filing, and reporting. The organization had shrunk so much in a decade that Congress had to remind itself every year what this organization was and why it kept asking for money. On January 11, 1930, the House floor discussed how much to budget for MID as part of the larger Army appropriations bill.[72] Opponents of MID funding took the position of many government officials and senior military officers regarding the stereotypical military attaché: they took extended vacations in Europe, wining and dining at expensive parties and socializing with host country elites for personal gain.[73] Dwight D. Eisenhower, at the time still a major, had a different opinion. He criticized the caliber of the attaché corps, stating that only officers with independent means could serve as Army representatives overseas. Eisenhower said they were usually "estimable, socially acceptable gentlemen" but often did not know the essentials of intelligence work.[74] The lack of funds for the Army's representatives overseas was not a new problem in MID's history. It was just more noticeable during the Great Depression as the government wrestled with saving capitalism while (in)adequately funding its agencies.

Meanwhile, MID's reputation as a spy-catching organization continued to grow, even if G-2s had not overseen substantial counterintelligence work in years. Americans flocked to motion pictures such as *Mata Hari* (1931) starring popular actress Greta Garbo, which equated intelligence with spying. Increasingly, the culture demonstrated a fascination with mysterious actors within the Department of War outsmarting radicals and spies and saving the day. By the mid-1930s, spy movies and novels were mainstream and portrayed a romantic image of military intelligence that did not exist in reality.

Two movies glamorize the Army intelligence investigator as the hero in the mid-1930s. *Marie Galante* (1934) is an interwar spy story of the titular character, a Frenchwoman accidently abducted by a drunken sea captain, who escapes to Central America and is forced to find work in the Panama Canal Zone. She becomes embroiled in an espionage plot to sink the US Fleet. Characters such as a Japanese merchant, a German competitor, and a British diplomat confuse Galante about who the real spy is. Fortunately, an undercover American intelligence officer, played by a young Spencer Tracy, comes to her aid to help her save the fleet from the saboteur. The movie depicted spies threatening the American military and reinforced the idea that only intelligence officers could save Americans from these bad actors. In 1935, MGM produced *Rendezvous*, with an Army intelligence officer as the protagonist. Lieutenant Bill Gordon, an expert in codes and code-breaking, deploys to France for frontline duty. The assistant secretary of war finds out about his skillset and reassigns him to breaking enemy codes. He becomes entangled with Russian and German spies when he tries to retrieve a stolen codebook. In this Hollywood-created spy world, mysterious and heroic American intelligence officers could do no wrong and had little trouble outsmarting the typical German and Japanese villains of the period. If movie directors had (more accurately) depicted MID officers overstepping legal and patriotic bounds to capture spies, they would neither exhibit American democratic ideals nor be better than the spies they caught.

Dime store novels and books also tried to capture the intrigue of what authors perceived as counterintelligence work by Army officers. Major General George A. White, writing under the pen name Ared White, tried to portray for his American readers Army intelligence efforts during the Great War. He wrote short stories for pulp magazines, such as *Adventure*, *Everybody's Magazine*, and *The Saturday Evening Post*. In the pulp fiction *Agent B-7*, the American Secret Service (possibly a fictional representation of MID) attempts to identify and destroy a German spy ringleader. Protagonist Lieutenant Fox Elton, an Army intelligence officer, seems more interested in the spy world than in information gathering. Colonel Rand, Elton's boss and chief of the service, may very well be a fictional representation of Colonel Dennis E. Nolan, head of the American Expeditionary Force's G-2, with whom White may have served in the AEF headquarters in France.

By 1936, MID and ONI's counterintelligence efforts had rebooted. With the services of both agencies over the next four years, the US government convicted twelve suspects for espionage. Naval and Army intelligence officers made the initial investigations and then turned over the cases to the FBI for eventual Department of Justice prosecution.[75] Popular culture documented this increase in espionage work in fiction and nonfiction. The *Dan Fowler G-Man* series, written by Major George F. Eliot between 1936 and 1953, blurred the lines separating the military and civilian domestic security. To the American audience, it did not matter which organization Detective Fowler belonged to. The Department of Justice G-Man had characteristics of both an ONI or MID officer. Eliot himself served in the Great War and was a reserve Army intelligence officer in the 1920s and early 1930s. His first Dan Fowler novel appeared in the *G-Men Detective* pulp magazine under the title *The Purple Legion*. Eliot wrote fourteen of the first twenty-three Dan Fowler adventures, including the first four stories of the series.

Newspapers further highlighted ONI and MID's counterintelligence reputation. In mid-July 1936, the Navy arrested two service members for spying. Hanson W. Baldwin wrote an editorial on July 19 for the *New York Times* praising military intelligence's efforts in this case and in domestic security in general. He talked about the secret war waged behind the scenes between the United States and other nations.[76] Baldwin described the expanding budget of naval intelligence, which was by this point $100,000 more than the previous fiscal budget. In his interpretation, the primary duty the Departments of the Navy and of War placed on military intelligence was counterintelligence, as ONI and MID "stand instantly ready to aid in investigation, pursuit or prosecution of the spy or foreign agent."[77]

Here once again, the media interpreted military intelligence agents as the good guys, mirroring their portrayal in popular spy novels and movies.

Media and Hollywood continued to enhance ONI and MID's reputation for being secret domestic services. Asian countries were at war, and it began to look like Hitler would plunge Europe into another great war. William M. Pinkerton wrote an editorial praising military and civilian intelligence work against spies. First, he villainized the spy with spooky descriptions.[78] But against this sinister threat of "cunning and intrigue," he pointed to four agencies—FBI, MID, ONI, and the State Department—collaborating as a heroic band, working together to arrest spies and unpatriotic Americans.[79] Media also reported that Roosevelt favored larger appropriations to ONI and MID for counterintelligence within the United States.[80] In the film *Smashing the Spy Ring* (1938), starring Ralph Bellamy as John Baxter, the FBI spy-smasher seeks to root out an enemy agent operating a ring in the United States. The movie centers on FBI activities investigating villains with German accents but not identified as Germans. The director furthers the plot with the murder of Phil Dunlop, a G-2 operative, whom the hero Baxter calls "a soldier of peace."[81] In another example, author Francis Van Wyck Mason created the Captain Hugh North series in the 1930s. North, eventually promoted to colonel, was an Army intelligence agent and had some of the same characteristics as Ian Fleming's James Bond character: tough, athletic, well-dressed, well-spoken, and an excellent fighter. In *The Man from G-2*, three pulp-fiction novels in one tome, Mason assumes that G-2 officers spied in other countries, which they were specifically restrained from doing under Roosevelt. Mason also describes North's boss, Colonel Lewis Blount, as "one of the great gods that preside over the destinies of what is cryptically known as G-2—a certain bureau of the United States Army which seeks publicity as a cinema actress courts exposure to smallpox."[82] Although Mason had military experience in the Great War, it is apparent in his North series that he did not know MID missions that well. This did not stop him or others within popular culture from perpetuating the legend of strategic military intelligence organizations as glorious spy-catchers. For instance, the film *Cipher Bureau* (1938) portrays a vibrant organization loosely based on naval intelligence, although the Cipher Bureau engages only codebreaking and counterintelligence missions. It has the power to conduct investigations, which is important to the plot: a staff intelligence officer's brother falls for a German seductress spy. The reality of course was quite different, which did not prevent audiences from relishing the film's hardly recognizable portrayal of ONI.

While the fictional ONI and MID agents daily saved the day fighting evil, foreign villains in the cinemas and dime stores, real-life intelligence professionals grappled with questions of how to be more effective in their service to the federal government and Americans in general. Perhaps a revival of domestic security concerns would help military intelligence obtain more money, stature, and opportunities to conduct other missions. Events in Poland in September 1939 changed DNI and G-2s' calculus.

The next chapter details strategic military intelligence's more intense preparations, spurred by government support of military restructuring in the New Deal Age, for conflict many officers assumed would come. Historians have studied thoroughly how the Japanese surprised the US military at Pearl Harbor—both the lead-up to and the actual attack. Could military intelligence have conducted affairs differently in the interwar period to be better prepared for Japan's surprise tactics? The short answer is probably not.

Besides being preoccupied with domestic concerns, DNIs had not set up ONI as a strategic warnings and operational intelligence organization. Between 1919 and 1939, an underfunded and undermanned office reeling from the effects of demobilization, isolationism, and Great Depression struggled in its role as an information gatherer and intelligence producer. Notably, according to Thomas C. Mahnken, ONI suffered from bogus analytical constructs and preconceived beliefs about how Japan would fight a war, incomplete and inaccurate information, and a misunderstanding of how naval warfare had changed with new technologies.[83] At the same time, Mahnken notes that US naval intelligence understood Japanese naval strategy and incorporated it into the US plan for war with Japan, and the Naval War College utilized it in wargames.[84] Mahnken gives ONI too much credit. ONI intelligence could not predict such outcomes as where and when Japan would attack. DNIs, when not sidetracked by catching spies and subversives, directed ONI to collect generic strategic and general military intelligence of the great naval powers without engaging in much analysis, if any.

Likewise, MID had the same funding and manpower issues in the interwar period as ONI, only worse. G-2s barely kept the organization running. Powe writes that the division had difficulties deciding if it was a planning or operations outfit; in his view, if old military pioneers such as Van Deman had run MID throughout the 1920s and 1930s, organizational problems would not have occurred.[85] This assessment is too generous.

MID, reeling from the budget shortfalls forced by the Great Depression, was in no condition to make advanced assessments of Japanese future strategic moves, much less gather the necessary intelligence for war planners to drive strategy or even inform department leaders of routine, daily intelligence.

Strategic military intelligence organizations performed basic functions to get by in a decade of isolation and economic hardship. The spirit of New Deal programs spurred them to make mobilization plans for war and dream of future glory. Meanwhile, DNIs and G-2s convinced their superiors to allow them to dabble in domestic security duties. ONI and MID would have to strengthen in size, funding, and capabilities to prepare for an expected war.

Chapter Eight
1939–1941:
ONI and MID's Inability to Warn

"It was a bad day all around; and if there is anyone I would not like to be, it is Chief of Naval Intelligence."
—Adolf A. Berle, *Navigating the Rapids, 1918–1971: From the Papers of Adolf A. Berle*

Assistant Secretary of State Adolf A. Berle wrote this assessment of director of naval intelligence's position in his diary on December 7, 1941, in the aftermath of Japan's attack on Pearl Harbor.

The attack marked the transition of government-instituted change in the American economy and way of life under the New Deal to an awakened America on a war footing. The New Deal changed the paradigms of American capitalism and democracy, as the federal government grew in complexity and boldness. Government imposed programs and bureaucracy on the chaos of failed individualism in an attempt to restore order and faith in the system so that a wrecked economy could recover. In the case of the military intelligence, organizations grew by fits and starts due to individuals' peculiar personalities and skill sets, but they also gradually worked out a proper balance of missions. Politicians and theorists infused Taylorism and the other traits of progressivism into American society, and military intelligence cultivated institutional efficiency, through trial and error, to prepare for World War II. They created organizational structures and processes to mobilize when necessary and protect Americans from subversive threats within. However, military intelligence did not yet have the tools to warn of an attack by an audacious enemy from without.

Berle's initial reaction to Pearl Harbor reflects many decisionmakers' hasty comments featuring intelligence as the scapegoat. The eyes and ears of America had failed them, they argued. The benefits of New Deal government efficiency on military intelligence did translate into the agencies being able to warn of immediate foreign threats. Historians have covered the surprise attack in excruciating detail for over eighty years, seeking to explain how the Japanese caught the US government unprepared and who was to blame. Renowned historian Roberta Wohlstetter argued that there was an inundation of signals or "noise"—relevant and irrelevant—for the US authorities to sift through, making it impossible to anticipate the Pearl Harbor attack.[1] According to another prominent historian, Gordon W. Prange, the surprise occurred because Americans did everything wrong, and Japan did what it had to do.[2] The historiography, in short, ranges far and wide in the offered explanations.

The scholarship on the Office of Naval Intelligence (ONI) and Military Intelligence Division (MID)'s role in the lead-up to the attack is just as eclectic. Often ONI is portrayed as an inadequate and undervalued strategic military intelligence organization. In the view of historian Jeffrey M. Dorwart, ONI knew enough to predict the attack and may have been the only agency with all the tools for prediction.[3] James R. Green assessed the intelligence failure as stemming from the inability to evaluate and disseminate the materials they had.[4] For his part, command historian Wyman H. Packard argued that the leadership turnover of four DNIs in 1941 and 1942 contributed to a rudderless analytical effort at ONI.[5] Packard, Prange, Dorwart, and Edward Miller wrote that Admiral Richmond K. Turner, War Plans Division director, succeeded in taking ONI's evaluation power away from the DNIs, making estimates of possible Japanese attacks almost impossible.[6] There were many deficiencies reflected in ONI's intelligence setup, contemporary naval intelligence officer Captain Ellis M. Zacharias indicated.[7] These deficiencies revealed themselves by happenstance in personality conflicts and performance ineptitude, but there is more to ONI's missteps. By no fault of their own, the architects of the New Deal and their emphasis on processes and bureaucracy set up naval intelligence to prepare for a probable future war with empty billets and an imaginary budget. The era had not taught ONI to plan for that which was not predictable: the ability to provide timely, strategic warnings.

Likewise, MID was not organized, after a decade of changes in government practices brought on by the New Deal and Taylorism, for this type of intelligence. The historiography on Army intelligence facets of the Pearl Harbor attack indicates that the G-2 may have had some indicators of attack but had coordination problems with agencies such as ONI and encountered organizational obstacles in effectively evaluating and disseminating intelligence. Colonel Bruce W. Bidwell argued MID obtained much advanced information but failed to evaluate it accurately.[8] Scholars Marc B. Powe and Edward E. Wilson stated that although intelligence was available to determine Japanese intentions, MID did not have the system to make the intelligence understandable to national decision-makers.[9]

Their assessment is probably the most accurate for both ONI and MID. To have given adequate strategic warning, the organizations needed the equivalent of modern watch floors, indicator checklists, and personnel dedicated to finding signals among the noise. Watch floors are offices that are open twenty-four hours a day and monitor near real-time information to make quick intelligence assessments for customers. Indicator lists are events that would have to occur to predict what actions adversaries will pursue. If those events do occur, an intelligence analyst will warn the decision-makers before the adversary acts. Bureaucratic changes, brought on by government reforms, had not yet created an equilibrium of capabilities, missions, and doctrine at ONI and MID that would have left them prepared in the event of surprise.

The size and capabilities of military intelligence increased between 1939 and December 7, 1941, as the US government sensed war was inevitable. ONI and MID wanted a larger role in war planning support, but their reputation and lack of leadership hindered them. Stellar officers stayed away from intelligence tours of duty. But the office and division were minor entities and not even on many distribution lists.[10] At the same time, they had an important proponent in President Franklin D. Roosevelt. The DNI and G-2 had direct access to Roosevelt through daily intelligence briefs. The president wanted ONI and MID to be involved heavily in counterintelligence. However, toward the end of 1941 the President looked to other sources for intelligence, perhaps sensing military intelligence had not caught up with the complexities of a post–Great Depression international environment. Congress exhibited little interest in strategic military intelligence's successes and failures before December 7. But legislators keyed in on military intelligence's advancing domestic capabilities and encouraged them. Still, even though they had influence with the president, ONI and MID lacked access to the secretaries of the Navy and War. The DNI and G-2 were unable to convince the secretaries that they needed intelligence for decision making.[11] The departments' senior military leaders also were hesitant to use ONI and MID's intelligence. Chief of Naval Operations Admiral Harold R. Stark, for example, looked to Turner's War Plans Division for analysis and assessments, instead of naval intelligence.[12]

Strategic military intelligence officers had to have felt like pariahs in national security affairs. But MID grew throughout 1939 and 1941, coinciding with the increased US alert status and fulfillment of government reform–driven mobilization plans. G-2s Colonel E. R. Warner McCabe and Brigadier General Sherman Miles were content to fill the empty billets of MID's reactivated sections. They viewed the danger of the world environment manifesting into domestic threats to department properties. The G-2s also relied on military attachés and filing officers and clerks at headquarters to compile and disseminate intelligence on foreign militaries. But MID was neither organized, nor trained, to conduct strategic warning. Neither Army nor naval intelligence considered this a central function.[13] DNIs struggled to define ONI's missions and concentrated on internal security and information-gathering duties. ONI's bosses needed them to evolve further as other agencies did based on initiatives inspired by the New Deal and Great Depression. Confidence deteriorated in both ONI and MID prior to December 7, 1941. But their failures taught them lessons, born out of Taylorism, to continue efficient mobilization efforts and improve organizational structures during wartime.

The strategic military intelligence organizational apparatus was in flux in the years leading up to the Pearl Harbor attack. The Marine Corps' intelligence organization morphed to fit the evolving commandant's general staff, while ONI and MID executed decades-old mobilization plans to fill skeleton sections and activate others. New strategic nonmilitary intelligence organizations arose to challenge ONI, MID, and the FBI's influence on national security. Intelligence centralization became a real possibility, whether military intelligence chiefs wished for it or not. Meanwhile, President Roosevelt required strategic intelligence to cooperate on domestic issues. Weak leadership hampered ONI and MID's ability to meet these challenges.

Since 1920, the United States Marine Corps had a miniscule Intelligence Section that nominally qualified as a strategic military intelligence organization. The section could be compared to the initially tiny ONI that emerged in the Bureau of Navigation in 1882 and the small MID that sprouted from the Adjutant General's Office in 1885. But the lack of archival history on the Intelligence Section suggests it only performed staff work and relied heavily on ONI for intelligence to provide to its marine leadership.

In 1939, the section received a promotion of sorts. On April 1, Marine Corps Commandant Major General Thomas Holcomb changed the name of the Operations and Training Division to the Plans and Policies Division (popularly known as the "Pots and Pans" Division), designating it the Marine Corps' planning agency.[14] The new division included the M-2 or the "Intelligence Section," the equivalent in organizational rank to the G-2 on the Army's general staff. Major David A. Stafford became the first director of M-2.[15] M-2's creation was a step up for Marine Corps intelligence, as the service's leadership recognized it as an essential part of a general staff with a role in planning and policy. M-2's place in the division and at headquarters would remain undisturbed throughout World War II.

Through much of 1939, ONI was an organization in transition, similar to its Marine counterpart. Roosevelt ordered the Departments of War and of the Navy to complete the Rainbow and mobilization plans. On April 24, the CNO sent a message to the naval district commandants reiterating the basic requirements for manning and organizing naval intelligence within the United States. This statement of readiness put districts on notice to conduct such domestic security missions as plant protection and local investigations along the East and West Coasts. In May, DNI Rear Admiral Ralston S. Holmes worked on a wartime proposal that would include over six hundred more personnel and a budget of close to $400,000.[16] This ambitious mobilization plan mirrored his belief that international tensions would allow naval intelligence to expand rapidly and soon. But Rear Admiral Walter S. Anderson relieved Holmes before he could bring his expansion plans to completion.

Anderson had intelligence experience as naval attaché in London in 1934 through 1937 and was prepared to deal with the bureaucracy that was sure to come from future ONI enlargements. Believing the United States would become entangled in a potential European war soon, he set out to prepare naval intelligence for this eventuality. He expanded the naval attaché corps to include nations to which the Navy had no representation and made sure to assign attachés for each member of the British Commonwealth.[17] He created a Strategic Information Section to handle requests for information from customers.[18] The Department of the Navy transferred this section over to the Office of Strategic Services in 1942.[19]

Anderson's organizational skills were impressive, but ONI still had many demands placed upon it. The war planners required information for the Rainbow plans. Roosevelt wanted to tighten domestic security processes. And the department sought to enlarge its covert services at home and abroad. The DNI felt the pressure but was optimistic regarding its ability to prepare the office for war. Anderson prepared a secret memorandum on August 31 titled "Are You Ready" for the General Board. In it, the DNI stated that ONI was close to adequate in performing its duties because of increases in funds and personnel.[20] He told naval leadership that ONI was building, as the department requested, an undercover presence abroad to supplement naval attaché reporting. He also acknowledged, although reluctantly, participation in detentions of foreigners in the United

States.²¹ To exacerbate all the challenges Anderson faced, he answered to a new CNO, Admiral Harold R. Stark, starting in August. Stark was not as capable as Admiral William D. Leahy had been, nor as friendly to intelligence.

In the fall and winter of 1939 to 1940, Anderson and ONI dealt with the repercussions as war finally broke out in Europe. Adolf Hitler's army invaded Poland on September 1; two days later Britain and France declared war on Germany. The US Navy immediately went into alert status. Anderson sent a memorandum to all naval district intelligence officers and naval attachés on September 3, informing them that ONI's primary concern was the security of the United States and asking for information on threats to the United States or its naval interests as well as the disposition, plans, and operations of the belligerent powers.²² The DNI and CNO sought information promptly, in brief dispatches and with caveats about the reliability of sources. The Navy's interest in the war increased considerably when Roosevelt proclaimed a Limited National Emergency on September 8.

At first, the country was stunned by the news that another great war had befallen the world. What would the future bring for Americans in this conflict?²³ Anderson, who expected war promptly, prepared his organization for tasks from department leadership and was proactive about suggesting new policies. The same day Roosevelt issued the limited emergency declaration, Anderson proposed the commander in chief create a National Defense Committee, to consist of the president, the secretaries of state, war, Navy, and treasury, the chief of staff of the Army, and the CNO to evaluate national defense plans.²⁴ Nothing resulted from this recommendation. The office continued mobilization plans in September and kept its data collectors on high alert.

The DNI also simplified his organization in 1939 and 1940. He reactivated the Commerce and Travel Section (OP-16-5) to help the Navy enforce neutrality laws. Reservists updated twenty-year-old training manuals on commercial ocean travel and how the United States would monitor it. Anderson reorganized ONI December 5 placing the Foreign Intelligence Branch (OP-16-F) under the command of his assistant, with the following sections: F-1, British Empire; F 2, Far East; F-3, Western Europe; F-4, Central Europe; F-5, Eastern Europe; F-6, the Balkans and the Near East; F-7, Latin America; and F-8, Enemy Trade.

Meanwhile Germany's defeat of France in May 1940 served as a stimulus for finishing US Navy mobilization plans. Anderson completed his fundamental directives portion, "Principal Naval Intelligence Service

Operating Plan (General)," or WPDNI-8, just before the Phony War ended in April. On May 21, he gave a progress report to naval department leadership titled "Readiness of the Naval Establishment to Meet a Serious Emergency?" The DNI gave a status update on intelligence plans for the Public Relations Administration. He was positive about naval intelligence's readiness, saying the operating plans were sufficient to execute the task assigned ONI in Basic War Plans.[25] But the DNI warned the existing office currently could not meet existing conditions for want of personnel, office space, and funds.[26] While true, every ONI director since 1882 had requested more to meet their mission challenges. What Anderson asked for was no different.

With world events rapidly occurring overseas, Anderson continued to tie up loose ends on mobilization plans; perhaps, he would need them sooner rather than later. He updated the Department of the Navy on June 10 with another memorandum titled "Are We Ready?" In it, he stated that ONI was in a better position to meet an emergency than in months past. Anderson declared the office's operating plans were sufficient and effective to execute task assigned in Basic War Plans; ONI was in a fair state of readiness.[27] But Anderson still worried about the ability to procure higher caliber personnel to meet war needs. The DNI also had apprehensions on the office's competence to obtain covert information in wartime.[28] But Anderson seemed to be more optimistic of naval intelligence's readiness than he had been ten months previously.

Like most DNIs, Anderson wished to go back to sea as soon as he arrived at ONI. Rear Admiral Chester W. Nimitz, chief of personnel, came to his office in late 1940 and told Anderson he would be promoted to vice admiral and assigned to a different post.[29] When Roosevelt heard of Anderson's impending departure, he offered him a permanent job as DNI, which he graciously declined.[30] DNI Anderson departed early January 1941.[31]

Captain Jules James filled in temporarily when Anderson left. He had orders to command the US naval base in Bermuda in the spring. The department had not settled on a permanent replacement for Anderson; leadership was unconcerned with filling this relatively minor post. Nonetheless, James attempted to preserve ONI's integrity. His friendship with Roosevelt helped maintain daily briefs to the president. He also set up a Special Activities Branch for covert intelligence work in January.

Captain Alan G. Kirk talked to Anderson in January about changing naval intelligence posts. Anderson told Kirk that he was not staying in London as naval attaché because the department was posting someone as DNI who was currently a naval attaché. Kirk said later, "I was dumb enough not to realize he was talking about me."³² Nimitz sent him his orders on January 23 to report as DNI.³³ Kirk had returned from London on temporary duty in January and February as a consultant. He made the briefing rounds to Stark, Secretary of the Navy William F. Knox, and Undersecretary James V. Forrestal, giving his impression of the situation in Europe. Kirk also updated Roosevelt, having received a warning from his friend Holmes on how to get in a word edgewise before the meeting.³⁴ And Kirk did have to interrupt the president.³⁵ He also joined Rear Admiral Robert L. Ghormley, Turner, and Miles for the first of fourteen sessions of the American-Britain Conversations in Washington on January 29. Kirk's speech on strengthening Anglo-American defense measures was one of his last acts as naval attaché. Kirk believed these high-profile January meetings convinced superiors to make him the next DNI.³⁶ He was a logical choice, as a seasoned naval attaché who had become conversant in the larger strategic intelligence questions surrounding this next great war. Of course, he did not want the position and wanted to go back to sea; most naval officers assigned as DNI did not want the job.³⁷ He received both congratulations and condolences (sometimes in the same written letters) for the desk job.³⁸ Ominously for his future in the position, his rank as captain made it easier for department admirals to order him around.

Kirk took on DNI responsibilities with great apprehension; his six-month record as director was full of missteps. There was no standard operating procedure that explained step-by-step how to be DNI. Kirk did not receive much assistance in the turnover from Anderson and James.³⁹ He also experienced a brief illness that hindered aggressive leadership from the beginning. He discovered immediate personnel and administrative issues to tackle, such as replacing four rotating and veteran section heads. He also moved the entire division in April to a new naval department facility, which did not have enough space for all fifty-three naval officers and the dozens of civilians; he had to relocate his censorship section elsewhere. Kirk found ONI to be an expansive agency, with conflicting missions and overlapping jurisdictions with other agencies.⁴⁰ How could he juggle these issues—learning the job, domestic security, and the international crisis—all at the same time?

ONI experienced additional organizational developments as well, such as air intelligence liaisons and plant protection duties. The Navy's Bureau of Aeronautics (BUAER) set up an Aviation Intelligence Branch in the Administrative Division, with two sections: Air Intelligence and Technical Applications. Their principal sources of information were ONI and

MID, and the section's officers kept a close liaison with the two organizations. The Aviation Intelligence Branch's initial functions were operational and tactical information gathering and reporting for BUAER and naval air station customers.[41] The branch eventually became the Air Intelligence Group during World War II, with the director doubling as the assistant DNI. In August, the Senate and House of Representatives charged ONI with plant protection for naval shore establishments, reinforcing popular perception of ONI as an investigative agency.[42] And just as these institutional changes occurred, personnel rotations shook up an already demoralized ONI.

Kirk took the advice of his friend Rear Admiral Adolphus Andrew and petitioned Stark, his assistant Rear Admiral Royal E. Ingersoll, and Forrestal for sea duty and they eagerly accepted his proposal.[43] Kirk's tour at ONI only lasted six months compared to an average DNI tenure of two to three years. The department wanted a more senior captain or junior admiral to match rank with the MID and FBI and someone who was more malleable to Stark's and Turner's demands. Now that Kirk had put in his request, the change would be that much easier to accomplish.[44] He paid his regards to colleagues and government agency partners and departed for sea October 15.[45]

Rear Admiral Theodore S. Wilkinson sat at the DNI's desk next. Wilkinson became known as the naval officer who presided over ONI during the greatest military intelligence failure in US history. New bureaucratic processes had not set up the office for success in strategic warning, which would have required watch floors, indicator lists, and more sophisticated, unavailable technology capable of alerting tactical and operational units simultaneously. Instead, the new DNI headed an organization that collected information overseas as a secondary duty to domestic security. Wilkinson had no idea why the Navy chose him for the job; he wanted to go to sea. Stark probably selected him to lead the Navy's efforts for centralized intelligence under military leadership and hoped he would be the senior member and chairman of the Joint Intelligence Committee (JIC).[46] As a sign of good faith, Stark and Ingersoll promised Wilkinson ready access to their office. Wilkinson's reputation as popular, amiable, and smart may have been wasted on a post often regarded by line officers as a bureaucratic desk job. But his selection held promise for a change at ONI.

Wilkinson had no experience relevant to the job and had little time to get adjusted. The new DNI had just a few days' turnover with Kirk and spent only several hours meeting with individual sections, including the crucial Far Eastern Section. One of his first tasks was to improve the morale of ONI, which had lost analytical evaluation functions and was confused about its mission. It did not help that ONI had physically moved portions of the organization four times in the previous two months. The moves benefited more important divisions, according to the department, which needed the prime office spaces.

By early December, ONI had 230 officers, 75 enlisted men, and 300 civilians organized into three branches: Intelligence, Domestic Intelligence, and Administrative. The attaché system had 133 officers, 200 enlisted men, and 29 civilians. There were 1,835 intelligence officers on active duty in the fleets and headquarters around the globe. Japan's early morning raid on Oahu ensured that this number would jump greatly.

The situation at MID was not much better. Future G-2 Major General George V. Strong spoke poorly of MID's condition and morale in 1939.[47] MID was a hollowed out, small outfit looking for a brighter future. G-2 Colonel McCabe was the caretaker of a moribund division awakening from a two-decade long slumber. The Department of War acknowledged the resurgence of foreign espionage activity within the United States by allowing for a separate MID counterintelligence branch in 1939. Yet, the fact remained that a division of only seventy-nine personnel headed by a colonel within a general staff of at least one-star division heads was not ready for war.

MID's expansion occurred more quietly than ONI's development in the winter of 1939 and 1940. Shortly after Roosevelt's proclamation of a limited national emergency, McCabe initiated mobilization plans. Considering how small MID had become, Army intelligence officers knew that any expansion of their offices brought benefits. There was a noteworthy increase of Army intelligence representation in foreign countries, akin to ONI's observer system. Additionally, MID set up four branch offices in the United States. Their mission was to liaison with other government agencies within their respective cities. Retired Army officers ordered to active duty were usually placed in charge of the branch offices. The department also selected them because they knew the city or the region.[48] In the nine reorganizations of MID from 1940 to 1944, G-2s did not integrate the branch offices into the Washington MID structure.[49]

A G-2 turnover accelerated MID's mobilization and expansion. Brigadier General Sherman Miles relieved McCabe April 30, 1940, after serving a half year as the military attaché to Great Britain. His priorities were mobilization and domestic security. Miles discovered quickly that MID had the vacant billets and sections available for a time of crisis; he would have to fill them as department requirements dictated. Most significant to the division's rejuvenation was Miles's rank. Not since Brigadier General Dennis E. Nolan left MID in September 1921 had MID possessed a G-2 the Department of War had selected specifically for his flag credentials.

MID expanded slowly in 1940. It had 200 officers with 848 civilians by the end of the year. A New York branch was established as soon New Orleans and San Francisco branches came online. But Miles knew the division's growth was taking too long. Unfortunately for the G-2, the history of the US Army's mobilizations for major wars suggested that expansion occurred best after a disastrous event. Miles had a decent rapport with the Army War Plans Division but was not in the loop with War Plans or the general staff on important policy decisions.[50] The G-2 and his staff were preoccupied with domestic security; data management of foreign intelligence was secondary.

In September, Miles reorganized the division vertically. He had an executive officer and a Special Study Group (later the Propaganda Branch) directly underneath his purview. The Administrative, Intelligence, Counter-intelligence, Plans and Training, and Censorship Branches reported to him through his executive officer.[51] The Intelligence Branch, the largest of the branches, comprised sections related to the Balkans and Near East, the British Empire, Central Europe, Eastern Europe, Far East, Latin America, and Western Europe. The other important branch, Counterintelligence, possessed the functional sections of Domestic Intelligence, Investigation, and Plant Intelligence. Compared to the wartime MID post-December 7, MID at this stage was a relatively simple organization.[52] Until the fall of 1941, MID activity was somewhat routine. Miles and his staff spent the year trying to rectify its deficiencies in manpower and mission. Their efforts did not include strengthening the division's ability to provide strategic warnings.

The line between strategic and tactical air intelligence often blurred. The G-2 and the chief of the Army Air Forces realized that separation of responsibilities was necessary. The air branch of the Army had an intelligence organization, the Intelligence Office, which, however, focused on tactical and operational issues. Nonetheless, authorities needed to draw a line between the strategic and lower echelon intelligence, between MID and the Intelligence Office. Adjutant General Major General Emory S. Adams ordered MID to conduct information gathering and prepare comprehensive military studies and estimates, that is, characteristically strategic functions.[53] The Intelligence Office would compile and evaluate technical and tactical air information received from sources, such as MID.

Adams and senior military officials expected both organizations to cooperate to exchange information.[54]

Roosevelt forced ONI, MID, and the FBI to liaise in 1939. The president lumped MID into a landmark effort to increase coordination among US government intelligence agencies. In July 1939, FDR ordered that all espionage, counterintelligence, and sabotage matters be handled by the FBI, MID, and ONI.[55] Roosevelt was concerned about the cost and efficiency of duplication of effort among the three agencies. FBI Director J. Edgar Hoover wanted to expand his investigations beyond the country's borders and often had the president's ear. On a regular basis Roosevelt invited the DNI and G-2 to visit the White House to brief him on various intelligence matters as well. The president was too fond of what these organizations had to offered decommission any one of them but rather wanted all three to work together on domestic security issues.

The chiefs of ONI, MID, and FBI immediately held a series of conferences to plan coordination of counterintelligence operations. DNI Anderson increased his meetings with Roosevelt and convened once a week with the MID director, State Department intelligence liaison Berle, and Hoover. Hoover fascinated Anderson and often influenced the DNI to side with the FBI on intelligence policy. The DNI ordered his personnel to share all investigational information with FBI agents.[56] The G-2 McCabe's rank as colonel hampered MID's representation at these conferences. Veteran intelligence officer Hoover dominated the discussions and emerged as the supreme authority on domestic intelligence.[57] By direction of the CNO, Anderson also promulgated guidance on how headquarters and the districts should comply with the president's direction of close liaison between ONI, MID, and the FBI. He ordered the District Intelligence Officers (DIO) to maintain a close liaison with each FBI divisional field office and Army Corps Area Headquarters.[58]

In 1940, Roosevelt set up an informal intelligence committee meeting once a week and required intelligence briefings daily. Anderson recalled that he found the committee "very interesting and rewarding."[59] Berle was cautiously optimistic about what benefits could come out of committee meetings, such as a centralized intelligence agency.[60] Roosevelt charmed the DNI with his respect and knowledge of intelligence. Anderson and MID gave Roosevelt daily intelligence briefs in the president's private office in a relaxed atmosphere.[61]

At the end of June, Roosevelt issued another executive order for ONI, MID, and FBI to coordinate further in domestic security. He assigned the FBI intelligence work in the Western Hemisphere, while military intelligence covered the rest of the world. The agencies coordinated the draft previously, with the resulting "Proposal for Coordination of MID, ONI, and FBI" signed by all concerned on June 28. Contemporaries commonly referred to the order as the "Delimitation Agreement." Despite authorizations from higher levels, strategic intelligence organizations made no real progress on solving intelligence jurisdictions or coordinating doctrine. The vagueness of the agreement gave the FBI more territory to monitor. Yet, ONI and MID still had internal counterintelligence responsibilities; the agreement only required them to coordinate with the FBI. They hired more agents to cover ground the FBI could not. It would take several years for the agencies to have more delineated boundaries.[62] Anderson tried to find ways to improve coordination among himself, Miles, and Hoover. Indeed, all the directors earnestly wanted to synchronize domestic security efforts because the president ordered it. Staff officer Paul M. Robinett, who served in the Plans and Training Branch of G-2, later said, "No differences of view came to my attention, certainly not in the fields in which I was working, and if they occurred in other fields I was not aware of it."[63]

Other organizations threatened to squeeze intelligence agencies out of their traditional responsibilities. General William J. Donovan's Office of the Coordinator of Information (COI) was aggressive, creative, brilliant, and proactive. Donovan had almost unlimited access in high places, both in Europe and America, the most prominent being Roosevelt and Churchill. His irregular methods and disregard for intelligence boundaries frustrated ONI, MID, and the FBI. Intelligence heads Kirk, Miles, and Hoover worried that Donovan would attempt to subvert or even erase their agencies with a centralized strategic intelligence organization. When a presidential order created the COI, the directive mandated that all government agencies share information related to national security with it, but also that Donovan's office not interfere with the duties of the military and naval advisors to Roosevelt.[64] The president ordered Donovan's office to collect and analyze strategic information and carry out vaguely described special intelligence activities. ONI had operated mostly in the strategic domain since 1882 and a bureaucratic competitor's invasion of its territory, Kirk probably believed, threatened ONI's reason for being.

ONI and MID defended themselves repeatedly against proponents of centralized intelligence and joint reorganization in 1941. Miles wrote to the chief of staff, General George C. Marshall, on July 2 to address rumors that strategic customer Roosevelt thought military intelligence inadequate. He argued that Roosevelt observed strategic military intelligence organizations through simple, but important, "spot" news reports and briefs. The characterization was unfair even though Roosevelt did prefer short papers. According to Miles, MID and ONI did not try to compete with the media's short articles.[65] He further stated that not even the secretaries of War and Navy saw all the mass of intelligence produced by MID and ONI, such as attaché reporting, technical intelligence, support to war planning, counterintelligence, and monographs.[66] ONI's and MID's reputation and very existence was on the line.

The cries disparaging strategic intelligence were loud enough for military intelligence leaders to take action. The G-2 and DNI recommended that the Army and Navy create a joint intelligence committee to serve the Joint Board. The Joint Board approved this proposal, making it coequal with the Joint Planning Committee. The board tasked the JIC with preparing daily intelligence summaries and important intelligence reports to the president and other senior government officials.[67] MID manned the JIC with four representatives, while ONI provided three. The senior-ranked representative served as the chairman. The Navy provided spaces adjacent to ONI offices in the Main Navy Building abutting the National Mall. By December, the JIC had a complement of fifteen personnel comprising officers, analysts, and stenographers.[68] Perhaps the JIC, Miles and Kirk thought, would help preserve military intelligence from Donovan's intrusions into military intelligence's affairs. The JIC was a logical step in the long-term trend of Taylorism: increasing the efficiency of military organizations to expediently provide information to customers and cut down on bureaucratic obstacles.

The naval attaché to London had always been an influential post in the Department of the Navy. Lieutenant Commander French E. Chadwick set a precedent in 1882 in making it a position that exerted great sway in the amount and quality of information filtering from the European continent to ONI in Washington, DC. The post was challenging and rewarding because Great Britain, by virtue of having the most powerful navy in the world, had a bounty of naval technological information to collect. Therefore, most US naval officers did not complain when the department ordered them to London. In the late 1930s, this premier billet's heavy productivity exemplified the frantic efforts of naval attachés in Asia and Europe to establish partnerships and acquire data on the war that might be important to the United States.[69] The Department of the Navy needed competent representatives in the United Kingdom in 1939.

Roosevelt and the Navy had uneasy relations with Great Britain before Winston Churchill became prime minister in May 1940. The US Navy was a competitor with the British Navy, and the two countries were not officially allies. The United States desired secret and overt information regarding British technologies such as radar and mining equipment, while the Admiralty reluctantly realized His Majesty's waning Navy needed American help against the rising fascist and communist powers.

In this environment, DNI Anderson picked his friend Kirk to be the naval attaché to London, and Kirk was eager to fulfill his orders.[70] The DNI and Kirk corresponded almost daily and formed a strong professional bond. Kirk arrived in London in June with the task of strengthening ties with British naval officials and collecting technical data. He sought out a partnership with senior Captain John H. Godfrey, director of the Naval Intelligence Division, for information on radars.[71] Godfrey gave the naval attaché a tour of the operational intelligence center bunker, war rooms, and radar stations but nothing too technically secret. In turn, the NID director convinced Kirk and Anderson to allow British attaché visits to US naval installations. Although US and British naval intelligence seemed to be playing a game of keeping secrets, these visits nevertheless laid the groundwork for a closer partnership in World War II after America's entry into the conflict.

Meanwhile, the DNI sought to send naval observers worldwide proposing a list of places to the CNO, the secretary of the Navy, the secretary of state, and the president for approval. He had difficulty getting his plans implemented through the State Department.[72] After some negotiations, Anderson was able to outline and activate this observer network with heavy representation in both Western Pacific and European countries. He chose likely locations based on Rainbow plans that military war planners created. At home, the DNI called on the foreign chiefs of mission in Washington and developed close relations with at least some of them.[73] Anderson would also use his foreign emissary contacts to get approval for observers within their countries. With the prospects of steady information coming into headquarters, the question was whether intelligence professionals could keep up.

The speed and changes of the European war during the spring and summer of 1940 captivated not only the naval establishment and governments' interest but much American public attention as well. Anderson, by virtue of his post, and Kirk, due to his location, had particularly good perches to view events and collect information. On May 14 Kirk wrote to Anderson that the war was gradually intensifying and that his letter would be moot by the time the DNI read it.[74] He testified to the ineffectiveness of Dutch and Belgian resistance against the German war machine. Kirk recommended that the American ambassador start evacuating Americans from the British Isles. The naval attaché was pessimistic about the situation on the Continent.[75] Perhaps it was this negativity and inexperience that caused Roosevelt to send Rear Admiral Robert L. Ghormley to London as the senior naval representative of the United States, in a move reminiscent of President Woodrow Wilson's selection of Admiral William S. Sims to represent American naval interests in London in World War I.

In just a few weeks, the ground situation in Europe changed considerably.[76] Kirk reported the German blitzkrieg was powerful and dangerous.[77] Eventually, Kirk and the US embassy relocated to Headley Park outside of London when the Luftwaffe targeted the British Isles. Other naval attachés had a prominent vantage point for the German onslaught in Western Europe. Lieutenant Commander Ole Hagen, Captain John A. Gade, Captain Monroe Kelly, Commander Roscoe Hillenkoetter—representing the US Navy in Scandinavia, Belgium, Holland, and France, respectively—all experienced tribulations in reporting and escaping the fighting in their host countries.[78]

Kirk continued to express his pessimism about the Allied war effort with his most dour message, on June 11.[79] He advised the DNI that the United States needed to watch out for its vital interests as the German war machine moved quickly and conquered in days what took months in World War I.[80] After the British evacuation of Dunkirk and Churchill's rise to prime minister in May, the British realized they needed the Americans. Godfrey intensified the charm offensive on Kirk by offering him information regarding operational details of British war damage and combat data and full access to him and his deputy, Captain W. D. Stephens. Anderson probably took the naval attaché report's opinions of the need for an Atlantic-first strategy straight to Roosevelt.[81]

Miscommunications and protocol led to two naval attachés in London serving concurrently. Kirk was uninformed of Ghormley's orders until August.[82] He later described the situation as "a little awkward" and "a little embarrassing."[83] The DNI apologized to Kirk for how the Navy handled the situation.[84] Ghormley was Roosevelt's personal envoy and the situation had to be rectified. The protocol confusion perturbed Ambassador to the United Kingdom Joseph P. Kennedy; he was used to coordinating naval intelligence only with Kirk, not two naval attachés. Roosevelt's informal emissary to Great Britain William J. Donovan stepped in on Kirk's behalf at the White House; Roosevelt renamed

Ghormley as a special naval observer (SPENAVO) to Great Britain, placating all the egos involved.[85]

Back in Washington, while Germany's successes caused anxiety, the Department of the Navy was still focused on Japanese activities. In 1940 American military policymakers chose a Rainbow war plan centered on an offensive war in the Atlantic while defending in the Pacific. But ONI still treated Far East information gathering as just as imperative as that from Europe. Japan, throughout the interwar period, was a tough collection target. Naval attaché to Tokyo Henri H. Smith-Hutton and his assistant Lieutenant Commander Donald McCallum had difficulties traveling because of strong Japanese counterintelligence efforts and often stayed near the US embassy. US ambassador Joseph C. Grew put tight restrictions on intelligence collections to try to keep good relations with his host country. The only sources ONI had consisted of international media and diplomats.[86] Therefore, Japan's military capabilities soon became an enigma. If ONI could not solve the attaché collections problems overseas, naval intelligence's most reliable source, how much use would the office be to war planners and decision-makers?

The importance of the attaché position to strategic military intelligence organizations spoke to the importance of the data collection mission. Both ONI and MID relied upon information from abroad to help headquarters collate, analyze, and report strategic intelligence to customers. MID had more autonomy to provide estimates to the Department of War than ONI to Navy leaders. By late 1941, the War Plans Division took ONI's analytical capabilities away. But military intelligence's main missions, set by superiors and agreed upon by intelligence professionals, were still domestic. It was also a distraction from the mission the United States needed and what strategic intelligence could not provide: strategic warning.

Between 1939 and late 1941, ONI leaders enjoyed carrying out domestic security missions. The office took its cue from Roosevelt, who displayed an affinity for the espionage business. When he was assistant secretary of the Navy, he employed reserve intelligence officers as secret agents on the home front during the Great War. Now, as president, FDR hired private secret agents, such as Vincent Astor, to spy on domestic affairs.[87] ONI also worked closely with patriotic societies to help monitor subversives and pacifistic groups' activities. With a president expressing such great interest, the DNI activated the Counterintelligence Branch (OP-16-B) in 1939, which included Naval Censorship (B-2); Investigations (B-3); Security of

Naval Information (B-4); Commerce and Travel (B-5); Sabotage, Espionage, and Counterespionage (B-7); and Coastal Information (B-8). ONI's domestic security program was approaching the size it had ballooned to in the Great War.

From Roosevelt's point of view, ONI was one of only three agencies in the United States responsible for domestic security. And the DNI took this charge seriously. Anderson followed the DIOs' activities closely and encouraged them to handle cases independently of FBI assistance, especially in naval matters. The DNI required them to create their own suspect list and files on Nazis, fascists, communists, Japanese, and other suspected subversives. He wanted DIOs to use informants to uncover unpatriotic comments and threats to naval interests.[88] Anderson also welcomed help from the civilian commercial sector to find spies and saboteurs. He cited the presidents of Pan-American and Massachusetts Institute of Technology as Americans who wished to help.[89] The Navy was concerned about spies stealing secrets, whether it be war plans or naval technologies. The *Wilmington Morning Star* reported on November 12, 1940, that the Department of the Navy had recently begun photographing all its employees "to guard against possible sabotage of Uncle Sam's rapidly expanding Navy."[90]

Based on recent activity, the DNI, G-2, and FBI director decided to cooperate more often. In New York City, ONI, MID, and the FBI conducted their own separate and confidential investigations; there was much confusion and duplication of effort.[91] In December, Anderson hired businessman Warren B. Phillips to create a covert intelligence collection organization in the city. The DNI allowed him to set up an office there. Anderson told Phillips to be in close contact with Major F. D. Sharp, the head of MID's New York Branch Office. With Miles's approval, Sharp let Phillips use some of his office space for intelligence operations. Instances like this show that coordination was a priority.

Kirk did not get along with Hoover as well as he did with Anderson. In March 1941, he discovered that the FBI violated the agreement by having agents investigate cases within ONI's jurisdiction in the Western Pacific. Kirk believed it was another example of Hoover trying to control intelligence issues.[92] Kirk knew that turf battles occurred in the past with previous DNIs, but he could not tactfully and diplomatically make concessions in intelligence meetings with the other agencies, siding more often with MID than the FBI on domestic security issues.

Be that as it may, the three agencies became more intertwined in domestic affairs and bureaucratic issues in mid-1941. This trend was a logical extension of the 1930s as government agencies butted up against each other as they fulfilled roles under the New Deal. The three domestic security agencies approved a "Third Agency Rule" May 14, placing stricter rules on information-sharing with outside entities. They intended to stave off advocates of centralized intelligence with these types of agreements. The three heads told their superiors that coordination was going smoothly and the appointment of a coordinator of the three intelligence services would offer only negligible advantages.[93] Throughout, Kirk, Miles, and Hoover sensed that Donovan was plotting in the shadows.

The Department of the Navy viewed Kirk's ONI as a domestic security agency. This was once more made clear when the Navy finalized Rainbow V and Plan Dog by June. These plans and another "Are We Ready" memorandum confirmed ONI would mostly watch the home front. The Navy expected ONI to guard against sabotage on Navy bases, especially those associated with the Lend-Lease Act.[94] Kirk relied on DIOs to monitor and conduct inspections of piers and docks associated with Navy ships or commercial businesses that had contracts with the department. He expanded the staff of the DIO offices and the Domestic Intelligence Branch to meet the reporting coming from the districts. The DNI, as expected by superiors, treated domestic affairs as ONI's priority.

When not focused on these responsibilities, ONI carried out its traditional information-gathering duties. As in World War I, naval intelligence was particularly interested in U-boat operations and their threat to American commercial shipping. The Department of the Navy also worried about German Navy surface raiders, such as the *Graf Spee*. Officers at ONI headquarters analyzed German ships by obtaining technical specifications and designs through overseas sources. This is reminiscent of ONI's efforts in the 1880s and 1890s, when the US Navy improved technologically with the help of naval intelligence.[95] As in the nineteenth century, the Navy's technical bureaus needed information to compare how US naval ships, equipment, and weaponry stacked up against the belligerents.

Naval department leaders often disregarded intelligence estimates, the final step in the intelligence cycle of converting information into intelligence useful for policymakers. The analytical tension between ONI and the rest of CNO's staff mounted throughout the 1930s. The friction escalated when Admiral Turner took over the post as director of the War Plans Division in October 1940. Turner had a condescending attitude toward ONI and tried to dominate the DNIs by reducing them to librarians, only providing information for war planners. CNO Stark and his assistant Rear

Admiral Royal E. Ingersoll supported Turner, with Stark stating on November 15 that the evaluation process of information was not within the purview of ONI.[96] Therefore, not only was ONI forbidden to help create plans and policies but intelligence officers could not even provide analysis and assessments of the information to the War Plans Division.

But the DNI still had some analytical jurisdiction. Anderson met almost daily with Roosevelt and continued to provide him with analytical assessments. In an oral interview later, he said he felt no pressure and that there had been no restrictions on the dissemination of information. Anderson also stated that he had no personal issues with Turner in late 1940.[97] Yet, the outgoing DNI was distracted by other domestic and administrative matters. The evaluation fight was not Anderson's priority.

Stark desired to increase the flow of information within his staff and the fleet to increase efficiency.[98] He ordered each bureau and division to establish an intelligence liaison section to coordinate with ONI on circulating intelligence within their organization.[99] The CNO, War Plans Division, General Board, and technical bureaus desperately wanted the latest on the European air picture, Atlantic submarine movements, and other war news. In early 1941 DNI James advised the department that ONI placed no credence on rumors of any attacks on Pearl Harbor.[100] James's estimate irked Turner. The War Plans director came to James's office and told ONI to make no estimates of enemy intentions for the CNO and only pass information to Turner's office to make the required assessments. James pushed back, arguing existing instructions required intelligence to furnish the estimates.[101] This staved off Turner's attacks for the time being.

DNI Kirk also managed the daily routines to make assessments of foreign information. He imitated the British Admiralty's Operational Intelligence Centre from his days in London and brought a "chart room" concept for routine tracking of US and foreign ship movements to the Department of the Navy. Secretary of the Navy Knox did Kirk a favor and removed the Office of Public Relations from ONI's purview on April 28. Throughout ONI's history, public relations had been an on-again, off-again mission. On the eve of entry into a world war, it benefited the DNI not to have this mission; his staff was busy.

Roosevelt declared an unlimited national emergency May 27 in response to the Atlantic naval war's threat to American Western Hemisphere interests. As part of the deepening crisis, Kirk expanded Anderson's initiative to acquire more daily information overseas. His office oversaw the technicians, observers, and subject-matter experts who complemented the Lend-Lease program. In mid-1941, when Hitler initiated Operation

Barbarossa against the Soviet Union, Kirk sent Lieutenant Commander Ronald H. Allen and Lieutenants Samuel B. Frankel and George D. Roullard to the Eastern front as observers. ONI presented new information each morning for Knox's meeting. Kirk ordered that each information report receive a reliable rating from "A" to "D," with D meaning questionable trustworthiness.[102] Foreign intelligence was to be where ONI rebuilt its reputation. Akin to the NID and the Admiralty's combined intelligence and war planning organization, ONI would be the center of planning to aid operational commanders and strategic policymakers.

Kirk hoped Godfrey's visit in July to Washington would rejuvenate ONI's morale and offer suggestions on making ONI the hub of an operational intelligence center within the Department of the Navy. Godfrey and his assistant, Commander Ian Fleming (later creator of the iconic James Bond character), came for combined joint staff meetings with other British representatives. Kirk orchestrated meetings for the British intelligence officers with Hoover and Berle. He also gave them a tour of ONI, showing them a sprawling, expanding organization of six branches and twenty-one subordinate sections.[103] But Kirk's hopes of a perfect reunion between him and Godfrey and perhaps ONI's ascension in department stature did not come to fruition. Kirk became suspicious of Godfrey's meetings with Roosevelt and Fleming's discussions with Donovan.[104] The NID representatives were unimpressed with ONI and the lack of integration between intelligence, operations, and planning. They believed the Department of the Navy had isolated Kirk's staff from other divisions. It did not help the DNI that each division jealously guarded its information. Kirk did not have a Commodore John G. Walker–type champion to cut through the bureaucracy to collect data from the rest of the naval establishment. Godfrey apparently did not give much advice to Kirk or tell the Department of the Navy of ONI's faults. It was not Godfrey's place to do so.

The War Plans director went to Stark to ask that he take away ONI's responsibility of assessment. Turner argued that ONI was just an information collection office and no more, whereas the War Plans Division was the premier division on the CNO's staff and the nerve center for operations, planning, and enemy estimates. Never mind that neither Turner himself nor his officers had any analytical experience. He reasoned that his opinion and his staff's estimates were just as good, if not better, than those of any other office in the Navy. Kirk tried to fight back saying that ONI always had the expertise to analyze enemy intentions and was best suited in the department for this role.[105] Kirk's protests fell upon deaf ears.

By July, the War Plans director made estimates on international issues without consulting naval attaché or observer information streaming into ONI's office. One such assessment was Turner's belief that Japan would attack north into Russia instead of pursuing a campaign against Southeast Asia.[106] Kirk could not persuade Stark who, by default, sided with Turner by not restraining the War Plans Division from making estimates. By the end of July, the DNI could not consult with Washington's strategic customers who mattered the most in his chain of command: Roosevelt and Stark.

The suppression of ONI's analytical capabilities continued into the fall of 1941. Commander Arthur H. McCollum of the Far East Section published an intelligence digest negating Turner's assessment of a probable Japanese attack on Siberia. Subsequently, Turner and Stark sent out a directive in October that ONI could not send out evaluations but only report facts.[107] Turner's division continued daily strategic estimates without ONI having a chance to review them before their publication. ONI's officers learned of War Plans Division's assessments through lower-level contacts.[108]

Army intelligence attachés had the same data collections issues in Tokyo as their naval counterparts. They were effectively quarantined by Japanese counterintelligence; the information on the Japanese diminished to almost nothing but overt methods. The G-2 discovered he and his staff had to find other ways to acquire data. Historian Bidwell said MID did "too little too late" in increasing military collection in the Far East.[109] The division tried in vain with other sources, such as "Magic" intelligence. Magic was a US government cryptanalysis effort against Japanese codes. Efforts like this, though, could hardly offset the lack of human intelligence from attachés in Japan. Just as in domestic security duties, MID was not effective in information gathering in 1941.

ONI and MID's overall usefulness to the Departments of the Navy and of War in the late 1930s was negligible. As President Roosevelt's confidence in strategic military intelligence organizations waned, the military establishment followed suit. The chief of naval operations and, to a lesser extent, chief of staff did not trust in ONI's and MID's analytical capabilities. But they gave these intelligence agencies a greater tether in domestic concerns, believing ONI and MID were more successful in these areas. Likely, ONI's and MID's superiors also believed they could measure military intelligence effectiveness not through the peaceful administrative years of the Depression era but via mobilization and wartime performance. The media already identified military intelligence as successful agencies nurtured under New Deal optimism, especially when it came to spy catching. They often confused these professionals with the more prominent FBI.

Prewar culture reflected Americans' identification of naval intelligence with counterintelligence. W. T. Lackey Productions released *Navy Secrets*, a film starring Fay Wray and Grant Withers, in February 1939. Howard Bretherton directed the spy comedy-romance-thriller, based on a short story "Shore Leave" by Steve Fisher and published in the *International Cosmopolitan*. Wray's character, a Naval Intelligence Department operative, and Withers's role, also that of a Naval Intelligence Department operative, work together to break up a spy ring trying to gain US military secrets. Both naval intelligence professionals are so undercover that neither knows the other is also working for naval intelligence and detailed to the FBI. ONI is not mentioned by name in the movie but implied. A woman as a naval intelligence operative was unheard of in the late 1930s but served to enhance the plot and the love story subplot. The movie gave the impression to the audience that naval intelligence specialized in counterintelligence and nothing else.

When not depicting the MID as a nest of government agents, the media of early 1941 portrayed the division as a growing intelligence collection agency. A March 4 *New York Times* editorial discussed the work of overseas military attachés and observers, as well as headquarters in Washington. The *Times* said of the fifty-six military officers in forty countries around the globe that they were key observers for American soldiers in a future war. The editorial noted MID was increasing in size to help analyze and correlate attaché reporting and work closely and "harmoniously" with ONI.[110] In reality, MID was still inadequate for the growing crisis, especially in East Asia. The G-2 fretted in April that the division had not grown fast enough and was still far below the strategic military intelligence standard of a great power.[111]

The FBI dictated the narrative of American intelligence in the popular culture. When spy novels and films of 1939 illustrated US domestic counterintelligence efforts, the FBI figured prominently, with military intelligence either in a supporting role or not mentioned at all. In *Seven Tickets to Singapore*, Ared White penned a narrative of FBI agents pursuing spies who have stolen a "detonation ray." Around the same time, the fictional Japanese detective Mr. Moto returned to the silver screen in the film *Mr. Moto's Last Warning*. It was the sixth installment of eight films with the character created by John P. Marquand. Although there were no FBI or US military intelligence agents in *Mr. Moto's Last Warning*, this film presented US strategic intelligence, especially the FBI craft, through a counterintelligence lens. For their part, the films *Confessions of a Nazi* and *Espionage Agent* represented Americans' fears of foreign spies stealing military secrets or sabotaging America's industrial capability. Only civilian agents such as Edward Renard in *Confessions* and Barry Corvall in *Espionage Agent* could save the day. In Hollywood's eyes, ONI and MID took a supporting role in FBI's domestic security program.

Publicly, the counterintelligence team of ONI, MID, and FBI presented a united front. FBI Director Hoover was a master at public relations, building an image of himself and his agency as crime-fighters. Motion pictures and novels depicted G-Men as heroes. Hoover wrote opinion articles in the media about spies and the value of counterintelligence. In a July 1941 edition of the *Week Magazine*, he wrote "Is There a Spy Menace?" His response to his own title was "emphatically yes" and that it is "a menace in every sense of the word."[112] He implored American citizens to not underestimate the threat and advocated protecting America by building up national defenses and internal security mechanisms. Hoover portrayed an image of ONI, MID, and the FBI working together effectively.[113] Hoover, of course, exaggerated the seamless coordination of the three agencies in the public eye. But compared to just a year previous, when each investigative service worked separately, coordination efforts had indeed improved.

Society lumped ONI, MID, the FBI, and other government agencies together as the frontline defense against spies and subversives. Author Bruno Branzel wrote a serial set of cliffhangers for syndication called "That We May Live." The story details the life of a private detective named Kay Dennis. In the course of her investigative work, she occasionally talks shop with FBI agents and other undercover operatives.[114] At the start of the new decade, Branzel and other detective genre writers viewed strategic military intelligence as part of a community dragnet. In the film *Murder in the Air* actor and future president Ronald Reagan plays one of two secret service agents from the Treasury Department. His boss orders him to stop a plot by presumably German agents to destroy the dirigible airship Mason, which carries a top secret US defense weapon called the "inertia projector."[115] Even though the film does not mention military intelligence specifically, the tone of interagency intrigue is apparent in director Lewis Seiler's portrayal of spy-catchers. Reagan's character could have easily been from MID or ONI.

ONI, MID, and FBI aggressively promoted their domestic security efforts. The agency heads petitioned the House of Representatives in June to expand a 1918 statute restricting border movements, which aimed to prevent anyone from departing or entering the country during war. The intelligence organizations asked for an updated amendment to this law to become operative whenever the president found it necessary. Kirk, Miles, and Hoover sent a statement to the Foreign Affairs Committee with their requests. Representative Luther A. Johnson (Texas) responded that, based on intelligence's reports, subversive activities happened daily and the bill amendment was a necessity.[116] Frederick R. Barkley, an opinion writer for the *New York Times*, wrote a piece to inform and influence Americans on the value of ONI, MID, and the FBI.[117] Recent arrests, he argued, showed spies were within the borders. Likely this advertisement for the three agencies was orchestrated by master promoter Hoover.[118] Barkley reported that the military intelligence organizations were trained, alert, and fully funded to confront espionage threats against the military.[119] Newspapers and the public believed Americans spy novels and movies: strategic military intelligence organizations were spy catchers.

The operational and tactical narratives of intelligence failures leading up to Pearl Harbor are well-known and will not be discussed here. What is important in understanding ONI and MID's actions at the strategic level is the two organizations' incapacity to warn of the specificities of the Japanese attack. The managerial atmosphere of the 1930s and early 1940s under the New Deal had set up strategic intelligence well in the domestic security sphere and in organizational planning. But the environment was not conducive to preparing for surprise. This conclusion arises once one looks at the agencies' organizational setups and explicitly stated functions.

Naval leaders did not prepare ONI for predicting the unpredictable in late 1941. ONI did not have either a twenty-four-hour office to monitor the latest information or mechanisms to warn superiors in a timely fashion of operational and tactical information of importance. Moreover, it was not even tasked with such a mission. Plus, key decision-makers in the Department of the Navy hampered Wilkinson and his staff by limiting access to key information and customers.

When Wilkinson took control in mid-October 1941, he set about changing the organization of ONI. He looked at ways to be more responsive to the Department of the Navy's requirements. Wilkinson accepted the responsibility for the interrogation and handling of prisoners of war.

He assigned the duty to the Special Intelligence Section. But the DNI soon got bogged down in department politics and the crises that arose every day.

Wilkinson attempted to work around the War Plan Division's restrictions on assessments and regain access to senior leaders in the department. In late October, he engaged Ingersoll again, but the assistant CNO repeated the CNO's policy that War Plans had the responsibility of estimates. However, he allowed Wilkinson's staff to attach analytical summaries to department weekly information reports, a positive step for naval intelligence. Stark had promised more access to the DNI than his predecessor and that was fulfilled. Wilkinson used the CNO's aide Samuel N. Moore as an intermediary to send ONI estimates. And to appease Turner, Wilkinson sent him the same estimates as a primary recipient.[120]

ONI's analyst expected war to be imminent and most likely starting in hotspots in Southeast Asia or the South Pacific, such as the Philippines, Malay Peninsula, or Marianas Islands. Wilkinson continued to rely upon networks that Anderson and Kirk helped to build up in Asia to feed information to his officers: businessmen, media, American expatriates, scholars, and naval attaché and observers. Operational intelligence, by means of radio intercepts captured by fleet intelligence assets in the Pacific, filtered back to ONI. Analysts were not totally blind to lower-echelon intelligence, but the latest information was slow to arrive. The DNI also arranged for the daily preparation of Magic-decoded message traffic for his superiors as well. ONI's Japanese-language translator program, managed since the beginnings of Anderson's tenure, matured under Wilkinson's watch. Also, Wilkinson attempted to improve his office's dissemination processes for more on-time delivery for operators and planners.[121]

As the calendar changed from October to November, overwhelmed analysts tried to decipher Japanese plans. There were mass amounts of noise among the valuable signals coming from overseas sources. As best they could decipher, Japan's military interests still lay in the Western Pacific. Planners questioned if Japan planned to attack at all. Naval attaché reporting noted many sailors in Tokyo in November, who, after the attack, naval intelligence learned were soldiers dressed in naval uniforms.[122] ONI's budding translator section aided the Army and Navy's communications departments in deciphering Japanese diplomatic traffic under the Magic program. Simultaneously, while some sections of the ONI looked to East Asia, others focused on potential U-boat dangers from the Atlantic war and counterintelligence threats in the Western Hemisphere, such as the Panama Canal Zone. It was a busy time for naval intelligence.

In the last prewar week at ONI, signals of an impending Japanese strike began to coalesce. The Navy learned through intercepted messages that Japanese foreign offices in New York and Washington had burned codes and confidential papers to close their delegations. McCollum rationalized, based on Japan's recent diplomatic rupture and odd call sign changes in radio traffic, that something was afoot. He sent out department and fleet-wide messages between December 1 and 5 to be alert for an imminent attack.[123] Captain John R. Beardall, Roosevelt's naval aide, made sure the president saw ONI's messages. ONI sent a directive to exposed outposts in the Pacific to destroy sensitive materials. They were ordered to confirm with ONI officials and operational commanders in the Pacific that they had taken these serious prewar steps.[124] The US government was ready for war, but the question was from "where" and "when" the attack would come.

Naval intelligence historians such as Jeffrey M. Dorwart argue that ONI was the best suited in the Navy for deciphering Japanese intentions. He pointed to the volumes of intelligence kept on Japan since the Russo-Japanese War, the many hours of analytical discussions at various naval intelligence venues, the constant intelligence revisions of War Plan Orange, and numerous decoded messages as reasons that Wilkinson and his team should have answered the "where" and "when" question.[125] But having target country intelligence only goes so far in deciphering intentions. Surprise was a well-known tactic from Japan's doctrine, which rendered impossible a total understanding of Japanese tendencies. The issue was a lack of a centralized around-the-clock watch within ONI to that could take in all the data, filter out the noise, and make assessments that would make a warning possible. But even if ONI's officers had the answers to stop a Japanese attack on Pearl Harbor, would the naval establishment listen?

On the Army intelligence front, Miles was well-established as the G-2 in the late fall of 1941. He had fifteen years of intelligence-related duties in his career. The G-2's organization was growing, but nothing in his charter or organizational setup prepared his officers to alert decision-makers immediately. MID, and the nation for that matter, had not experienced a foreign adversary boldly raiding US territory since the War of 1812; it is not therefore that surprising that the division was not well-equipped to act.

Scholars have argued that Magic intercepts were the key to understanding Japanese intentions. And there may be truth to this. But only two officers in MID—Miles and his assistant G-2—were privileged to this secret program. The intelligence chief, Colonel Hayes A. Kroner did not even have access to this information. Instead, MID's East Asia experts made strategic estimates based on traditional intelligence gleaned from attachés and open-source reporting. Although analysts' assessments were appropriate for understanding the geopolitical and military capabilities environment, they could not dive into tactical and operational information easily to assess and then alert authorities.

In November and early December 1941, MID did not have a watch floor, much less a central dissemination office. The Administrative Branch parsed out publications to distribution lists that the branches deemed as suitable, but senior officials set no guidance.[126] Miles and his senior staff did not explore new approaches to dissemination methods suitable for rapid turnaround of urgent information. And the idea of setting aside officers and clerks to man an office space twenty-four hours a day to determine strategic signals from noises was not yet a concept at the strategic level. Even if Miles somehow took the initiative and built such a structure within MID, would Secretary of War Henry L. Stimson and Marshall have listened? MID's assessments had less weight compared to more prestigious divisions like War Plans. MID had improved its processes in foreign intelligence since Roosevelt's limited emergency proclamation in 1939, procedures born from bureaucratic processes promulgated in the New Deal era, but they were not nearly advanced enough for strategic warning.

The organizational chart of MID on December 5 was its usual alignment of functional shops designed for practicality and for future expansion. MID had not changed much from the summer, with Intelligence and Counterintelligence Branch being the most important of its six branches.[127] The organizational chart had no centralized nexus for information essential to sounding alerts of a strategic, operational, or tactical nature. Why would it? This was not a MID function instituted in reforms and planning of the New Deal era. There was no feasible way MID could have predicted and warned of the Japanese attack on Pearl Harbor.

The immediate years before US entry into World War II were hectic ones for strategic military intelligence. ONI and MID increased in size, equipment, and funding, while retaining a super-agent persona publicly, all by-products of governmental infusion of money, resources, and bureaucracy under the New Deal. Yet, both lost prestige, analytical responsibilities, and a sense of mission during this period. Most significantly, the two agencies failed to warn superiors about the Pearl Harbor attack, a mission they were not equipped to handle or even ordered to carry out.

New agency rivalries in Washington exacerbated MID's travails between 1939 and 1941. When Donovan's COI invaded the field of military intelligence, he created a mix of jealousy and irritation.[128] Yet, Army intelligence was much better off entering this war than the previous world war; MID did not even exist in April 1917. MID was more organized and suited to expand than the MID of August 1918 thanks to government-welcomed reforms and experimentation in the 1930s. But the division's organizational problems in 1942 and 1943 demonstrated the G-2 had more work to do.

ONI's rapid leadership changes, domestic security responsibilities, and squabbles with other divisions—side effects of finding the bureaucratic equilibrium evolving under the New Deal—hampered its ability to be a larger part of department strategy and planning before World War II. Too many unexceptional officers filled the DNI post in such a short period of time. Naval intelligence also became too eager to take on domestic security missions, to the neglect of traditional roles. "Gumshoe approaches" and "snooping" for "cases of petty thievery and casual lechery among personnel at Naval shore establishments" was not what naval intelligence pioneers like Lieutenant Commander Theodorus B. M. Mason and Walker envisioned when developing ONI.[129] In 1941, ONI lost favor with the president even in domestic affairs issues; Roosevelt often used private naval spies for information and turned to Donovan for strategic intelligence. Finally, ONI lost the Department of the Navy's confidence that it could give sound analytical assessments. This rejection of naval intelligence's expertise can be attributed to the average line officer's ignorance of the intelligence profession. By December 7, 1941, naval intelligence officers became a frustrated and disillusioned cadre.[130]

A chance at redemption lay before ONI and MID in World War II. Could military intelligence, infused with manpower surges and funding increases planned for in the peaceful New Deal era, meet wartime information demands? The ultimate challenge would be whether strategic military intelligence organizations could produce operational intelligence, a test they had failed in the Spanish-American War and World War I.

Chapter Nine
1941–1945:
ONI and MID Sidelined Again

In a bold foreign attack on US soil, the Japanese silenced the isolationist and pacifistic elements in America. In war, most Americans became internationalist. The supposed "paper tiger" began to recuperate and tackled the business at hand.

Complex government agencies in wartime were just an extension of what New Dealers accomplished in President Franklin D. Roosevelt's America, only applied more specifically to the needs of a nation embroiled in a mass-production war. When World War II arrived, the government poured much-needed money into the economy as war contracts and military service brought full employment. The war washed away the Great Depression, ending it for good. New Deal safeguards ensured the new prosperity did not turn into the unrestrained capitalism that had led to the economic calamities of the 1930s. The Office of Naval Intelligence (ONI) and Military Intelligence Division (MID) were beneficiaries of the explosion of government infusion of resources and managerial organization applied specifically to the war.

As Roosevelt's administration moved forward, many government officials looked back in December 1941 to cast blame. Naturally, the supposedly omniscient ONI and MID dealt with the repercussions of supposed failure. To make matters worse, the agencies just started full mobilization after the United States declared war. Their ability to collect, analyze, and disseminate intelligence had to improve much above peacetime capabilities. The strategic military intelligence organizations received new competition from intelligence agencies, such as the Office of Strategic Services (OSS), that vied for access to senior government leaders. Managerial reforms of the New Deal era had taught ONI and MID to adjust their organizations and budget their congressional allotments for eventualities of potential war. But the heads of the agencies—the DNI and G-2—still found themselves catching up to the intelligence demands of war.

The war tested the ONI's ability to support the fleet in battle and to increase collection and production capabilities. True, manpower and financial resources poured into the office as the DNI so carefully planned in the 1930s. The question was what to do with it. Strategic naval intelligence had not been helpful in the Spanish-American War as ONI's officers went to sea, resulting in a nearly empty office. During World War I, Admiral William S. Sims managed his own Intelligence Section for operational intelligence, leaving ONI with only domestic security functions. Naval intelligence pioneers did not design ONI for operational intelligence, information urgently needed by fleet-level naval commanders for planning and conducting operations. From the beginning, the Department of the Navy charged the DNIs and their staffs to provide broad-brush, strategic intelligence on foreign navies for the consumption of its senior leaders. With the breakout of World War II, ONI was once again ill-suited, as such organizations as Commander-in-Chief, US Fleet (COMINCH) and Commander-in-Chief, Pacific Fleet (COMPACFLT) set up their own operational intelligence sections. In Washington, radio intelligence organizations like OP-20-G (Communications Security Section) effectively shut ONI out of lower-level intelligence, leaving the office with basic strategic information-gathering duties.[1] Plan Orange, the blueprint for war with Japan, did not have an intelligence annex for the collection and production of intelligence; DNIs had to improvise. ONI scrambled to find methods to be useful to the Navy. One historian stated that ONI was limited to a domestic security agency throughout the war.[2] While an oversimplification, there is some truth to the idea that Department of the Navy leaders largely excluded it from the main intelligence efforts. Still, through trials and tribulations, the office found its way by the end of the war to a satisfactory balance of missions.

MID ballooned from a small organization into a wartime behemoth almost overnight. Prewar mobilization plans called for the G-2 to fill billets and activate sections, but reality changed the nature of the plans. G-2s had tried to infuse New Deal organizational skills and Taylorist efficiency to prepare MID prior to the war. The swelling of new personnel did not solve expertise deficiencies and the fact that prewar planners had not addressed information gaps such as orders-of-battle, military capabilities, maps, and dissemination processes when establishing ghost sections.[3] Stuck in a seemingly never-ending loop of inefficiency so much despised by past and present reformers, MID's solution was to reorganize repeatedly. Whenever the general staff revised its structure or a new G-2 came into the position, the MID realigned again.[4] Another G-2 fallback solution consisted of requesting more personnel, to tap into the near bottomless manpower pool the government created with the draft, even when reallocation from one portion of MID to another would have better served the agency. It did not benefit the division that it was led by four different G-2s between 1941 and 1944. MID's main shortcomings in World War II were poor organizational structure and ill-defined missions. It would take the division most of the war to achieve institutional efficiency.

Most government officials held ONI and MID in low regard, especially after December 7, generally thinking of these organizations as information libraries and counterintelligence agencies useless at the strategic level. Once a huge supporter of ONI and MID, Roosevelt moved on to other sources of strategic intelligence such as Donovan's OSS. Congressmen perceived military intelligence as investigative agencies; legislation from the era on military intelligence focused on domestic security. The Secretaries of the Navy and War let the senior staff officers handle intelligence matters and overlooked the office and the division. The COMINCH and general staff were ONI's and MID's masters throughout the war. ONI's superiors blamed much of the Pearl Harbor attack on ONI.[5] Making matters worse, most commanders did not understand how to use intelligence in war. Admiral Ernest J. King, chief of naval operations and COMINCH, ignored ONI and ran his own operational intelligence outfit. Army commanders also held MID in low esteem—even more so after the war broke out. Some historians have simplified MID's role in the war to a fault; Russell F. Weigley believed the division was just an agency to serve the planning division of the general staff.[6] Senior officials' low opinions of military intelligence especially at the beginning of the war were visible symptoms of strategic military intelligence organizations attempting to calibrate themselves in the aftermath of organizational reshufflings, byproducts of the New Deal.

Eager to right their organizations, both the DNIs and G-2s readily heeded their respective departments' encouragement to work together. Their combined strength could help take on rival OSS. There were several believers in naval intelligence, including Captain Ellis M. Zacharias, who wanted to alter ONI's mission from strategic, long-term intelligence to consumable and urgent intelligence in real-time tracking of the enemy.[7] ONI's efforts at this mission were more successful later in the war. Zacharias's labors exemplified military intelligence recalibrating in difficult circumstances. But in the main war effort, military leaders sidelined ONI and MID in favor of fleet and field intelligence units until 1944, when military intelligence found its niche in a more complex intelligence community emerging out of the American "Arsenal of Democracy."

An organizational merry-go-round ensued because ONI and MID still did not know what their superiors wanted from them; nor were they sure what they wanted to accomplish themselves. Even as the nation needed stability in the military intelligence community, the agencies floundered to find purpose within the massive wartime government. At the same time, joint and centralized intelligence advocates pitched for super intelligence agencies to fill in intelligence gaps among existing institutions, to the detriment of ONI and MID.

Even though ONI was ill-prepared for the strategic warning role because the government reforms of the 1930s did not imagine such a role for naval intelligence, its staffers felt great culpability for the stunning Pearl Harbor raid. Wilkinson had been a rising admiral in the Department of the Navy, partly due to his amiability, confident demeanor, and impeccable reputation, but the raid shattered this image. Other naval officers, he probably thought, would blame him and his staff and eventually start an investigation. In early wartime JIC meetings, which the CNO asked Wilkinson to assertively chair, the Coordinator of the Office of Information William J. Donovan controlled the flow of conversation.[8]

While the DNI fended off attacks and dealt with his demons, other administrative changes occurred at the Department of the Navy and ONI after the US entry into the war. Established war plans automatically activated the Commerce and Travel (OP-16-B-5), Plant Protection (OP-16-B-6), and Censorship (OP-16-D) Sections. Roosevelt chose Byron J. Price as director of Censorship on December 19, 1941. The Cabinet Committee on Censorship, with an ONI representative, met with Price four days later to coordinate the censorship effort.[9] Senior ONI staffer Captain Paul Cassard recommended to the DNI that ONI also set up a foreign liaison section, similar to MID's efforts.[10] Meanwhile, the president appointed Admiral Ernest J. King as the first COMINCH on December 20, a momentous restructuring of the naval department. Three months later King also obtained the CNO title after relieving Stark. COMINCH acquired operational functions, such as planning. His new organization required intelligence, but it was unclear if ONI would or could provide it.

Wilkinson's failure to improve ONI's reputation for operational intelligence and domestic security defined the agency's fortunes in the first half of 1942. The DNI stumbled to regain the respect of his department. He was more apt to believe all pieces of gathered information, even the outlandish ones. Although not suited for strategic warning and operational threats to the coast, ONI and district intelligence officers dutifully sifted through paranoid civilian eyewitness accounts of enemy sightings along the eastern seaboard.[11] Wilkinson did not want to be surprised again; he knew Roosevelt and others were unhappy with ONI's performance.

The department assigned operational missions of aerial reconnaissance and decryption to COMINCH, reaffirming ONI's niche as a domestic security, information-gathering agency in early 1942. COMINCH created an Operational Information Section (F-35) in the Operations Division under Commander George C. Dyer. He had access to the COMINCH assistant chief of staff for plans and his intelligence section worked with planners to satisfy operational requirements, a symbiosis between intelligence and planning ONI had lost long ago.[12] Meanwhile, from a meeting with King and Stark the DNI understood his organization's role as an information-gathering library, the ONI's traditional mission since 1882. The department sidelined ONI again, at least until it could adjust to the realities of a postindustrial revolutionary United States at war. COMINCH was the closest the Navy had come to a general staff system, one in which past naval theorists hoped ONI would be a prominent fixture.[13] But the office was on the outside of war efforts looking in. ONI relied on Dyer's intelligence because his staff had communications intercepts to which ONI did not have access. But even then, like all naval organizations of the period, COMINCH kept much of the intelligence to itself.[14] As prewar plans dictated, ONI expanded to 488 military personnel at headquarters and 4,934 employees altogether by April 1, 1942.[15] Overall, under Wilkinson's watch, ONI lost intelligence functions, endured criticism from admirals and senior officials, and lost bureaucratic battles with rising intelligence organizations. Wilkinson departed for command in the South Pacific in June, a job he had wanted all along. The Department of the Navy probably believed his talents best served frontline command. Another dejected DNI longing for sea duty left the post.

Rear Admiral Harold C. Train arrived in the Office of the Chief of Naval Operations in June 1942, received orders to ONI on July 18, and reported for duty as DNI two days later. During the first weeks, while the Department of the Navy stashed Train in CNO's offices, naval intelligence veteran Zacharias also reported aboard ONI as the head of the Foreign Section. Zacharias wanted Train's job and openly petitioned for it, which made for an awkward coupling at the top of ONI's organizational chart. Zacharias was the most qualified intelligence officer in the Navy. He had spent over twenty years in various intelligence billets, from ONI to Japan. He expected the department to promote him to rear admiral and name him DNI. The combination of his brashness and department bureaucracy probably contributed to Zacharias not getting his dream job.[16] Zacharias had nothing but disparaging words for Train, calling him a passed-over captain with no intelligence experience, lamenting he would shoulder all the work of ONI as Train's assistant.[17] In these circumstances, Zacharias set out to be a de facto second DNI, often working around Train.

For his part, Train was a diplomatic, agreeable officer who was primarily selected to manage almost ten thousand naval intelligence personnel with a healthy budget of almost $5,000,000 and to coexist peacefully with the interagency community in Washington.[18] He was exactly what ONI needed, someone who could apply managerial skills to handle the infusion of resources brought on by war. FBI director J. Edgar Hoover's relationship with Zacharias was a good example of why Train was a better pick than Zacharias. Train sensed at once that Hoover disliked Zacharias. Hoover's refusal to let the assistant DNI into his office was the first sign.[19] Train, who developed a solid friendship with Hoover and George V. Strong, played buffer between them and the loose cannon underneath him.

Meanwhile, Zacharias tried to undermine the DNI's authority. Taylorist Zacharias wanted to overhaul the office to make it efficient in war.[20] He thought he would receive Train's support but was disappointed when Train seemed to ignore his advice. So, Zacharias pushed on alone.[21] Zacharias did not realize (or ignored) that he was borderline insubordinate to Train.

Train carried out his own plans and obligations. He played the dutiful host to British, Russian, Free French, and other Allied naval representatives visiting ONI as per Roosevelt's desire for the US military forces to strengthen relations with other members of the coalition. Throughout Train's tenure, he cooperated with consultants and efficiency experts on ways to reorganize ONI to better meet the challenges of interagency cooperation and ONI's more complex customers. He also took selections for the naval attaché billets seriously.[22] Despite the turmoil of war, Train also moved ONI to the newly constructed Pentagon, to which the rest of the CNO staff transferred to in November. His organization took up 160,000 square feet in the building's massive space.[23]

Zacharias brought efficiency to ONI in early 1943 while Train was busy with the external coordination matters. He instilled new programs at ONI such as psychological warfare, special operations, propaganda, and operational intelligence, creating unique organizational branches.[24] In March, Zacharias formed the Operational Intelligence Section to push his main effort of supporting the fleet. On April 14, Vice CNO (VCNO) Frederick Horne approved placing three groups (Services, Intelligence, and Counterintelligence) underneath Train and Zacharias. The Intelligence Group had geographic sections and new functional sections, with Operational Intelligence playing a prominent role.

The reorganization was probably the most extensive since ONI's founding and created a positive buzz in the Navy, especially the operational intelligence measures.[25] However, ironically, an efficiency expert threatened ONI's existence in April 1943. The president directed the Navy to conserve manpower and cut down expansion of agencies in the department. Secretary Frank Knox asked his friend and president of Gulf Oil Rawleigh Warner to investigate Train's operation.[26] His subsequent recommendations to COMINCH were devastating to ONI.[27] He advised that ONI should give domestic security to the FBI, share foreign information collection duties with MID and OSS, and cede its nascent operational intelligence capabilities to COMINCH, which would leave ONI without any missions. Although both organizations harbored thoughts of a prospective merger with MID, ONI senior leaders preferred that this be accomplished from a position of strength, versus outside forces pulling missions away from naval intelligence. Train realized that if the department carried out the Warner Report recommendations, the Navy would decommission ONI.[28] He fought back with memoranda; eventually King and Horne conceded that wartime was not the time for such major alterations to naval intelligence.[29]

This scare had both Train and Zacharias on edge. Even with reorganizations and improvements to operational intelligence, the senior officers worried that they needed to justify ONI's existence. As part of Roosevelt's manning reduction directives, ONI had to cut 20 percent of its staff. On May 8, Zacharias ordered the office's officers to fill out a survey of their duties and explain their importance. Zacharias needed to defend ONI to senior department officers who had a "deep-seated obtuseness and a lack of appreciation" of the organization they manned, trained, and equipped.[30] The deputy DNI solution was to show the naval leadership job sheets for each officer's responsibilities to convince them of the significance of ONI missions.

Zacharias was pleased with the progress he made in improving ONI. Oblivious to the debates among senior ONI officers about the worth of his initiatives, he pushed Train to implement his ideas. Near the end of the summer, the department abruptly ordered Zacharias to sea to command the battleship *New Mexico*. Reassignment surprised him and his subordinates, especially when he was realizing the fruits of his labors and planning new ones. He wondered if he became too powerful for ambitious individuals and agencies in Washington.[31] Train recalled a much different story, one where Zacharias attempted a bureaucratic coup while the DNI was on a business trip.[32] Train sought proof of insubordination by Zacharias; supposedly Zacharias sent a letter that demonstrated disloyalty to Train and King and even the president. The letter's recipient brought it to his superiors, and eventually it made its way to Admiral King. An angered King wished to send Zacharias to "Timbuctoo" but settled for a quick dismissal of Zacharias and an end to his long career in naval intelligence.[33]

By then, though, Train was ready to vacate the post after such a long, tough year.[34] He was frustrated that the Navy's top officers thought they were their own best intelligence officers and still ignored ONI's assessments. Train also stated that he would get requests for information from the White House and other agencies, not exactly knowing who sent it and why.[35] ONI still had not quite found its place in wartime America. The transition from Train to newly minted Rear Admiral Roscoe E. Schuirmann in late September went smoothly. Schuirmann retained the F-2 (intelligence) billet at COMINCH, an effective arrangement; the DNI could monitor the fuzzy line of responsibilities between strategic and operational. His position straddled the line between ONI and COMINCH and allowed for better coordination and mutual support.[36]

Schuirmann's long-term task was to prepare for demobilization. After eleven years of the government and military's efforts to inflate the economy and manpower reservoirs brought on by depression and war, senior US leaders recognized that they had to slow down or turn off the spigot of resources to government agencies. ONI bloated to peak wartime manpower levels with 65 officers, 240 enlisted men, and 358 civilians at headquarters in March 1943. This number dwarfed the 49 officers, 10 enlisted men, and 38 civilians on September 1, 1939. Civilians were so plentiful that the VCNO ordered a freeze on recruitment of additional personnel.[37] Although there was more war to fight, the Navy knew that soon the nation would want the military to contract to peacetime manning levels. The office would eventually have to downsize; this was guaranteed. Immediately upon assuming his duties, the new DNI faced Department of the Navy's calls for surveys and manpower cutback studies. Schuirmann knew that even in these circumstances he had to maintain a solid organizational structure and a large naval attaché corps. The DNI was similar in demeanor to Train—patient, cooperative, and an able administrator—helpful characteristics for dealing with Navy bureaucracy and the complex joint environment.[38] He would use these skills to ponder ONI's future missions. Wartime ONI also reached a point where staffers automatically handled established processes and routines. The standard daily regimen gave the DNI and his staff time to ponder ONI's true missions. Would the office continue to function as an information-gathering library and a nest for counterintelligence agents, or would it dive into more fleet intelligence issues? Schuirmann made it an organizational priority (behind demobilization) in his one-year tenure to figure this out.

The DNI wrote a series of memoranda in January 1944 regarding his vision for ONI's demobilization. Schuirmann said that to understand how naval intelligence would appear postwar, one should consider ONI's participation in World War II as the key to knowing the office's mission and tasks.[39] His emphasis appeared to be in domestic security and war planning, with foreign intelligence being implied. His war planning initiatives probably reflected the fact that he also worked at COMINCH. The DNI also indicated that he wanted a larger nucleus of trained personnel after the war, than prior to 1941. Specifically, Schuirmann hoped ONI could retain 488 personnel in peacetime. He identified a few uncertainties of the postwar era with which ONI would have to grapple. Could naval intelligence divorce itself from domestic investigation functions? Would air intelligence organizations scattered throughout the department be merged with ONI? And would there be a merger of OSS, MID, and ONI after the hostilities?[40] It was hard for Schuirmann or other intelligence professionals to answer any of the questions while the nation was at war.

Schuirmann's staff drew an organizational chart for the CNO's staff and again described ONI's mission. For the unclassified chart of the naval department's Manual of Organization Charts publication, the DNI described ONI's mission as roughly the collection and evaluation of information for the department and for other naval activities. It was a generic statement for a standard manual. In Schuirmann's view, ONI's duties were equal amounts of foreign information gathering and domestic security. There was no mention of fleet and tactical interests.[41]

On October 21, 1944, Rear Admiral Leo H. Thebaud took the helm from Schuirmann. Thebaud was mindful of the limitations that demobilization might place on ONI's pursuit of potential enemies or certain other missions. Thebaud's ONI prepared for the postwar in earnest in 1945. ONI, nominally called the Division of Naval Intelligence since 1915, officially reverted to the title of "Office of Naval Intelligence" in April. Most naval officers called it by the latter title unofficially anyway. Thebaud's staff was in constant dialogue with the Office of the CNO regarding the size of ONI after the war. He told his assistant directors on May 3, 1945, to prepare statements for the Planning Branch of the mission and specific tasks of their activity in peacetime and wartime, their necessity, and logistical requirements for expanding to fulfill wartime needs. Thebaud wanted his staff's frank opinions of weaknesses and strengths in organization and methods.⁴²

Demobilization truly began on August 15, 1945. The same day, the DNI celebrated the war victory and was honest with his personnel.⁴³ Thebaud told them that demobilization—with readjustments, reassignments, cutbacks, roll-ups, and releases—would be difficult and have confusing and conflicting directives. The director also addressed the postwar outlook for ONI and its relations with other branches of the government.⁴⁴ Essentially, Thebaud did not know.

On the Army side, MID licked its wounds within the Department of War in December 1941. The G-2, Brigadier General Sherman Miles, and his staff were frustrated and apprehensive. As some blame for the Japanese attacks on US territories fell on them, they acted as the misunderstood and underappreciated martyr of the intelligence business. Senior Army officers in the department saw Army intelligence in disarray at the start of the war.⁴⁵ Miles's division had to regroup somehow to gain the trust of the general staff.

According to senior Army intelligence officers, the reformers' usual solution of reorganization was the first step. Restructuring and increasing manpower became go-to mechanisms for MID throughout the war whenever there were perceived deficiencies in customer support, just as in the New Deal era. Miles and his staff began realignment discussions to coincide with larger general staff changes immediately after December 7 and developed plans throughout the winter. Meanwhile, the Army intelligence failures seemed to mount. Places such as the Philippines fell into Japanese hands, evidence that MID and other Allied intelligence agencies underestimated their foe's ability to wage an offensive war in the Western Pacific.⁴⁶ It would take much effort for MID to gain the faith of its superiors in its ability to collect information and offer insightful assessments about the Western Pacific.

The division tried to rediscover its purpose as the Department of War reorganized in February 1942, with Army intelligence following suit. In February, G-2 Brigadier General Raymond E. Lee and Intelligence Branch Chief Colonel Hayes A. Kroner schemed to establish a separate operating agency under direct control of MID but working alongside the War Plans Division.⁴⁷ The directing staff would retain title heads of the new organizations, but most of the functions would be under assistant chiefs. The title of this subordinate organization harkened back to World War I: the Military Intelligence Service (MIS). At a conference for the

Department of War's reorganization on February 21, Major General Joseph T. McNarney, chairman of the War Department Reorganization Committee of the War Plans Division, told Lee that MIS would not be a part of the general staff but a command underneath MID. There would be a distinction between operating and staff functions, with MID retaining the latter role and MIS taking over the former. McNarney emphasized MIS's operational duties; staff officers were supposed to steer clear of MIS.[48] The problem with the relationship between MIS and MID, which haunted them throughout the war, stemmed from disagreements as to who owned the evaluation and assessment function.[49]

In March 1942, the Department of War changed the appearance of strategic Army intelligence. Most MID personnel transferred to MIS, except for a few commissioned officers. Kroner became MIS's new chief. MIS collected information from the attachés and other sources and produced intelligence. It also administered to the semiautonomous American Intelligence Service in Miami and managed secret communications intercepts.[50] MIS organized under four groups: Administrative, Intelligence, Counterintelligence, and Operating, and Administrative. The Foreign Liaison Branch and the Military Attaché Section reported directly to the chief.[51] This setup changed multiple times in the next few years.

One immediate complication from the reorganization was the rapid growth of the Air Intelligence Staff in the Army Air Force. Officers in both organizations quickly noticed some overlapping responsibilities and duplication of effort. The underlying problem was the line between strategic and operational intelligence. Army Air Force intelligence officers needed information for daily operations and planning of missions. The architects of the MIS air elements designed them to be manned with air officers and to provide the Air Force with strategic air intelligence. But strategic bombing operations overseas required the Air Intelligence Staff to grow so that it rivalled the G-2's structure in size, creating fuzzy boundaries between the strategic and the operational. Throughout the war, the staffs came to a mutual understanding through many agreements about who was responsible for which type of intelligence.[52]

Major General George V. Strong had the respect of the military and civilian establishment alike in the US government.[53] On May 5 this esteemed general became the next assistant chief of staff, G-2. Chief of Staff General George C. Marshall was keenly aware of the shortcomings of strategic intelligence on his staff and saw Strong as a solution to them.[54] A few days after being appointed, Strong addressed his division. He told them he did not like a separate MIS under the G-2 and wanted it abolished. Strong believed that MID should perform the evaluation duties and could not accomplish this if divorced from information compiling groups.[55] Furthermore, Strong judged that he could not provide intelligence advice to Marshall without control over collections residing in MIS. Strong delayed MIS's full implementation and its separation from MID. There were two separate organizational charts under Strong, a chart for his bosses to see and a true chart showing actual command and control relationships.[56]

During the first five months of the new G-2's tenure, he molded MID and a nominal MIS to his sensitivities, merging the two along functional lines. On October 22 he announced more major changes to the MID-MIS structure. After the dust settled, Strong's staff issued a chart showing the various modifications. He retained the G-2 staff and the chief of the MIS became the deputy, G-2. Strong and Kroner had four assistant chiefs— Intelligence, Training, Administrative, and Security.[57] The MIS portion of Strong's organization also moved into 193,870 square feet of assigned office space in the Pentagon.[58] The new arrangement reflected Strong's desire to keep MID and MIS together, if he could not totally abolish the latter.

MID also handled the headaches of sending liaisons to OSS and manning branch offices. The Army in fact provided OSS with most of its intelligence cadre. More MID branch offices opened in the United States to supplement the office in New York City. The San Francisco, Miami, and New Orleans offices came online in 1942 and 1943.[59] Three of the branches closed at the end of the war and Miami's outlet closed soon thereafter.

Strong tinkered with his organizational chart in 1943. Kroner amended organizational charts with a new flow chart between MID and MIS on January 25.[60] This change brought MIS even further into the MID structure, reflecting Strong's disapproval of a separate MIS. The latest chart showed the MIS Administrative Group abolished and its functions moved to MID. Four new sections appeared under the G-2: Policy, Evaluation and Dissemination, Administrative, and Joint Intelligence Committee.[61] Strong made it challenging for future G-2s to separate the functions of MID and MIS. Also, the G-2 short-circuited MIS by linking the Evaluation and Dissemination Section directly to members of the Intelligence Group.[62]

The chief of staff's office tasked the general staff divisions in late April to provide an update to the general staff's biennial report. This gave Strong a platform to reflect on MID's growth from an underutilized organization to a gigantic division under his watch. In his view, it was regrettable that there were only a few competent intelligence professionals at the start of the war, as true in 1941 as it had been in 1917.[63] Strong believed that strategic military intelligence should be just as powerful and prolific in peacetime as in war. He argued that decisionmakers need conditioning in how to use intelligence. Strong advocated that after the war the Army should maintain a comprehensive strategic military intelligence organization.[64] This is the biggest "lesson learned"—as military professionals traditionally call operational errors—that MID and its superiors took from Army intelligence's wartime performance. By June 1943, the Army was already thinking about postwar institutions and set up a special planning division for such a purpose.

Strong could not abolish the MIS because the chief of staff had mandated its existence. So, the G-2 continued to bury it. On August 20, 1943, Strong made Kroner the deputy for administration, G-2, and Colonel Thomas J. Betts the deputy for intelligence, G-2.[65] Next, Strong revoked the previous organizational chart and molded the new organization around three deputies: administration, intelligence, and air.[66] Outside MID, organizational charts showed that MIS existed at least in name, and MIS signatures still adorned many memoranda delivered outside of Army intelligence. But this was a concocted facade to placate Strong's superiors.[67]

Strong made his last report to the general staff in early February 1944 on personnel strength and organization. The huge G-2 Division Headquarters had 480 officers, 30 enlisted men, 22 Women's Army Corps, and 1,306 civilians to manage.[68] Strong left this gigantic organization to General Major General Clayton Bissell on February 21, retiring after forty years of service. As a legendary G-2, Strong had revitalized MID, made it larger, and did what he felt was right for Army intelligence. Bissell had a tough act to follow. But he was determined to make MID his own command . . . , which meant another reorganization.

Bissell had a fundamentally different opinion from Strong about the MID organization and MIS's place within it.[69] The new G-2 and the Adjutant General James A. Ulio were eager to change the division once Strong was gone. They established two boards of officers in March to plan yet another reorganization. By March 10, the acting chief of MIS had supervision over the Counterintelligence group, the Geographic Branch, the Propaganda Branch, and Special Branch, all of which had previously reported directly to the G-2. MIS seemed active again. The changes lasted until the end of the war. The boards decided to separate MID and MIS to keep the policymaking elements at the G-2 level distinct from the collection of information and production of intelligence at the Chief, Military

Intelligence Service level. The architects of the new structure emphasized that personnel in both organizations had to avoid rigid compartmentalization. Assistant Deputy Chief of Staff Major General Otto L. Nelson Jr. ordered Army intelligence to implement the changes by the end of April.

By separating MID and MIS, Nelson stressed to Bissell that policy-making and intelligence production roles had to be completely divorced. Nelson ordered MIS to prioritize an information structure that flowed intelligence direct from source to user and allowed for flexibility and lateral cooperation.[70] MID's reorganization committee planned a division with a chief, deputy, and four subordinate groups, of which the MIS was the largest component. MIS was to be MID's operating agency, manned by a chief, a deputy, and three directors (administration, information, and intelligence). The concept included a supervised specialist aided by research groups to produce intelligence within MIS. What separated this reorganization from other transformations was its emphasis on concrete techniques and procedures rather than the addition of more personnel and sections. Bissell had to acquire new office spaces, relocate personnel and furniture, and rewire telephones to implement the plan, but by June he completed the overhaul of MID and MIS, leaving only minor alterations later in the year. At long last, the Department of War had an MIS structured as an operating agency and the MID as agency working for the policymakers and planners. It took most of the war, but MID found balance in its organization; its struggles were indicative of many agencies in the US government in a nation at war.

It took a few months to work out the kinks of reorganization, but a general staff circular in September helped accomplished it.[71] In December 1944, MID made the final organizational chart of the war, reflecting only minor alterations since the last great shake-up in the spring. By the close of the war, then, MID and its component MIS had an organization that could establish priorities and requirements and practice an early form of an intelligence cycle: determining requirements, collecting information, processing data into finished intelligence, and disseminating it, soon prompting a new set of requirements.[72] MID had resumed the intelligence management and planning missions it began in the 1880s and 1890s.

At the beginning of the war ONI and MID had to figure out not only the most optimal organizational structures but how to work together to fight of bureaucratic predators. In early 1942 President Roosevelt closed the COI and moved its functions over to the new OSS, a subordinate to the Joint Chiefs of Staff (JCS). This strategic intelligence creation received more attention and respect from superiors than ONI and MID.

Therefore, future battles with Donovan and the OSS were a given. The heads of the agencies realized they needed further refinements of the various joint intelligence committees to coordinate strategic intelligence efforts.

The US military officially formed the Joint Chiefs of Staff in February 1942. Naturally, the JCS required coordinated intelligence to function effectively. The JIC already existed and, in early 1942, took on the task of providing intelligence estimates to the JCS.[73] Yet, interservice and inter-Allied military operations demanded collaborative effort from the nascent intelligence community. But it was the intelligence leaders who would define what centralized intelligence really meant, all while trying to retain the independence of their own agencies.

There were positive developments in joint intelligence cooperation in April 1942.[74] Decades of informal contacts between ONI and MID became more official when the DNI named retired Rear Admiral Neil B. Nichols the ONI Liaison Officer with the G-2 organizations (later officially changed to representative of ONI with the AC/S, G-2). He moved into the Munitions Building, MID's home. Soon after the DNI replaced Nichols for health reasons with Captain Robert Henderson. Henderson's office acted as an information bureau for Army intelligence officers, supplying naval publications and answering requests for information or identifying the offices with the proper expertise.

Zacharias described the interagency and intelligence coordination scene as chaotic when he arrived, citing duplication, agencies doing their own thing, and theater commanders conducting their own intelligence programs.[75] Much of his description was true, but the situation had advanced considerably since 1939. Coordination improved throughout the rest of 1942 with the revitalized JIC and new domestic security agreements.

Crucial for strategic military intelligence's overall cooperation was Strong's deep friendship with Train. They had both served with the American delegation to the Preparatory Commission in Geneva for the League of Nations in 1927 and 1929. Train would later recall that they thought alike, informed each other of important developments, and never disagreed.[76] Strong and Train frequently developed joint initiatives. One such project was introducing legislation to "put some teeth" into the Espionage Act.[77] The two directors integrated Army-Navy sections of the Joint Army Navy Studies (JANIS) publications, which provided detailed information about foreign ports and harbors. Also, Train and Strong met with Hoover weekly to air grievances. Because of this DNI/G-2 partnership, ONI and MID became much closer in their philosophy and missions.

In the summer of 1942, the JIC solidified itself as a workable staff, which met weekly to discuss planning and policy sessions. The members included ONI, MID, the State Department, the Treasury Department, Office of War Information, the OSS, and Marine Corps M-2. The military intelligence heads stood together as a voting bloc in the JIC. Train developed a solid relationship with State representatives Berle and Ray Atherton.

Additionally, Train and Strong created the Joint Intelligence Collection Agencies (JICA) in 1942. The JICA sent officer teams to the war fronts to collect information from field commanders to bring it back to Washington. The JICAs became quite the success story for ONI and MID in 1943. The organizations were effective in eliminating duplication of collection efforts and sending timely information back to Washington from the war fronts so that ONI and MID could disseminate the data as valuable intelligence. Military intelligence instituted the first JICA with Eisenhower's consent and JCS approval by January 26, 1943, and by July 7 of that same year there were seven JICAs scattered throughout the operational theaters.[78] Because of the demand for more JICAs and their proven track record, Horne and McNarney, the joint deputy chiefs of staff, asked the commanding generals on the fronts to detail the capabilities, missions, and needs in theater of the JICA.[79] Strong suggested even experimenting with attaching senior economic representatives from the Office of Economic Warfare to various JICAs.[80] Strong was pleased that the JICAs functioned with such high proficiency and theater commander demand; he and the DNI could expand the missions of these teams with a supportive chain of command. Cooperation between ONI and MID was at its peak.[81]

Together they faced the bureaucratic threat from the OSS. Even though the military controlled the OSS, there was still animosity between it and military intelligence officers. At every level of the organizations, ONI and MID resisted cooperation in collections, centralized intelligence, and training of service members for unconventional operations.[82] What irked Train about OSS director Donovan was that he did not compromise and instead used political influence to get his way.[83] To alleviate bureaucratic headaches, Train was quite liberal in the number of officers he allocated to OSS. By 1943, there were fifty-six Navy intelligence officers assigned. The DNI and G-2 also monitored closely Donovan's efforts to create a centralized intelligence agency. His first proposals, which held the seeds of the future Central Intelligence Agency, came to the JIC in the summer. Train and Strong were weary of Donovan's recommendations because they "smacked too much of the

Gestapo," with negative effects on funding, manning, and missions for ONI and MID and the creation of an all-powerful strategic intelligence agency on strategic military intelligence.[84] To Train and Strong, OSS was not a coordinating agency as Donovan advertised it. It was just another competing and overlapping organization. Even worse, some government officials wanted to make ONI and MID adjuncts of the OSS.

The OSS threat and the spirit of cooperation generated momentum for an organization that harnessed both naval and Army intelligence capabilities. In response to questions from Admiral King, Zacharias recommended pooling military intelligence resources together to form an armed forces intelligence agency, and King approved.[85] Meanwhile, King and Marshall pushed for joint planning and closer liaison between similar agencies of both services in other matters as well. ONI and MID already had started this process with a liaison office, which in the fall moved to the Pentagon to continue its duties. But many advocates of joint intelligence believed that they required more synergy.

King suggested to Marshall on November 22 their intelligence heads find ways to merge intelligence activities and eventually create a unified intelligence agency.[86] Train and Strong appointed committees for ONI and MID to make plans for a merger. After study, the DNI and G-2 jointly suggested to King and Marshall that service-wide intelligence activity, including that undertaken by OSS, be housed under one roof. The JCS approved the proposal as an ultimate objective with gradual implementation. But there remained much work to make a joint intelligence agency a reality.[87]

Merger efforts between ONI and MID were in full stride early in 1943. Train and Zacharias agreed that a joint intelligence agency was beneficial for naval intelligence and Strong, who disliked OSS's intrusions into Army intelligence affairs, thought pairing with ONI was also advantageous to MID. COMINCH and the chief of staff agreed with the idea as late as March, when Roosevelt started requesting efficiency measures be implemented in the services. They believed there was wasteful duplication of effort between ONI and MID, which King and Marshall had wanted to address.[88] The DNI and deputy DNI designed March and April's reorganization of ONI to make it parallel to MID's setup. Strong told the chief of staff that MID concurred with the principle of placing the responsibility for merging with the JIC.[89] ONI and MID established coordinating subcommittees to plan integration efforts. Military intelligence was primed by late spring to begin the unification process.

But the efficiency inspection and subsequent Warner Report turned events against the merger. When Warner seemed to advocate for the dissolution of ONI, the DNI's support for joint intelligence agency faded. The COMINCH had taken the Warner Report under advisement, but apparently lost interest in a joint intelligence agency. Instead, he ordered ONI to coordinate with the other intelligence agencies and continue to enlarge the JICAs.[90] By November the JCS scrapped the merger proposal.

The breakdown in the drive for a fully integrated strategic military intelligence organization is not surprising. Even after ONI's reorganization, MID was not parallel to the naval office in structure. MID was part of a general staff whereas ONI was not. Plus, tradition hampered this joint initiative: years of independence and conditioning made the institutions cherish their distinctiveness. But the effort for cooperation was impressive nonetheless, given that a military intelligence leader had not attempted a merger in sixty years.[91]

The close partnership between ONI and MID ended with alterations in senior leadership and growing attention to demobilization. Schuirmann discontinued the office of the ONI representative to the G-2's spaces on February 10, 1944. The DNI needed to move the personnel to other parts of his staff due to personnel shortages. The Army used the office's services more often than the Navy did, as the representative was co-located with MID.[92] The successful program brought together Navy and Army intelligence officers in ways never attempted. And, although ONI and MID did not merge, the liaison greatly aided in the planning for this endeavor. With the elimination of the post, the two strategic military intelligence organizations lost the close relationship fostered over two years but still coordinated in the counterintelligence and foreign liaison sections.[93]

Donovan aggressively pressed to create a powerful centralized intelligence agency. Strategic military intelligence organizations had sensed the growing momentum in favor of such an agency. The consensus that war would soon end further convinced senior military intelligence leaders that change was going to happen to the intelligence community in peacetime. Thebaud and Bissell had to determine how much ONI and MID would cooperate with the centralized intelligence proposals. ONI's planning group first discussed the idea of a central intelligence agency in November 1944. In the coming months they saw no less than three different proposals: an Army-Navy report (JIS 89), a Foreign Economic Administration recommendation, and Donovan's plans. The branch talked over JIS 89 and the OSS proposal in earnest. In December they recommended to Thebaud that JIS 89's blueprint was more acceptable than the others. The JCS, in early 1945, approved the idea of a national intelligence agency.[94]

ONI's begrudging acceptance of a superior agency also reflected MID's opinion. A strategic intelligence agency would occur whether ONI and MID concurred or not. The question of how this would affect their missions was of chief concern next to demobilization challenges.

In the beginning months of the war, strategic customers closed doors to ONI and MID. Often blamed for some portion of the perceived Pearl Harbor debacle, the DNI and G-2 struggled to define their organizations' purpose. When the Departments of the Navy and of War did not request war planning help and directed the agencies to domestic security duties, they obediently turned to these tasks. ONI and MID refined their missions and coordinated with the FBI to deconflict responsibilities further. Of course, both military intelligence agencies, with the help of overseas observers, collected information for customers as had been the case since the 1880s. But this was not where the glory resided. In time ONI attempted to hone its operational intelligence skills. Naval intelligence had failed to provide lower-echelon intelligence in the Spanish-American War, and the theater intelligence center in London shut the office out of European affairs in World War I. This time, senior leaders at ONI sought inclusion and perhaps a niche after the war.

But in 1942, domestic security was where both ONI and MID excelled. DNI Wilkinson supported the interagency initiatives for broader wiretapping laws to investigate suspected national security offenses. He also sought permission for his investigators to review telegraph and cable company files.[95] The DNI further approved government initiatives to include American journalists and private citizens in protecting classified information from leaking. In the 1930s, ONI began observing Japanese American communities in Hawaii. ONI, MID, and FBI worked together before the war to create a database to track this community. But ONI's role in the internment of Japanese Americans in 1942 was minimal, as ONI concluded that Japanese Americans were not a security threat and internment was not necessary.[96] Other national security agencies took a much more prominent role in this controversial Roosevelt administration policy.[97] Nonetheless, in other domestic security issues, the allure of investigative work sucked in Wilkinson, as it had previous DNIs.

Zacharias embraced ONI's domestic security missions. He helped create the Counterintelligence Group in 1943, which defined its mission as obtaining information to protect the naval establishment and merchant shipping.[98] During July alone, ONI had 1,428 requests for investigations of civilian and service personnel; naval districts reported 392 actual investigations. The Counterintelligence Group claimed close cooperation with MID and the FBI and reported no enemy-inspired sabotage to naval establishment assets.[99]

MID and its subordinate units conducted domestic security missions well into 1944. A key feature to the MID-MIS 1944 reorganization was jettisoning domestic security missions from MIS. The operating portions of the division were finally free from a mission not naturally suited for strategic military intelligence.[100] The Security Branch handled domestic security under the G-2. But even this branch had many of its functions transferred to other Department of War agencies and was less active by the end of the war.[101]

In matters of domestic security, interagency cooperation adjusted unevenly during the war. FBI Director Hoover still desired to control discussions about intelligence matters with the DNI and G-2. Since early 1941, he had wanted to revise existing agreements so that the FBI had sole control of cases involving civilians within the United States.[102] The DNI and G-2 reluctantly settled to new guidelines after Pearl Harbor. The agreement was a major deterrent for military intelligence in resorting to excessive methods in domestic cases, especially those involving American citizens.[103]

The three agencies further agreed on the jurisdiction in the Western Hemisphere for the Special Intelligence Service (SIS), a covert counterintelligence branch of the FBI established by Hoover to monitor the activities of Nazi and pro-Nazi groups in Central and South America. He needed ONI and MID cooperation because of the attaché corps in those places. In early 1942 the three directors agreed that naval and military attachés would share SIS-pertinent information with the FBI and that the "knowledge of the existence of the Special Intelligence Service is closely held, and every effort will be made to safeguard its existence and responsibilities."[104] Years of negotiating responsibilities began to settle between America's senior intelligence organizations. On occasion, disagreements on domestic security issues flared in the field between ONI, MID, and FBI agents. In response, the agency heads worked out another agreement in late 1942 to charge the local field offices to settle their differences. Relations slowly improved.[105] At the same time, the counterintelligence sections of ONI and MID established an official liaison program, with each sending three officers to the other office. By late 1942, the three agencies had solved their four-year turf battle.

In information-gathering duties, the War Plans Director Rear Admiral

Richmond K. Turner continued to plague ONI as America entered World War II. He complained to CNO Admiral Harold R. Stark after Pearl Harbor that ONI failed to get intelligence to the people who needed it. He also questioned ONI's and MID's ability to supply the JIC with information. DNI Wilkinson countered that ONI still held the authority to distribute information throughout the CNO's offices and had the capability for collating and fact-checking that other divisions did not. In response, Turner insisted that the office spent too much time keeping data secret rather than parsing information.[106]

Despite snubs from some superiors, ONI continued conducting information gathering. ONI's Intelligence Group had an uneasy relationship with COMINCH, especially regarding the division of labor. Schuirmann, with King's blessing, set up a combat intelligence division in COMINCH in June. The new F-2, or assistant chief of staff for combat intelligence, realized that the line between his division and ONI would blur. But he believed ONI would handle its traditional strategic intelligence duties while his staff would focus on tactical and operational intelligence. He envisioned ONI would take its cue from the Combat Intelligence Division as to the priority of effort in the COMINCH. Train later reflected on his office's relationship with COMINCH intelligence as not close: ONI provided some intelligence, but the F-2 did not contact it frequently.[107] By 1943, there was no duplication of effort; Schuirmann's division was small compared to Train's office. And the two organizations, except for ONI's tiny Operational Intelligence element, stuck to their echelons of intelligence. The situation resolved itself when Schuirmann held both desks. The Intelligence Group reporting in September revealed that some of Zacharias's views of operational intelligence rubbed off on his subordinates, and the group hailed operational intelligence as the primary mission of ONI.[108]

When discussing ONI's World War II contributions, it would be a misstep not to mention overseas information gathering. In 1943, the office maintained 66 naval attaché posts manned by 336 officers worldwide except for Switzerland and enemy territories.[109] This was a significant expansion over prewar totals. In both previous major wars, the backbone of ONI's collection efforts had come from the networks abroad. The network was in full effect when the DNI post changed hand in late 1944. True, naval attachés, observers, and liaison officers had mixed success overseas. Improved radio communications and air travel allowed for almost instantaneous reporting from reporter to headquarters. Their information was more valuable to ONI Headquarters because of its timeliness. But an uncoordinated representation effort overseas, bureaucracy, the limited talents of some overseas agents, and naval officer bias against their reporting limited the networks' effectiveness in providing an accurate strategic picture for their customers.[110]

In 1945, DNI Thebaud pivoted the office's focus to the Soviet Union and communism, while also contracting ONI to an acceptable peacetime size. Communism attracted renewed interest in America as a potential adversary in the spring months of 1945 as relations with the Soviet Union strained. Roosevelt did not want any issue to upset relations with the ally, which meant curtailing investigations of Soviet agents within the United States or collecting detailed information on them abroad. Still, the DNI recognized that various forms of communism would be a concern for the Department of the Navy after the war. Thebaud instructed his office and overseas agents to start collecting information on the USSR, especially after Roosevelt died in April.[111] Information gathering on the erstwhile American ally intensified in the summer when President Harry S. Truman had tense interactions with Josef Stalin at the Potsdam Conference. The DNI then changed ONI's focus from Japanese aggression to the Soviet threat, which would remain the primary naval intelligence target for the next half century.

Navy administrators were more pleased with ONI in early 1945 than at any previous time during the conflict. ONI had finally adjusted to the institutional changes in the Navy brought on by the Great Depression and war. War planners asked for the office's assistance, a practice not considered in decades. JCS and theater commanders praised the JANIS product—produced jointly with MID—for assistance in planning operations.[112] Thebaud was eager to consolidate gains the staff made in ONI's reputation.

While ONI's foray into operational intelligence commenced in 1942, the office immediately became insignificant to the Department of the Navy's war effort when COMINCH came online. Fleet commanders needed operational intelligence, a requirement essential for the Navy in war. Outside organizations, like COMINCH, shut the ONI out of operational intelligence—a mission not naturally fitting to a strategically focused office.

Zacharias was a firm believer in operational intelligence. He thought that the office should put more emphasis on supporting the war effort directly with coastal information, near-real time data on enemy locations, and estimates on the adversary's current intentions. The assistant DNI determined that Navy leadership had kept his office out of these roles and was frustrated that the current, strategic setup of ONI's architecture would not allow it to conduct operational intelligence. There was no organization within ONI until mid-1943 that could obtain tactical information and then disseminate it to operating forces.[113] Zacharias set about to change the mindset of ONI's officers by training them at intelligence schools in Frederick, Maryland, and New York, and sending ONI personnel to operational theaters. He argued intelligence officers needed to know traditional ONI missions, but also switch mindsets to recognize types of ships and planes, know methods to track enemy movements, and be familiar with merchant patterns and security procedures. Zacharias understood what most prior senior naval intelligence officers had not: ONI's prestige in war was linked directly to its ability to support fleet commanders. With Zacharias's departure, Train backed away from ONI's operational interests. He cancelled the operational intelligence courses in the intelligence schools' curricula on September 11, 1943. In doing so, the DNI appeased a faction of ONI staffers who opposed the operational intelligence interpretation of ONI's major mission.[114] But Train departed for sea that month.

DNI Schuirmann freely assigned ONI officers to operational intelligence duties in COMINCH, while still providing strategic intelligence to national customers through officers already in place at ONI. This action pacified senior officers of ONI who were divided in their preference for either the strategic or operational focus. Although the DNI had inside access to COMINCH operational planning, theater commanders virtually shut out ONI headquarters from operational intelligence. For instance, ONI had little input to planning Operation Overlord, the Allied invasion of the German-occupied Normandy coast.

In 1944, DNI Thebaud conducted a self-assessment of the office to discover weaknesses when he took the post. He concluded that ONI was most deficient in operational intelligence.[115] This was the first time the DNI put priority of operational intelligence over any other type of intelligence. Because data flowed between Washington and the naval assets at sea much faster than ever before, he and other members of his staff realized that they could support the fleet much more efficiently. Thebaud decided to revive Zacharias's initiatives, such as an operational intelligence section and an operationally focused training curriculum at intelligence schools. ONI also launched such measures as supporting fleet watch officers with intelligence guides, sending intelligence officers on temporary assignments to naval ships on station, creating operational intelligence products, and instituting collections measures of operational value in the district intelligence offices.[116] ONI's renewed commitment to operational intelligence and support to department and fleet combatants made superiors happy.

The DNI realized too that a centralized intelligence agency was a probability, which would take away some of ONI's strategic focus. He looked for another environment where ONI could survive and thrive.

The Departments of War and of the Navy did not make ONI and MID a prominent part of the war effort. The government tasked the agencies to coordinate, especially in domestic security and data collections matters. They had not changed the image of military intelligence within society. Publicly, ONI and MID officers were not staffers and information-gatherers in the halls of the Pentagon. They were field agents pitted against spies and saboteurs.

Popular culture depicted a different side to the two agencies. In January 1942, the syndicated comic strip *The Spirit* featured Army intelligence as spy-catchers. This edition of the comic strip took place at the G-2, United States Office of Military Intelligence. Five counterintelligence agents under the charge of an unidentified Army captain were found dead and ten spies that the offices kept tabs on disappeared. The angry officer said, "I'd hoped to use regular channels, but I'm going to use the Army's trump card . . . The Spirit. Get The Spirit!!" he told an aide. "Army Intelligence requires his immediate aid!!"[117] In this fictional world, which probably gave Americans the most information about military intelligence, MID was a cloak-and-dagger outfit.

Wartime Hollywood continued to produce military films depicting Army intelligence officers as federal agents. In the thirteen-part serial *Adventures of the Flying Cadets*, flying students are suspected of a series of murders perpetrated by a Nazi agent known as the Black Hangman. The four cadets go on a world adventure in pursuit of the murderer and try to clear their own names. Captain Ralph Carson, identified as an Army intelligence officer in plain clothes, pursues the protagonists to thicken the plot. Carson typified Americans' perceptions of military intelligence. Authors John and War Hawkins wrote *Pilebuck*, a fictional account of an FBI agent investigating sabotage at a northwestern shipyard.[118] There is no mention of ONI or MID; for the sake of accuracy, the authors should have included naval intelligence agents as it was a maritime investigation. Nonetheless, the readers could easily have swapped an FBI agent for ONI and MID investigators and still have achieved the same effect. Media reporting of intelligence matters complemented the publicity Hollywood gave military intelligence. For instance, *New York Times* editorial writer Frances M. Collon reported on the Army Specialized Training Program, consisting of 100,000 personnel at 209 higher education institutions with many assigned to foreign area and language studies. Collon said the Army would order many of these students learning new languages to G-2.[119] The article implied that MID recruited such highly intelligent and specialized personnel with knowledge of another language as a prerequisite, which it did not. As was often the case, the inner workings of strategic military intelligence were a mystery to the average American.

MID and ONI were characterized by much fluidity throughout World War II. The explosion of resources and manpower the government provided strategic military intelligence organizations overwhelmed them—even when they prepared for war using efficiency methods in the 1930s. DNIs and G-2s spent much of the war perfecting their institution to handle what their customers needed. Some of the turmoil associated with their transformation factored into ONI and MID's decisions to be more willing to function in the operational military intelligence environment. ONI was an organization no official wanted to associate with in the first year of America's participation in the war. Therefore, the office's attention was on domestic security. Weak leadership and a poor reputation shut it out of the main war efforts in Washington. However, ONI's leader's willingness to work with the MID in joint affairs and to improve its operational capabilities under senior leaders such as Zacharias and Thebaud made ONI stronger as the war progressed. By 1944 and 1945, ONI maintained a robust operational network.[120] For its part, MID also suffered from a lack of prestige. Organizationally MID was a "mongrel," a mix of different chief of staff and G-2 philosophies.[121] Generous personnel allocations and ineffective methods aimed at solving its deficiencies nurtured MID's gigantic size. Once the clear separation of MID and MIS occurred under Bissell's watch and the organization jettisoned some duties, strategic Army intelligence became more fine-tuned. By 1945, ONI and MID were more receptive to altering their intelligence roles within the US government.

The year 1945 was a milestone for military intelligence. Almost every intelligence product or action ONI and MID contributed before the end of the war was for customers at the highest level. Afterward, their customers started to change and military intelligence's status as a strategic supplier of intelligence was not assured. The DNI and deputy DNI's experimentation in operational intelligence through COMINCH or internal mechanisms altered the mindset of the average naval intelligence officer.

Thebaud encouraged its importance to the office's future. Both military intelligence organizations felt threatened by a Donovan-led push to take over their strategic responsibilities. World War II was a formative era for many modern intelligence practices, from political estimation to strategic warning to covert action.[122] Military intelligence was not suited to these strategic intelligence initiatives. ONI's and MID's status as underlings to the Departments of the Navy and of War limited how DNIs and G-2s could provide strategic intelligence to levels above the secretaries—such as Congress and the president. Although the ONI and MID were not enthusiastic about it, the creation of a centralized intelligence agency could relieve military intelligence of its strategic burden and allow it to shape into organizations better suiting the Navy and Army. Reprioritization of missions was the best method strategic military intelligence organizations knew when the government itself evolved to serve Americans in the broader framework of societal development after the Industrial Revolution. Only this time, they had to reevaluate the level of government at which their customers resided.

Chapter Ten
1946–1947:
CIA Subordinates ONI and MID

Only a few years ago I asked a flag officer: "How is the intelligence work in your force, sir?" And he answered with a straight face, convinced he was giving the proper answer: "We don't need intelligence work. There are no Communists in our ships." His answer went far to reveal how little even a man with three or four stars understood the true meaning of the word and the task of intelligence. To him it was confined to one minor phase of counter-intelligence and investigation.
—Captain Ellis M. Zacharias, *Secret Missions: The Story of an Intelligence Officer*

Captain Ellis M. Zacharias's story underscores that even at the end of World War II, military intelligence had still not found its purpose within the US government. Inaccurate perceptions, misunderstandings, limitations, and reputations hampered the Office of Naval Intelligence (ONI)'s and the Military Intelligence Division (MID)'s ability to serve their strategic customers as late as 1945.

The Great Depression and war, just the latest societal and international events in a long line of sweeping changes to the industrial American landscape, once again altered the US government. By 1945, it had become a complex behemoth with a sprawling footprint in Washington, DC, and tentacles reaching out to nearly every American across the nation. Over the past two decades, government agencies and programs had sprung up everywhere to try to meet the challenges of the economy, the military, and society. Leaders often used managerial efficiency measures and bureaucratic tools developed since the 1870s. Some New Deal agencies remained focused on government programs to help ensure the Great Depression did not resume after the war. Military leaders installed Departments of the Navy and of War demobilization policies that did not permit the armed services to fall back to bare minimum resources post–World War II. Government social programs and policies thrived and multiplied to aid the average citizen in achieving the elusive American dream. The government also sought to improve strategic intelligence between 1945 and 1947 with centralized, managerial efficiency. This required creating yet another agency. The question was what would happen to ONI and MID in the process.

When the war ended, because of the continued confusion of mission and priorities, leaders within ONI, MID, and the general military establishment had to decide how to evolve military intelligence. Most intelligence professionals agreed that in anticipation of a future war the organizations needed to avoid peacetime neglect.[1] For decades strategic military intelligence organizations had struggled to find where they belonged; what the American public, presidents, congressmen, military leaders, and intelligence professionals had not understood was that ONI and MID did not fully function at the strategic level. There had to be an agency above the department level to truly meet the strategic requirements of national leaders. By the end of World War II, these actors discovered military intelligence served the Departments of the Navy and of War better in lower-echelon capacities.

Months of reckoning came to ONI and MID in late 1945 for their perceived failure to warn of the Japanese attack on Pearl Harbor. Military intelligence leaders, such as Major General Sherman Miles, testified before Congress that the Joint Intelligence Committee formed in October 1941 did not function properly because of interservice disagreements and lack of office space.[2] The Pearl Harbor hearings faulted strategic military intelligence, but there was much blame to go around. Publicly, the disaster was still a blow to ONI and MID's reputation. Was the ONI and MID persona of mysterious, all-knowing spy-catchers and wizards of intelligence in fact fallible?

For ONI, in the years following the war the DNI made widespread changes, from the cosmetic to more emphasis on operational matters. The DNIs began to realize from events of the last decade that ONI was not the strategic military intelligence organization equipped to meet the challenges of an increasingly complex government and society. Rear Admiral Leo H. Thebaud attempted to stay abreast of postwar planning himself rather than have others dictate ONI's fate. He tried to improve internal processes as his branch and section heads told Thebaud that the present organization was "clumsy and inadequate."[3] The staff did not resolve the debate among ONI officers since 1882 about whether ONI should be organized along functional or geographic lines. The staff called for future personnel to receive more focused training because of how specialized intelligence operations had become.⁴ And they complained about duties the Department of the Navy had burdened them with that were not naval intelligence, namely, domestic security.⁵

The DNI put forward the Navy Subsidiary Demobilization Plan for Intelligence to supplement the Navy's Basic Post-War Plan no. 1 as recommendations for ONI's duties in the demobilization in August. In it, he noted that ONI would supply foreign intelligence and, against his staff's opinions, domestic security.⁶ The description was not detailed; Thebaud did not have a clear vision. The document indicated relations would stay the same between the FBI, Department of War, State Department, and other intelligence agencies. He, like other intelligence professionals, did not know how the movement to a centralized intelligence agency would play out. The DNI and his staff's uncertainty about ONI's future is understandable: the smoke of war had not cleared.

In September, ONI's fate ceased being Thebaud's responsibility. New DNI Rear Admiral Thomas B. Inglis led the office into the new era. The Office of the Chief of Naval Operations (OPNAV) changed his title to chief of naval intelligence.⁷ Two years of demobilization planning crystalized into changes at the OPNAV and ONI levels. COMINCH organization dissolved in October and its intelligence organization responsible for operational intelligence slowly transferred to ONI over the next few months, boosting the effort to reorient ONI's focus away from the strategic environment. OPNAV assigned ONI to the deputy chief of naval operations and his OP-02 (Administration).⁸ ONI's OPNAV designator became OP-23. ONI's organization reshuffled into seven branches and two elements along functional lines (Administrative, Domestic, Foreign, Air, Special, Operational, Naval Records and Library, Liaison, and Plans).⁹

These modifications continued into November. ONI requested fifty-nine officers and enlisted men from the US Marine Corps to serve at ONI and naval attaché offices.¹⁰ ONI promulgated the Navy Subsidiary Post War Plan for intelligence based on OPNAV's Basic Post-War Plan no. 75. It called for the reduction of service members and the increase of civilians at ONI. In general, personnel numbers declined even as the international situation deteriorated at the start of the Cold War. As usual in a postwar naval intelligence environment, Inglis had to defend ONI from cuts in funds and manpower, scrambling to keep the organization afloat even as the threat from the USSR became more and more evident. The changes in October and November—most notably a functional reorientation and inheritance of a section from the defunct COMINCH—indicated a redirection toward operational intelligence.

ONI continued to morph and downsize in 1946. By February 15, 1946 the transfer of OP-32, the Combat Intelligence Section, to ONI was complete. It fit into the newly created Operational Branch (OP-23Y) nicely. A month later, Secretary of the Navy James Forrestal approved the creation of the US Navy Intelligence School housed at Anacostia in Washington, DC. The school gave the naval establishment a source of highly specialized intelligence officers and a foreign language program.[11] The Department of the Navy's initiative was a sign that even in the face of the reduction of naval intelligence's manpower, the quality and importance of intelligence would not diminish in peacetime. Also promising for ONI, Truman approved the *Advanced Changes to U.S. Navy Regulations of 1920* in June. This was the first time since 1882 that the Department of the Navy wrote into Navy Regulations ONI's duties and its relation to the rest of the Navy. The regulations emphasized operational duties and the Marine Corps intelligence's integration with ONI along with the office's traditional information management functions.[12] The Department of the Navy finally formalized naval attachés as a legitimate source for overt information. The naval establishment addressed in earnest the underfunding of US Navy's overseas representatives, especially for social interactions in foreign countries, by requesting Congress to increase attaché maintenance funds. In short, ONI continued to transform up until the next evolution in the realm of government reorganization of intelligence, namely, the creation of a centralized intelligence agency.

The immediate issue confronting MID in peace was demobilization, as part of the Army's larger initiative. In September 1945, the Department of War appointed a special board headed by Lieutenant General Alexander M. Patch to study Army-wide demobilization. It became known as the Patch Board and then later the Simpson Board under Lieutenant General William H. Simpson. The Patch Board drafted its first plans for review by the divisions within the general staff. On November 11, MID director Major General Clayton Bissell gave his recommendations to the board. His thoughts revealed where Army intelligence professionals perceived MID's role was in a postwar America. The G-2 emphasized his organization provided overall strategic intelligence, not just air or ground intelligence.[13] He also provided a revision of his job description.[14] The G-2's corrections reflect an organization not yet ready to change, a lack of realization that the complex strategic intelligence environment had grown too large for MID and its sister organization to handle.

Like naval intelligence, MID and the G-2 further pushed for more training for intelligence officers. After the Army phased out the Military

Intelligence Training Center in Maryland at the end of 1945, it moved operational intelligence training to the Army General School at Fort Riley, Kansas. The department continued its counterintelligence courses at Fort Holabird, Maryland, in 1945. The Army also established a strategic intelligence school in Washington in 1946 to train military attachés. The training initiatives were a microcosm of the changes happening at MID and in the larger Army in 1946. The Patch-Simpson Board submitted its recommendations for a postwar Army to Truman on January 24. Little direction came from the Department of War as to military intelligence's place within the Army, but changes would come.[15] Bissell would not oversee them as he moved on to become military attaché in London in late January.

Lieutenant General Hoyt S. Vandenberg, the highest-ranking officer ever to serve as head of MID, became G-2. He oversaw the major reorganization of the division in March through June, creating a special board to plan it in parallel with the secretary of war and the Patch-Simpson Board. Vandenberg approved the preliminary findings of the board on March 19; the recommendations fell in line with "The War Department Basic Plan for the Post-War Military Organization" (issued November 19) and the Simpson Board Report (issued November 29), the final foundation for reorganization of the Department of War, effective the spring of 1946. Vandenberg and his board told Robert B. Patterson that Army intelligence was inadequate for tasks that the department expected of them in the coming decades.[16] The G-2 stated May 15 that the Army had long suffered from a lack of appreciation of intelligence in modern warfare and thus the general quality of personnel assigned to intelligence was inferior to the rest of the branches of the service before the war. He further expressed the view that the Army must alter these attitudes toward his division and the current skillsets or face the consequences of potential defeat in a future war.[17]

The General Plan stated Army intelligence's functions were information gathering, domestic security, and war planning.[18] The statements were vague enough that MID had some room to adjust as its staff sorted out their place in the postwar Department of War. Vandenberg recommended that the MIS be amalgamated back into the MID under the G-2. The new structure of the Intelligence Division had the G-2 on top with a deputy director, executive director, and assistant executive director underneath him. Vandenberg and the board advised the secretary that the organization would house five groups: Security, Intelligence, Combat Intelligence and Training, Army Security Agency, and Collection. Combat Intelligence, another name often used interchangeably with tactical intelligence, was a new branch and reflected operational intelligence's growing importance to MID's mission. The new alignment was a fundamental departure from the wartime setup.

The department accepted all of Vandenberg's recommendations and reinstated the division to its prewar status as one of five divisions. It would serve in multiple capacities: an operating agency, planning organization, and policy staff. MID established all the intelligence requirements for the Army, conducted data management, and distributed finished products throughout the Army. These changes gave MID more power and respect as an organization than any time since its founding.[19] But these would weaken with the founding of the Central Intelligence Agency.

Strategic intelligence organizations were in retreat in late 1945. One agency even disappeared. The executive branch decided to look elsewhere for strategic intelligence support. This rejection reflected long-term governmental trends of centralization, efficiency, and preparedness combining to minimize military intelligence's role at the strategic level.

After President Franklin D. Roosevelt's death, Office of Strategic Services director William J. Donovan lost his protection and political influence in the government. He still had his enemies, such as FBI Director J. Edgar Hoover and most Army intelligence officers in MID. Unfortunately for Donovan, he made another enemy in Truman in April when the new president took office. Donovan's proposals for a centralized intelligence agency seemed too all-powerful and "Gestapo"-like to Truman. The director's brash and bold personality also conflicted with Truman's sensibilities. Donovan attempted to persuade Truman a few times between May and August through personal meetings and the media, but Truman was not convinced. The president liquidated the OSS and dismissed Donovan on September 20.[20] After a decade of favor at the highest levels of government, Donovan was unceremoniously kicked out of power.

Potential threats and innovations—such as Soviet sneak attacks, jet propulsion, and atomic bombs—made collaboration between ONI and MID and the formation of a new strategic intelligence agency even more imperative.[21] On November 14, the Joint Chiefs of Staff approved of the Joint Army-Navy Air Intelligence Division (JANAID), which allowed for the ONI and Army Air Force coordination of air intelligence products. There was a four-month gap between October 1, 1945, and January 1946 where the United States did not have a strategic intelligence agency akin to the OSS. ONI and MID had always pretended to be that type of organization but continually fell short. Truman assigned the leading role in creating a centralized intelligence agency to Secretary of State James Byrnes. He and the secretaries of the Navy and of war formed an interdepartmental group to make it a reality. Bureaucratic rivalries characterized the staffing process.[22] ONI and MID leaders' defensive attitude, even as they tried to figure out their own missions and organizations, contributed to the proposal delays into the next year.

The Departments of the Navy, War, and State finally reached an agreement for a centralized intelligence agency. Truman gave much of the credit to Souers from ONI for coordinating the final proposal.[23] The president held a series of meetings at the White House to finalize the agreement. Truman designated the departments' secretaries as part of the National Intelligence Authority (NIA) on January 18 and then issued an executive order four days later establishing the Central Intelligence Group (CIG). The president named Fleet Admiral William D. Leahy as his representative to the NIA and appointed Rear Admiral Sidney W. Souers (a friend of Truman's) to be the first director of central intelligence (DCI). The NIA activated the CIG on February 8 with a presidential directive. Although a nominal successor to the OSS, the group was no serious threat to replace ONI and MID as the government's strategic intelligence agency. Truman meant the CIG to be the go-to centralized place for strategic intelligence, but the organization failed because it had only limited legal power to conduct such a mission. CIG's faults came from a lack of manning, defined missions, funding, and legitimacy. Because the organization lacked congressional legal authority, the Pentagon and the State Department questioned its legitimacy and military intelligence professionals soured to working with the CIG staff.[24]

Souers was eager to retire to civilian life in Missouri and Truman relented. Not even six months on the job as G-2, Vandenberg followed Truman's order to become the second DCI. Surprisingly, Vandenberg was a leading proponent for a respectable central intelligence agency even though he came from an agency continually wary of a powerful, civilian strategic intelligence organization. Vandenberg immediately pushed forward with plans for legislation in Congress for a successor to the CIG. He hounded the White House staff to include such an agency in the upcoming national security bill. Truman was reluctant to have the CIG tinkered with because the group gave him everything he wanted: a centralized place to get his classified news. Yet, from his lofty perch he had not observed the bureaucratic infighting. ONI and MID were less than eager for a more formidable CIG; they preferred the status quo as the sole foreign intelligence providers in government. But Vandenberg persisted in getting the Central Intelligence Agency on the bill.

Vandenberg and his staff politically stumped Congress. Most members of Congress believed that the CIA was essential; in the wake of the Pearl Harbor hearings, they wanted to prevent another such incident. The CIA was the potential solution.[25] During the deliberation stages in the summer of 1947, ONI and MID realized that once Congress expressed support of the CIA, they did not have much say. Besides, they were too engrossed in their own reorganization and search for purpose. And since the CIA would not conduct intelligence operations within the United States, FBI leaders were satisfied Congress would not disturb their internal functions.[26] The two houses overwhelmingly passed the National Security Act of 1947 by voice vote. Truman signed the act into law aboard Truman's VC-54 C presidential aircraft "Sacred Cow" on July 26. The CIA became an official organization September 18, establishing the first strategic intelligence organization in American history formed and approved by the executive and legislative branches. Incidentally, the National Security Council (NSC) also created in the same Act lessened ONI's and MID's influence; the council was one more layer between military intelligence and national policymakers.[27] Army intelligence lost its air component to the new Air Force. The CIA subordinated both ONI and MID to a new intelligence community, a position of strategic inferiority to which ONI and MID officers were unaccustomed. These officers perhaps foresaw their demotion as inevitable considering a decades-old trend of government enlargement and reforms to meet industrial age challenges. The CIA's emergence and the formation of the NSC forced military intelligence to become more operationally focused.

The CIA was the death knell of the uneasy wartime strategic intelligence triumvirate of the ONI, MID, and OSS. The film *13 Rue Madeleine*, released in 1947, was the last movie to feature the old counterintelligence spy system made popular during World War I in American culture. James Cagney plays an unassuming OSS agent and training instructor charged by his superiors to find a German spy within a US agent school and subsequently in occupied France before D-Day. The OSS received all the glory in this American spy thriller, which included authentic OSS film footage. In the end credits, however, the filmmakers paid tribute to Army intelligence.[28] Furthermore, the film indirectly recognized naval intelligence; a scene at the National Archives reveals a file cabinet with case files labeled

"ONI." After this film, Hollywood reoriented its focus on the CIA as the Cold War intensified, leaving military intelligence in the shadows again. American filmmaking echoed the demotion of ONI and MID to a lower echelon of intelligence work.

From the formation of the CIA through the rest of the decade, ONI adjusted to more operational customers and roles. Several layers of government separated ONI from the president: the NSC, CIA, secretary of the Navy, and the Office of the Chief of Naval Operations. Naval intelligence's superiors above the department level did not request broad-brush political and economic intelligence from them. Most requests were from the CNO's level and fleet and theater-level commanders regarding adversaries' fleets, naval capabilities, and ship technical specifications. To be sure, ONI received tasks from the department and above occasionally, but not as often as military intelligence professionals were used to. Naval intelligence in Washington drifted into unfamiliar work somewhere closer to the operational environment.

ONI's organization shrank in the closing months of 1947. Staffers still acquired information from abroad, but their efforts were not about collections against an enemy such as Japan and Germany, but a new one in the Soviet Union. As part of ONI's shift to helping the fleet, the officers in Washington became more specialized to avoid conflict with or overlap efforts by Army and State Department intelligence agencies, the FBI, and the recently formed CIA. ONI sought to acquire a continuous flow of technical data about the principal foreign naval establishments, including forces afloat, units under construction, and naval aviation. Also, this operational pivot allowed the office to acquire up-to-the-minute information about unrelated subjects such as hydrography, cartography, and meteorology.[29] This specialization changed the naval intelligence profession in the process. In September 1947, ONI filled all intelligence billets with graduates of the Intelligence School. Congress, through the Officer Procurement Act of 1947, created the personnel designator "1630" for restricted line officers in intelligence. In 1948, a selection board designated ten regular officers as 1630s from a pool of restricted line officers. The number of professional naval intelligence officers climbed into the thousands by the end of the century. The evolution of the naval intelligence officer corps solved a problem plaguing ONI since the beginning: enticing officers away from sea duty to a position not beneficial to their careers.

ONI's transformation continued. On November 1, 1948, Inglis reverted the title chief of naval intelligence back to the director of naval intelligence, with the CNO Admiral Louis E. Denfeld's approval. The DNI cited the nomenclature of other agencies—the "directors" of the Army, Air Force, FBI, and CIA—as the reason to change the name.[30] In the next month, ONI fully moved to the Pentagon from the Main Navy Building. Inglis also changed the office's mission statement and promulgated it to his staff on March 1, 1949. The customer, he told them, was the "Naval authority."[31] Presumably this meant the Department of the Navy, but one could reasonably interpret it as commanders in the fleet and theaters. ONI's missions, Inglis contended, were to information gather, war plan, and conduct domestic security.[32] In objectives he provided, the DNI was specific in maintaining an operational intelligence section, a new key feature for ONI. The office revised the missions and objectives of this document in September 1950. The only added mission was "(d) to contribute the Naval components to National Intelligence."[33] Although it is unclear what "naval components" implies, it suggests operational intelligence from naval intelligence assets at the fleet and tactical units filtering through a receptive ONI. The organizational chart of September 21, 1950, was complicated and large, a very distant relative to the four-man office of ONI in 1882. Senior naval intelligence officials organized it by functionality to handle technical and enemy capabilities request for intelligence. The operational intelligence section sits prominently in the middle of the Intelligence Branch on the chart.[34] ONI's shift from the purely strategic military intelligence organization in the 1880s to a hybrid of strategic intelligence and the operational duties was complete. Government complexity to meet the challenges of societal transformation was the catalyst for ONI's conversion.

For two years after the war, MID had great autonomy reconstituting itself during demobilization as a co-equal division of the general staff. Then, in 1946 and 1947, MID lost its air intelligence functions to the independent Army Air Forces. Also, the shakeout from the Pearl Harbor hearings put military intelligence on the defensive. CIA's formation was the final factor in MID's retreat to a mixture of strategic and operational intelligence missions.

The CIA subordinated the division further down the chain of command, as the new agency now coordinated finished intelligence with the NSC for the president. More significantly, the CIA reoriented MID away from national economic and political intelligence—missions MID gravitated toward to fill a void where a strategic civilian intelligence organization did not exist. The Haislip Board Report explained MID's new role in 1947: "The War Department Intelligence Division, working in conjunction with the Central Intelligence Agency is responsible for obtaining information of a military nature concerning the capabilities and probable intentions of potential enemies."³⁵ The report had not quite captured MID's subordinate role to the CIA in coordination matters. But soon MID found itself relegated to purely Army intelligence–related tasks. The *Annual Report of the Secretary of the Army for the Fiscal Year 1948*, the first report of this secretary after the creation of the secretary of defense, was nondescriptive of the MID's duties because the department did not know yet how the CIA and NSC would affect Army intelligence.³⁶ Although Army intelligence officers judged in 1948 that MID was on its way to providing "a world-wide basis military intelligence" to help formulate plans for national policy, the new strategic intelligence apparatus pushed MID down the ladder. No fewer than five layers separated the main customer, the president, from the G-2. The director of intelligence's role in influencing national policy was decidedly reduced.³⁷ MID's main customers became the chief of staff and the generals in the field. They were more interested in adversarial locations and capabilities and forced Army intelligence to become more attuned to theater operations. MID followed ONI's path—buried under layers of parent organizations as part of the US government's centralization initiatives.

Assessment

A review of strategic military intelligence organizations between 1882 and 1947 indicates the reason the American public, government and military leaders, and intelligence professionals chronically struggled to define their missions and had competing ideas of what strategic military intelligence should be and do was because they were never truly strategic organizations in nature. Intelligence organizations were a novelty for much of this period, floating without defined purpose in an ever-changing industrialized society. The idea of collecting intelligence on foreign countries, especially in peacetime, was not natural to a democratic, open society. The average American barely knew that intelligence organizations existed until they began spying on citizens in World War I. Presidents and congressmen tasked intelligence from ONI and MID that often was strategic and nonmilitary in nature because there was no other agency to fill the void until the OSS in the early 1940s. Leaders of the Departments of the Navy and of War generally had no conception of what intelligence agencies could do for planning and strategy; therefore, many generals and admirals treated them with misunderstanding and derision. "What type of honorable officer spies on foreign officers behind closed doors?" was a common question throughout this period. And since there were no intelligence organizational templates for military officers to follow in the 1880s, they were often confused about what echelons of intelligence the organizations should operate, much less what they were supposed to do. Strategic military intelligence organizations' missions changed as society evolved. There were almost always visions of what the agencies should be in the minds of individual actors, even though often there was no agreement among the ideas of the different individuals involved. Most of these actors possessed professional pragmatism that allowed them to compromise their visions. They were working toward concepts inspired by the cultural ideas of the time, which ultimately formed the military intelligence structures.

Military intelligence organizations endured a myriad of challenges over the decades in response to the societal forces at work in America. Prior to World War I, the beginning stages of American's response to the Industrial Age, ONI and MID were tiny organizations with simple tasks. The managerial revolution of the early 1880s birthed ONI and MID to meet the challenges of a modernizing Navy and Army. The two agencies had growing pains in the late 1880s and early 1890s as part of the chronic struggle in American history between the Jeffersonian and Hamiltonian ethos. In this contest for the direction of America, ONI and MID followed the Hamiltonian navalists' and reformists' lead. The Hamiltonian vision of America won as the nation's bounty of riches now had boundaries; to get past those barriers, many Americans believed they had to look overseas to thrive economically. The Spanish-American War exemplified this expansionist dream. Yet, military intelligence organizations were unable to totally fulfill their strategic and operational intelligence missions in war, a wartime trend that would continue through World War II. Progressivism, which harnessed the untapped potential of government regulation to push a wide-ranging agenda—in politics, economy, society, and the military—nearly reformed and overregulated ONI and MID out of existence. But military preparedness and domestic security concerns in the Great War resuscitated military intelligence to help Americans fight in a war beyond their borders. In forty years, ONI and MID expanded in size and complexity to attempt to meet the challenges of an American society in flux.

The trend of military intelligence's adjustments to a changing America continued in the next three decades after World War I. In the 1920s, three converging streams of American thought and experience—the Red

Scare, the isolationist movement, and demobilization—solidified ONI's and MID's ready acceptance of untraditional missions in domestic security to remain relevant in a fluid American society. The stock market crashed in 1929, plunging the United States into the Great Depression, New Deal politics, and isolationism. ONI and MID's recovery during the New Deal lay in planning for the future with mobilization for when the money and manpower flowed again. American society's response to ailing capitalism—the New Deal—drove the evolution of the military intelligence agencies. As government imposed itself in everyday affairs to restore order and faith in the system, military intelligence organizations grew by fits and starts just prior to World War II due to individuals' peculiar personalities, but larger governmental trends of efficiency and bureaucracy gradually helped ONI and MID find an acceptable balance of missions. World War II allowed the government, with the full backing of Americans, to throw resources into the war effort. ONI and MID benefited from the manpower and money but struggled organizationally to find their niche and foundered in the operational realm. After the war, the many decades of government expansion finally buried military intelligence under numerous managerial layers, causing military intelligence professionals to reevaluate not only their missions but their customers. It was this continual societal churn, a response to an industrializing America throughout military intelligence's existence, that kept military intelligence agencies refining their raison d'être.

Historiographic Essay

There is a relatively small and incomplete historiography covering strategic military intelligence organizations stretching from their infancy to the beginning of the Cold War. Much of the scholarship fails to account for how they relate to American society. The Department of the Navy formed the Office of Naval Intelligence (ONI) in March 1882, making it the oldest US government intelligence agency still functioning in Washington, DC. As significant as ONI is to the advent of American military intelligence organizations and intelligence in general, it is a relatively obscure agency in the United States. There are few accounts of its origin, birth, and development. Likewise, relatively little has been written about the Military Intelligence Division (MID), and the historical accounts are disjointed. Apart from a few monographs, there has been no in-depth analysis of the intelligence agencies through the whole period covered in this study, and there have been no accounts linking the two organizations. More generally, not one work highlights how these organizations fit into American historical trends, much less military growth. Major ONI and MID histories are a mix of historians' narratives and official government accounts. Historians generally have written about the problems of both organizations; the government authors are neutral in their interpretations. They barely touch upon this work's key issue: the changing missions of strategic military intelligence organizations between 1882 and 1947.

ONI or naval intelligence historiography is dominated by Jeffrey M. Dorwart's *The Office of Naval Intelligence: The Birth of America's First Intelligence Agency, 1865–1918* and *The U.S. Navy's Intelligence Dilemma, 1919–1945: Conflict of Duty*. In 2019, he and the US Naval Institute Press combined the two books into one volume titled *Dorwart's History of the Office of Naval Intelligence 1865–1945*. Dorwart provides an in-depth, well-researched analysis of ONI throughout the period. In *The Office of Naval Intelligence*, he argues that "the Office of Naval Intelligence had an occasional effect on the course of naval and national policy. But while policymakers periodically consulted the office, most refused to recognize the importance of intelligence or to employ it in decision making, planning, and operations."[1] He concludes that even at the earlier stages of ONI's development, the office "evinced disturbing proclivities" and gravitated toward "spying, counterespionage, domestic snooping."[2]

Dorwart continued the theme of domestic security's primacy in *The U.S. Navy's Intelligence Dilemma*, which he called an agonizing contradiction that ONI had to face as it carried out missions both of foreign intelligence and domestic security.[3] Dorwart was the first historian to remark on ONI's place in military history, but he had a clear agenda: to show the seedier side of naval intelligence. As such, he probably makes too much of this supposed dilemma. Domestic security was a mission that ONI staff performed based on the requirements of society, their bosses, and their natural inclinations. He does not incorporate societal trends such as Progressivism and Taylorism to enrich his analysis. Doing so might have helped Dorwart arrive at a better-rounded conclusion as to ONI's purpose and mission.

Three other major pieces of scholarship discuss all or portions of the period of strategic naval intelligence covered in this book. In 1963, James R. Green wrote his master's thesis "The First Sixty Years of Naval Intelligence" while at American University. The former US Naval Intelligence School instructor attempted the first academic treatment of the agency and, for the most part, did a satisfactory job introducing strategic naval intelligence to academia. Green argued that in 1963 ONI's missions included data collection and processing, domestic security, and criminal investigation.[4] ONI's missions change over time, and his assessment does not accurately reflect military and societal trends even fifteen years before his writing. Historian Peter Karsten's much heralded *The Naval Aristocracy: The Golden Age of Annapolis and the Emergence of Modern American Navalism* touches upon ONI briefly in its efforts to define the nature of naval officers. His book treats the early pioneers of the naval intelligence organization as aggressive, patriotic, young Turks bent on modernizing the US Navy. His discussion of navalists and governmental reforms forms a major component of the trends examined in chapters 1 and 2. Brian T. Crumley's dissertation, "The Naval Attaché System of the United States, 1882–1914," is also a useful source for understanding early ONI as well as the naval attaché corps, the information-gatherers of naval intelligence in the era of the managerial revolution. All three works, together with Dorwart's books, make up the most important scholarship of ONI, making for a meager library to research.

Two other scholars penned articles on strategic naval intelligence. Robert G. Angevine from George Washington University wrote "The Rise and Fall of the Office of Naval Intelligence: A Technological Perspective," in which he provided a technological viewpoint of ONI's functions, arguing that in the 1880s ONI was thriving because the growing Navy required technical intelligence that naval intelligence could provide through its attaché reports. But when the improved Navy did not need the office's intelligence as much, ONI stagnated as an organization. The officers then struggled through the next few decades to find its purpose.[5] This technological perspective is valuable, but there were other factors—such as culture, economics, and, as he admits, bureaucratic considerations—at the strategic level that confused the functions and purpose of ONI. Historian Mark R. Shulman addresses the bureaucratic issues in "The Rise and Fall of American Naval Intelligence, 1882–1917." In his assessment, by the 1890s, most ONI officers were disciples of Captain Alfred T. Mahan's sea power theories. They stopped providing valuable technical data and became a public relations office.[6] Shulman is correct that ONI conducted public relations as a mission, but it was one of several duties in the 1890s depending on the shifting requirements of the Department of the Navy. Both Angevine and Shulman complement Dorwart in their negative judgements of ONI's effectiveness in the early years, but their time window is too narrow to understand what was truly happening with strategic naval intelligence throughout the decades.

Another set of writings on the ONI subject put forward an objective interpretation of the organization's past: official histories. These are unapologetic in their sterile treatment of ONI's performance of its duties. This is unsurprising, given that ONI either commissioned the authors or the historians worked for the agency themselves; in such circumstances, criticism would be in bad form, if not forbidden. Captain Wyman H. Packard wrote the definitive encyclopedia *A Century of U.S. Naval Intelligence* for the Department of the Navy.[7] His tome is a must-read on naval intelligence today because of Packard's years of research. However, the material is mundane, with no assessment of ONI's purpose relating to the larger American experience.[8] Randy Goguen was the command historian for two decades; her articles also take a necessarily impartial, perhaps even positive, view of ONI. For instance, she wrote "U.S. Navy Owes T.B.M. Mason" for *Naval History* in 2005, in which she spoke glowingly of Mason's contributions to ONI and the larger Navy. The value of ONI command histories lies in information coming directly from the agency itself and in showing how its employees view their own past. Still, one should not expect an unfiltered assessment of ONI's missions from these sources.

MID's historiography is small as well. Colonel Bruce W. Bidwell, Roy

Talbert, Marc B. Powe, and James L. Gilbert wrote major works on the division's history. The MID and the Office of Military History commissioned Bidwell to write the *History of the Military Intelligence Division, Department of the Army General Staff: 1775–1941*. While this technically is a command history, it is also the most authoritative account of the division in the scholarship. Like Packard, he was thorough and took an impartial view of MID and its missions. The work is strictly an institutional history, with little to no economic, political, or cultural research added. Scholar Roy Talbert wrote of the perceived "misdeeds" of MID— notably during the Red Scare in 1919 and 1920—in *Negative Intelligence, the Army and the American Left, 1917–1941*.[9] In his assessment, MID's missions were mostly in the domestic security; he was not too kind in describing MID's morality, paying little attention to the division's foreign intelligence functions. Colonel Marc B. Powe wrote semiofficial accounts of MID, such as *Evolution of American Military Intelligence*, with his most academic work being his master's thesis "The Emergence of a War Department Intelligence Agency" for Kansas State University in 1974.[10] Tracing MID's development as a microcosm of the increasingly bureaucratic American society between 1885 and 1917, Powe framed his argument within the trends of centralization and organization. Hence, he judged that MID's main missions were the centralization of information and then dissemination of intelligence. He did not, however, focus on the division's other missions.[11] James L. Gilbert's 2012 book *World War I and the Origins of U.S. Military Intelligence* noted that the Department of the Army lacked "an intelligence presence during the years leading up to World War I."[12] Although Gilbert was a former command historian at US Army Intelligence and Security Command (INSCOM), a descendant of MID, he did not hold back on the effectiveness (or lack thereof) of strategic military intelligence, especially before World War I. His discussions of MID's missions are mostly confined to that war and have limited value for other periods of this research.

Two articles stand out in the historiography of the division. Military intelligence historian Angevine wrote "Mapping the Northern Frontier: Canada and the Origins of the US Army's Military Information Division, 1885–1898," in which he theorized that the Army created MID in part "to collect intelligence enabling it to strike Canada in the event of conflict with Great Britain."[13] He cited leadership statements, collection methods, intelligence objectives, organizational structures, and officer backgrounds between 1885 and 1897 as evidence of the Department of War's fascination with Canada. The topographical mission to map Canada weighs heavy in his argument, but the Army and MID leadership had other functions in additional regions of concern from MID's inception, such as information-gathering in Europe, militia tracking within US borders, and cataloguing information in the division files. Archivist Elizabeth Bethel, assistant to the records supervisor of the War Records Office at the National Archives, published one of the first scholarly histories of the division in *Military Affairs* in April 1947. Only eight pages, the article provides a narrative of how MID came to be but is devoid of details of how MID related to the historical trends of the Gilded Age occurring around intelligence officers.[14] Bethel concentrates her efforts on the data management mission. Because she wrote to enlighten general readership about a limited time period in the organization's existence, her article is valuable more for its informational qualities rather than for a discussion of MID's purpose within US society and government.

Army institutions have also provided some helpful histories on MID. The US Army Center of Military History kept a detailed folder on events between 1884 and 1944 called the George W. Auxier Historical Manuscript File, named for the historian who maintained it in the 1940s. It comprises of organizational charts, personnel logs, funding information, and a document titled "Materials on the History of Military Intelligence in the U.S., 1884–1944." INSCOM historian John P. Finnegan wrote a prominent account of the Army's military intelligence programs in general, titled *Military History: A Picture History*. The volume employs historical pictures to enhance the narrative written for military intelligence specialists but does not detail the division's place in American society.[15] INSCOM command historian, Michael E. Bigelow, has written such informative articles as "Van Deman" and "A Short History of Army Intelligence." All these histories are meant to inform but not to detail MID's mercurial functions in relation to the society it serves.

US Marine Corps strategic intelligence historical accounts are almost nonexistent because the subject itself is not that robust. Nonetheless, there are a few notable secondary sources on the topic. The most valuable article and the most recent is Michael H. Decker and William Mackenzie's 2019 article for the *Marine Corps History*, "Birth and Early Years of Marine Corps Intelligence." Their main contention is that Marine Corps intelligence predates most accounts that cite the 1939 reorganization of HQMC and the creation of the "M-2" as the birth of Marine Corps Intelligence.[16] Another source is Laurence M. Nelson III's master's thesis "Innovation in Intelligence: An Analysis of U.S. Marine Corps Intelligence Modernization during the Occupation of Haiti, 1915–1934." Nelson briefly references military intelligence innovations and key players from the early years who would help form the Intelligence Section at Marine Corps headquarters. *A Brief History of Headquarters Marine Corps Staff Organization*, written by Kenneth W. Condit, Major John H. Johnstone, and Ella W. Nargele, provides context for how Marine Corps intelligence fits into the service's staff structure. Overall, the paucity of scholarship on Marine Corps strategic intelligence is striking, but secondary sources are only as good as the archival documents available. The Intelligence Section lacked the size and significance to leave much of a paper trail.

Military intelligence general histories are too few and have too wide of an aperture to be informative on strategic military intelligence missions. Most of these historians group ONI and MID within the larger intelligence communities past and present, alongside such organizations as the Secret Service, FBI, State Department analysts, the CIA, the Office of Strategic Services, and others. ONI and MID are inherently different agencies than the rest of the community. G. J. A. O'Toole briefly discussed ONI and MID as central repositories of information within a larger intelligence world of secret agents in his *A History of US Intelligence, Espionage, and Covert Action from the American Revolution to the CIA*. Nathan Miller's *Spying for America: The Hidden History of U.S. Intelligence* is helpful in contextualizing ONI and MID within the larger environment of American strategic intelligence but does not adequately describe their role in his chosen historical eras. In *Donovan and the CIA: A History of the Establishment of the Central Intelligence Agency*, famed CIA historian Thomas Troy depicts ONI and MID as on the one hand weak, ineffective organizations in the 1920s and 1930s, but necessary organizational steps for the formation of the ultimate U.S. strategic intelligence organization on the other.[17] Another prominent historian of the CIA, Rhodri Jeffreys-Jones, discussed ONI and MID in the context of spying leading up to the creation of the CIA. His research in *American Espionage: From Secret Service to CIA* is especially valuable for understanding strategic military intelligence's role in the Red Scare of 1919 and 1920.

Archival records provide the backbone of this research, but there are some significant firsthand accounts. Rear Admiral Alfred P. Niblack, a navalist and early reformer of our focus period, penned the first history of ONI in 1920. He originally intended the essay "ONI: Its History and Aims" as a state of the office address, but it essentially separates the story of ONI between that of a more innocent, straightforward organization of the past and of a more complex, perhaps extralegal outfit in the post–World War I period. For his part, Captain Ellis M. Zacharias wrote *Secret*

Missions: The Story of an Intelligence Officer in 1946, an insightful look into the inner bureaucracy of the Department of the Navy from 1920 to 1945.

In the interwar and World War II periods, Rear Admiral Walter S. Anderson, Rear Admiral Harold C. Train, and Captain Alan G. Kirk directed ONI. Columbia University captured their accounts of the World War II era in oral history interviews in the early 1960s. Their recollections of office politics at ONI shed light on the organizational troubles the office had to overcome in finding and performing missions in the New Deal and World War II eras. Additionally, the Department of the Navy ordered its staffs to record the events of their office during World War II. *The U.S. Naval Administrative Histories of World War II*, specifically the four volumes of the "Office of Naval Intelligence," are an important resource for comprehending how the ONI staff reflected on their performance throughout the war.

In Army intelligence accounts, Colonel Arthur L. Wagner provided the first written American theory of military intelligence, a prescription for how to effectively manage the craft, in his 1893 book *The Service of Security and Information*. Major General Ralph H. Van Deman, also known as the "Father of Military Intelligence" and a protégé of Wagner's, wrote his Memoranda series at the end of the 1940s and early 1950s to chronical his extensive, illustrious career in Army intelligence. The memoirs help us understand how MID fit into the trends and events of the period. Finally, Lieutenant Colonel Walter C. Sweeney looked to capitalize on the advancements of Army intelligence during World War I, writing *Military Intelligence: A New Weapon in War*, which was acclaimed by his contemporaries. His book encapsulates the excitement of Army intelligence officers at a time they believed their craft had turned a corner to respectability and their representatives received a prominent seat on the general staff. But MID's positive reputation was short-lived in the period of the retreat from foreign entanglements, demobilization, and disillusion that marked America in the 1920s.

Hopefully, this work gives more richness to the small and incomplete historiography of strategic military intelligence organizations from 1882 to 1947. To build upon the scholarship, this writing attempts to shows how these organizations fit into the broader thread of American history. Additionally, it reveals the changing missions of strategic military intelligence organizations. Broadly, bureaucratic and societal demands forced their leaders to engage in more operational tasks near the end of the period.

Notes

Notes on Terminology

1. Jonathan M. House, *Military Intelligence: 1870–1991*, Research Guides in Military Studies 6 (Westport, CT: Greenwood Press, 1993), 2.
2. House, *Military Intelligence*, 3.
3. Henry H. Ransom, *Central Intelligence and National Security* (Cambridge, MA: Harvard University Press, 1958), 12, and House, *Military Intelligence*, 3.
4. House, *Military Intelligence*, 3.
5. House, *Military Intelligence*, 4.
6. Ransom, *Central Intelligence and National Security*, 13.

Introduction

1. US Naval Administrative Histories of World War II, Office of the Chief of Naval Operations, "Office of Naval Intelligence," 4 vols., Archives Branch, Naval History and Heritage Command, Washington, DC (hard copy) and Nimitz Library, United States Naval Academy, Annapolis, MD (microfiche), 1–2.
2. Louis Galambos, "Emerging Organizational Synthesis in Modern American History," *Business History Review* 44, no. 3 (Autumn 1970): 288.
3. John Patrick Finnegan, *Military History: A Picture History*, 2nd ed. (Fort Belvoir, VA: US Army, 1992), 2.
4. Marc B. Powe, "The Emergence of a War Department Intelligence Agency" (MA thesis, Kansas State University, 1974), 2.
5. Finnegan, *Picture History*, 2.
6. Colonel Bruce W. Bidwell, *History of the Military Intelligence Division, Department of the Army General Staff: 1775–1941* (Frederick, MD: University Publications of America, 1986), 56.
7. Nathan Miller, *Spying for America: The Hidden History of U.S. Intelligence* (New York: Paragon House, 1989), 160.
8. Powe, "Emergence," 4.
9. Bidwell, *History*, 23.
10. Edwin C. Fishel, "Myths That Never Die," *International Journal of Intelligence and Counterintelligence* 2, no. 1 (January 1988): 29.
11. Powe, "Emergence," 4.
12. Finnegan, *Picture History*, 3.

13. Stephen E. Ambrose, *Upton and the Army* (Baton Rouge: Louisiana State University Press, 1964), viii.

14. Captain Wyman H. Packard, USN (Ret.), *A Century of U.S. Naval Intelligence* (Washington, DC: Office of Naval Intelligence, 1996), 1.

15. Jeffery M. Dorwart, *Dorwart's History of the Office of Naval Intelligence: 1865–1945* (Annapolis, MD: Naval Institute Press, 2019), 9.

16. Dorwart, *Dorwart's History*, 11.

17. Dorwart, *Dorwart's History*, 14–15.

18. John Walker to William H. Hunt, August 10, 1881, container 1, John Grimes Walker Papers, Naval Historical Foundation Collection, Manuscript Division, Library of Congress, Washington, DC.

Chapter 1. 1882–1885: Emergence of ONI and MID

1. Walter Millis, *Arms and Men: A Study of American Military History* (New York: Mentor Books, 1956), 126.

2. Renowned American historian Robert H. Wiebe wrote extensively on this theme in his 1967 seminal work *The Search for Order: 1877–1920* (New York: Hill and Wang, 1967).

3. James L. Abrahamson, *America Arms for a New Century: The Making of a Great Military Power* (New York: Free Press, 1981), 47.

4. Captain Peter M. Swartz, "Looking Out Over the Promised Land: The U.S. Naval Institute Proceedings, 1880–1889," *U.S. Naval Institute Proceedings* 140, no. 6 (June 2014): 16. Swartz also noted that sail-powered ships were more prevalent in the American fleet, as sail power was a very economical propulsion system if one needed to get from Pensacola to all points east, south, and west.

5. Swartz, "Looking Out Over the Promised Land," 17.

6. Sidney E. Dean, "New Navy, New Power," *Naval History* 27, no. 1 (February 2013): 57.

7. Captain Wyman H. Packard, USN (Ret.), *A Century of U.S. Naval Intelligence* (Washington, DC: Office of Naval Intelligence, 1996), 2.

8. Captain J. M. Ellicott, "Theodorus Bailey Meyers Mason: Founder of the Office of Naval Intelligence," *U.S. Naval Institute Proceedings* 78, no. 3 (March 1952): 265.

9. Ellicott, "Theodorus Bailey Meyers Mason," 266.

10. Packard, *Century of U.S. Naval Intelligence*, 2.

11. Jeffery M. Dorwart, *Dorwart's History of the Office of Naval Intelligence: 1865–1945* (Annapolis, MD: Naval Institute Press, 2019), 17.

12. Peter Karsten, *The Naval Aristocracy: The Golden Age of Annapolis and the Emergence of Modern American Navalism* (New York: Free Press, 1972), 299–300.

13. Robert G. Angevine, "The Rise and Fall of the Office of Naval Intelligence, 1882–1892: A Technological Perspective," *Journal of Military History* 62, no. 2 (April 1998): 293.

14. For the full order see page 2 of Packard, *Century of U.S. Naval Intelligence*, 2.

15. James R. Green, "The First Sixty Years of the Office of Naval Intelligence" (MA thesis, American University, 1963), 5.

16. Packard, *Century of U.S. Naval Intelligence*, 2.

17. Dorwart, *Dorwart's History*, 17.

18. Dorwart, *Dorwart's History*, 17.

19. Packard, *Century of U.S. Naval Intelligence*, 3.

20. Packard, *Century of U.S. Naval Intelligence*, 18–19.

21. Brian T. Crumley, "The Naval Attaché System of the United States, 1882–1914" (PhD diss., Texas A&M University, 2002), 28.

22. French E. Chadwick to John Walker, October 28, 1882, Records of the Office of the Chief of Naval Operations, record group 38, entry 90, stack 10WR, row 12, compartment 12, shelf 1, Naval Attaché London, vol. 1, National Archives, Washington, DC. The handwriting is almost illegible, but what is important in Chadwick's report is how promptly he started his duties upon arrival in London.

23. Crumley, "Naval Attaché System," 29.

24. Rear Admiral Alfred P. Niblack, "The History and Aims of the Office of Naval Intelligence," Ibiblio.org, 1920, 4, accessed May 23, 2019, http://www.ibiblio.org/hyperwar/NHC/History-Aims-ONI-1920/History-Aims-ONI-1920.html.

25. "A Busy Diplomatic Attaché," *Evening Star*, September 2, 1884, 1.

26. Rear Admiral A. G. Berry, "The Beginning of the Office of Naval Intelligence," *Proceedings of the United States Naval Institute* 63, no. 1 (January 1937): 102.

27. Biographies in ONI Register of Personnel, 1882–1918, Records of the Office of the Chief of Naval Operations, record group 38, entry 120, stack 10WR, row 13, compartment 5, shelf 4, vol. 1, National Archives Building, Washington, DC. The ONI Register is an undated logbook without a specific author. It most likely resided in ONI spaces for decades with clerks filling out personnel entries as officers came and went. Because ONI was not a large institution before World War I, the registry is quite small. There are only 144 officers listed as working at ONI between 1882 and 1918.

28. Berry, "Beginning of the Office of Naval Intelligence," 102.

29. Berry, "Beginning of the Office of Naval Intelligence," 102.

30. John Walker to Washington I. Chambers, October 16, 1882, container 1, Washington I. Chambers Papers, Naval Historical Foundation Collection, Manuscript Division, Library of Congress (hereafter Chambers Papers).

31. Theodore B. M. Mason to Albert Gleaves, November 6, 1882, container 6, Albert Gleaves Papers, Naval Historical Foundation Collection, Manuscript Division, Library of Congress.

32. Theodore B. M. Mason to Washington I. Chambers, December 9, 1882, container 1, Chambers Papers.

33. Theodore B. M. Mason to Washington I. Chambers, February 9, 1883, container 1, Chambers Papers.

34. Dorwart, *Dorwart's History*, 19.

35. Ensign Charles C. Rogers, "Naval Intelligence," *Proceedings of the United States Naval Institute* 9 no. 4 (April 1883): 659.

36. Rogers, "Naval Intelligence," 659–660.

37. Rogers, "Naval Intelligence," 671.

38. Rogers, "Naval Intelligence," 680–689.

39. Rogers, "Naval Intelligence," 690.

40. John Walker to William S. Sims, March 19, 1885, container 12, William S. Sims Papers, Naval Historical Foundation Collection, Manuscript Division, Library of Congress.

41. Charles M. Thomas to Washington I. Chambers, April 3, 1884, container 1, Chambers Papers.

42. Randy C. Goguen, "U.S. Navy Owes T.B.M. MASON," *Naval History* 19, no. 3 (June 2005): 29.

43. Richard Deacon, *The Silent War: A History of Western Naval Intelligence* (London: Grafton, 1988), 44–45.

44. Swartz, "Looking Out Over the Promised Land," 17.

45. Commodore Stephen B. Luce, "War Schools," *Proceedings of the United States Naval Institute* 9, no. 4 (December 1883): 634.

46. John Walker to Stephen B. Luce, May 3, 1884, container 8, Stephen B. Luce Papers, Naval Historical Foundation Collection, Manuscript Division, Library of Congress.

47. Mahan stated, "The College will produce good results in three principal directions. 1st. There will be a small body of selected officers who, during the time they are attached to the College, will be giving their whole attention and abilities to the study of naval war and the method of carrying it on; considering both the general problems of war and the special interests and dangers of the U.S. 2nd. The results of the extensive reading and thought, thus ensured by the organization of the college, will be imparted in a condensed methodized form to classes of officers yearly ordered. . . . 3rd. Besides the officers specially attached to the College as students and instructors, particular subjects of investigation are assigned to others stationed elsewhere throughout the naval service. The result of this is to promote and stimulate thought and the study of the Art of War by men who will have to wage it, if the United States is ever engaged in a naval war." Alfred T. Mahan, "What Is the Use of the Naval War College," box 3, William D. Puleston Papers, Archives Branch, Naval History and Heritage Command, Washington, DC.

48. "Army and Navy News: Orders to Officers—A Naval Office of Intelligence—Other Matters," *New York Times*, March 26, 1882, 2.

49. US Department of the Navy, "Annual Report of the Secretary of the Navy," Washington, DC, US Government Printing Office, 1884, 164. Secretary Chandler requested $10,000 "for the publication of current technical information for the instruction of the personnel of the Navy and mercantile marine," $900 for the salary of a copyist, and $660 for a laborer.

50. *North American*, editorial, June 27, 1884, 1.
51. Berry, "Beginning of the Office of Naval Intelligence," 102.
52. Berry, "Beginning of the Office of Naval Intelligence," 102.
53. Rear Admiral Albert Gleaves, *Life and Letters of Rear Admiral Stephen B. Luce, U.S. Navy* (New York: Putnam, 1925), 172–173.
54. Rear Admiral Seaton Schroeder, *A Half Century of Naval Service* (New York: D. Appleton, 1922), 171.
55. Rear Admiral Richard Wainwright, "The General Board," *Proceedings of the United States Naval Institute* 48, no. 2 (February 1922): 192.
56. Ellicott, "Theodorus Bailey Meyers Mason," 267.
57. Marc B. Powe, "The Emergence of a War Department Intelligence Agency" (master's thesis, Kansas State University, 1974), 14–15.
58. Powe, "Emergence of a War Department Intelligence Agency," 15.
59. "The Army Bureau of Intelligence: Steps That Have Been Taken to Establish Such a Bureau," *Evening Star*, October 6, 1885, 1.
60. Some historians believe that the Army was just trying to match the Navy. Historian Elizabeth Bethel stated that the Department of War had not even thought about collecting and storing military information about foreign armies until one day in the fall of 1885. Specifically, one day Secretary of War William C. Endicott requested that Drum furnish him immediately with some information on a certain foreign army. Drum sheepishly replied that he did not have the information and that it would require some time to compile it, time the secretary did not have. Major General Ralph H. Van Deman wrote another account perpetuating this legend. In his telling, the secretary suggested to Drum to set up a bureau to collect, collate, and report military information to prevent such an embarrassment from occurring again. For his part, Admiral Berry described an incident at ONI in the fall of 1885: "One day General Drum (Adjutant General I think) visited the office and was shown all that had been done and how it was filed on the cards. He was surprised and expressed much pleasure, finally remarking that he did not believe that any officer in the Army knew anything about Mexico, except those who had served during the Mexican War." Elizabeth Bethel, "The Military Information Division: Origin of the Intelligence Division," *Military Affairs* 11 (April 1947): 17; Ralph H. Van Deman, "Memorandum," April 8, 1949, Records of the Army Staff, record group 319, entry 1071, stack 270, row 15, compartment 4, shelf 23, box 3, 4, National Archives at College Park, MD; Berry, "Beginning of the Office of Naval Intelligence," 102–103.
61. Robert G. Angevine, "Mapping the Northern Frontier: Canada and the Origins of the US Army's Military Information Division, 1885–1898," *Intelligence and National Security* 16, no. 3 (September 2001): 121–122.
62. James L. Gilbert, *World War I and the Origins of U.S. Military Intelligence* (Lanham, MD: Scarecrow Press, 2012), 8.
63. Angevine, "Mapping the Northern Frontier: Canada and the Origins of the US Army's Military Information Division, 1885–1898," 130.
64. Bethel, "Military Information Division," 17–18.

65. US Department of the Navy, "Annual Report of the Secretary of the Navy," Washington, DC, US Government Printing Office, 1885, 94. The salaries of all the clerks at ONI amounted to $1,560 in 1885. "and had simple missions": Missions such as counterintelligence, censorship, security, and others—all of which the public, the military establishment, and the organizations themselves debated as to whether they were essential strategic military intelligence duties—did not surface in these offices until later decades.

66. ONI personnel loved writing essays. Ten of the fifteen first prize winners for the *Proceedings* annual contest between 1882 and 1900 worked for ONI.

Chapter 2. 1885–1895: Growing Pains of ONI and MID

1. Richard Hofstadter, *The Age of Reform: From Bryan to F. D. R.* (New York: Knopf, 1955), 5.

2. Mark R. Shulman, *Navalism and the Emergence of American Sea Power, 1882–1893* (Annapolis, MD: Naval Institute Press, 1995), 2 and 7–8.

3. Peter Karsten, *The Naval Aristocracy: The Golden Age of Annapolis and the Emergence of Modern American Navalism* (New York: Free Press, 1972), 385.

4. Stephen E. Ambrose, *Upton and the Army* (Baton Rouge: Louisiana State University Press, 1964), 153–154.

5. Karsten, *Naval Aristocracy*, 296.

6. Captain J. M. Ellicott, "Theodorus Bailey Meyers Mason: Founder of the Office of Naval Intelligence," *U.S. Naval Institute Proceedings* 78, no. 3 (March 1952): 266.

7. Jeffery M. Dorwart, *Dorwart's History of the Office of Naval Intelligence: 1865–1945* (Annapolis, MD: Naval Institute Press, 2019), 25.

8. Dorwart, *Dorwart's History*, 25. Dorwart said that Colwell could be quite brooding, irreverent, and radical, while Buckingham was manageable but disparaging of the Navy.

9. Rear Admiral Seaton Schroeder, *A Half Century of Naval Service* (New York: D. Appleton, 1922), 171–172.

10. Captain Wyman H. Packard, USN (Ret.), *A Century of U.S. Naval Intelligence* (Washington, DC: Office of Naval Intelligence, 1996), 6.

11. Rear Admiral Albert Gleaves, *The Life of an American Sailor: Rear Admiral William Hemsley Emory* (New York: George Doran, 1923), 121.

12. Mark R. Shulman, "The Rise and Fall of American Naval Intelligence, 1882–1917," *Intelligence and National Security* 8, no. 2 (April 1993): 218.

13. Robert G. Angevine, "The Rise and Fall of the Office of Naval Intelligence, 1882–1892: A Technological Perspective," *Journal of Military History* 62, no. 2 (April 1998): 312.

14. Dorwart, *Dorwart's History*, 47.

15. Dorwart, *Dorwart's History*, 47.

16. Nathan Miller, *Spying for America: The Hidden History of U.S. Intelligence* (New York: Paragon House, 1989), 161–162.

17. Robert G. Angevine, "Mapping the Northern Frontier: Canada and the Origins of the US Army's Military Information Division, 1885–1898," *Intelligence and National Security* 16, no. 3 (September 2001): 127. Angevine's thesis was that MID was mainly created because of the Canada threat. Naturally, in his assessment of Taylor's selection, the historian would focus on the captain's Canada knowledge and deep suspicion of Great Britain's designs in North America. Canada was indeed important to MID's initial mission, but it was only part of MID's task in coming years. The choice of Taylor as division chief probably was due to Drum's broader hope for MID efficiency and stability. And it may have been that Drum just got along better with Taylor than Volkmar.

18. Order by R. C. Drum, April 12, 1889, Records of the War Department General and Special Staffs, record group 165, entry 65, microfilm M1024, file 639, roll 1, National Archives at College Park, MD.

19. Elizabeth Bethel, "The Military Information Division: Origin of the Intelligence Division," *Military Affairs* 11 (April 1947): 19.

20. Memorandum by Stephen B. Elkins, January 20, 1892, Records of the War Department General and Special Staffs, record group 165, entry 65, microfilm M1024, file 639, roll 1, National Archives at College Park, MD, 1.

21. Memorandum by Stephen B. Elkins, January 20, 1892, 2.

22. 23rd Cong. Rec. H2273 (daily ed. March 21,1892).

23. Outhwaite convinced Holman that MID needed a clerk as "this clerk is necessary, because this information which the bureau collects comes from all quarters of the globe. It is information relative to the organization of armies in every country, and it comes in different languages. This clerk is supposed and expected to be a master of three or four or more of these languages, so as to be able to translate and collate this information." 23rd Cong. Rec., H2273–2274 (daily ed. March 21, 1892).

24. Bethel, "Military Information Division," 20.

25. Confidential report by J.B. Babcock, "Plan for the Systematic Work and Subdivision into Sections of the Military Information Division, Adjutant General's Office," September 28, 1893, Records of the War Department General and Special Staffs, record group 165, entry 65, microfilm M1024, file 639, roll 1, National Archives at College Park, MD, 2.

26. Babcock, "Plan for the Systematic Work and Subdivision into Sections," 4–5.

27. Babcock, "Plan for the Systematic Work and Subdivision into Sections," 6.

28. Marc B. Powe, "The Emergence of a War Department Intelligence Agency" (MA thesis, Kansas State University, 1974), 28.

29. Benjamin H. Buckingham to John Walker, December 17, 1885, Records of the Office of the Chief of Naval Operations, record group 38, entry 90, stack 10WR, row 12, compartment 12, shelf 1, Naval Attaché Paris volume, National Archives Building, Washington, DC.

30. Benjamin H. Buckingham to John Walker, December 18, 1885, Records of the Office of the Chief of Naval Operations, record group 38, entry 90, stack

10WR, row 12, compartment 12, shelf 1, Naval Attaché Paris volume, National Archives Building, Washington, DC.

31. An Act Making Appropriations for the Naval Service for Fiscal Year Ending June Thirtieth, Eighteen Hundred and Eighty-Nine, and for Other Purposes, Chapter 991 (September 7, 1888).

32. In 1892 and 1893, Sargent picked up Berlin responsibilities, reflecting the realization by the US Navy that a naval attaché should report on the Triple Alliance formed by Germany, Italy, and Austria-Hungary in 1882.

33. Dorwart, *Dorwart's History*, 38.

34. 20th Cong. Rec. H169 (daily ed. February 28, 1889).

35. Dorwart, *Dorwart's History*, 38.

36. Gleaves, *Life of an American Sailor*, 123.

37. Gleaves, *Life of an American Sailor*, 124.

38. Dorwart, *Dorwart's History*, 49.

39. Soley told Chadwick that the CIO's request to increase the allowance of naval attachés from $100 to $125 would not be honored, as "the condition of the appropriation 'Pay Miscellaneous 1893,' from which the allowance is paid, will not admit of the increased expenditure recommended." James R. Soley to French E. Chadwick, December 30, 1892, Naval Records Collection of the Office of Naval Records and Library, record group 45, entry I-18 277, stack 11WR, row 10, compartment 4, shelf 2, vol. 1, National Archives Building, Washington, DC.

40. 19th Cong. Rec. H5332 (daily ed. June 16, 1888).

41. An Act Making Appropriations for the Naval Service for Fiscal Year Ending June Thirtieth, Eighteen Hundred and Eighty-Nine, and for Other Purposes, Chap. 1027, 483 (September 22, 1888).

42. Instructions by William C. Endicott, March 2, 1889, George W. Auxier Historical Manuscript File.

43. John F. Votaw, "United States Military Attachés, 1885–1919: The American Army Matures in the International Arena" (PhD diss., Temple University, 1991), iv. Only a few of the 207 officers who served as attachés in the first three decades were career agents overseas.

44. Ellicott, "Theodorus Bailey Meyers Mason," 267.

45. Ellicott, "Theodorus Bailey Meyers Mason," 267.

46. Memorandum by R. C. Drum, November 13, 1886, Records of the War Department General and Special Staffs, record group 165, entry 65, microfilm M1024, file 639, roll 1, National Archives at College Park, MD.

47. Circular by Redfield Proctor, April 19, 1889, Records of the War Department General and Special Staffs, record group 165, entry 65, microfilm M1024, file 639, roll 1, National Archives at College Park, MD.

48. Colonel Bruce W. Bidwell, *History of the Military Intelligence Division, Department of the Army General Staff: 1775–1941* (Frederick, MD: University Publications of America, 1986), 56.

49. Powe, "Emergence of a War Department Intelligence Agency," 20.

50. Headquarters of the Army, Adjutant Generals Office, General Order no. 23 (March 18, 1892).

51. US War Department, "Annual Report of the Secretary of War," Washington, DC, US Government Printing Office, 1892, 7.

52. Memorandum by Robert Williams, May 7, 1892, Records of the War Department General and Special Staffs, record group 165, entry 65, microfilm M1024, file 639, roll 1, National Archives at College Park, MD.

53. Angevine, "Mapping the Northern Frontier," 124–125.

54. Bidwell, *History of the Military Intelligence Division*, 60.

55. Dorwart, *Dorwart's History*, 42.

56. Dorwart, *Dorwart's History*, 43.

57. "The Navy in Excitement: Lively Times in All Branches at the Department," *New York Times*, January 15, 1892, 1.

58. Charles O. Paullin, "A Half Century of Naval Administration in America, 1861–1911," *Proceedings of the United States Naval Institute* 39, no. 4 (December 1913): 1498.

59. Rear Admiral Stephen B. Luce, "Naval Administration," *Proceedings of the United States Naval Institute* 14, no. 3 (July 1888): 577.

60. Dorwart, *Dorwart's History*, 40.

61. US Department of the Navy, "Annual Report of the Secretary of the Navy," Washington, DC, US Government Printing Office, 1889, 299.

62. Shulman, *Navalism*, 32.

63. Shulman, *Navalism*, 1–2.

64. Commander French E. Chadwick, "Naval Department Organization," *Proceedings of the United States Naval Institute* 20, no. 3 (July 1894): 493.

65. Chadwick, "Naval Department Organization," 499.

66. Captain Arthur L. Wagner, *The Service of Security and Information* (Kansas City: Hudson-Kimberley, 1893), 2.

67. Wagner, *Service of Security and Information*, 3.

68. Wagner, *Service of Security and Information*, 5.

69. John Walker to Stephen B. Luce, July 18, 1887, container 1, John Grimes Walker Papers, Naval Historical Foundation Collection, Manuscript Division, Library of Congress.

70. Angevine, "Mapping the Northern Frontier," 125.

71. US Department of the Navy, Annual Report of the Secretary of War, Washington, DC, US Government Printing Office, 1889, 7. In his annual report to Congress, Secretary Tracy praised ONI's work.

72. Dorwart, *Dorwart's History*, 40.

73. US Department of the Navy, "Annual Report of the Secretary of the Navy," Washington, DC, US Government Printing Office, 1890, 43.

74. US War Department, "Annual Report of the Secretary of War, 1892–1908," Washington, DC, US Government Printing Office, 1892, 8.

75. General Kelton asked for more office rooms in Washington, DC, local buildings because it was "absolutely necessary for the full development of the

important work of the division of military information." US War Department, "Annual Report of the Secretary of War," Washington, DC, US Government Printing Office, 1892, 195.

76. US War Department, "Annual Report of the Secretary of War," Washington, DC, US Government Printing Office, 1893, 24.

77. US War Department, "Annual Report of the Secretary of War," 1893, 168.

78. Circular by Daniel S. Lamont, January 27, 1894, George W. Auxier Historical Manuscript File.

79. US War Department, "Annual Report of the Secretary of War," Washington, DC, US Government Printing Office, 1894, 22 and 182.

80. The 1894 Appropriations Act read, "For contingent expense of the military information division, Adjutant General's Office, and of the military attachés at the United States embassies and legations abroad, to be expended under the direction of the Secretary of War, three thousand six hundred and forty dollars." An Act Making Appropriations for the Support of the Army for Fiscal Year Ending June Thirtieth, Eighteen Hundred and Ninety-Five, and for Other Purposes, Chap. 228, 243, 53rd Cong. (August 6, 1894).

81. "Rams and Big Guns: Observations of United States Naval Officers in the South American War," *Saint Louis Daily Globe-Democrat*, October 5, 1885, 14.

82. "Navies of the Old World: How Our Government Obtains Information as to the Building of War-Ships," *Indianapolis Journal*, October 16, 1885, 1.

83. "Bureau of Naval Intelligence," *New York Times*, editorial, July 4, 1889, 4.

84. "Bureau of Naval Intelligence," 4.

85. "Another Army Dispute: Secretary Elkins' Decision Concerning the Inspection of Militia," *North Platte Tribune*, May 29, 1892, 1.

86. "Not Satisfied with Its Work: Mr. Lamont to Overhaul the Bureau of Military Information," *New York Times*, January 12, 1894, 9.

87. "Not Satisfied with Its Work," 9.

88. "German Army Organization: A Valuable Work upon This Topic Issued at Washington," *North American*, May 24, 1894, 8.

89. "The Armies of Europe: Official Figures of Interest Compiled by the War Department," *Goodland Republic*, April 12, 1894, 1.

90. Shulman, *Navalism*, 31.

Chapter 3. 1895–1900: Operational Tests for ONI and MID

1. Walter LaFeber, *The New Empire: An Interpretation of American Expansion 1860–1898* (Ithaca, NY: Cornell University Press, 1963), 64.

2. LaFeber, *New Empire*, vii.

3. Ernest R. May, *From Imperialism to Isolation, 1898–1919* (New York: Macmillan, 1964), 32.

4. "Capt. Mahan's Duty: His Assignment Will Be Made Congenial in This City," *Evening Star*, April 10, 1895, 1.

5. Captain Damon E. Cummings, *Admiral Richard Wainwright and the United States Fleet* (Washington, DC: Government Printing Office, 1962), 67.

6. James R. Green, "The First Sixty Years of the Office of Naval Intelligence" (MA thesis, American University, 1963), 30. The quotation came from the book *The Letters of Theodore Roosevelt*, ed. Elting E. Morison (Cambridge, MA: Harvard University Press, 1951).

7. Roosevelt praised Sims, stating, "Once more the Department's attention is called to the energy, zeal, and intelligence that you have displayed in the collection of so much valuable information in so short of time, meriting in a high degree the confidence reposed in you." Handwritten in the margins Roosevelt added, "I am very much pleased; you have done well; your report and enclosures were as interesting as anything I have recently read." Theodore Roosevelt to William S. Sims, December 2, 1897, container 12, William S. Sims Papers, Naval Historical Foundation Collection, Manuscript Division, Library of Congress.

8. Arthur L. Wagner Memorandum to the Adjutant General, September 28, 1897, Records of the War Department General and Special Staffs, record group 165, entry 65, stack 370, row 75, compartment 16, shelf 5, box 109, National Archives at College Park, MD, 6.

9. Arthur L. Wagner Memorandum to the Adjutant General, September 28, 1897, 7.

10. Wagner to the Adjutant General, September 28, 1897, 8.

11. Todd R. Brereton, "An Impractical Sort of Officer: The Army Career of Arthur L. Wagner, 1875–1905" (PhD diss., Texas A&M University, 1994), 6.

12. Elting E. Morison, *Admiral Sims and the Modern American Navy* (Boston: Houghton Mifflin, 1942), 40.

13. Singer praised Sims for his diligence. He told Sims, "Permit me to congratulate you on the general excellence and thoroughness of your reports, not only the regular Intelligence Reports, in which the details are so carefully worked out, but also your grasp of the salient points of general interest to the service and this office." Frederick Singer to William S. Sims, February 21, 1895, container 12, William S. Sims Papers, Naval Historical Foundation Collection, Manuscript Division, Library of Congress (hereafter Sims Papers).

14. Frederick Singer to William S. Sims, April 4, 1896, container 3, Sims Papers.

15. Kimball said, "Wainwright asked me about future men for this shop, and I told him *you were probably the best man in the Service for work here* if your eyes held out. . . . You can probably have any desk you choose and I think the work would amuse and interest you. Please let me know your wishes and especially when you would like to come, if you wish this duty." W. M. Kimball to William S. Sims, April 8, 1896, container 3, Sims Paper.

16. Sims wrote in the corner of the letter as a note to himself that he declined this invitation and the ONI requests before it. He also wondered where Kimball got the rumor that his eyes were not well. And in an uncomplimentary statement as to the reputation of ONI, Sims wrote on Kimball's letter, "The Intelligence

Office is probably hard up for men who will work. I am not formally acquainted with Mr. Kimball, and barely know Wainwright (Chief Int. Officer)." W. M. Kimball to William S. Sims, April 8, 1896.

17. Albert P. Niblack to Richard Wainwright, September 21, 1896, Naval Records Collection of the Office of Naval Records and Library, record group 45, entry I-18 280, stack 11WR, row 10, compartment 4, shelf 4, vol. 1, National Archives Building, Washington, DC.

18. Cummings, *Admiral Richard Wainwright*, 68–69.

19. Green, "First Sixty Years," 24.

20. William S. Sims to John D. Long, March 10, 1898, Naval Records Collection of the Office of Naval Records and Library, record group 45, entry 1–18 60, stack 11WR, row 6, compartment 8, shelf 3/4, vol. 1, National Archives and Research Administration, National Archives Building, Washington, DC. Sims reported on March 10 how Spanish naval officers tried to push an English ship-building firm to speed up a contract, to which Sims advocated diplomatic action to prevent the Spanish from succeeding, or there would be an "exorbitant price."

21. Sims said in the cable, "Have received information to the effect that the Spanish senior naval officer constructor at Paris yesterday confidentially expressed opinion as follows: 'The United States vessels not well armed, not well drilled. The Spanish ships much more efficient, they could secure an important victory, they assume that Cuba is lost, in any event will not be defended. They would attack coasts as soon as war was declared, inflicting penalty, as much damage as possible, not in expectation of successful termination of the war.'" Cable by William S. Sims, March 25, 1898, Records of the Office of the Chief of Naval Operations, record group 38, entry 100, stack 10WR, row 13, compartment 1, shelf 3, box 1, National Archives Building, Washington, DC.

22. Jeffery M. Dorwart, *Dorwart's History of the Office of Naval Intelligence: 1865–1945* (Annapolis, MD: Naval Institute Press, 2019), 61.

23. Cummings, *Admiral Richard Wainwright*, 77.

24. Captain Wyman H. Packard, USN (Ret.), *A Century of U.S. Naval Intelligence* (Washington, DC: Office of Naval Intelligence, 1996), 383.

25. Dorwart, *Dorwart's History*, 56–57.

26. "Not Unprepared for War: Coast Defenses in Better Condition Than Supposed," *New York Times*, December 19, 1895, 1.

27. Patrick E. McGinty, "Intelligence and the Spanish American War" (PhD diss., Georgetown University, 1981), 134. McGinty stated that MID had been unfairly criticized or even overlooked by many historians of the war because the Army itself did not prepare as well for a contest with Spain. McGinty erroneously separated the MID and the Army in this instance; MID had an important role in the Army's preparations by aiding in war plans.

28. Brereton, "An Impractical Sort of Officer," 126.

29. Later in his remarkable career, he described the inadequate physical spaces of the office: "At that time the office occupied three rooms on the main

floor of the old State, War, and Navy Building almost directly opposite the main entrance of the building." Ralph H. Van Deman, Memorandum, April 8, 1949, Records of the Army Staff, record group 319, entry 1071, stack 270, row 15, compartment 4, shelf 23, box 3, National Archives at College Park, MD, 3.

30. Elizabeth Bethel, "The Military Information Division: Origin of the Intelligence Division," *Military Affairs* 11 (April 1947): 24.

31. Marc B. Powe, "The Emergence of a War Department Intelligence Agency" (MA thesis, Kansas State University, 1974), 27–28.

32. Captain Thomas B. Mott, "The Organization and Function of a Bureau of Military Intelligence," *Journal of the Military Service Institution* 32, no. 122 (March–April 1903): 185.

33. Memorandum (unattributed), February 25, 1898, Records of the War Department General and Special Staffs, record group 165, entry 65, microfilm M1024, file 639, roll 1, National Archives at College Park, MD. Wagner changed the name of the outdated "Frontiers Section" to "Interiors Section" and assigned more officers to the "Military Progress Section," the MID branch that analyzed foreign information.

34. Michael E. Bigelow, "Van Deman," *Military Intelligence* 16, no. 4 (December 1990): 38.

35. Van Deman, memorandum, April 8, 1949, 4–5.

36. Historian Marc B. Powe commented, "Because there was no tradition in the American Army for systematic intelligence work, particularly not at the War Department, it did not occur to either the Commanding General, Nelson A. Miles, or the Secretary of War, Russell A. Alger, to direct MID to collect *any* information on Cuba." Powe, "Emergence of a War Department Intelligence Agency," 30.

37. Powe, "Emergence of a War Department Intelligence Agency," 31.

38. James L. Gilbert, *World War I and the Origins of U.S. Military Intelligence* (Lanham, MD: Scarecrow Press, 2012), 9.

39. Dorwart, *Dorwart's History*, 53.

40. Dorwart, *Dorwart's History*, 55.

41. G.J.A. O'Toole, *Honorable Treachery: A History of US Intelligence, Espionage, and Covert Action from the American Revolution to the CIA* (New York: Atlantic Monthly Press, 1991), 186–187.

42. George M. Wheeler, "Necessity for a General Staff," *Cosmopolitan*, August 1898, 464. In the 1890s, Army officers occasionally penned articles for a journal or magazine lamenting the lack of central authority in the Army institution. Major George M. Wheeler of the US Army Corps of Engineers did so in this article stating that, unlike all Continental armies, the Army lacked a general staff.

43. Brereton, "An Impractical Sort of Officer," 129.

44. Powe, "Emergence of a War Department Intelligence Agency," 31–32.

45. The secretary concluded, "The Intelligence Office is in a highly efficient condition. It has been most carefully and ably managed by the present officer in

charge and his predecessors, and is believed to be equal if not superior to any similar office abroad. It would be very hard to exaggerate its importance." US Department of the Navy, "Annual Report of the Secretary of the Navy," Washington, DC, 1896, 48–49.

46. Green, "First Sixty Years," 32. The author describes incidents where Roosevelt wrote unclassified letters to Long or ONI staffers containing secret information.

47. Dorwart, *Dorwart's History*, 55.

48. Theodore Roosevelt to William S. Sims, August 19, 1897, container 12, Sims Papers.

49. Morison, *Admiral Sims*, 50.

50. Roosevelt wrote, "Lieutenant-Commander Wainwright, while in charge of the Office of Naval Intelligence, has established a standard of faithful and intelligent work which I can say quite sincerely I do not believe can be surpassed by any incumbent who may hereafter hold the position, no matter what his zeal and ability. It would be impossible to overestimate the afficiancy [sic] with which Lieutenant-Commander Wainwright has performed his duties. . . . Not only has Mr. Wainwright fulfilled all the duties proper to his position in a way that left nothing to be required of the most exacting, but he has also shown a grasp and broad knowledge of the needs of the service and of the country, which have made him an invaluable adviser in all matters affecting the larger policies of the Department." Theodore Roosevelt to Richard Wainwright, November 6, 1897, Theodore Roosevelt Papers, Series 2: Letterpress Copybooks, 1897–1916, vol. 3, 1897, Oct. 15–Nov. 29, image 219–220, Manuscript Division, Library of Congress.

51. Theodore Roosevelt to Richard Wainwright, November 6, 1897, and Richard Wainwright to Theodore Roosevelt, November 10, 1897, Theodore Roosevelt Papers, Series 1: Letters and Related Material, 1759–1919; 1759, Aug. –1898, May, image 886, Manuscript Division, Library of Congress. Roosevelt flattered Wainwright with the attention; Wainwright told the go-getter politician so in a letter four days later.

52. US War Department, "Annual Report of the Secretary of War," Washington, DC, US Government Printing Office, 1895, 184.

53. Powe, "Emergence of a War Department Intelligence Agency," 27.

54. US War Department, "Annual Report of the Secretary of War," Washington, DC, US Government Printing Office, 1897, 16.

55. US War Department, "Annual Report of the Secretary of War," 1897, 215–216.

56. "Keeping Tabs of Navies All Over the World: Not a Vessel Moving in the Remotest Seas Escapes the Vigilance of the Office of Naval Intelligence," *Washington Times*, June 23, 1895, 3.

57. "Keeping Tabs of Navies All Over the World," 3.

58. "Spain's Navy: Two Strong Additions to Her Fighting Force," *Saint Paul Globe*, December 27, 1896, 1. The newspaper commented on how powerful these ships were compared to US naval assets.

59. "Quieter Yesterday: Less 'War' Excitement at the National Capitol," *Kansas City Journal*, March 14, 1898, 1.

60. "Working Day and Night: No Cessation of the Preparation for War," *Sun*, March 23, 1898, 1.

61. "Spain's Flotilla in a Gale: The Scattered Boats Put in at the Cape Verde Islands," *Sun*, April 3, 1898, 1. This article reported the arrival of the first section of a Spanish torpedo boat flotilla in St. Vincent in the Cape Verde Islands.

62. Associated Press, "Waiting the Message," *Los Angeles Herald*, April 10, 1898, 4. The Associated Press story said the naval board met again on April 10.

63. "Diplomats Talk: Navy Department Prepares for the War," *Herald* (Los Angeles), April 1, 1898, 1.

64. "Spain's Sea Strength: Col. Wagner Issues a Compilation of Her Available Naval Force—Speed and Armament," *New York Times*, April 3, 1898, 1 and "Spain's Flotilla in a Gale: The Scattered Boats Put in at the Cape Verde Islands," 1. The *Sun* commented, "Credit for the information and cuts is given to the Office of Naval Intelligence, Commander Richardson Clover, Chief Intelligence Officer. The pamphlet was compiled under the direction of Lieut.-Col. A. L. Wagner, Assistant Adjutant General and Chief of the Division of Military Information."

65. The *Sun* credited Clover as "one of the most earnest and active worker in the preparations for putting the navy into condition for a hostile emergency." "Assigned to the Bancroft: Commander Clover's Request for Sea Duty Is Complied With," *Sun*, April 8, 1898, 1.

66. Dorwart, *Dorwart's History*, 62.

67. US Department of the Navy, "Annual Report of the Secretary of the Navy," Washington, DC, US Government Printing Office, 1898, 374.

68. John R. Bartlett, "Watching for the Enemy in the Spanish War," *Century Illustrated Magazine*, October 1901, 907.

69. Packard, *Century of U.S. Naval Intelligence*, 383.

70. "Commander Mason Dead," *Salt Lake Herald*, October 16, 1899, 1, and Randy C. Goguen, "U.S. Navy Owes T.B.M. MASON," *Naval History* 19, no. 3 (June 2005): 30. ONI Command Historian Goguen commented on his legacy: "Although he died prematurely, Mason lived long enough to see his life's work and dream for his beloved service fulfilled. Just as he had envisioned in his 1876 *Proceedings* article, over the course of three decades he helped the Navy ascend from decrepitude to ride the waves of vindication with a great victory over Spain."

71. "Navy Intelligence Office," *Atchison Daily Globe*, February 3, 1899, 1.

72. Bartlett recalled, "Not long after I went to Washington a messenger came into my office and said: 'The compliments of the commissary general of subsistence of the army to Captain Bartlett, and can he tell him of some place where he can hire a Swedish nursegirl.' This is the answer that was sent back: 'Captain Bartlett's compliments to the commissary general of subsistence of the army, and he knows nothing about Swedish nurse girls, although he can tell him a lot about

army transport'." Captain Bartlett explained that the Navy once had a naval board on transports, which had collected information regarding vessels available for us as transports and the best ways to fit them out. The Army never called for this information however, and he feared his message was misunderstood. "Navy Intelligence Office," 1.

73. Brereton, "Impractical Sort of Officer," 136.

74. Powe, "Emergence of a War Department Intelligence Agency," 32.

75. Dorwart, *Dorwart's History*, 59.

76. John D. Long to William S. Sims and William H. Beehler, May 5, 1898, General Records of the Department of the Navy, record group 80, entry PC-31 194, stack 11WR, row 17, compartment 22, shelf 2, vol. 2, National Archives Building, Washington, DC.

77. Sims wrote, "The Spanish military attaché stated to French newspaper editors that the fleet from Cape Verde Islands, at Canary Islands and will remain until fleet from Cadiz, Spain is ready, in about one month. This is the general opinion here." William S. Sims to Theodore Roosevelt, May 7, 1898, Naval Records Collection of the Office of Naval Records and Library, record group 45, entry 1–18 60, stack 11WR, row 6, compartment 8, shelf 3/4, vol. 1, National Archives Building, Washington, DC.

78. Nathan Miller, *Spying for America: The Hidden History of U.S. Intelligence* (New York: Paragon House, 1989), 171.

79. Dorwart, *Dorwart's History*, 63.

80. Packard, *Century of U.S. Naval Intelligence, 384*.

81. Dorwart, *Dorwart's History*, 66.

82. Powe, "Emergence of a War Department Intelligence Agency," 33.

83. US Department of the Navy, "Annual Report of the Secretary of the Navy," 1898, 374.

84. US Department of the Navy, "Annual Report of the Secretary of the Navy," 1898, 374.

85. US Department of the Navy, "Annual Report of the Secretary of the Navy," 1898, 375.

86. US Department of the Navy, "Annual Report of the Secretary of the Navy," 1898, 377.

87. US Department of the Navy, "Annual Report of the Secretary of the Navy," 1898, 379.

88. US Department of the Navy, "Annual Report of the Secretary of the Navy," 1898, 379.

89. US Department of the Navy, "Annual Report of the Secretary of the Navy," 1898, 53.

90. "New Naval Regulations," *Anaconda Standard*, December 11, 1898, 1.

91. When William H. Beehler received orders to be the naval attaché to Berlin and Rome the Navy allotted him $150 per month for "the extraordinary expenses to which you will be subjected, by reason of your duties at Naval Attaché, and is to be considered as additional to the ordinary travelling and other expenses that

may be allowed." But this amount was a mere pittance of what he would half to spend per month. Arent S. Crowninshield to William H. Beehler, January 27, 1899, Records of the Office of the Chief of Naval Operations, record group 38, entry 90, stack 10WR, row 12, compartment 12, shelf 1, Naval Attaché Berlin, Rome, and Saint Petersburg volume, National Archives Building, Washington, DC.

92. Dorwart, *Dorwart's History*, 67.

93. Dorwart, *Dorwart's History*, 67.

94. Corbin wrote, "Recent events have demonstrated that our geographical isolation does not exempt us from foreign war, and that to neglect the employment of every known expedient for keeping abreast of the world's progress in the military art would be neglect of what is due the best interests of the people." US War Department, "Annual Report of the Secretary of War," Washington, DC, US Government Printing Office, 1898, 281–283.

95. Powe, "Emergence of a War Department Intelligence Agency," 33.

96. Robert H. Wiebe, *The Search for Order: 1877–1920* (New York: Hill and Wang, 1967), 241.

97. David F. Trask, *The War with Spain in 1898* (New York: Macmillan, 1981), 486.

Chapter 4. 1900–1915: The Nadir of ONI and MID

1. Michael McGerr, *A Fierce Discontent: The Rise and Fall of the Progressive Movement in America* (New York: Oxford University Press, 2003), xv.

2. Beverly Gage, *The Day Wall Street Exploded: A Story of America in Its First Age of Terror* (New York: Oxford University Press, 2009), 8.

3. McGerr, *Fierce Discontent*, xiv–xv.

4. Robert H. Wiebe, *The Search for Order: 1877–1920* (New York: Hill and Wang, 1967), xiii–xiv.

5. James L. Abrahamson, *America Arms for a New Century: The Making of a Great Military Power* (New York: Free Press, 1981), xiii–xiv.

6. Samuel Haber, *Efficiency and Uplift: Scientific Management in the Progressive Era, 1890–1920* (Chicago: University of Chicago Press, 1964), x.

7. Abrahamson, *America Arms for a New Century*, xiv.

8. Ronald J. Barr, *The Progressive Army: U.S. Army and Command and Administration, 1870–1914* (New York: St. Martin's Press, 1998), ix–x.

9. The *Ladies Home Journal*, a representative publication of a cross-section of American pop culture of 1903, presented a world primer for the housewife that stated, "The talk of the world is of trade or of lifting up the unfortunate masses. This change in the thought of mankind may be fairly credited to the United States. We have stood for peace. We have stood for work. We have stood for philanthropy. We have stood for the well-being of the man who toils." "The World and His Wife: A Popular Explanation of the Affairs of To-Day," *Ladies' Home Journal*, June 1903, 14.

10. The article specifically spoke about ONI in encyclopedic terms: "Our Government is fast forging ahead as a great naval power. A few years ago it was sixth in the list of nations in the fighting strength of its ships. In an official report made by Captain Sigsbee, Chief of the Office of Naval Intelligence, it was pointed out that we shall soon stand third." "World and His Wife," 14.

11. Marc B. Powe, "The Emergence of a War Department Intelligence Agency" (MA thesis, Kansas State University, 1974), 34.

12. Barr, *Progressive Army*, 196.

13. Jeffery M. Dorwart, *Dorwart's History of the Office of Naval Intelligence: 1865–1945* (Annapolis, MD: Naval Institute Press, 2019), 69.

14. US Department of the Navy, "Annual Report of the Secretary of the Navy," Washington, DC, US Government Printing Office, 1898, 525.

15. US Department of the Navy, "Annual Report of the Secretary of the Navy," 1898, 525–526.

16. Dorwart, *Dorwart's History*, 72.

17. Rear Admiral Seaton Schroeder, *A Half Century of Naval Service* (New York: D. Appleton, 1922), 270.

18. Schroeder, *Half Century of Naval Service*, 270–271.

19. Navy Department, General Order no. 128 (May 7, 1903).

20. James L. Gilbert, *World War I and the Origins of U.S. Military Intelligence* (Lanham, MD: Scarecrow Press, 2012), 16.

21. Powe, "Emergence of a War Department Intelligence Agency," 37.

22. John F. Votaw, "United States Military Attachés, 1885–1919: The American Army Matures in the International Arena" (PhD diss., Temple University, 1991), 39.

23. An Act to Increase the Efficiency of the Army, Chap. 553, 831 (February 14, 1903).

24. Barr, *Progressive Army*, 100.

25. Daniel R. Beaver, *Modernizing the American War Department: Change and Continuity in a Turbulent Era, 1885–1920* (Kent, OH: Kent State University Press, 2006), 30.

26. Memorandum (unattributed), June 11, 1903, Records of the War Department General and Special Staffs, record group 165, entry 65, microfilm M1024, file 639, roll 1, National Archives at College Park, MD. Although the memorandum had no signature, Simpson most likely wrote the report because he was the chief. His recommendations for the new division were not found in the archives but probably exist undiscovered.

27. Barr, *Progressive Army*, 115.

28. Orders by Elihu Root, August 8, 1903, Records of the War Department General and Special Staffs, record group 165, entry 65, microfilm M1024, file 639, roll 1, National Archives at College Park, MD; General Orders no. 120 by Elihu Root, August 14, 1903, Records of the Adjutant General's Office, record group 94, entry 25, stack 8W3, row 133, compartment 27, shelf 3, box 3,493, National Archives Building, Washington, DC.

29. Although department officers still called the Second Division by its old name for years.

30. Powe, "Emergence of a War Department Intelligence Agency," 43.

31. Carter wrote a circular on September 4 addressed to the department with the order: "With a view to extending the usefulness of our military attachés abroad, the chiefs of bureaus and offices of the War Department and individual officers of the Army at large will furnish the Second (Military Information) Division of the General Staff, from time to time, memoranda of such data respecting foreign armies as they desire in order that the attachés may be directed to investigate and report upon the same." Circular by William H. Carter, September 4, 1903, George W. Auxier Historical Manuscript File.

32. US War Department, "Annual Report of the Secretary of War," Washington, DC, US Government Printing Office, 1903, 136.

33. Gilbert, *Origins of U.S. Military Intelligence*, 9.

34. An Act Making Appropriations for the Support of the Army for Fiscal Year Ending June Thirtieth, Nineteen Hundred and Five, and for Other Purposes, Chap. 1485, 260 (March 23, 1904).

35. Beach argued, "The Army War College is not the General Staff legally or inferentially although its students have thus far been doing General Staff work and to now merge two divisions of this body into the War College which is generally understood to be an institution for the higher education of officers of the army and really obliterating their identity will surely militate against the prestige to say nothing of the usefulness of the entire General Staff." Memorandum (unattributed), May 31, 1904, Records of the War Department General and Special Staffs, record group 165, entry 65, microfilm M1024, file 639, roll 1, National Archives at College Park, MD.

36. Memorandum (unattributed), May 31, 1904.

37. Van Deman, "Memorandum," April 8, 1949, Records of the Army Staff, record group 319, entry 1071, stack 270, row 15, compartment 4, shelf 23, box 3, 4, National Archives at College Park, MD," 16. Van Deman returned to the intelligence division in 1904 for an official visit. One of his first recollections was that practically every morning a pushcart would appear at the War College full of material Third Division requested from the Second Division.

38. Phill Jones, "The Office of Naval Intelligence: Phill Jones Charts How the ONI Contributed to the Birth of the New US Navy," *History Magazine* 12, no. 3 (February/March 2014): 31.

39. Archivists maintain McCully's diary at the National Archives in downtown Washington, DC.

40. Seaton Schroeder to Newton A. McCully, March 10, 1904, Records of the Office of the Chief of Naval Operations, record group 38, entry 101, stack 10WR, row 13, compartment 10, shelf 4, vol. 5, National Archives Building, Washington, DC.

41. Seaton Schroeder to Newton A. McCully, March 10, 1904.

42. Seaton Schroeder to Newton A. McCully, March 17, 1904, Records of the

Office of the Chief of Naval Operations, record group 38, entry 101, stack 10WR, row 13, compartment 10, shelf 4, vol. 5, National Archives Building, Washington, DC.

43. Seaton Schroeder to Naval Attaché Tokyo, March 18, 1904, Records of the Office of the Chief of Naval Operations, record group 38, entry 101, stack 10WR, row 13, compartment 10, shelf 4, vol. 6, National Archives Building, Washington, DC.

44. Dorwart, *Dorwart's History*, 76.

45. Mark R. Shulman, "The Rise and Fall of American Naval Intelligence, 1882–1917," *Intelligence and National Security* 8, no. 2 (April 1993): 222.

46. ONI reported, "The behavior of all the Japanese is excellent and they seemed to be stirred by an all powerful [*sic* sense of loyalty to their nation." ONI memorandum to Theodore Roosevelt, May 18, 1904, reel 44, Theodore Roosevelt Papers, Manuscript Division, Library of Congress.

47. The memo said, "As an illustration of the confidence with which the Japanese began the war the following is quoted from letter of the Naval Attaché at Tokyo: 'A prominent foreigner on June 27th spoke to General Fukushima in congratulations of the heavy reduction in the Russian Army resulting from the last engagements' [i.e., the fighting near Telissu where fifteen thousand Russians are said to have been killed] which, if continued would soon leave the enemy without enough available men to resist the advance. Fukushima assented, but expressed some disappointment also, saying that if the Japanese plans had succeeded, absolutely as laid down, there would by this time 'be no Russian Army.'" H. W. Whittlesey to Theodore Roosevelt, July 22, 1904, reel 46, Theodore Roosevelt Papers, Manuscript Division, Library of Congress (hereafter Roosevelt Papers).

48. H. W. Whittlesey to William Loeb Jr., October 27, 1904, reel 49, Roosevelt Papers.

49. Dorwart, *Dorwart's History*, 79.

50. "Army and Navy Gossip: United States Navy," *Washington Post*, April 7, 1907, 20.

51. First Lieutenant Edwin R. Stuart, "The Organizations and Functions of a Bureau of Military Intelligence," *Journal of the Military Service Institution* 32, no. 72 (March–April 1903): 162.

52. Stuart, "Organizations and Functions," 162–164.

53. Captain Thomas B. Mott, "The Organization and Function of a Bureau of Military Intelligence," *Journal of the Military Service Institution* 32, no. 122 (March–April 1903): 184.

54. Brigadier General Theodore Schwan, "The Coming General Staff," *Journal of the Military Service Institution* 33, no. 123 (July–August 1903): 23.

55. Schwan, "Coming General Staff," 24.

56. W. D. Beach to United States Army Chief of Staff, September 13, 1904, Records of the War Department General and Special Staffs, record group 165, entry 65, stack 370, row 75, compartment 16, shelf 5, box 109, National Archives at College Park, MD, 7.

57. Military Information Division Memorandum to United States Army Chief of Staff, October 12, 1905, Records of the War Department General and Special Staffs, record group 165, entry 65, stack 370, row 75, compartment 16, shelf 5, box 109, National Archives at College Park, MD, 1.

58. Powe, "Emergence of a War Department Intelligence Agency," 47–50.

59. Memorandum by unidentified captain, October 26, 1906, Records of the War Department General and Special Staffs, record group 165, entry 65, microfilm M1024, file 639, roll 1, National Archives at College Park, MD.

60. Van Deman, "Memorandum," 20.

61. 33rd Cong. Rec. H4238 and H4268 (daily ed. April 16, 1900). It was common between 1890 and 1920 for ONI to provide tables and charts of the Navy's growth compared to other foreign naval powers for the congressional debates on naval appropriations. For instance, a house debate on April 16, 1900, referenced ONI data and a report on "Notes of Naval Progress" provided earlier that year.

62. Dorwart, *Dorwart's History*, 71–72.

63. Memorandum by Stephen B. Luce, March 1, 1900, container 10, Stephen B. Luce Papers, Naval Historical Foundation Collection, Manuscript Division, Library of Congress, 1.

64. Memorandum by Stephen B. Luce, March 1, 1900, 5–6.

65. Luce argued, "The Secretary issue an order to the War College and Office of Naval Intelligence that their work shall be regarded as directly connected and interdependent, and that the chiefs of the two institutions and their first assistants and the Chief of Bureau of Navigation shall constitute a permanent board of five members, who shall meet frequently and consult as to war plans and information. That one-half of the Intelligence Office force shall pass four months of each year at the War College, and one-half the War College force four months at the Intelligence Office." Memorandum, March 1, 1900, 9.

66. Navy Department, General Order no. 544 (March 13, 1900).

67. Paul Y. Hammond, *Organizing for Defense: The American Military Establishment in the Twentieth Century* (Princeton, NJ: Princeton University Press, 1961), 54–55.

68. Rear Admiral Albert Gleaves, *Life and Letters of Rear Admiral Stephen B. Luce, U.S. Navy* (New York: Putnam, 1925), 238.

69. The *Sun* argued, "The work begun seventeen years ago by Admiral then Commodore Luce Is bearing fruit; the Secretary of the Navy has issued an order creating a Naval General Staff and assigning Admiral Dewey to duty as its chief. This is one of the most important peace orders ever issued in the Navy and places the capstone on the structure begun by Admiral Luce so long ago." "The Naval General Staff," *Sun*, March 22, 1900, 1.

70. Dorwart, *Dorwart's History*, 77.

71. Representative George B. McClellan (New York) was one of these supporters. He said in an Army appropriation debate of the House floor on March 26, 1900, "We have no general staff, no military brain to assist the general commanding, whoever he may be, in the military problems he is called upon to solve.

The Secretary of War, thoroughly realizing existing conditions in our so-called 'staff' departments, has begun the organization of what he calls a war college, but which when complete will be nothing more and nothing less than one of the sections of the Prussian general staff. Our Adjutant-General's Department, with the military information division and the war college, will by indirection become a general staff." 33rd Cong. Rec. H3323 (daily ed. March 26, 1900).

72. Powe, "Emergence of a War Department Intelligence Agency," 40.
73. Barr, *Progressive Army*, 90.
74. Barr, *Progressive Army*, 41.
75. Barr, *Progressive Army*, 40.
76. 36th Cong. Rec. H2315 (daily ed. February 17, 1903). Sigsbee sent Representative George E. Foss (Illinois), Chairman of the Committee on Naval Affairs, large amounts of data on January 2, 1903, to advise the House on potential threats before discussions on naval appropriations.
77. "Second in Naval Power: The United States is Near the Head of the List on Sea Power," *Minneapolis Journal*, March 24, 1903, 1.
78. "Navies of the World: Capt. C.D. Sigsbee's Record of the Work Recently Done," *New York Times*, September 3, 1901, 8. The newspaper reported ONI's ability, through naval attaché information, to publish modernization among great world powers. The newspaper neglected to state the other reason to publish intelligence data: ONI's attempts to capture the public's attention and therefore obtain further funds from Congress.
79. C. F. Goodrich, "Naval Intelligence during War," *Proceedings of the United States Naval Institute* 29, no. 2 (April 1903): 358.
80. Goodrich, "Naval Intelligence during War," 359.
81. 39th Cong. Rec. H2572 (daily ed. February 15, 1905).
82. "Interests President: He Discusses with Experts Progress of Naval War in the Far East," *Washington Post*, May 21, 1905, 13.
83. "Look Now for Peace: Effect of Rojestvensky's Great Defeat," *Evening Star*, May 29, 1905, 1.
84. "Shows Tonnage of Navies: Office of Naval Intelligence Gives Relative Rank of Powers," *Washington Post*, November 6, 1907, 4.
85. 42nd Cong. Rec. A112 (daily ed. April 10, 1908) (appendix).
86. 42nd Cong. Rec. H4579 (daily ed. April 10, 1908).
87. US War Department, "Annual Report of the Secretary of War," Washington, DC, US Government Printing Office, 1900, 21.
88. US War Department, "Annual Report of the Secretary of War," 1900, 21.
89. "Proposed Army War College: Probable That It Will Be Located in Washington," *Tazewell Republican*, August 22, 1901, 1. Ironically, it would be military intelligence that Army leaders placed under the supervision of the Army War College in 1908.
90. John E. Jenks, "A Government Picture-Book," *Youth's Companion*, August 29, 1901, 419.
91. Van Deman, "Memorandum," 23. There was only one automobile available

to the Third Division and the Army assigned the "White Steamer" to the president of the college.

92. US War Department, "Annual Report of the Secretary of War," 1907, Washington, DC, US Government Printing Office, 184.

93. Barr, *Progressive Army*, 169.

94. Memorandum by J. Franklin Bell, June 27, 1908, George W. Auxier Historical Manuscript File.

95. Van Deman, "Memorandum," 20. Van Deman stated that Bell had a prejudice against military information work, which he had acquired while provost marshal of the Philippines. Bell had indeed inherited distaste for MID when dealing with the Manila branch; he may have experienced the humiliation of his anti-intelligence opinion rejected by superiors in support of MID.

96. Powe, "Emergence of a War Department Intelligence Agency," 54–56.

97. Van Deman, "Memorandum," 25–26.

98. US War Department, "Annual Report of the Secretary of War," Washington, DC, US Government Printing Office, 1908, 358.

99. US War Department, "Annual Report of the Secretary of War," 1908, 358.

100. An Act Making Appropriations for the Support of the Army for Fiscal Year Ending June Thirtieth, Nineteen Hundred and Eleven, Chap. 112, 244 (March 23, 1910).

101. Lt. Col. Walter C. Sweeney, *Military Intelligence: A New Weapon in War* (New York: Frederick A. Stokes, 1924), 87.

102. Colonel Bruce W. Bidwell, *History of the Military Intelligence Division, Department of the Army General Staff: 1775–1941* (Frederick, MD: University Publications of America, 1986), 91–92.

103. Marc B. Powe and Edward E. Wilson, *The Evolution of American Military Intelligence* (Fort Huachuca, AZ: US Army Intelligence Center and School, 1973), 16.

104. James R. Green, "The First Sixty Years of the Office of Naval Intelligence" (MA thesis, American University, 1963), 107.

105. Congress continued to consume ONI data for naval appropriations discussions. For instance, Senator Claude A. Swanson (Virginia) advertised ONI's tables "showing the relative strength of the navies of the various nations of the world and the authorized increases of those navies for the next several years." 48th Cong. Rec. S7851 (daily ed. June 8, 1912).

106. Commander W. S. Crosley, "The Naval War College, the General Board, and the Office of Naval Intelligence," *Proceedings of the United States Naval Institute* 39, no. 3 (September 1913): 969.

107. Crosley, "Naval War College," 969.

108. Dorwart, *Dorwart's History*, 90.

109. The article "Trained Initiative and of Action: The True Bases of Military Efficiency" ran in the March 1913 edition of *Proceedings*.

110. Memorandum by James H. Oliver, August 12, 1914, reel 57, Josephus

Daniels Papers, Naval Historical Foundation Collection, Manuscript Division, Library of Congress.

111. 52nd Cong. Rec. H2687 (daily ed. January 29, 1915).

112. John Biddle to United States Army Chief of Staff, September 26, 1911, Records of the War Department General and Special Staffs, record group 165, entry 65, stack 370, row 75, compartment 16, shelf 5, box 109, National Archives at College Park, MD, 2.

113. John Biddle to United States Army Chief of Staff, September 26, 1911, 7.

114. Memorandum by Office of the Chief of Staff, February 3, 1912, Records of the War Department General and Special Staffs, record group 165, entry 65, microfilm M1024, file 639, roll 1, National Archives at College Park, MD.

115. Powe, "Emergence of a War Department Intelligence Agency," 65.

116. Gilbert, *Origins of U.S. Military Intelligence*, 14.

117. Gilbert, *Origins of U.S. Military Intelligence*, 14.

118. Karen Kovach, *The Life and Times of MG Dennis E. Noland, 1872–1956: The Army's First G2* (Fort Belvoir, VA: History Office, Office of the Chief of Staff, US Army Intelligence and Security Command, 1998), 22.

119. Gilbert, *Origins of U.S. Military Intelligence*, 14–15.

120. Dorwart, *Dorwart's History*, 84.

121. Acting Secretary of the Navy to Templin M. Potts, October 6, 1910, Naval Records Collection of the Office of Naval Records and Library, record group 45, entry I-18 29, stack 11WR, row 1, compartment 8, shelf 4/5, vol. 5, National Archives Building, Washington, DC.

122. Acting Secretary of the Navy to Templin M. Potts, October 6, 1910.

123. Dorwart, *Dorwart's History*, 85.

124. George von Lengerke Meyer to Templin M. Potts, "Preparation of War Portfolios," October 26, 1911, Naval Records Collection of the Office of Naval Records and Library, record group 45, entry I-18 29, stack 11WR, row 1, compartment 8, shelf 4/5, vol. 5, National Archives Building, Washington, DC.

125. Dorwart, *Dorwart's History*, 87.

126. Green, "First Sixty Years," 49.

127. Churchill said, in 1920, "We failed to see that correct military information is unattainable except as a result of correct staff organization, highly-trained specialized intelligence personnel and complete governmental teamwork." Brigadier General Marlborough Churchill, "The Military Intelligence Division, General Staff," *Journal of the United States Artillery* 52, no. 4 (April 1920): 315.

128. Churchill, "Military Intelligence Division," 295–296.

Chapter 5. 1915–1919: The Resuscitation of ONI and MID

1. Manuel Franz, "Preparedness Revisited: Civilian Societies and the Campaign for American Defense, 1914–1920," *Journal of the Gilded Age and the Progressive Era* 17, no. 4 (October 2018): 673.

2. James L. Gilbert, *World War I and the Origins of U.S. Military Intelligence* (Lanham, MD: Scarecrow Press, 2012), 10.

3. Marc B. Powe, "The Emergence of a War Department Intelligence Agency" (MA thesis, Kansas State University, 1974), vi.

4. Roy Talbert, *Negative Intelligence: The Army and the American Left, 1917–1941* (Jackson: University Press of Mississippi, 1991), 44–45.

5. ONI historian Captain Wyman H. Packard said of naval intelligence in the Great War, "When the United States entered World War I, the Allies already had operational intelligence systems functioning in support of their convoy routing and antisubmarine operations. Allied operational intelligence was made available to the United States, making it unnecessary for the Office of Naval Intelligence to become extensively involved in processing operational intelligence." Captain Wyman H. Packard, USN (Ret.), *A Century of U.S. Naval Intelligence* (Washington, DC: Office of Naval Intelligence, 1996), 215.

6. According to the *Washington Post*, "The United States government must go further than it has gone in the prevention of spying if it is to equal the precautions taken by other belligerents. The prevention of spying and the detection of spies is the duty of every individual in the government. The making of drastic laws will not serve as a substitute for individual vigilance." "Put None but Americans on Guard!" *Washington Post*, May 31, 1917, 6.

7. Gilbert, *Origins of U.S. Military Intelligence*, 97.

8. Lt. Col. Walter C. Sweeney, *Military Intelligence: A New Weapon in War* (New York: Frederick A. Stokes, 1924), 4.

9. Jeffery M. Dorwart, *Dorwart's History of the Office of Naval Intelligence: 1865–1945* (Annapolis, MD: Naval Institute Press, 2019), 169.

10. Gilbert, *Origins of U.S. Military Intelligence*, 74.

11. "Spies and Thieves Barred from U.S. Office Buildings: Loss of State Secrets from State, War and Navy Departments Forces Officials to Adopt Strict Regulations against Prowlers—Important Papers Stolen," *Washington Herald*, July 19, 1915, 1. The article reported that thieves stole plans for a new battleship off a drafting table, among other papers that had disappeared around the building.

12. Memorandum by James H. Oliver, "Report of Progress," June 26, 1915, reel 38, Josephus Daniels Papers, Naval Historical Foundation Collection, Manuscript Division, Library of Congress.

13. Dorwart, *Dorwart's History*, 95.

14. Laurence M. Nelson III, "Innovation in Intelligence: An Analysis of U.S. Marine Corps Intelligence Modernization during the Occupation of Haiti, 1915–1934" (MA thesis, Utah State University, 2017), 25.

15. Van Deman, "Memorandum," April 8, 1949, Records of the Army Staff, record group 319, entry 1071, stack 270, row 15, compartment 4, shelf 23, box 3, 4, National Archives at College Park, MD, 31.

16. Clarence C. Clendenen, *Blood on the Border: The United States Army and the Mexican Irregulars* (London: Macmillan, 1969), 332.

17. Marc Powe notes that "no individual contributed more to American intelligence organization or doctrine than Van Deman. He quite literally led American intelligence into the twentieth century." Marc B. Powe, in *The Final Memoranda: Major General Ralph H. Van Deman, USA Ret., 1865–1952*, ed. by Ralph E. Weber (Wilmington, DE: A Scholarly Resources Imprint, 1988), xxii.

18. Weber, *Final Memoranda*, 103. Van Deman's March 2, 1916, memorandum is reprinted here in its entirety.

19. Weber, *Final Memoranda*, 113–114.

20. Nathan Miller, *Spying for America: The Hidden History of U.S. Intelligence* (New York: Paragon House, 1989), 185.

21. General Orders no. 15, April 25, 1916, George W. Auxier Historical Manuscript File.

22. Powe, "Emergence of a War Department Intelligence Agency," vi.

23. Colonel Bruce W. Bidwell, *History of the Military Intelligence Division, Department of the Army General Staff: 1775–1941* (Frederick, MD: University Publications of America, 1986), 98.

24. Gilbert, *Origins of U.S. Military Intelligence*, 28.

25. Russell F. Weigley, *The American Way of War: A History of United States Military Strategy and Policy* (Bloomington: Indiana University Press, 1973), xxii.

26. Powe, "Emergence of a War Department Intelligence Agency," vi.

27. Dorwart, *Dorwart's History of*, 96.

28. James H. Oliver to William S. Benson, "Collection of Industrial Information within the United States," February 12, 1916, General Records of the Department of the Navy, record group 80, entry PC-31 19, stack 11W3, row 15, compartment 32, shelf 3, box 2617, National Archives Building, Washington, DC, 1.

29. Oliver to Benson, "Collection of Industrial Information," 3.

30. Dudley Knox to William S. Sims, February 16, 1916, container 69, William S. Sim Papers, Naval Historical Foundation Collection, Manuscript Division, Library of Congress.

31. Dorwart, *Dorwart's History*, 96.

32. Captain W. H. Packard, "ONI Centennial," April 1982, Records of the Office of the Chief of Naval Operations, record group 38, entry UD-09D 19, stack 270, row 82, compartment 21, shelf 1, box 116, National Archives at College Park, MD, 11.

33. "Thousands of Spies Are Here: Estimated that 100,000 Are in the United States Who Need Watching," *Ogden Standard*, February 19, 1917, 1. The article cited Senator Lee S. Overman (North Carolina) regarding this inflated number. He said that Congress had to enact these drastic laws to protect naval assets and bases.

34. Bidwell, *History of the Military Intelligence Division*, 109–110.

35. Van Deman stated later, "The Chief of Staff said he could see no reason for the United States Army to have any such thing as a military information service

and that if as explained the British and French armies had such organizations and were receiving the necessary information concerning the enemy." Van Deman, "Memorandum," 33.

36. Van Deman, "Memorandum," 34.
37. Van Deman, "Memorandum," 34.
38. Van Deman, "Memorandum," 36.
39. "Work and Activities of the Military Intelligence Division, General Staff," October 1, 1918, Records of the Army Staff, record group 319, entry 1071, stack 270, row 15, compartment 4, shelf 23, box 22, National Archives at College Park, MD, 2. Cited hereafter as "Work and Activities of the Military Intelligence Division, General Staff."
40. Van Deman, "Memorandum," 36.
41. Changes no. 7, War College Department Manual, May 3, 1917, Records of the War Department General and Special Staffs, record group 165, entry 65, microfilm M1024, file 639, roll 1, National Archives at College Park, MD.
42. Powe, "Emergence of a War Department Intelligence Agency," 88.
43. Van Deman, "Memorandum," 36.
44. "Work and Activities of the Military Intelligence Division, General Staff," 3.
45. Bidwell, *History of the Military Intelligence Division*, 112.
46. John Patrick Finnegan, *Military History: A Picture History*, 2nd ed. (Fort Belvoir, VA: US Army, 1992), 2.
47. "Work and Activities of the Military Intelligence Division, General Staff," 4.
48. War Department, General Order no. 14 (February 9, 1918).
49. "Military Intelligence Branch, Executive Division, General Staff," 1918, Records of the Army Staff, record group 319, entry 1071, stack 270, row 15, compartment 4, shelf 23, box 22, National Archives at College Park, MD.
50. War Department, General Order no. 40 (April 23, 1918). The MIB took on new responsibilities as well. On April 26, the War Department directed the chief of the MIB to be the representative of the Cooperating Committee of Representatives of the Fire-Prevention Section of the War Industries Board. The secretary of war ordered the department bureaus to direct their questions and issues of plant protection, especially related to sabotage and incendiarism, to the MIB.
51. Van Deman, "Memorandum," 57.
52. March said the work "required a character of work for which authors, college professors, students of languages, were peculiarly fitted, and before the war was over its roster resembled a Who's Who of writers. This brilliant collection of educated men and women thus did their bit in the war, in capacities where their brains could be used, instead of being square pegs in round holes, in camp or the field, performing duties which could be done better by some husky son of the soil." Major General Peyton C. March, *The Nation at War* (Garden City, NJ: Doubleday, Doran, 1932), 40.
53. March, *Nation at War*, 226–227.
54. "News of Army and Navy," *Washington Post*, May 5, 1918, 3.

55. Talbert, *Negative Intelligence*, 28, and Miller, *Spying for America*, 201.

56. Van Deman said of Churchill, "He had little experience in Intelligence but was favorably known to the Chief of Staff, General Peyton C. March, who selected him as the best officer known to him to take over the intelligence work. That the Chief of Staff made a very excellent selection is amply proven by the work that Lt. Col. Churchill did as the head of the Military Intelligence Branch of the Executive Section of the General Staff as well as that performed following the restoration of the Military Intelligence to its proper place in the General Staff organization and his promotion to Brigadier General. Too little has been said concerning the most excellent work done by Marlborough Churchill from the time he took over the head of the Military Branch of the Executive Division of the General Staff up to the time that an attack of sleeping sickness acquired from a clerk in his office caused his retirement." Weber, *Final Memoranda*, 43.

57. After only three months, MIB moved again from Monroe Courts to the upper floors of the Hooe Building at 1330 F Street, NW, just two blocks east of the White House. The building offered a larger space for an expanding organization rumored for promotion to division size.

58. Marlborough Churchill to Ralph H. Van Deman, August 26, 1918, Records of the War Department General and Special Staffs, record group 165, entry 65, MID file 9954–50, National Archives at College Park, MD.

59. War Department, General Order no. 80 (August 26, 1918).

60. March, *Nation at War*, 40–41.

61. Gilbert, *Origins of U.S. Military Intelligence*, 89.

62. Memorandum by A. B. Coxe, "Memorandum no. 64," August 28, 1918, Records of the Army Staff, record group 319, entry 1071, stack 270, row 15, compartment 4, shelf 23, box 3, National Archives at College Park, MD.

63. Memorandum by A. B. Coxe, "Memorandum no. 64."

64. "Work and Activities of the Military Intelligence Division, General Staff," 1.

65. Brigadier General Marlborough Churchill, "Credit for Bolshevist Disclosures," letter to the editor, *New York Times*, October 5, 1918, 12. He wrote to correct the paper, which credited the "American Intelligence Department" instead of MID for recent intelligence work.

66. John J. Pershing to Ralph H. Van Deman, November 29, 1918, Records of the Army Staff, record group 319, entry 1071, stack 270, row 15, compartment 4, shelf 23, box 3, National Archives at College Park, MD. Pershing thought highly of Van Deman's work during his brief stint in the AEF. Despite this, Pershing stated that the War Department had discontinued all general officer–grade promotions after the Armistice and therefore he regretted to inform the colonel he could not get his star yet. The Army would not promote Van Deman for another nine years.

67. Marlborough Churchill to Ralph H. Van Deman, November 30, 1918, Records of the War Department General and Special Staffs, record group 165, entry 65, MID file 2412–5, National Archives at College Park, MD.

68. March, *Nation at War*, 229. The chief of staff stated that MID developed

a great efficiency and reputation through its reports. This prestige made it easy for March to send MID personnel to France with the president.

69. Bidwell, *History of the Military Intelligence Division*, 248.

70. Dorwart, *Dorwart's History*, 99.

71. Dorwart, *Dorwart's History*, 102.

72. An Act Making Appropriations to Supply Urgent Deficiencies in Appropriations for Military and Naval Establishments on Account of War Expenses for the Fiscal Year Ending June Thirtieth, Nineteen Hundred and Seventeen, and for Other Purposes, chap. 29, 202 (June 15, 1917).

73. Talbert, *Negative Intelligence*, 29.

74. Memorandum by Roger Welles, "Enrollment of Officers for the Office of Naval Intelligence and the Offices of Naval Attachés at London, Paris, and Madrid," July 7, 1917, reel 38, Josephus Daniels Papers, Naval Historical Foundation Collection, Manuscript Division, Library of Congress.

75. Welles, "Enrollment of Officers."

76. A wartime ONI also grappled with space issues at its 1734 New York Avenue address. The office made its third move in the organization's history February 1918 and settled into new spaces at the Corcoran Court annexes.

77. Niblack wrote, "These reports soon increased in number so that it became necessary to mimeograph the compilations made from them, and to distribute them to the fleet and others concerned. First, we got out a mimeograph compilation once a month; then twice a month, and later, these got so bulky that it was necessary to print them." Rear Admiral Alfred P. Niblack, "The History and Aims of the Office of Naval Intelligence," Ibiblio.org, 1920, 23, http://www.ibiblio.org/hyperwar/NHC/History-Aims-ONI-1920/History-Aims-ONI-1920.html.

78. "Censoring, Except Radio, Is Ended: All Military Suspension of Messages Discontinued," *Sun*, November 16, 1918, 8.

79. Dorwart, *Dorwart's History*, 113.

80. Karen Kovach, *The Life and Times of MG Dennis E. Noland, 1872–1956: The Army's First G2* (Fort Belvoir, VA: History Office, Office of the Chief of Staff, US Army Intelligence and Security Command, 1998), 24.

81. John Patrick Finnegan and Romana Danysh, *Military Intelligence* (Washington, DC: Center for Military History, United States Army, 1998), 24.

82. Gilbert, *Origins of U.S. Military Intelligence*, 88.

83. Marlborough Churchill to Dennis E. Nolan and Ralph H. Van Deman, September 16, 1918, Records of the War Department General and Special Staffs, record group 165, entry 65, MID file 10560–235 3, National Archives at College Park, MD.

84. Ralph H. Van Deman to Marlborough Churchill, October 20, 1918, Records of the War Department General and Special Staffs, record group 165, entry 65, MID file 10560–235 5, National Archives at College Park, MD.

85. An Act to Punish Acts of Interference with the Foreign Relations, the Neutrality, and the Foreign Commerce of the United States, to Punish Espionage,

and Better to Enforce the Criminal Laws of the United States, and for Other Purposes, chap. 30. (June 15, 1917).

86. Dorwart, *Dorwart's History*, 99.

87. Circular by Josephus Daniels, "Reporting of Information to the Office of Naval Intelligence," October 10, 1917, Records of the Office of the Chief of Naval Operations, record group 38, entry NM-63 86, stack 10W4, row 2, compartment 2, shelf 5, box 1, National Archives Building, Washington, DC.

88. Daniels, "Reporting of Information to the Office of Naval Intelligence."

89. Packard, *Century of U.S. Naval Intelligence*, 250.

90. Dorwart, *Dorwart's History*, 110.

91. Dorwart, *Dorwart's History*, 111.

92. Assistant naval attaché to Madrid Reserve Lieutenant George A. Dorsey congratulated his Ivy League friend August 17. He also said that Rear Admiral Alfred P. Niblack, the future DNI, spoke highly of ONI and Welles. Dorsey reported, "He (Niblack) remarked that the change that had come over O. N. I. since you took hold of it was one of the finest things in recent naval achievements." George A. Dorsey to Roger Welles, August 17, 1918, container 3, Roger Welles Papers, Naval Historical Foundation Collection, Manuscript Division, Library of Congress.

93. ONI transferred to the Navy Building in Potomac Park in September 1918.

94. Van Deman, "Memorandum," 40.

95. Finnegan, *Picture History*, 21.

96. Gilbert, *Origins of U.S. Military Intelligence*, 77.

97. Powe defended the chief, stating, "While these activities may appear too severe today, two points need to be made: first, as Van Deman always stressed, Americans had no previous experience with German-style intelligence operations; second, MI Section seems to have made considerable effort to insure that investigations were complete and that no one would be smeared." Nathan Miller said that "in defending a free and open society, intelligence officials must often pursue methods inimical to these very freedoms. Moreover, once the line between protection of the national security and domestic snooping is crossed, it becomes difficult to stop short of outright lawbreaking." Powe, "Emergence of a War Department Intelligence Agency," 88; and Miller, *Spying for America*, 200.

98. Powe, "Emergence of a War Department Intelligence Agency," 88; Miller, *Spying for America*, 200; and Talbert, *Negative Intelligence*, 18–19.

99. Talbert, *Negative Intelligence*, 19.

100. Memorandum by Ralph H. Van Deman, April 2, 1918, Records of the War Department General and Special Staffs, record group 165, entry NM-84-310, stack 370, row 75, compartment 19, shelf 2, box 124, National Archives at College Park, MD.

101. Memorandum by Ralph H. Van Deman, April 2, 1918.

102. Dorwart, *Dorwart's History*, 111.

103. Dorwart, *Dorwart's History*, 107.

104. The article stated, "It was felt that the functions of censorship have been

too widely separated under various offices, when they might naturally be centralized in the bureau of military intelligence." "Col. Churchill New Censor: Power Consolidated under Plans of General Staff Consolidation," *Washington Post*, June 22, 1918, 6.

105. March, *Nation at War*, 227–228.

106. "Keep Watch on Spies: Gregory, Bielaski and Churchill Warn against Relaxation," *Washington Post*, November 10, 1918, 18.

107. The *New York Times* wrote, "For weeks the officers assigned to the intelligence service have been quietly at work listing the enemy aliens whose liberty they had reason to believe constituted a menace to the safety of the country. Not until their case was complete and they were ready to act did the naval investigators call upon the Secret Service agencies of the Government and the Police Department of the city." "More Germans to Be Interned: Ninety-One Taken Wednesday Night Are Searched and Examined," *New York Times*, September 28, 1917, 1.

108. The *Tribune* editorial said, "If there are German naval spies in America they have thus far eluded the Department of Justice and the Naval Intelligence Bureau, it was learned authoritatively to-day. It was stated at the Navy Department that not a single bona fide German naval spy has been arrested in the United States since this country entered the war. It is feared, however, that dangerous enemy aliens have been released by the Department of Justice after having been apprehended." "No Naval Spies Caught Here, Says Intelligence Bureau," *New York Tribune*, January 23, 1918, 4.

109. "Spy Suspect Is Seized Here in Secret Raid: Wilhelm Korthaus, Ostensibly Employed by German Dye Firm, Held," *New York Tribune*, March 12, 1918, 1.

110. The *Post* reported, "Several officers of the naval intelligence bureau who speak German went to the restaurant Saturday night as customers of the place. They mingled freely with the Germans and Austrians about the tables, and were astounded by what they heard. Several times the orchestra played a parody or travesty on the 'Star-Spangled Banner,' and the enemy aliens hilariously sang 'Der Stern Spangled Bana.' Repeatedly they sang 'Die Wacht am Rhein' and 'Deutschland Über Alles.' There was no police interference with the proprietor for selling drinks after midnight, and at 2 o'clock in the morning the naval lieutenant in command of the 'spy catchers' gave a signal and his men stood up, ordered the orchestra to cease and commanded all in the place, men and women, to stand against the wall. The aliens obeyed, but protested, saying they had a right to have a celebration." "Aliens Parody Anthem: Sing 'Der Stern Spangled Banana' in N.Y. Saloon," *Washington Post*, April 2, 1918, 4.

111. Lawrence Semon, dir., *Huns and Hyphens* (Vitagraph Company of America, 1918).

112. 57th Cong. Rec. H2698 (daily ed. February 4, 1919).

113. Powe, "Emergence of a War Department Intelligence Agency," 98.

114. War Department, Bulletin no. 74 (December 31, 1917).

115. War Department, Bulletin no. 74 (December 31, 1917).

116. Brigadier General Marlborough Churchill, "The Military Intelligence Division, General Staff," *Journal of the United States Artillery* 52, no. 4 (April 1920): 296.

117. Dorwart, *Dorwart's History*, 168.

Chapter 6. 1919–1929: ONI and MID Navigate the Rapids

1. Beverly Gage, *The Day Wall Street Exploded: A Story of America in Its First Age of Terror* (New York: Oxford University Press, 2009), 3.

2. Robert H. Wiebe, *The Search for Order: 1877–1920* (New York: Hill and Wang, 1967), 301–302.

3. William L. Langer and S. Everett Gleason, *The Challenge to Isolation: 1937–1940* (New York: Harper and Brothers, 1952), xi.

4. Langer and Gleason, *Challenge to Isolation*, 15.

5. Brian M. Linn, "The American Way of War," *Magazine of History*, October 2008, 19–20.

6. Captain Ellis M. Zacharias, *Secret Missions: The Story of an Intelligence Officer* (New York: G. P. Putnam's, 1946), 165.

7. "How We Abused the Loyalty of Our Foreign-Born," *New Ulm Post*, editorial, April 4, 1919. The *New Ulm Post*, based out of New Ulm, Minnesota, served the heavy German immigrant population and naturally was not supportive of the government intruding on German immigrants' lives. The editorial commented, "The Department of Justice had already in the field a large, intelligent, and well-trained organization; there was also the Secret Service of the Treasury swiftly sprang Military Intelligence, Naval Intelligence, Shipping Board Intelligent, etc., etc.; and, by way of climax, the American Protective League, an organization of two hundred and fifty thousand 'citizen volunteers' formed with the sanction of the Attorney-General and operating under the direction of the Bureau of Investigation. Never was a country so thoroughly contra-espionaged! Not a pin dropt [sic] in the home of any with a foreign name but that it rang like thunder on the inner ear of some listening sleuth!"

8. Rhodri Jeffreys-Jones, *American Espionage: From Secret Service to CIA* (New York: Macmillan, 1977), 121.

9. Marc B. Powe, "The Emergence of a War Department Intelligence Agency" (MA thesis, Kansas State University, 1974), 106.

10. Jeffery M. Dorwart, *Dorwart's History of the Office of Naval Intelligence: 1865–1945* (Annapolis, MD: Naval Institute Press, 2019), 169.

11. Henry H. Ransom, *Central Intelligence and National Security* (Cambridge, MA: Harvard University Press, 1958), 51.

12. According to Zacharias, "The United States was very fortunate in having in the persons of its DIO's energetic and alert men." Zacharias, *Secret Missions*, 200.

13. Zacharias, *Secret Missions*, 21–22.

14. James R. Green, "The First Sixty Years of the Office of Naval Intelligence" (MA thesis, American University, 1963), 66–67.

15. Dorwart, *Dorwart's History*, 174.

16. Dorwart, *Dorwart's History*, 176. Dorwart hypothesizes that perhaps Niblack was jealous of Sims's reputation, rapid advancement, and higher rank during the war. More importantly, Niblack tried to curry favor with Daniels to be the next CNO. Dorwart may be right, but historians may never know.

17. Alfred P. Niblack, "Request of Major Earl. H. Ellis for Intelligence Duty in South America and in the Pacific Ocean," September 4, 1920, Earl H. "Pete" Ellis Collection, COLL 3247, row 13, section B, shelf 6, box 2, folder 12, Archives Branch, Marine Corps History Division, Quantico, VA.

18. Captain Wyman H. Packard, USN (Ret.), *A Century of U.S. Naval Intelligence* (Washington, DC: Office of Naval Intelligence, 1996), 14.

19. Niblack argued, "It has been the aim of the office to use only reputable business methods and avoid anything savoring of 'gum-shoe' methods. This point cannot be too strongly emphasized." Rear Admiral Alfred P. Niblack, "The History and Aims of the Office of Naval Intelligence," Ibiblio.org, 1920, 6, http://www.ibiblio.org/hyperwar/NHC/History-Aims-ONI-1920/History-Aims-ONI-1920.html.

20. Niblack reasoned MID was better suited for internal affairs "since enemy activities in our own country are more rigidly watched through military posts distributed throughout the country than through naval stations which are merely on the coasts." Niblack, "History and Aims," 24.

21. Niblack, "History and Aims," 12.

22. Niblack, "History and Aims," 6.

23. Dorwart, *Dorwart's History*, 177.

24. Green, "First Sixty Years," 107–108.

25. Dorwart, *Dorwart's History*, 195.

26. Zacharias would later write, "The new director of Naval Intelligence was learning his job. The office of Naval Intelligence continued its protracted hibernations, and nobody in the Navy Department showed other than slightly amused interest in my experiences and ideas." Zacharias, *Secret Missions*, 71.

27. Memorandum by Henry H. Hough, "Data for Annual Report," June 19, 1924, Records of the Office of the Chief of Naval Operations, record group 38, entry 79, stack 10WR, row 1, compartment 3, shelf 5, box 8, National Archives Building, Washington, DC.

28. Zacharias, *Secret Missions*, 83.

29. Zacharias, *Secret Missions*, 83.

30. Roy Talbert, *Negative Intelligence: The Army and the American Left, 1917–1941* (Jackson: University Press of Mississippi, 1991), 97.

31. Marc B. Powe, in *The Final Memoranda: Major General Ralph H. Van Deman, USA Ret., 1865–1952*, ed. by Ralph E. Weber (Wilmington, DE: A Scholarly Resources Imprint, 1988), 91.

32. Memorandum by War Department Information Section, August 20, 1920,

Records of the War Department General and Special Staffs, record group 165, entry 65, MID file 24–461 10, National Archives at College Park, MD, and Memorandum by T. C. Cook, "Memorandum No. 130," September 1, 1920, Records of the War Department General and Special Staffs, record group 165, entry 65, MID file 10560–469 1, National Archives at College Park, MD.

33. Karen Kovach, *The Life and Times of MG Dennis E. Noland, 1872–1956: The Army's First G2* (Fort Belvoir, VA: History Office, Office of the Chief of Staff, US Army Intelligence and Security Command, 1998), 38.

34. *Intelligence Regulations, 1920*, Records of the War Department General and Special Staffs, record group 165, entry NM-84–310, stack 370, row 75, compartment 19, shelf 2, box 124, National Archives at College Park, MD.

35. *Intelligence Regulations, 1920*.

36. Powe, "Emergence of a War Department Intelligence Agency," 106.

37. Colonel Bruce W. Bidwell, *History of the Military Intelligence Division, Department of the Army General Staff: 1775–1941* (Frederick, MD: University Publications of America, 1986), 256.

38. War Department personnel still used MID as an unofficial title for decades.

39. "The American Legion: News: Local, State, National," *New York Tribune*, October 3, 1921, 4. The newspaper reported that Army intelligence aided the police department in tracking down unregistered immigrants in the fall of 1921.

40. Heintzelman ghost-wrote for Pershing: "I would like to call your attention to the great importance of the work being done by the Military Intelligence Division. Before the World War, we were rather like a silent partner in world affairs, and our interest in other countries' doings was rather academic, provided we were not disturbed, and all went well. But all did not go well, and we were violently disturbed and are now an active partner, as the present Conference on the Limitations of Armaments shows." Memorandum by Stuart Heintzelman, December 7, 1921, Records of the War Department General and Special Staffs, record group 165, entry 65, MID file 32–167 24, National Archives at College Park, MD.

41. Memorandum by Heintzelman, December 7, 1921.

42. Bidwell, *History of the Military Intelligence Division*, 339–340.

43. William K. Naylor to Bigby, January 4, 1923, Records of the War Department General and Special Staffs, record group 165, entry 65, MID file 271-A-7 88, National Archives at College Park, MD.

44. Lt. Col. Walter C. Sweeney, *Military Intelligence: A New Weapon in War* (New York: Frederick A. Stokes, 1924), v.

45. Sweeney, *Military Intelligence*, v–vi.

46. Sweeney, *Military Intelligence*, 12.

47. "The Gossip Shop," *Bookman*, December 1924, 4.

48. Lejeune called Feland and Ellis "two officers who had served with distinction" while they were stationed in Santo Domingo, Haiti. Feland commanded

the Second Brigade of Marines, while Ellis was Feland's Chief of Staff. Major General John A. Lejeune, *The Reminiscences of a Marine* (Philadelphia: Dorrance, 1930), 468.

49. Memorandum by John A. Lejeune, December 1, 1920, Records of the Office of the Chief of Naval Operations, record group 127, entry 38, stack 11W1, row 6, compartment 16, shelf 4, box 32, National Archives Building, Washington, DC.

50. Feland recalled, "November 1920: The Major General Commandant, at a conference, stated in the best and simplest terms the purpose of the Division. He announced that it was desired to provide for the study of purely military questions arising in the Marine Corps through the establishment of this office." Brigadier General Logan Feland, "The Division of Operations and Training Headquarters U.S. Marine Corps," *Marine Corps Gazette* 7, no. 1 (March 1922): 41.

51. Feland, "Division of Operations," 41–42.

52. Niblack stated, "The result is, the Office has a good deal to recover from to get back to its old status of getting information from abroad. It is a question of getting the raw meat for the use of Operations vs. the running of a baled hay and canned goods department that I am for the moment up against. In other words, I have got to start in and reorganize the Office of Naval Intelligence along fresh and more energetic lines. So many activities have been added to the Office which only cripple it that I have a big job ahead of me." Alfred P. Niblack to William S. Sims, June 19, 1919, container 76, William S. Sims Papers, Naval Historical Foundation Collection, Manuscript Division, Library of Congress (hereafter Sims Papers).

53. Dorwart, *Dorwart's History*, 172.

54. Sims wrote, "I am sorry to hear your account of the retrenchment and reform in the Office of Naval Intelligence, but I suppose we must expect this for some years to come in all branches of the Navy." William S. Sims to Alfred P. Niblack, June 21, 1919, container 76, Sims Papers.

55. Dorwart, *Dorwart's History*, 173.

56. "Senate Committee for Full Inquiry: Daniels Declares Admiral Sims Must Make Good His Allegations," *Richmond Times-Dispatch*, January 20, 1920, 1.

57. "Involve Naval Heads: Newport Charges Bring Daniels and Roosevelt into Case," *Washington Post*, March 3, 1920, 11.

58. US Naval Administrative Histories of World War II, Office of the Chief of Naval Operations, "Office of Naval Intelligence," 4 vols., Archives Branch, Naval History and Heritage Command Washington Navy Yard (hard copy) and Nimitz Library, United States Naval Academy. Annapolis, MD (microfiche), 150–151.

59. US Naval Administrative Histories of World War II, 150–151.

60. Dorwart, *Dorwart's History*, 196–197.

61. Dorwart, *Dorwart's History*, 198.

62. Dorwart, *Dorwart's History*, 198

63. "On Pacifist List, but Serve Nation: Others Recorded in the 'Who's Who in Radicalism' Are Now in Jail," *New York Times*, January 26, 1919, 8.

64. "Senate Will Probe Reds' Moves Here," *New York Tribune*, February 5, 1919, 1.

65. "Senate Will Probe Reds' Moves Here," 1.

66. Talbert, *Negative Intelligence*, 126.

67. "Army Has Charts of Red Activities: Gen, Churchill Shows Senate Military Committee the Haunts in New York," *New York Times*, June 18, 1919, 19.

68. "Foiled Spies in Army: Intelligence Service Routed Germans, Churchill Says," *Washington Post*, June 18, 1919, 3.

69. Talbert, *Negative Intelligence*, 29.

70. Van Buren said that "one room in the department headquarters at Chicago was piled almost ceiling high with documentary evidence of I. W. W., Bolshevist and other radical activities in Gary, a mass so great that it will take months to translate it all and get it in order." "Reveals Plotting of Gary Radicals: Army Intelligence Officer Gives Senate Committee Results of Investigation," *New York Times*, October 25, 1919, 1.

71. Memorandum by C. H. Mason, "Sinister Inertia in Present United States Situation," October 31, 1919, George W. Auxier Historical Manuscript file.

72. Mason, "Sinister Inertia."

73. Mason, "Sinister Inertia."

74. Talbert, *Negative Intelligence*, 141–142.

75. Brigadier General Marlborough Churchill, "The Military Intelligence Division, General Staff," *Journal of the United States Artillery* 52, no. 4 (April 1920): 294.

76. Churchill, "Military Intelligence Division," 294.

77. Churchill, "Military Intelligence Division," 295.

78. Churchill, "Military Intelligence Division," 299.

79. Churchill, "Military Intelligence Division," 314–315.

80. "572 Slackers Sought in D. C.: War Department Prepares to Round Up 100,000 throughout U. S.," *Washington Herald*, July 27, 1920, 1.

81. General Orders no. 48, August 12, 1920, George W. Auxier Historical Manuscript file.

82. Reeves said, "It is desired to accentuate the service rendered by the Military Intelligence Division for it is essentially a service and supply agency." Lecture by James H. Reeves, "Problems of the Military Intelligence Division," January 4, 1927, Records of the War Department General and Special Staffs, Record Group 165, entry 65, MID file 10560–737 16, National Archives at College Park, MD, 1.

83. Reeves, "Problems of the Military Intelligence Division," 2.

84. Reeves, "Problems of the Military Intelligence Division," 2.

85. Reeves, "Problems of the Military Intelligence Division," 6.

86. Ford assumed the post on May 1, 1927.

87. Van Deman argued, "As I was the man who had to handle this subject

when we entered the war, I really think it is up to me to tell what I know about the matter, for I know that no such plan as that will work. I have tried it myself and had to give it up very early in the game." Ralph H. Van Deman to Stanley H. Ford, December 15, 1928, Records of the War Department General and Special Staffs, record group 165, entry 65, MID file 271-A-9 127, National Archives at College Park, MD.

88. Stanley H. Ford to Ralph H. Van Deman, January 8, 1929, Records of the War Department General and Special Staffs, record group 165, entry 65, MID file 271-A-9 127, National Archives at College Park, MD.

89. Ford to Van Deman, January 8, 1929.

90. Ford to Van Deman, January 8, 1929.

91. W. Evans, J. T. Thompkins, and Harry Yarnell, "Organization of a War Plans Section of the Office of Naval Operations," April 24, 1919, container 1, Harry E. Yarnell Papers (1909–1958), Naval Historical Foundation Collection, Manuscript Division, Library of Congress.

92. Josephus Daniels to Alfred P. Niblack, July 31, 1919, reel 57, Josephus Daniels Papers, Naval Historical Foundation Collection, Manuscript Division, Library of Congress.

93. "United States Now Second in Navy Strength: Building Program during War, Coupled with Germany's Surrender, Makes Us British Contender," *Pensacola Journal*, August 18, 1919, 1.

94. Niblack stated, "The fundamental assumption of the Office of Naval Intelligence has been that it exists largely for the benefit of, and for the support of, the naval attachés abroad, because loyal service can only be had by loyal support of the attachés." Lecture by Alfred P. Niblack to the Army War College, October 17, 1919, Records of the War Department General and Special Staffs, record group 165, entry P 128, stack 270, row 19, compartment 15, shelf 6, box 1, National Archives at College Park, MD, 4.

95. Niblack lecture to the Army War College, 5.

96. Niblack lecture to the Army War College, 6.

97. According to command historian Packard, "The monographs were postbound, loose leaf folios of related papers on a given topic and, as time went on, often grew to almost unmanageable size." Packard, *Century of U.S. Naval Intelligence*, 14.

98. Representative Joseph J. Mansfield's (Texas) intent when mentioning the pamphlet was to show "England's losses during the war were far greater than the average person has any conception of." England, according to ONI, lost 219 naval vessels. 60th Cong. Rec. H811 (daily ed. April 29, 1921).

99. Dorwart, *Dorwart's History*, 180.

100. Dorwart, *Dorwart's History*, 193.

101. Dorwart, *Dorwart's History*, 183.

102. Dorwart, *Dorwart's History*, 187.

103. 69th Cong. Rec. H4657 (daily ed. March 12, 1928).

104. Memorandum by A. W. Johnson, April 11, 1928, Records of the Office

of the Chief of Naval Operations, record group 38, entry UD1, stack 370, row 14, compartment 35, shelf 3–4, box 1, National Archives at College Park, MD. A staff officer mentioned these duties in the memorandum regarding the relation between communications and naval intelligence. Johnson asked his staff to review the paper and give comments and recommendation. The duties the staff officer referenced came from US naval policy approved December 1, 1922, by the secretary of the Navy. Johnson did not dismiss these duties outright when asking his officers to comment. Therefore, he seemed comfortable with the mention of both traditional and counterintelligence duties.

105. Alfred W. Johnson, "The Duties of Naval Attachés," 1928, Records of the Office of the Chief of Naval Operations, record group 38, entry NM-63 86, stack 10W4, row 2, compartment 2, shelf 5, box 1, National Archives in Washington D.C.

106. Captain Wyman H. Packard, "ONI Centennial," July 1982, Records of the Office of the Chief of Naval Operations, Record Group 38, entry UD-09D 19, stack 270, row 82, compartment 21, shelf 1, box 116, National Archives at College Park, MD, 9–10.

107. Packard, *Century of U.S. Naval Intelligence*, 16.

108. Lecture by James H. Reeves, "The Military Intelligence Division, War Department General Staff," September 4, 1924, Records of the War Department General and Special Staffs, record group 165, entry 65, MID file 10560–328 186, National Archives at College Park, MD, 1. Reeves took over from Naylor as ACoS G-2 in July.

109. Reeves, "Military Intelligence Division," 2.

110. Bidwell, *History of the Military Intelligence Division*, 300–301.

111. Major Michael H. Decker (ret.) and Sergeant (ret.) William Mackenzie, "Marine Corps Intelligence," *Marine Corps Gazette* 103, no. 9 (September 2019): 11.

112. G. A. Johnson, "Duties of the Intelligence Section," April 30, 1921, Records of the US Marine Corps, record group 127, entry 38A, stack 11W1, row 11, compartment 1, shelf 2, box 5, National Archives Building, Washington, DC, 3.

113. Johnson, "Duties of the Intelligence Section," 6.

114. Johnson, "Duties of the Intelligence Section," 7.

115. Allan R. Millett, *Semper Fidelis: The History of the United States Marine Corps* (New York: Macmillan, 1980), 325.

116. Ellis explained the plans purpose and his thinking on page 1e: "In order to impose our will upon Japan, it will be necessary for us to project our fleet and land forces across the Pacific and wage war in Japanese waters. To effect this requires that we have sufficient bases to support the fleet both during its projection and afterward. As the matter stands at present, we cannot count upon the use of any bases west of Hawaii except those which we may seize from the enemy after the opening of hostilities. Moreover, the continued occupation of the Marshalls, Caroline, and Pelew Islands by the Japanese (now holding them under mandate of the League of Nations) invests them a series of emergency bases flanking any

line of communications across the pacific throughout a distance of 2300 miles. The reduction and occupation of these islands and the establishment of the necessary bases therein as a preliminary phase of the hostilities is practically imperative." Earl H. Ellis, "Advanced Base Operations in Micronesia," July 23, 1921, Historic Amphibious Files, COLL 3634, row 23, section F, shelf 2, box 1, folder 165/6075, Archives Branch, Marine Corps History Division, Quantico, VA.

117. Packard, *Century of U.S. Naval Intelligence*, 15, 334, and 389.

118. "Bombs Made in Germany: U. S. Naval Bureau Identifies Infernal Machines as Imported Product," *Tonopah Daily Bonanza*, May 1, 1919, 1.

119. 62nd Cong. Rec. S943 (daily ed. December 27, 1922).

120. 62nd Cong. Rec. S943–944 (daily ed. December 27, 1922).

121. Poindexter argued, "My opinion is that instead of being useless men, as he describes them, men who are interested only in drawing their pay, there are no harder-working officers of the Government, no more competent or able, officers, and none more successful in performing the services for which they are employed and for which their office is established. They gather information from all parts of the world for the use of the Navy in the bearing it may have on naval activities." 62nd Cong. Rec. 944 (daily ed. December 27, 1922).

122. 57th Cong. Rec. H3307 (daily ed. February 13, 1919).

123. An Act Making Appropriations for the Support of the Army for Fiscal Year Ending June 30, 1920, and for Other Purposes, Chap. 8, 105 (July 11, 1919).

124. 60th Cong. Rec. H827 (daily ed. April 29, 1921).

125. Stuart Heintzelman to O. N. Solbert, March 6, 1922, Records of the War Department General and Special Staffs, record group 165, entry 65, MID file 2632-A-18 2, National Archives at College Park, MD.

126. The division head argued, "If the Military Intelligence Division is to perform its functions in any adequate fashion during the coming fiscal year, it is essential that the appropriation should be $225,000—the amount allotted by the budget, and on more than one occasion approved by the Secretary of War." Memorandum by Stuart Heintzelman, April 17, 1922, Records of the War Department General and Special Staffs, record group 165, entry 65, MID file 32–167 63, National Archives at College Park, MD.

127. Memorandum by Stuart Heintzelman, April 17, 1922.

128. Citing complaints to the War Department from nine separate State Department missions, Weeks told Hughes, "It would appear that the service rendered by the Military Intelligence Division of the General Staff, as represented in foreign countries by the Military Attachés, is an essential adjunct to the service of information carried on by the Department of State, and that the Department of State is vitally interested in the continuance of its functions." John W. Weeks to Charles E. Hughes, May 19, 1922, George W. Auxier Historical Manuscript File.

129. Weeks wrote, "Such being the case, I feel that I can with propriety suggest to you that, when the Army appropriations bill is being considered by the Senate Committee on Military Affairs, you come to the assistance of the War

Department in this matter by conveying to this committee a statement of the value of the service of the Military Intelligence Division to the Department of State and requesting that special consideration be given to the needs of the Division in connection with appropriations, on account of the fact that it serves both Executive Departments. If sufficient appropriations are provided, nothing will give me greater pleasure than to concur in the views of the Department of State with respect to the continuance of Military Attachés at important embassies and legations." John W. Weeks to Charles E. Hughes, May 19, 1922.

130. 64th Cong. Rec. H3066 (daily ed. February 5, 1923).

131. 64th Cong. Rec. S3261 (daily ed. February 8, 1923).

132. John Patrick Finnegan and Romana Danysh, *Military Intelligence* (Washington, DC: Center for Military History, United States Army, 1998), 4.

133. Finnegan and Danysh, *Military Intelligence*, 43.

134. Ransom, *Central Intelligence and National Security*, 54.

Chapter 7. 1929–1939: Storm on ONI and MID's Horizon

1. Richard Hofstadter, *The Age of Reform: From Bryan to F. D. R.* (New York: Knopf, 1955), 11.

2. William L. Langer and S. Everett Gleason, *The Challenge to Isolation: 1937–1940* (New York: Harper and Brothers, 1952), 11.

3. Dwight D. Eisenhower, *Crusade in Europe* (New York: Doubleday, 1948), 32.

4. Author Myron J. Smith Jr. said of the industry's growth in the 1930s, "Although spy-adventures have been long been widely read in America, it was not until comparatively recently that Yankee writers penned very many of them." Myron J. Smith Jr., *Cloak-and-Dagger Bibliography: An Annotated Guide to Spy Fiction, 1937–1975* (Metuchen, NJ: Scarecrow Press, 1976), 10.

5. *ONI Review*, April/May 1957, record group 38, entry UD-09D 19, stack 270, row 82, compartment 21, shelf 1, box 116, National Archives and Research Administration, National Archives at College Park, MD, 178.

6. Jeffery M. Dorwart, *Dorwart's History of the Office of Naval Intelligence: 1865–1945* (Annapolis, MD: Naval Institute Press, 2019), 212.

7. Zacharias said after his return to ONI as head of the Far East Section, "When I departed in 1931 I left a section still understaffed and overworked, woefully inadequate as a truly effective part of our defense system. But now in 1934 there was a different atmosphere, a refreshing breeze filling for the first time the sails of Naval Intelligence." Captain Ellis M. Zacharias, *Secret Missions: The Story of an Intelligence Officer* (New York: G. P. Putnam's, 1946), 147.

Zacharias, 148. Zacharias also commented that Puleston was one of the greatest DNI's in ONI's history and the years he had the post witnessed the "greatest years of development in our intelligence field."

8. Dorwart, *Dorwart's History*, 214.

9. Former DNI Baldridge said of Sims, "I have always thought of Sims as an

iconoclast. Was he not one who attacked cherished beliefs as shams; was he not radical rather than liberal?" Captain Harry A. Baldridge, "Sims—The Iconoclast," *Proceedings of the United States Naval Institute* 62, no. 2 (February 1937): 183.

10. Dorwart, *Dorwart's History*, 244–245.

11. Dorwart, *Dorwart's History*, 245.

12. US Naval Administrative Histories of World War II, Office of the Chief of Naval Operations, "Office of Naval Intelligence," 4 vols., Archives Branch, Naval History and Heritage Command, Washington, DC (hard copy) and Nimitz Library, United States Naval Academy, Annapolis, MD (microfiche), 36.

13. US Naval Administrative Histories of World War II, 61.

14. Memorandum by Alfred T. Smith, "Cooperation between Army and Navy," September 15, 1932, Records of the War Department General and Special Staffs, record group 165, entry 65, MID file 10560–875 1, National Archives at College Park, MD.

15. Lincoln argued, "Without an information service we cannot keep abreast of developments in foreign armies nor profit by the lessons learned by them. We cannot prepare war plans nor solve intelligently the problems of organization, equipment and supply of the forces to be used therein until we have reasonably complete and accurate information on the potential enemy. That is G-2's job." Lecture by Francis H. Lincoln, "The Military Intelligence Division, War Department General Staff," January 5, 1937, Records of the War Department General and Special Staffs, record group 165, entry 65, MID file 10560–873 39, National Archives at College Park, MD, 1.

16. Lincoln, "Military Intelligence Division," 2.

17. He specifically explained to the audience, "You will notice the absence of certain functions which this division was called upon to perform during the World War; notably such activities as espionage and counter-espionage among the civil population, graft and fraud prevention, protection of civilian plants and public utilities against sabotage. These functions pertain to civilian agencies of the government and were taken over by the War Department due to the inability of the civil authorities to meet the situation." He later clarified his remarks, arguing that "the suppression of communism is not a function of the War Department. The Department, however, is most sympathetic towards those individuals and groups which, stirred by patriotism, actively combat those engaged in subversive attacks upon our system of National Defense." Lincoln, "Military Intelligence Division," 2 and 11.

18. As noted in chapter 6, the National Defense Act of 1920 allotted only four general billets for the staff's division chiefs. When General John J. Pershing reorganized the staff to five divisions, circumstances forced the MID to have colonels as chief.

19. Memorandum by Francis H. Lincoln, "Increase in Number of 'Assistants to the Chief of Staff,'" June 19, 1937, George W. Auxier Historical Manuscript File.

20. Lincoln, "Increase in Number of 'Assistants to the Chief of Staff.'" Naval intelligence had just transitioned DNIs, and the new director was a rear admiral in 1937.

21. Marc B. Powe, "The Emergence of a War Department Intelligence Agency" (MA thesis, Kansas State University, 1974), 108.

22. 72nd Cong. Rec. H1973 (daily ed. January 20, 1930). One such January 15 ONI table appeared before the House when congressmen debated the merits of the London Conference on the floor.

23. Alfred W. Johnson to All Naval Attachés, "Naval Attaché Reports," February 5, 1930, Records of the Office of the Chief of Naval Operations, record group 38, entry 193, stack 10WR, row 13, compartment 5, shelf 3–4, box 1, National Archives Building, Washington, DC.

24. Dorwart, *Dorwart's History*, 203.

25. Captain Wyman H. Packard, USN (Ret.), *A Century of U.S. Naval Intelligence* (Washington, DC: Office of Naval Intelligence, 1996), 17.

26. Packard, *Century of U.S. Naval Intelligence*, 17.

27. Dorwart, *Dorwart's History*, 207.

28. Dorwart, *Dorwart's History*, 217.

29. Dorwart, *Dorwart's History*, 217.

30. Dorwart, *Dorwart's History*, 248.

31. Dorwart, *Dorwart's History*, 210.

32. Dorwart, *Dorwart's History*, 211.

33. Hayne Ellis to J. V. Babcock, August 25, 1932, Records of the Office of the Chief of Naval Operations, record group 38, entry UD1, stack 370, row 14, compartment 35, shelf 3–4, box 1, National Archives at College Park, MD.

34. Hayne Ellis to J. V. Babcock, August 25, 1932.

35. 75th Cong. Rec. H120 (daily ed. December 7, 1932). One tried and true method of ONI attempting to influence congressional thinking was providing figures for use in floor debates. On December 7, the House used an ONI-produced table of new ships England, Japan, France, and Italy were constructing and how much money those countries appropriated to the navies in 1932.

36. Historian Edward Miller argued, "War Plan Orange, the secret program of the United States to defeat Japan, was in my opinion history's most successful war plan. In plans developed before the war, Japan was code-named Orange, the United States, Blue, hence the name of the plan developed over nearly four decades by the best strategic minds of the military services. As it was implemented in World War II, it was remarkably successful, especially considering the difficulties of Pacific geography and the many political and technological changes that occurred over the years. The prewar plans of other great powers proved, by and large, to be costly failures." Edward Miller, *War Plan Orange: The U.S. Strategy to Defeat Japan, 1897–1945* (Annapolis, MD: Naval Institute Press, 1991), xix.

37. Dorwart, *Dorwart's History*, 240.

38. Colonel Bruce W. Bidwell, *History of the Military Intelligence Division*,

Department of the Army General Staff: 1775–1941 (Frederick, MD: University Publications of America, 1986), 345.

39. Howell said, "I was amazed at the ease with which we entered this building and the offices of the Inspector. Of course we did this with the assistance and connivance of the superintendent and watchmen, who were only too glad to assist us—first, because of their patriotic duty, and second, because they hate the Japs so." Glenn F. Howell Log, September 1, 1929, box 15 LXVII, Archives Branch, Naval History and Heritage Command, Washington, DC.

40. Howell boasted in his log, "The grand thing about the whole performance is that they haven't the slightest suspicion that we have this stuff, for they are still using the same old secret code, and of course we are getting first hand information as to what they are really thinking and saying and planning." Glenn F. Howell Log, September 1, 1929.

41. Glenn wrote exactly how he felt about his target. He said, "I have been following Communism for months, and I am convinced that it is the severest menace the United States have. These damned skunks acting under the orders of Moscow presume to come over here and preach their sedition and overthrow of government. If they don't like this country let them go back to the rat holes whence they crept, but I went at this raid entirely cold-bloodedly." Glenn F. Howell Log, September 1, 1929.

42. Glenn bragged, "I invite your attention to the clippings in this section to see what happened, for I had chosen them to fit a possible reunion between the opposing forces of Foster and Lovestone. What happened was beyond my fondest expectations, for the raid, largely by luck, was blamed instantly on Lovestone—the ass sent a cable last May which I knew about and which directed a member of his gang to seize the very records which we seized. So it was that the Navy was, the last force suspected of seizing these records . . . this is a grand move because they are more than ever convinced that Lovestone stole these records, and nothing he can say or do will ever convince these Reds that he didn't do the . . . raid. We just happened to select the psychological moment—that's all, and I think we were luck although that is exactly what I wanted." Glenn F. Howell Log, September 1, 1929.

43. Dorwart, *Dorwart's History*, 200.

44. Tammany Hall was a New York City political organization founded in 1786. It was the Democratic Party political machine that helped control New York politics.

45. Glenn F. Howell Log, May 21, 1930, box 15 LXX, Archives Branch, Naval History and Heritage Command, Washington, DC.

46. Glenn F. Howell Log, May 21, 1930.

47. Glenn F. Howell Log, May 28, 1930, box 15 LXX, Archives Branch, Naval History and Heritage Command, Washington, DC.

48. Howell lied to the manager, "Mr. Meehan," after establishing himself as an American agent. Howell said, "So I established my identity to his satisfaction, asked him if he desired to do his country a patriotic service, and upon his eager

affirmation told him that in his building were working the agents of a foreign government against our own United States. I explained to him that it was essential that I get at the files of these foreigners and that I probably would need to photostat some papers." Glenn F. Howell Log, June 25, 1930, box 15 LXX, Archives Branch, Naval History and Heritage Command, Washington, DC.

49. The room they broke into was "absolutely empty" according to Howell. O'Brien had taken flight a couple days earlier and moved to another place "on Greenwich Avenue." Howell said that he appeared to have "fallen on evil days" after shadowing him. Howell believed that O'Brien told Tammany Hall that he "had the goods on Hoover" but was just stringing them along. Tammany realized O'Brien was lying and took away his rent for the office building, effectively kicking him to the curb. Glenn F. Howell Log, June 25, 1930.

50. Glenn F. Howell Log, June 25, 1930.

51. Dorwart, *Dorwart's History*, 208.

52. Dorwart, *Dorwart's History*, 231.

53. Dorwart, *Dorwart's History*, 232.

54. Dorwart, *Dorwart's History*, 217–218.

55. Dorwart, *Dorwart's History*, 221.

56. "Army and Navy Criticism Curbed by President, Church Group Says: Complaint over Naval Memorandum Asserting that Federal Council Is Aiding Communism Is Declared to Have Brought Order by Executive after Conference," *New York Times*, December 7, 1935, 1.

57. Dorwart, *Dorwart's History*, 229.

58. "Navy Men Tighten Vigilance on Spies: Espionage Activity Always Increases in the Expansion Periods, Says Standley," *New York Times*, July 26, 1936, 27.

59. "Navy Men Tighten Vigilance on Spies," 27.

60. Dorwart, *Dorwart's History*, 234.

61. Dorwart, *Dorwart's History*, 227.

62. Major George F. Eliot, *The Navy Spy Murders* (New York: Dodge, 1937), 68. This dime store novel features protagonist Agent Dan Fowler masquerading as Lieutenant Daniels, a naval reserve officer, even though he is an FBI agent. The FBI receives most of the credit in this book for counterintelligence, but Eliot gives nods to ONI with the character of naval intelligence officer Captain Upshaw. Further, the book references ONI and FBI conducting joint surveillance operations on civilian houses.

63. Dorwart, *Dorwart's History*, 234.

64. Ralph H. Van Deman to Alfred T. Smith, December 9, 1933, Records of the War Department General and Special Staffs, record group 165, entry 65, MID file 271-A-9 168, National Archives at College Park, MD.

65. Van Deman to Smith, December 9, 1933.

66. Smith stated, "I may state that within the limits of the United States the Department of Justice is charged with the investigation of civilians who may be disloyal citizens or enemy agents operating among the civil population. The

Army is responsible for preventing enemy agents from gaining military information from any military personnel. The Military Intelligence personnel is responsible for making investigations concerning disloyalty within the Army and also among civilians who may be employed within military camps, stations or installations. In border-line cases, the duties of the Department of Justice and of the Military Intelligence personnel will be very closely allied. The policy of the War Department is that no activities which might savor in the slightest degree of military espionage of our own people will be permitted in time of peace. Information relative to groups and organizations which might be involved in internal disorder or aiding an enemy will be obtained through civil officials and by scrutiny of the press." Alfred T. Smith to Ralph H. Van Deman, January 25, 1934, Records of the War Department General and Special Staffs, record group 165, entry 65, MID file 271-A-9 168, National Archives at College Park, MD.

67. Smith to Van Deman, January 25, 1934.

68. Michael E. Bigelow, "Van Deman," *Military Intelligence* 16, no. 4 (December 1990): 41.

69. Zacharias said of his meeting, "I found General Van Deman to be a reservoir of information, experience, and good counsel. It was natural that I should spend many hours in the little office of his home drinking in the words of wisdom not available anywhere else, even in the most extensive libraries." Zacharias, *Secret Missions*, 204.

70. Zacharias, *Secret Missions*, 204.

71. John P. Marquand, *No Hero* (Boston: Little and Brown, 1935), 77.

72. 72nd Cong. Rec, H1467 (January 11, 1930).

73. Representative William H. Stafford (Wisconsin) grumbled, "Ah, if it is merely for the expense of these nicely adorned military attachés who are connected with the courts of Europe, that is one thing, but if it is for military intelligence of the Army, that is another." 72nd Cong. Rec, H1467 (January 11, 1930).

74. Eisenhower, *Crusade in Europe*, 32.

75. James R. Green, "The First Sixty Years of the Office of Naval Intelligence" (MA thesis, American University, 1963), 85–86.

76. Baldwin said, "It is a war of espionage versus counter-espionage, spy and undercover man versus agent and officer, and it rarely breaks through the screen of mystery which surrounds it." Hanson W. Baldwin, "U.S. Alert to Spy Out Spies: Army and Navy Intelligence Staffs Keep Constant Vigil Against Foreign Prying," *New York Times*, July 19, 1936, E10.

77. Baldwin, "U.S. Alert to Spy Out Spies," E10.

78. Pinkerton wrote, "The shadow of the spy, which darkens the coffee houses and drawing rooms of lands abroad, is falling today on the far-flung defenses of the United States. About half a hundred spies—professional, disciplined foreign agents—hover about the arsenals, flying fields and coast defenses of a Nation new to intrigue. Beyond them are the petty "Informers"—Workmen, business men, housewives perhaps, who will sell a secret for a price—to anybody. No one knows how many of these amateurs there are." William M. Pinkerton, "Foreign

Spies Pit Cleverness against Four Big Agencies: F. B. I., G-2, O. N. I. and State Department's Special Agencies, Always on Alert. Spite Is Greatest Problem," *Sunday Star*, May 15, 1938, C-3.

79. Pinkerton, "Foreign Spies Pit Cleverness against Four Big Agencies," C-3.

80. Roosevelt stated to press reporters that counterintelligence meant to him "running down foreign spies in the United States"; however, he stressed that he did not "sanction espionage by American agents abroad." "President Urges Fund to Fight Spies: Favors Large Increase in Army and Navy Agencies—Deplores Sale of FBI Story," *New York Times*, June 25, 1938, 1.

81. Christy Cabanne, dir. *Smashing the Spy Ring* (Columbia Pictures, 1938).

82. Francis Van Wyck Mason, *The Man from G-2* (New York: Reynal and Hitchcock,1938), 168.

83. Thomas G. Mahnken, "Gazing at the Sun: The Office of Naval Intelligence and Japanese Naval Innovation, 1918–1941," *Intelligence and National Security* 11, no. 3 (July 1996): 424–425.

84. Mahnken, "Gazing at the Sun," 435.

85. Powe, "Emergence of a War Department Intelligence Agency," 108–109.

Chapter 8. 1939–1941: ONI and MID's Inability to Warn

1. Roberta Wohlstetter, *Pearl Harbor: Warning and Decision* (Stanford, CA: Stanford University Press, 1962), 387.

2. Prange wrote, "On the one hand, bountiful human errors of great variety, false assumptions, fallacious views, a vast store of intelligence badly handled; on the other, precise planning, tireless training, fanatical dedication, iron determination, technical know-how, tactical excellence, clever deception measures, intelligence well gathered and effectively disseminated, plain guts—and uncommon luck." Gordon W. Prange, *At Dawn We Slept: The Untold Story of Pearl Harbor* (New York: McGraw-Hill, 1981), xv–xvi.

3. Jeffery M. Dorwart, *Dorwart's History of the Office of Naval Intelligence: 1865–1945* (Annapolis, MD: Naval Institute Press, 2019), 318.

4. James R. Green, "The First Sixty Years of the Office of Naval Intelligence" (MA thesis, American University, 1963), 89.

5. Captain Wyman H. Packard, USN (Ret.), *A Century of U.S. Naval Intelligence* (Washington, DC: Office of Naval Intelligence, 1996), 21.

6. Packard, *Century of U.S. Naval Intelligence*, 25; Prange, *At Dawn We Slept*, 88; Jeffery M. Dorwart, *The U.S. Navy's Intelligence Dilemma, 1919–1945: Conflict of Duty* (Annapolis, MD: Naval Institute Press, 1983), 183; and Edward Miller, *War Plan Orange: The U.S. Strategy to Defeat Japan, 1897–1945* (Annapolis, MD: Naval Institute Press, 1991), 269. According to Packard, Turner tried to make ONI "a mere collection" agency without evaluation capability, which contributed to gaps in Navy' readiness. Prange argued that, in privileging its role as a collecting and distributing clearinghouse, the Navy removed ONI from evaluating Japanese intentions even though they were best suited for the job; naval

intelligence knew Japan, being familiar with its language and armed forces. Miller stated further, "The Office of Naval Intelligence, lacking prestige and suffering rapid turnover of leadership, played a minor role in prewar planning." Miller, *War Plan Orange*, 353.

7. Captain Ellis M. Zacharias, *Secret Missions: The Story of an Intelligence Officer* (New York: G. P. Putnam's, 1946), 253.

8. Colonel Bruce W. Bidwell, *History of the Military Intelligence Division, Department of the Army General Staff: 1775–1941* (Frederick, MD: University Publications of America, 1986), 456 and 525. The historian argued that collecting information on Japan were not as defined as ONI and MID wished them to be. Therefore, US military intelligence organizations risked intruding on each other's turf. There was no joint intelligence committee at the time that would have allowed for a better picture of Japanese planning.

9. Marc B. Powe and Edward E. Wilson, *The Evolution of American Military Intelligence* (Fort Huachuca, AZ: US Army Intelligence Center and School, 1973), 41.

10. Wohlstetter, *Pearl Harbor*, 279.

11. Alan H. Bath, *Tracking the Axis Enemy: The Triumph of Anglo-American Naval Intelligence* (Lawrence, KS: University Press of Kansas, 1998), 4–5.

12. "ONI itself was seriously affected by its exclusion from the evaluation and policy decisions of War Plans" because "its usefulness to the Navy was in direct proportion to the use it could make of raw intelligence." Wohlstetter, *Pearl Harbor*, 323.

13. Wohlstetter, *Pearl Harbor*, 279.

14. Headquarters Memorandum no. 1 by T. Holcomb, "Staff Organizations and Procedures," April 21, 1939, National Archives and Research Administration, National Archives at College Park, MD (Courtesy of Maj Michael H. Decker [ret]).

15. Major Michael H. Decker (ret.) and Sergeant (ret.) William Mackenzie, "Marine Corps Intelligence," *Marine Corps Gazette* 103, no. 9 (September 2019): 12.

16. Dorwart, *Dorwart's History*, 262.

17. Walter S. Anderson, interview by John Mason Jr., 1962, Naval History Project, Oral History Archives at Columbia, Columbia University in the City of New York, 225. Hereafter known as "Anderson Oral History Interview."

18. Anderson Oral History Interview, 226.

19. Anderson Oral History Interview, 227.

20. Memorandum by Walter S. Anderson, "Are We Ready?" August 31, 1939, US Naval Administrative Histories of World War II, Office of the Chief of Naval Operations, "Office of Naval Intelligence," 4 vols., Archives Branch, Naval History and Heritage Command, Washington, DC (hard copy) and Nimitz Library, United States Naval Academy, Annapolis, MD (microfiche), 1.

21. Anderson, "Are We Ready?" August 31, 1939, 2.

22. Memorandum by the Chief of Naval Operations, "Intelligence—Prompt

Forwarding of Important Reports," September 3, 1939, General Records of the Department of the Navy, record group 80, entry UD-8, stack 11W3, row 22, compartment 13, shelf 6, box 31, National Archives Building, Washington, DC.

23. Kirk remembered, "But you see, at the beginning of the war, the sentiment in this country, and especially in Washington, was rather dubious about whether we were going to be in it and how it was going to come out. It wasn't very popular to support the British cause." Alan G. Kirk, interview by John Mason Jr., 1962, Naval History Project, Oral History Archives at Columbia, Columbia University in the City of New York, 133. Hereafter known as "Kirk Oral History Interview."

24. Packard, *Century of U.S. Naval Intelligence*, 225.

25. Memorandum by Walter S. Anderson, "Readiness of the Naval Establishment to Meet a Serious Emergency?" May 21, 1940, US Naval Administrative Histories of World War II, Office of the Chief of Naval Operations, "Office of Naval Intelligence."

26. Anderson, "Readiness of the Naval Establishment."

27. Memorandum by Walter S. Anderson, "Are We Ready?" June 10, 1940, US Naval Administrative Histories of World War II, Office of the Chief of Naval Operations, "Office of Naval Intelligence."

28. Anderson wrote, "We have at present no intelligence network abroad other than Naval Attachés. When and if the need for 'agents' appear[s], I believe we can handle the situation." Anderson, "Are We Ready?" June 10, 1940.

29. Anderson Oral History Interview, 235.

30. Anderson would remember, "I was very gratified by this, but as my interests and ambitions lay along the lines of regular Navy duty, especially sea duty, I expressed my deep appreciation and thanks, but declined to consent to a permanent job as director of naval intelligence." Anderson Oral History Interview, 274.

31. Anderson was proud to have served as DNI and received accolades from superiors and peers. He was particularly proud of a letter from a characteristically stoic FBI Director J. Edgar Hoover, who called him "a dear personal friend." Hoover gushed, "I do want you to know that I am from a selfish viewpoint sorry to see you leave the position of Director of Naval Intelligence in order to return to sea duty. While I am glad for your sake that this transfer has come to you, because I know that by your very splendid record and tremendous ability you well merit this promotion, I nevertheless feel that in your transfer from Washington the Bureau is losing a fine official friend and supporter and I will be separated from a dear personal friend. Our relationship during the entire tenure of your assignment to the Office of Naval Intelligence has been an ideal one, and I feel that greater progress has been made in real coordination and cooperation of the Intelligence agencies during this period than at any time heretofore." J. Edgar Hoover to Walter S. Anderson, January 11, 1941, record group 38, entry 30, stack 170, row 65, compartment 23, shelf 2, box 2, National Archives and Research Administration, National Archives at College Park, MD.

32. Kirk Oral History Interview, 168.

33. Chester W. Nimitz to Alan G. Kirk, "Change of Duty," January 23, 1941, Records of the Office of the Chief of Naval Operations, record group 38, entry 30, stack 170, row 65, compartment 23, shelf 2, box 5, National Archives at College Park, MD.

34. Kirk recounted that Holmes said, "'Now, Alan, I want to tell you something. You may think this is something that you shouldn't do, but I warn you, President Roosevelt loves to talk, and he will begin on almost anything when you sit down, and he'll talk for twenty-five minutes of your half hour.' He said, 'Rude though it may sound, you've just got to break in, if you really want to tell him anything, and you should.'" Kirk Oral History Interview, 174.

35. Kirk continued the story on his briefing: "So in some fear—and trepidation, I went over to the White House. President Roosevelt was seated, of course, behind his desk, with his long cigarette holder and so on. He threw up his hands and said, 'Alan, my boy, I'm glad to see you back!' Then he launched into some long discourse, I forget what it was. Whereupon I broke in, after two or three minutes: 'Sir, I've really got some things I want to tell you about.' 'Oh,' he said. 'Well, go ahead.' Then I told him these various things." Kirk Oral History Interview, 175.

36. Alan G. Kirk to J. L. Kauffman, March 17, 1941, Records of the Office of the Chief of Naval Operations, record group 38, entry 30, stack 170, row 65, compartment 23, shelf 2, box 4, National Archives at College Park, MD. He said to a friend that his selection was a great surprise to him, and the Navy made the decision without consulting Kirk at all.

37. Kirk stated later, "I was a blue water sailor. I'd only been a Naval Attaché once, and I really had no yearning for the cloak and dagger trade or anything else." Kirk Oral History Interview, 177–178.

38. One friend told him, "I know that you wanted to go to sea and I don't blame you. However, there are lots of people that can go down to the sea in ships who could not do the job you have been selected for. Outside your personal feelings in the matter you have nothing to worry about as your career is an assured thing." Kirk returned a letter to another friend, future DNI Captain Harold C. Train, saying, "Thanks very much for your pleasant letter of February 17 and your congratulations. This is the first time I ever changed shore jobs. I must say it is with some trepidation, as it causes me to lose my chance to go to sea. You and the other fellows who have commands at this time are very fortunate." J. L. Kauffman to Alan G. Kirk, February 12, 1941, Records of the Office of the Chief of Naval Operations, record group 38, entry 30, stack 170, row 65, compartment 23, shelf 2, box 4, National Archives at College Park, MD, and Alan G. Kirk to Harold C. Train, March 11, 1941, Records of the Office of the Chief of Naval Operations, record group 38, entry 30, stack 170, row 65, compartment 23, shelf 2, box 5, National Archives at College Park, MD.

39. Walter S. Anderson to Alan G. Kirk, March 11, 1941, Records of the Office

of the Chief of Naval Operations, record group 38, entry 30, stack 170, row 65, compartment 23, shelf 2, box 2, National Archives at College Park, MD.

40. Dorwart, *Dorwart's History*, 295.

41. Packard, *Century of U.S. Naval Intelligence*, 171.

42. An Act to Authorize a Plant-Protection Force for Naval Shore Establishments, and for Other Purposes, Chap. 352, 616 (August 11, 1941).

43. Forrestal told him, "Well, I think you can get it. That will be done. All right. I think the Secretary is ready to see a change in Naval Intelligence, not that he doesn't think you've done a good job, but he thinks, you know, we ought to have some fresh blood." Kirk Oral History Interview, 182–183.

44. Kirk Oral History Interview, 183. Kirk justified in his own mind his decision. He believed that nobody was staying at ONI because of its officers' reputation as "striped pants, cookie-pushers, going to parties and so on, especially abroad."

45. Kirk wrote to Miles on October 14, "I want to take this occasion to express to you and M.I.D. my warm appreciation for the close cooperation and kind assistance you have given me personally and this Division generally." Alan G. Kirk to Sherman Miles, October 14, 1941, Records of the Office of the Chief of Naval Operations, record group 38, entry 30, stack 170, row 65, compartment 23, shelf 2, box 4, National Archives at College Park, MD.

46. Dorwart, *Dorwart's History*, 312.

47. Strong stated, "It was apparent from the very beginning of the national emergency, which preceded our formal entry into the war, that the data and records on file were not only inadequate in many of the intelligence subjects required by total war, but much information on regions where our national interest had been considered remote was almost non-existent so far as modern up-to-date intelligence was concerned. This condition was the direct result of the years of neglect of the Military Intelligence organization in our Army." Memorandum by George V. Strong, "Biennial Report," May 9, 1943, George W. Auxier Historical Manuscript File.

48. "History of the Branch Offices of MID, 1940–1945," Undated, Records of the Army Staff, record group 319, entry 1071, stack 270, row 15, compartment 4, shelf 2–3, box 13, National Archives at College Park, MD, 2.

49. "History of the Branch Offices of MID, 1940–1945," 2.

50. Wohlstetter, *Pearl Harbor*, 289.

51. US War Department, General Staff, Military Intelligence Division, *A History of the Military Intelligence Division 7 December 1941—2 September 1945*, 1946, 6. Hereafter known as *History of the Military Intelligence Division*.

52. *History of the Military Intelligence Division*, 9.

53. Memorandum by E. S. Adams, "Delineation of Intelligence Responsibilities," September 10, 1941, George W. Auxier Historical Manuscript File.

54. Adams, "Delineation of Intelligence Responsibilities," September 10, 1941.

55. Memorandum by Franklin D. Roosevelt, June 26, 1939, Records of the

Office of the Chief of Naval Operations, record group 38, entry UD16, stack 370, row 17, compartment 4, shelf 2, box 33, National Archives at College Park, MD.

56. Dorwart, *Dorwart's History*, 263.

57. Roy Talbert, *Negative Intelligence the Army and the American Left, 1917–1941* (Jackson: University Press of Mississippi, 1991), 172.

58. Memorandum by Chief of Naval Operations, "Cooperation with the Federal Bureau of Investigation and Military Intelligence Division, and the Training of I-V(S) Officers in Connection Therewith," December 7, 1939, Records of the Office of the Chief of Naval Operations, record group 38, entry UD1, stack 370, row 14, compartment 35, shelf 3–4, box 5, National Archives at College Park, MD, 1.

59. Anderson Oral History Interview, 230–231.

60. In Berle's June 4, 1940, diary entry he discussed a meeting at Hoover's office on how to coordinate intelligence. He said, "This may transfer some of this paranoid work into positive and useful channels. We likewise decided that the time had come when we would have to consider setting up a secret intelligence service—which I suppose every great foreign office in the world has, but we have never touched." Adolf A. Berle, *Navigating the Rapids, 1918–1971: From the Papers of Adolf A. Berle*, ed. Beatrice B. Berle and Travis B. Jacobs (New York: Harcourt Brace Jovanovich, 1973), 321.

61. Anderson Oral History Interview, 231.

62. Talbert, *Negative Intelligence*, 173–175. The author noted that even with a general officer as G-2, Miles was no match for Hoover, an intelligence and bureaucratic veteran of over twenty years. Miles arrived at MID with no counterintelligence experience. He even asked retired military intelligence pioneer Major General Ralph Van Deman to come to Washington to give Miles tips on how to manage domestic security.

63. Paul M. Robinett to Bruce W. Bidwell, September 9, 1954, Records of the Army Staff, record group 319, entry P 128, stack 270, row 19, compartment 15, shelf 6, box 1, National Archives at College Park, MD.

64. Packard, *Century of U.S. Naval Intelligence*, 22.

65. Memorandum by Sherman Miles, "Appreciation of Military and Naval Intelligence," July 2, 1941, George W. Auxier Historical Manuscript File.

66. Miles pleaded with the general, "I bring this to your attention because I think it is a point of great importance in the matter now under consideration, and I suggest that, if a fitting occasion should arise. It be brought to the attention of higher authority." Miles, "Appreciation of Military and Naval Intelligence."

67. Packard, *Century of U.S. Naval Intelligence*, 225.

68. Joint Intelligence Center Organizational Chart, December 1, 1941, Records of the Office of the Chief of Naval Operations, record group 38, entry UD2, stack 370, row 14, compartment 35, shelf 67, box 1, National Archives at College Park, MD.

69. The naval attaché post sent out on average of 1,440 to 1,700 reports annually in the late 1930s.

70. Kirk stated, "I'd always wanted to do that. Captain Anderson, who'd been

the Naval Attaché in London at one time, was my friend in this matter, and he was head of the Office of Naval Intelligence at the time, so I had a good word put in for me from that angle, in that area. The Department felt it would be a good appointment." Kirk Oral History Interview, 118.

71. Kirk stated, "I knew how little *we* knew. And of course, they themselves were pretty careful not to give too much, because they didn't want it to leak out to possible enemies." Kirk Oral History Interview, 133.

72. The DNI called on his State Department friends Ray Atherton and Berle, and they called a conference. Anderson recalled the meeting: "I was asked to state my difficulties, and said what they were. They said, 'For example, tell us where you went to send your observers. I said, 'Well, to take a place at random, Darwin, Australia.' The administrative officer spoke up and said, 'We haven't a consul there,' at which Mr. Berle made a forcible comment and asked what that had to do with it. This is an illustration of some of the internal difficulties that an administrative officer may encounter." Anderson Oral History Interview, 227–228.

73. Anderson Oral History Interview, 228–229.

74. Alan G. Kirk to Walter S. Anderson, May 14, 1940, Records of the Office of the Chief of Naval Operations, record group 38, entry 30, stack 170, row 65, compartment 23, shelf 2, box 2, National Archives at College Park, MD.

75. Kirk lamented, "I dislike always being gloomy, but it is my personal view that the Germans will attempt an invasion of these islands. . . . But that the German soldier will be on this Island in some force before next Fall, I am willing to offer 2–1 money . . . The trouble with the whole show is that not enough people foresaw the terrible military machine Mr. Hitler was building in time to take effective counter measures. They are too late over here in everything they undertake. I hope this lesson will not be lost sight of in our own country." Alan G. Kirk to Walter S. Anderson, May 14, 1940.

76. Kirk reported the latest situation on May 30, "As I write this, the remnants of the B.E.F. are being retrieved from the Belgian Coast. In less than three weeks the Dutch, Belgian, and British Armies, plus fragments of two French Armies have been completely wiped out. This is staggering, indeed." Alan G. Kirk to Walter S. Anderson, May 30, 1940, Records of the Office of the Chief of Naval Operations, record group 38, entry 30, stack 170, row 65, compartment 23, shelf 2, box 2, National Archives at College Park, MD.

77. Kirk judged, "Whoever tries to take it on must be prepared for a terrific struggle. No one should take it on unless they are ready to offer a heavy challenge for supremacy in the air." Kirk to Anderson, May 30, 1940.

78. Dorwart, *Dorwart's History*, 274–275.

79. Kirk said gloomily, "This war over here is going sour so fast that I hope my position with you is perfectly clear. It is my considered opinion that the war effort of the British and French has been so badly organized, badly planned, and badly led that the individual superiority of the Frenchmen and Englishmen against the Germans will give way, very rapidly, to sheer weight of numbers. The two

Democracies have not prepared themselves for the kind of war the Germans are waging and they are paying the penalty. They are short of airplanes, of tanks, of heavy artillery, of motorized transport, of anti-aircraft weapons—in short, they lack adequate supplies of anything and everything needed to combat the German war machine." Alan G. Kirk to Walter S. Anderson, June 11, 1940, Records of the Office of the Chief of Naval Operations, record group 38, entry 30, stack 170, row 65, compartment 23, shelf 2, box 2, National Archives at College Park, MD.

80. He displayed his anxiety to Anderson by saying, "Of course, no one is more distressed personally than I to have to write things like this, but that is what I believe and I think you are entitled to know." Kirk to Anderson, June 11, 1940.

81. Dorwart, *Dorwart's History*, 285–286.

82. The Navy Department's request to designate Ghormley as naval attaché to London confused the Department of State. Why was the Navy keeping Kirk there in that capacity? Their Division of European Affairs sent an internal memorandum around the State Department, stating, "It has never been the policy of the Department to have two Naval or Military Attachés at the same Mission and the Department may not wish to initiate a practice at the present time which would set a precedent for other of our Missions or which would give other countries a basis for asking us to accept two Naval or Military Attachés from them." The State Department concluded that the Navy could neither make a rear admiral an assistant attaché nor positionally demote Captain Kirk. Their recommendation was to designate two naval attachés to London. Department of State Division of European Affairs Memorandum, July 27, 1940, Records of the Office of the Chief of Naval Operations, record group 38, entry 30, stack 170, row 65, compartment 23, shelf 2, box 5, National Archives at College Park, MD.

83. Ghormley was an old friend of his. Kirk believed the Navy Department thought Kirk was too young to deal with British authorities at this high of level. He stated, "It was perfectly silly, because almost all the Board of Admiralty were just as old as I was or just as young as I was. Nevertheless, in terms of rank, it wouldn't do, so they sent over Ghormley." Roosevelt and the Navy probably did need someone of higher rank, but also an officer with a less depressing, more objective look at Great Britain's situation. Kirk Oral History Interview, 166–167.

84. Anderson said, "I want to make it clear that everybody's heart was in the right place here, but I thought their technique left something to be desired. . . . I want to assure you once more that all of us here, of high and low degree, appreciate the fine job you are doing over there. "Walter S. Anderson to Alan G. Kirk, August 29, 1940, Records of the Office of the Chief of Naval Operations, record group 38, entry 30, stack 170, row 65, compartment 23, shelf 2, box 2, National Archives at College Park, MD.

85. Dorwart, *Dorwart's History*, 286.

86. Dorwart, *Dorwart's History*, 279.

87. Dorwart, *Dorwart's History*, 261.

88. Dorwart, *Dorwart's History*, 266–267.

89. Anderson Oral History Interview, 229–230.

90. "Navy Guards against Spies," *Wilmington Morning Star*, November 12, 1940, 1.

91. Bidwell, *History*, 400.

92. Kirk said of March and April incidents, "I ran afoul of my friend Edgar Hoover, who maintained that inside the United States, the FBI was paramount, and that outside, Naval Intelligence and Military Intelligence were paramount. It was a long-standing feud. It never got really serious, but It might have, and in this particular case Naval Intelligence rather wiped the eye, so to speak, of the FBI, because our men found it out and we acted very promptly." Kirk Oral History Interview, 181.

93. Sherman Miles to Alan G. Kirk, May 29, 1941, Records of the Office of the Chief of Naval Operations, record group 38, entry UD16, stack 370, row 17, compartment 4, shelf 2, box 33, National Archives at College Park, MD.

94. Dorwart, *Dorwart's History*, 292–293.

95. Dorwart, *Dorwart's History*, 271.

96. Dorwart, *Dorwart's History*, 299.

97. Packard, *Century of U.S. Naval Intelligence*, 21–22.

98. Stark said in a memorandum November 26 that the war emphasized "the need of (1) dispatch in acquiring, evaluating and disseminating information, (2) insuring that it be promptly, carefully and completely considered, and (3) that, where indicated as desirable, actual and prompt application be made in order to improve the efficiency of our naval service." Memorandum by Harold R. Stark, "Naval Intelligence—Application and Dissemination of within Bureaus and Offices of the Navy Department," November 26, 1940, Records of the Office of the Chief of Naval Operations, record group 38, entry UD33, stack 370, row 15, compartment 1, shelf 2–6, box 8, National Archives at College Park, MD.

99. Stark, "Naval Intelligence—Application and Dissemination," November 26, 1940.

100. Packard, *Century of U.S. Naval Intelligence*, 21.

101. Prange, *At Dawn They Slept*, 87.

102. Dorwart, *Dorwart's History*, 297–298.

103. Office of Naval Intelligence Organization Chart, July 11, 1941, Records of the Office of the Chief of Naval Operations, record group 38, entry UD33, stack 370, row 15, compartment 1, shelf 2–6, box 26, National Archives at College Park, MD.

104. Phyllis L. Soybel, "A Necessary Relationship: The Development of Anglo-American Cooperation in Naval Intelligence" (PhD diss., University of Illinois at Chicago, 1997), 182.

105. Kirk later described his difficulties dealing with Turner: "He had the confidence of Ingersoll, the Assistant Chief of Naval Operations, and Admiral Starks. A very strong personality. . . . He felt he knew a great deal about the Japanese. We were clashing right along. It wasn't a very happy time there for me. I couldn't really persuade people." Kirk Oral History Interview, 179–180.

106. Dorwart, *Dorwart's History*, 300.

107. Packard, *Century of U.S. Naval Intelligence*, 22.

108. Wohlstetter, *Pearl Harbor*, 322.

109. Bidwell, *History*, 439.

110. "Eyes of Our Army," *New York Times*, March 4, 1941, 22.

111. John Patrick Finnegan and Romana Danysh, *Military Intelligence* (Washington, DC: Center for Military History, United States Army, 1998), 56.

112. J. Edgar Hoover, "Is There a Spy Menace?" *Week Magazine*, July 14, 1940, 2.

113. Hoover, "Is There a Spy Menace?" 2.

114. One FBI investigator told Dennis, "Certain information picked up and pieced together by the various United States intelligence services, the F.B.I. Military Intelligence and Naval Intelligence prove that secret agents of a certain group of foreign powers are at work in this country, and that they have a deadly Intrigue aimed directly at the security and future of the United States." Bruno Branzel, "That We May Live," *Sunday Star*, November 3, 1940, B-9.

115. Lewis Seiler, dir., *Murder in the Air* (Warner Bros., 1940). The inertia projector supposedly made the US "invincible in war." One can surmise that the device was decades ahead of its time similar, to the Star Wars defense program conceptualized during Reagan's administration.

116. 87th Cong. Rec. H5052 (daily ed. June 11, 1941).

117. Frederick R. Barkley, "Close Watch on Spies Revealed by Arrests: FBI, Army and Navy Act When Secret Agents Become a Real Menace," *New York Times*, editorial, July 6, 1941, E8.

118. Barkley, "Close Watch," E8.

119. Barkley, "Close Watch," E8.

120. Dorwart, *Dorwart's History*, 312.

121. Dorwart, *Dorwart's History*, 316.

122. Green, "First Sixty Years," 85.

123. Green, "First Sixty Years," 98.

124. Packard, *Century of U.S. Naval Intelligence*, 23.

125. Dorwart, *Dorwart's History*, 318.

126. Bidwell, *History*, 485.

127. "Annex to Organization Chart, General Staff (G-2)," December 5, 1941, Records of the Army Staff, record group 319, entry P 128, stack 270, row 19, compartment 15, shelf 6, box 4, National Archives at College Park, MD.

128. Robinett recalled, "It was no longer a question of the coordination of the old established intelligence agencies because the situation had been confused by the emergence of a number of new agencies which distracted existing agencies and contributed nothing constructive to the solution of the pressing intelligence problems. The confusion merely became confounded." Paul M. Robinett to Bruce W. Bidwell, September 9, 1954.

129. R. A. Kotrla, "Naval Intelligence Specialists Trained on Post-Graduate

Level," *Proceedings of the United States Naval Institute* 73, no. 9 (September 1947): 1061.

130. Dorwart, *Dorwart's History*, 310.

Chapter 9. 1941–1945: ONI and MID Sidelined Again

1. John Prados, *Combined Fleet Decoded: The Secret History of American Intelligence and the Japanese Navy in World War II* (New York: Random House, 1995), 354.

2. Sergeant David J. Ferrier, *ONI and OSS in World War II* (Washington, DC: Navy and Marine Corps WWII Commemorative Committee, Navy Office of Information, 1995), 1.

3. US War Department, General Staff, Military Intelligence Division, *History of the Military Intelligence Division 7 December 1941–2 September 1945*, 1946, 2.

4. *History of the Military Intelligence Division*, 9. This continual reshuffle resulted from wartime demands pressuring reallocations of functions.

5. Captain Ellis M. Zacharias, assistant to the DNI in 1942–1943 said, "Only perfunctory use was made of the Office of Naval Intelligence; the old prejudices carried over into war; and we had to fight for recognition, virtually sell our material to the staffs, no matter how valuable it might have been. Captain Ellis M. Zacharias, *Secret Missions: The Story of an Intelligence Officer* (New York: G. P. Putnam's, 1946), 294.

6. Russell F. Weigley, *History of the United States Army* (New York: Macmillan, 1967), 459.

7. Zacharias, *Secret Missions*, 296.

8. Jeffery M. Dorwart, *Dorwart's History of the Office of Naval Intelligence: 1865–1945* (Annapolis, MD: Naval Institute Press, 2019), 323.

9. Captain Wyman H. Packard, USN (Ret.), *A Century of U.S. Naval Intelligence* (Washington, DC: Office of Naval Intelligence, 1996), 302.

10. Memorandum by Paul Cassard, "Organization of M.I.D.," December 30, 1941, Records of the War Department General and Special Staffs, record group 165, entry UD33, stack 370, row 15, compartment 1, shelf 2–6, box 2, National Archives at College Park, MD.

11. Dorwart, *Dorwart's History*, 323.

12. Packard, *Century of U.S. Naval Intelligence*, 204.

13. Memorandum for Self by William D. Puleston, "The Changes and Fundamental Organization of the War and Navy Departments," March 10, 1042, box 1, William D. Puleston Papers, Archives Branch, Naval History and Heritage Command, Washington, DC.

14. Dorwart, *Dorwart's History*, 329.

15. Memorandum by A. D. Chandler, "Report of Officers, Enlisted Men, Civilian Agents and Civil Service Employees on Active Duty and Employed throughout the Entire Naval Intelligence Organization," April 1, 1942, Records of the Office of the Chief of Naval Operations, record group 38, entry UD21,

stack 370, row 15, compartment 6, shelf 2–3, box 1, National Archives at College Park, MD. The total personnel accounts for attachés, district offices, and investigative agents.

16. Dorwart, *Dorwart's History*, 334.

17. Zacharias, *Secret History*, 288.

18. Dorwart, *Dorwart's History*, 334.

19. Train recalled in a later oral history interview, "I don't think Mr. Hoover thought he was a good intelligence officer, even with all his aggressiveness, all his Japanese language things and everything. I just don't think he thought he was, and he disliked his actions. Zacharias was very aggressive, too aggressive." Harold C. Train, interview by John Mason Jr., 1965, Naval History Project. Oral History Archives at Columbia, Columbia University in the City of New York, 281. Hereafter known as "Train Oral History Interview."

20. Zacharias, *Secret History*, 288–289.

21. Zacharias recalled, "I was compelled to wage an uphill fight; even so I was able to carry out at least a part of my program, fighting, as I went, against obstruction and inertia." Zacharias, *Secret History*, 288–289.

22. Train specifically stated later, "to pick out a man that you thought would be an acceptable representative of our country to the particular country he's going to, speak the language if possible; also the factor of his wife entered into it a great deal. I think the fact was lost sight of many times, in sending an officer to be naval attaché; we made a mistake sometimes as regard the qualifications of his wife, and we had a couple of cases that didn't work out too well then. That's the basic thing—to get a man that would be an acceptable representative." Train Oral History Interview, 304–305.

23. O. L. Nelson to Joseph T. McNarney, "Space Needs of the Military Intelligence Service and the Office of Naval Intelligence," November 5, 1942, Records of the War Department General and Special Staffs, record group 165, entry 175, stack 390, row 35, compartment 6, shelf 5, box 346, National Archives at College Park, MD.

24. Dorwart, *Dorwart's History*, 338.

25. Dorwart, *Dorwart's History*, 340.

26. Train recalled, "Mr. Warner came to see me one time and said he'd been directed to inspect ONI. He was very apologetic. He was embarrassed. He said he knew absolutely nothing about the workings of intelligence, any more than I knew about the working of Gulf Oil, if I were directed to conduct an inspection of that company. I told him to go ahead and opened up everything I could for his inspection." Train Oral History Interview, 293–294.

27. Memorandum by Rawleigh Warner, "Summary Report of Intelligence Functions," April 29, 1943, Records of the War Department General and Special Staffs, record group 165, entry 175, stack 390, row 35, compartment 6, shelf 5, box 347, National Archives at College Park, MD, 1–2.

28. US Naval Administrative Histories of World War II, Office of the Chief of Naval Operations, "Office of Naval Intelligence," 4 vols., Archives Branch, Naval

History and Heritage Command, Washington, DC (hard copy) and Nimitz Library, United States Naval Academy, Annapolis, MD (microfiche), 93.

29. Dorwart, *Dorwart's History*, 338.

30. Ellis M. Zacharias, "Remarks of Captain E.M. Zacharias, USN, Deputy Director of Naval Intelligence upon Occasion of Conference with 'A' Branch Officers in Re: Personnel Audit," May 8, 1943, Records of the Office of the Chief of Naval Operations, record group 38, entry UD21, stack 370, row 15, compartment 6, shelf 2–3, box 1, National Archives at College Park, MD.

31. Zacharias, *Secret History*, 315–316.

32. Train recalled, "The first day in the office on my return, General Strong informed me that while I was gone Zacharias had done his best to get my job, but had failed. I was also tipped off by J. Edgar Hoover. I'd sort of suspected that he might try to do just that, but it came as a shock to me that one of my most senior officers would be so disloyal as to do such a thing behind my back." Train Oral History Interview, 315.

33. Train Oral History Interview, 315, and Jeffery M. Dorwart, *The U.S. Navy's Intelligence Dilemma, 1919–1945: Conflict of Duty* (Annapolis, MD: Naval Institute Press, 1983), 204–205. King, of course, did not send Zacharias to Africa. Despite efforts of King to reassign him to a minor post, Zacharias appealed to friends in Congress to put pressure on Knox to give him sea command. After sea duty, Zacharias still was involved heavily in the war effort, including propaganda broadcasts to Japan. Zacharias received a promotion to a "tombstone admiral" or advanced one rank as a commendation of service after retirement. Train called him too ambitious and too determined to be DNI and deplored Zacharias's methods of attaining his goals.

34. Train stated, "I've always expressed my opinion of ONI, that it's a frustrating job." Train Oral History Interview, 325.

35. Train Oral History Interview, 307–308.

36. Captain W. H. Packard, "ONI Centennial," October 1982, Records of the Office of the Chief of Naval Operations, record group 38, entry UD-09D 19, stack 270, row 82, compartment 21, shelf 1, box 116, National Archives at College Park, MD, 7.

37. Memorandum by N. M. Pigman, "History," November 17, 1943, Records of the Office of the Chief of Naval Operations, record group 38, entry UD21, stack 370, row 15, compartment 6, shelf 2–3, box 1, National Archives at College Park, MD, 3.

38. Dorwart, *Dorwart's History*, 351.

39. Memorandum by R. E. Schuirmann, "Post-War Demobilization Planning—Navy Basic Demobilization Plan No. 1," January 5, 1944, Records of the Office of the Chief of Naval Operations, record group 38, entry UD21, stack 370, row 15, compartment 6, shelf 2–3, box 5, National Archives at College Park, MD.

40. Schuirmann, "Post-War Demobilization Planning," January 5, 1944.

41. Memorandum by director of naval intelligence, "Revision of Manual of Organizational Charts of Bureaus and Offices in the Navy Department," January

8, 1944, Records of the Office of the Chief of Naval Operations, record group 38, entry UD33, stack 370, row 15, compartment 1, shelf 2–6, box 1, National Archives at College Park, MD.

42. Memorandum by Leo H. Thebaud, "Post-War and Demobilization Plans," May 3, 1945, Records of the Office of the Chief of Naval Operations, record group 38, entry UD33, stack 370, row 15, compartment 1, shelf 2–6, box 25, National Archives at College Park, MD.

43. Thebaud said, "The conclusion of active warfare makes it appropriate for Naval Intelligence officers to give careful consideration to their immediate and long-range future. Being fully aware of the patriotism which prompted you to enter the Navy, and of the very gratifying results which our intelligence personnel have achieved, I wish to assist you in every appropriate manner to realize your personal wishes." Memorandum by Leo H. Thebaud, August 15, 1945, Records of the Office of the Chief of Naval Operations, record group 38, entry UD21, stack 370, row 15, compartment 6, shelf 2–3b, Box 5, National Archives at College Park, MD.

44. Memorandum by Thebaud, August 15, 1945.

45. General Dwight D. Eisenhower said in his book *Crusade in Europe*, "Initially the Intelligence Division could not even develop a clear plan for its own organization nor could it classify the type of information it deemed essential in determining the purposes and capabilities of our enemies. The chief of the division could do little more than come to the planning and operating sections of the staff and in a rather pitiful way ask if there was anything he could do for us." Dwight D. Eisenhower, *Crusade in Europe* (New York: Doubleday, 1948), 32.

46. Colonel Bruce W. Bidwell, *History of the Military Intelligence Division, Department of the Army General Staff: 1775–1941* (Frederick, MD: University Publications of America, 1986), 480.

47. Lee was a temporary fill as G-2 after Miles rotated. He would only hold the post for three months.

48. *History of the Military Intelligence Division*, 12–13.

49. *History of the Military Intelligence Division*, 14–15.

50. John Patrick Finnegan, *Military History: A Picture History*, 2nd ed. (Fort Belvoir, VA: US Army, 1992), 61.

51. "Organization, Military Intelligence Service, War Department," March 14, 1942, Records of the Army Staff, record group 319, entry P 128, stack 270, row 19, compartment 15, shelf 6, box 4, National Archives at College Park, MD.

52. Major General Otto L. Nelson Jr., *National Security and the General Staff* (Washington, DC: Infantry Journal Press, 1946), 524.

53. Eisenhower said of Major General George V. Strong that he was "a senior officer possessed of keen mind, a driving energy, and ruthless determination." Assistant to the Secretary of State Assistant Adolf A. Berle reported in his journal, "The more I see of General Strong, the better I like him. He is a sound, solid citizen." Eisenhower, *Crusade in Europe*, 33–34 and Adolf A. Berle, *Navigating*

the Rapids, 1918–1971: From the Papers of Adolf A. Berle, ed. Beatrice B. Berle and Travis B. Jacobs (New York: Harcourt Brace Jovanovich, 1973), 410.

54. Eisenhower, *Crusade in Europe*, 33–34.

55. *History of the Military Intelligence Division*, 18.

56. John Patrick Finnegan and Romana Danysh, *Military Intelligence* (Washington, DC: Center for Military History, United States Army, 1998), 64.

57. *History of the Military Intelligence Division*, 20.

58. *History of the Military Intelligence Division*, 20.

59. The command history of the branch offices stated, "These offices were set up to collect information of intelligence value to the War Department from sources peculiar to the location selected, and to perform other functions, such as liaison with foreign personnel, dictated by the characteristics of the industries and traffic of their locations." "History of the Branch Offices of MID, 1940–1945," undated, Records of the Army Staff, record group 319, entry 1071, stack 270, row 15, compartment 4, shelf 2–3, box 13, National Archives at College Park, MD, 1.

60. Memorandum by Hayes A. Kroner, "Organization of G-2—MIS," January 25, 1943, George W. Auxier Historical Manuscript File.

61. *History of the Military Intelligence Division*, 25.

62. *History of the Military Intelligence Division*, 28.

63. Strong wrote, "It should be recognized that the proper time for a great nation to be a highly proficient and widely flung intelligence service is before it becomes engaged in war." Memorandum by George V. Strong, "Biennial Report," May 9, 1943, George W. Auxier Historical Manuscript File.

64. Strong, "Biennial Report," May 9, 1943.

65. *History of the Military Intelligence Division*, 28–29.

66. *History of the Military Intelligence Division*, 30.

67. *History of the Military Intelligence Division*, 31–32.

68. "Position Summary," February 5, 1944, Records of the War Department General and Special Staffs, record group 165, entry 175, stack 390, row 35, compartment 6, shelf 5, box 347, National Archives at College Park, MD.

69. *History of the Military Intelligence Division*, 32–33.

70. *History of the Military Intelligence Division*, 38–40.

71. *History of the Military Intelligence Division*, 57.

72. Finnegan and Danysh, *Military Intelligence*, 5.

73. US Naval Administrative Histories of World War II, 1, 428.

74. Berle commented on the spirit of coordination on April 14, "The military intelligence work is coming along fairly well; the Joint Intelligence Committee looks as though it might get somewhere." Berle, *Navigating the Rapids*, 407.

75. Zacharias, *Secret History*, 296.

76. Train Oral History Interview, 288.

77. Train Oral History Interview, 286.

78. US Naval Administrative Histories of World War II, 98.

79. Joint Deputy Chiefs of Staff (Frederick J. Horne and Joseph T. McNarney)

to Commanding General, August 5, 1943, Records of the War Department General and Special Staffs, record group 165, entry 185, stack 390, row 35, compartment 17, shelf 3, box 131, National Archives at College Park, MD.

80. George V. Strong to William T. Stone, August 26, 1943, Records of the War Department General and Special Staffs, record group 165, entry 185, Stack 390, row 35, compartment 17, shelf 3, box 125, National Archives at College Park, MD.

81. US Naval Administrative Histories of World War II, 306.

82. Marc B. Powe and Edward E. Wilson, *The Evolution of American Military Intelligence* (Fort Huachuca, AZ: U.S. Army Intelligence Center and School, 1973), 44.

83. Train Oral History Interview, 296.

84. Train Oral History Interview, 310–311.

85. Zacharias, *Secret History*, 291.

86. US Naval Administrative Histories of World War II, 88.

87. US Naval Administrative Histories of World War II, 89–90.

88. Thomas F. Troy, *Donovan, and the CIA: A History of the Establishment of the Central Intelligence Agency* (Frederick, MD: University Publications of America. 1984), 316.

89. Memorandum by George V. Strong, "Joint Intelligence Agency," April 10, 1943, Records of the War Department General and Special Staffs, record group 165, entry 175, stack 390, row 35, compartment 6, shelf 5, box 347, National Archives at College Park, MD.

90. US Naval Administrative Histories of World War II, 95.

91. Finnegan and Danysh, *Military Intelligence*, 64.

92. Packard, *Century of U.S. Naval Intelligence*, 227.

93. US Naval Administrative Histories of World War II, 98.

94. Packard, *Century of U.S. Naval Intelligence*, 235.

95. Dorwart, *Dorwart's History*, 328.

96. Nathan Miller, *Spying for America: The Hidden History of U.S. Intelligence* (New York: Paragon House, 1989), 185.

97. Miller, *Spying for America*, 255. MID, likewise, did not play a role in the Japanese American Internment Camps. Military intelligence legend retired Major General Ralph H. Van Deman called the relocation unnecessary, impractical, and one of the craziest propositions he ever heard. His lack of concern over the loyalty of these American citizens also reflected MID's disinterest.

98. Memorandum by Office of the Chief of Naval Operations, "Functions and Accomplishments of the C.I. Group of O.N.I.," August 26, 1943, Records of the Office of the Chief of Naval Operations, record group 38, entry UD1, stack 370, row 14, compartment 35, shelf 3–4, box 4, National Archives at College Park, MD, 1.

99. Memorandum by Office of the Chief of Naval Operations, "Functions and Accomplishments of the C.I. Group of O.N.I.," August 26, 1943, 6.

100. *History of the Military Intelligence Division*, 59–60.

101. *History of the Military Intelligence Division*, 48.

102. Edward A. Tamm to J.B.W. Waller and John T. Bissell, February 9, 1942, Records of the Office of the Chief of Naval Operations, record group 38, entry UD1, stack 370, row 14, compartment 35, shelf 3–4, box 5, National Archives at College Park, MD, 3.

103. Roy Talbert, *Negative Intelligence the Army and the American Left, 1917–1941* (Jackson: University Press of Mississippi, 1991), 178–179.

104. Raymond E. Lee, Theodore S. Wilkinson, and J. Edgar Hoover, "Agreement between MID, ONI and FBI for Coordinating Special Intelligence Operations in the Western Hemisphere," March 5, 1942, Records of the Army Staff, record group 319, entry 1071, stack 270, row 15, compartment 4, shelf 2–3, box 13, National Archives at College Park, MD.

105. US Naval Administrative Histories of World War II, 70–71.

106. Dorwart, *Dorwart's History*, 325.

107. Train Oral History Interview, 306–307.

108. Memorandum by Office of the Chief of Naval Operations, "The Division of Naval Intelligence: Its Contribution to the War Effort," September 2, 1943, Records of the Office of the Chief of Naval Operations, record group 38, entry UD1, stack 370, row 14, compartment 35, shelf 3–4, box 4, National Archives at College Park, MD, 1.

109. Memorandum by Office of the Chief of Naval Operations, "The Division of Naval Intelligence: Its Contribution to the War Effort," September 2, 1943, 4.

110. Dorwart, *Dorwart's History*, 343.

111. Dorwart, *Dorwart's History of the Office of Naval Intelligence: 1865–1945*, 355.

112. Dorwart, *Dorwart's History*, 355.

113. US Naval Administrative Histories of World War II, 824.

114. Dorwart, *Dorwart's History*, 342.

115. Packard, *Century of U.S. Naval Intelligence*, 219.

116. Dorwart, *Dorwart's History*, 354.

117. "The Spirit," *Evening Star*, comic strip, January 18, 1942, 2. The Spirit is a fictional masked crimefighter and vigilante created by cartoonist Will Eisner.

118. Pilebucks is slang for men who lay timber shipways on which vessels are built and launched.

119. Frances M. Collon, "Army Studies Alien Tongues," *New York Times*, October 17, 1943, E7.

120. David A. Pfeiffer, "Sage Prophet or Loose Cannon?: Skilled Intelligence Officer in World War II Foresaw Japan's Plans, but Annoyed Navy Brass," *Prologue Magazine* 40, no. 2 (Summer 2008): 12.

121. Nelson, *National Security and the General Staff*, 526.

122. Prados, *Combined Fleet Decoded*, xxii.

Chapter 10. 1946–1947: CIA Subordinates ONI and MID

1. US Naval Administrative Histories of World War II, Office of the Chief of Naval Operations, "Office of Naval Intelligence," 4 vols., Archives Branch, Naval History and Heritage Command, Washington, DC (hard copy) and Nimitz Library, United States Naval Academy, Annapolis, MD (microfiche), 151.

2. William S. White, "Army-Navy Balked Joint Intelligence Till after Dec. 7, '41: Committee Authorized Oct. 1 Blocked by Bickering before Pearl Harbor, Says Miles," *New York Times*, December 4, 1945, 1.

3. Memorandum by G. P. Simons, "Recommendations for Post-War Organization of the Division of Naval Intelligence," June 10, 1940, US Naval Administrative Histories of World War II, Office of the Chief of Naval Operations, "Office of Naval Intelligence," 2.

4. Memorandum by G. P. Simons, "Recommendations for Post-War Organization of the Division of Naval Intelligence," June 10, 1940, 6–7.

5. Simons, "Recommendations," 10.

6. Navy Subsidiary Demobilization Plan, August 1945, Records of the Office of the Chief of Naval Operations, record group 38, entry UD33, stack 370, row 15, compartment 1, shelf 2–6, box 12, National Archives at College Park, MD, 1.

7. Memorandum by F. S. Cookson, "Designation of Chief of Naval Intelligence," November 1, 1945, Records of the War Department General and Special Staffs, record group 165, entry 185, stack 390, row 35, compartment 17, shelf 3, box 132, National Archives at College Park, MD.

8. Captain Wyman H. Packard, USN (Ret.), *A Century of U.S. Naval Intelligence* (Washington, DC: Office of Naval Intelligence, 1996), 26.

9. Office of Naval Intelligence Organization Chart, October 29, 1945, Records of the Office of the Chief of Naval Operations, record group 38, entry UD33, stack 370, row 15, compartment 1, shelf 2–6, box 26, National Archives at College Park, MD.

10. Memorandum by Chief of Naval Operations, "The Navy Subsidiary Post-War Plan—Intelligence," November 29, 1945, Records of the US Marine Corps, record group 127, entry UD-WW 24, stack 370, row 24, compartment 12, shelf 5, box 16, National Archives at College Park, MD.

11. R. A. Kotrla, "Naval Intelligence Specialists Trained on Post-Graduate Level," *Proceedings of the United States Naval Institute* 73, no. 9 (September 1947): 1,062.

12. Packard, *Century of U.S. Naval Intelligence*, 26–27.

13. Memorandum by Clayton Bissell, "Comments of MID on Plan of Reorganization of War Department," November 11, 1945, Records of the War Department General and Special Staffs, record group 165, entry 32, stack 390, row 30, compartment 17, shelf 1, box 926, National Archives at College Park, MD.

14. Bissell wrote, "The Director of Intelligence is the advisor to and assistant of the Chief of Staff for all War Department matters relating to military intelligence and counterintelligence of the Army. The Director of Intelligence is

the responsible overall War Department instrumentality for the performance of intelligence and counterintelligence." Memorandum by Clayton Bissell, "Comments of MID on Plan of Reorganization of War Department," November 11, 1945.

15. Robert B. Patterson to Harry S. Truman, January 24, 1946, Records of the War Department General and Special Staffs, record group 165, entry 32, stack 390, row 30, compartment 17, shelf 1, box 926, National Archives at College Park, MD, 1.

16. "General Plan, Organization of the Intelligence Division, War Department General Staff," May 15, 1946, Records of the Army Staff, record group 319, entry P 128, stack 270, row 19, compartment 15, shelf 6, box 4, National Archives at College Park, MD.

17. "General Plan, Organization of the Intelligence Division, War Department General Staff," May 15, 1946.

18. "General Plan, Organization of the Intelligence Division, War Department General Staff," May 15, 1946.

19. John Patrick Finnegan and Romana Danysh, *Military Intelligence* (Washington, DC: Center for Military History, United States Army, 1998), 103.

20. Scott A. Moseman, "Truman and the Formation of the Central Intelligence Agency," *Journal of Intelligence History* 19, no. 2 (June 2020): 151–153.

21. Jeffery M. Dorwart, *Dorwart's History of the Office of Naval Intelligence: 1865–1945* (Annapolis, MD: Naval Institute Press, 2019), 358.

22. Moseman, "Truman and the Formation of the Central Intelligence Agency," 154–155.

23. Moseman, "Truman and the Formation of the Central Intelligence Agency," 155.

24. Moseman, "Truman and the Formation of the Central Intelligence Agency," 156–157.

25. Moseman, "Truman and the Formation of the Central Intelligence Agency," 159.

26. Samuel A. Tower, "Intelligence Net to Be World-Wide: For First Time in History This Country Plans an Effective and Permanent Service," *New York Times*, August 3, 1947, E5.

27. The NSC is a board that answers questions and provides advice to the president on national security matters. They help allocate fiscal and manpower resources and assist in crises planning.

28. The *13 Rue Madeleine* credits state, "No single story could ever pay full tribute to the accomplishments of U.S. Army Intelligence in World War II. Working secretly behind enemy lines, in close cooperation with our Allies, its brilliant work was an acknowledged factor in the final victory." Henry Hathaway, dir., *13 Rue Madeleine* (Twentieth Century Fox, 1947).

29. Kotrla, "Naval Intelligence Specialists," 1,062.

30. Packard, *Century of U.S. Naval Intelligence*, 28.

31. Memorandum by Thomas B. Inglis, March 1, 1949, Records of the Office

of the Chief of Naval Operations, record group 38, entry UD33, stack 370, row 15, compartment 1, shelf 2–6, box 6, National Archives at College Park, MD.

32. Memorandum by Thomas B. Inglis, March 1, 1949.

33. Memorandum by J. M. Ocker, "Statement of ONI Mission and Objectives—Revision of," September 27, 1950, Records of the Office of the Chief of Naval Operations, record group 38, Entry UD33, stack 370, row 15, compartment 1, shelf 2–6, box 25, National Archives at College Park, MD.

34. Office of Naval Intelligence Organization Chart, September 21, 1950, Records of the Office of the Chief of Naval Operations, record group 38, entry UD33, stack 370, row 15, compartment 1, shelf 2–6, box 26, National Archives at College Park, MD.

35. "Final Report: War Department Policies and Programs Review Board," August 11, 1947, Records of the US Joint Chiefs of Staff, record group 218, entry UD3, stack 190, row 1, compartment 16, shelf 3–7, box 9, National Archives at College Park, MD, 17.

36. The report stated, "Within the Department of the Army, the Intelligence Division of the General Staff directs and coordinates intelligence, security, and counterintelligence operations." *Annual Report of the Secretary of the Army for the Fiscal Year, 1948*, 1948, Records of the U.S. Joint Chiefs of Staff, record group 218, entry UD3, stack 190, row 1, compartment 16, shelf 3–7, box 9, National Archives at College Park, MD.

37. Finnegan and Danysh, *Military Intelligence*, 105.

Historiographic Essay

1. Jeffery M. Dorwart, *Dorwart's History of the Office of Naval Intelligence: 1865–1945* (Annapolis, MD: Naval Institute Press, 2019), 160.

2. Dorwart, *Dorwart's History*, 160.

3. The dilemma for ONI between 1918 and 1945 Dorwart continually raises is that "the security side led to secret conduct, domestic operations, and snooping—often within the United States itself—that might violate the constitutional obligations and freedoms that every naval officer had pledged to uphold and defend. More dangerous from the navy's perspective, concentration on the security function might interfere with ONI's primary obligation to provide the freshest possible data about foreign military technology and war plans." Jeffery M. Dorwart, *The U.S. Navy's Intelligence Dilemma, 1919–1945: Conflict of Duty* (Annapolis, MD: Naval Institute Press, 1983), ix–x. Furthermore, Dorwart argued, "In order to defend a free and open society, sometimes U.S. intelligence had to pursue secret operations inimical to that very freedom. Moreover, once crossing the line between lawful conduct and extralegal measures, it became difficult to stop short of criminal activity. On its part, naval intelligence faced its own version of the dilemma" (5).

4. James R. Green, "The First Sixty Years of the Office of Naval Intelligence" (MA thesis, American University, 1963), 1–2.

5. Robert G. Angevine, "The Rise and Fall of the Office of Naval Intelligence, 1882–1892: A Technological Perspective," *Journal of Military History* 62, no. 2 (April 1998): 291–192.

6. Specifically, Shulman argued, "the ONI continued in its role as chief propagandist for the Blue-Water navy throughout the era to 1940. Frequently it would provide just the information needed for publications to list the foreign threats and the relative strength of the American fleet—as carefully arranged by the ONI." Mark R. Shulman, "The Rise and Fall of American Naval Intelligence, 1882–1917," *Intelligence and National Security* 8, no. 2 (April 1993): 223–224.

7. Packard said of his book, "It should be reiterated and emphasized that this book is intended as an introductory reference work on U.S. Naval Intelligence." Captain Wyman H. Packard, USN (Ret.), *A Century of U.S. Naval Intelligence* (Washington, DC: Office of Naval Intelligence, 1996), 455.

8. An example of the encyclopedic nature of *A Century of U.S. Naval Intelligence* is Packard's definition of naval intelligence and its purpose: "Naval intelligence is the accumulated knowledge on the naval science and developments in all maritime countries; the naval capabilities, activities, and intentions of all potentially hostile and friendly countries; and the characteristics of all possible areas of naval operations. It has been a requirement within the U.S. Navy ever since intelligence was used to justify the procurement of the Navy's first ships. Additionally, naval intelligence includes the Navy's contribution to joint military and national intelligence efforts." Packard, *Century of U.S. Naval Intelligence*, xix.

9. Roy Talbert, *Negative Intelligence the Army and the American Left, 1917–1941* (Jackson: University Press of Mississippi, 1991), 12.

10. Powe died on August 2, 2020, of COVID-19, after having served in the US Army for nearly thirty years as a military intelligence officer.

11. Powe contended, "This thesis will attempt to demonstrate that the Military Information Division established in 1885 was both theoretically and practically the parent of the World War I agency." Marc B. Powe, "The Emergence of a War Department Intelligence Agency" (MA thesis, Kansas State University, 1974), vii.

12. Gilbert added, "In light of the Army's failure during its first 125 years to recognize the need for a viable means of collecting secrets, it is easy to see why many have labeled World War I the beginning of military intelligence." James L. Gilbert, *World War I and the Origins of U.S. Military Intelligence* (Lanham, MD: Scarecrow Press, 2012), 6 and 202.

13. Robert G. Angevine, "Mapping the Northern Frontier: Canada and the Origins of the US Army's Military Information Division, 1885–1898," *Intelligence and National Security* 16, no. 3 (September 2001): 121–122.

14. Elizabeth Bethel, "The Military Information Division: Origin of the Intelligence Division," *Military Affairs* 11 (April 1947): 17.

15. In Finnegan's words, "This history is designed as a tool to perpetuate the rich heritage of military intelligence for the individual soldier. It is hoped that it will be found useful at all levels of command and in various training programs."

US Army, US Army Intelligence and Security Command, Deputy Chief of Staff, Operations, History Office, John Patrick Finnegan, *Military History: A Picture History*, 2nd ed. (Fort Belvoir, VA: US Army, 1992), 5.

16. Major Michael H. Decker and Sergeant William Mackenzie, "Birth and Early Years of Marine Corps Intelligence," *Marine Corps History* 5, no. 2 (Winter 2019): 40–41.

17. Thomas F. Troy, *Donovan, and the CIA: A History of the Establishment of the Central Intelligence Agency* (Frederick, MD: University Publications of America, 1984), 7–9.

Bibliography

Primary Sources

Archival Sources

NATIONAL ARCHIVES

General Records of the Department of the Navy. Record Group 80. National Archives Building, Washington, DC.
Naval Records Collection of the Office of Naval Records and Library. Record Group 45. National Archives Building, Washington, DC.
Records of the Adjutant General's Office. Record Group 94. National Archives Building, Washington, DC.
Records of the Army Staff. Record Group 319. National Archives at College Park, MD.
Records of the Office of the Chief of Naval Operations. Record Group 38. National Archives at College Park, MD.
Records of the Office of the Chief of Naval Operations. Record Group 38. National Archives Building, Washington, DC.
Records of the US Joint Chiefs of Staff. Record Group 218. National Archives at College Park, MD.
Records of the US Marine Corps. Record Group 127. National Archives at College Park, MD.
Records of the US Marine Corps. Record Group 127. National Archives Building, Washington, DC.
Records of the War Department General and Special Staffs. Record Group 165. National Archives at College Park, MD.

LIBRARY OF CONGRESS

Washington I. Chambers Papers. Naval Historical Foundation Collection. Manuscript Division. Library of Congress. Washington, DC.
Josephus Daniels Papers. Naval Historical Foundation Collection. Manuscript Division. Library of Congress. Washington, DC.
Albert Gleaves Papers. Naval Historical Foundation Collection. Manuscript Division. Library of Congress. Washington, DC.
Stephen B. Luce Papers. Naval Historical Foundation Collection. Manuscript Division. Library of Congress. Washington, DC.
Theodore Roosevelt Papers. Manuscript Division. Library of Congress. Washington, DC.

Roger Welles Papers. Naval Historical Foundation Collection. Manuscript Division. Library of Congress. Washington, DC.
John Grimes Walker Papers. Naval Historical Foundation Collection. Manuscript Division. Library of Congress. Washington, DC.
Harry E. Yarnell Papers (1909–1958). Naval Historical Foundation Collection. Manuscript Division. Library of Congress. Washington, DC.
William S. Sims Papers. Naval Historical Foundation Collection. Manuscript Division. Library of Congress. Washington, DC.

MARINE CORPS HISTORY DIVISION
Ellis, Earl H. "Advanced Base Operations in Micronesia." Historic Amphibious Files. Archives Branch. Marine Corps History Division. Quantico, VA.
Niblack, Alfred P. "Request of Major Earl. H. Ellis for Intelligence Duty in South America and in the Pacific Ocean." Earl H. "Pete" Ellis Collection, Archives Branch, Marine Corps History Division. Quantico, VA.

NAVAL HISTORY AND HERITAGE COMMAND
Glenn F. Howell Log. Archives Branch. Naval History and Heritage Command. Washington, DC.
William D. Puleston Papers. Archives Branch. Naval History and Heritage Command. Washington, DC.

UNITED STATES ARMY CENTER FOR MILITARY HISTORY
George W. Auxier Historical Manuscript File. "Materials on the History of Military Intelligence in the U.S., 1884–1944." US Army Center of Military History. Washington, DC.

Published Primary Sources
Baldridge, Captain Harry A. "Sims—The Iconoclast." *Proceedings of the United States Naval Institute* 62, no. 2 (February 1937): 183–190.
Berle, Adolf A. *Navigating the Rapids, 1918–1971: From the Papers of Adolf A. Berle*. Edited by Beatrice B. Berle and Travis B. Jacobs. New York: Harcourt Brace Jovanovich, 1973.
Berry, A. G. "The Beginning of the Office of Naval Intelligence." *Proceedings of the United States Naval Institute* 63, no. 1 (January 1937): 102–103.
Chadwick, Commander French E. "Naval Department Organization." *Proceedings of the United States Naval Institute* 20, no. 3 (July 1894): 493–529.
Churchill, Brigadier General Marlborough. "The Military Intelligence Division, General Staff." *Journal of the United States Artillery* 52, no. 4 (April 1920): 293–315.
Crosley, Commander W. S. "The Naval War College, the General Board, and the Office of Naval Intelligence." *Proceedings of the United States Naval Institute* 39, no. 3 (September 1913): 965–74.
Feland, Brigadier General Logan. "The Division of Operations and Training

Headquarters U.S. Marine Corps." *Marine Corps Gazette* 7, no. 1 (March 1922): 41–45.

Gleaves, Rear Admiral Albert. *The Life of an American Sailor: Rear Admiral William Hemsley Emory.* New York: George Doran, 1923.

———. *Life and Letters of Rear Admiral Stephen B. Luce, U.S. Navy.* New York: Putnam, 1925.

Goodrich, Captain C. F. "Naval Intelligence during War." *Proceedings of the United States Naval Institute* 29, no. 2 (April 1903): 357–368.

Kotrla, Commander R. A. "Naval Intelligence Specialists Trained on Post-Graduate Level." *Proceedings of the United States Naval Institute* 73, no. 9 (September 1947): 1061–1063.

Lejeune, Major General John A. *The Reminiscences of a Marine.* Philadelphia: Dorrance, 1930.

Luce, Commodore Stephen B. "War Schools." *Proceedings of the United States Naval Institute* 9, no. 4 (December 1883): 633–657.

Luce, Rear Admiral Stephen B. "Naval Administration." *Proceedings of the United States Naval Institute* 14, no. 3 (July 1888): 561–588.

March, Major General Peyton C. *The Nation at War.* Garden City, NJ: Doubleday, Doran, 1932.

Mott, Captain Thomas B. "The Organization and Function of a Bureau of Military Intelligence." *Journal of the Military Service Institution* 32, no. 122 (March–April 1903): 184–208.

Niblack, Rear Admiral Alfred P. "The History and Aims of the Office of Naval Intelligence." Ibiblio.org, 1920. http://www.ibiblio.org/hyperwar/NHC/History-Aims-ONI-1920/History-Aims-ONI-1920.html.

Rogers, Ensign Charles C. "Naval Intelligence." *Proceedings of the United States Naval Institute* 9, no. 4 (April 1883): 659–692.

Roosevelt, Theodore. *The Letters of Theodore Roosevelt.* Edited by Elting E. Morison. Cambridge: Harvard University Press, 1951.

Schroeder, Rear Admiral Seaton. *A Half Century of Naval Service.* New York: D. Appleton, 1922.

Schwann, Brigadier General Theodore. "The Coming General Staff." *Journal of the Military Service Institution* 33, no. 123 (July–August 1903): 4–30.

Stuart, First Lieutenant Edwin R. "The Organizations and Functions of a Bureau of Military Intelligence." *Journal of the Military Service Institution* 32, no. 72 (March–April 1903): 158–183.

Sweeney, Lieutenant Colonel Walter C. *Military Intelligence: A New Weapon in War.* New York: Frederick A. Stokes, 1924.

US Naval Administrative Histories of World War II, Office of the Chief of Naval Operations. "Office of Naval Intelligence." Vols. 1–4. Archives Branch. Naval History and Heritage Command. Washington Navy Yard. (Hard Copy) and Nimitz Library. United States Naval Academy, Annapolis, MD (Microfiche).

US War Department, General Staff, Military Intelligence Division. *Functions of the Military Intelligence Division*, October 1, 1918.

———. *A History of the Military Intelligence Division 7 December 1941—2 September 1945*, 1946.
Van Deman, Major General Ralph H. *The Final Memoranda: Major General Ralph H. Van Deman, USA Ret., 1865–1952*. Edited by Ralph E. Weber. Wilmington, DE: Scholarly Resources Imprint, 1988.
Wagner, Captain Arthur L. *The Service of Security and Information*. Kansas City: Hudson-Kimberley, 1893.
Wainwright, Rear Admiral Richard. "The General Board." *Proceedings of the United States Naval Institute* 48, no. 2 (February 1922): 189–201.
Zacharias, Captain Ellis M. *Secret Missions: The Story of an Intelligence Officer*. New York: G. P. Putnam's, 1946.

Oral History Interviews

Anderson, Walter S. Interview by John Mason Jr. 1962. Naval History Project. Oral History Archives at Columbia, Columbia University in the City of New York.
Kirk, Alan G. Interview by John Mason Jr. 1962. Naval History Project. Oral History Archives at Columbia, Columbia University in the City of New York.
Train, Harold C. Interview by John Mason Jr. 1965. Naval History Project. Oral History Archives at Columbia, Columbia University in the City of New York.

Government Publication, Legislation, and General Orders

An Act to Authorize a Plant-Protection Force for Naval Shore Establishments, and for Other Purposes. *US Statutes at Large*, 1941–1942 (August 11, 1941).
An Act to Increase the Efficiency of the Army. *US Statutes at Large*, December 1901 to March 1903 (February 14, 1903).
An Act Making Appropriations for the Naval Service for Fiscal Year Ending June Thirtieth, Eighteen Hundred and Eighty-Nine, and for Other Purposes. *US Statutes at Large*, December 1887 to March 1889 (September 7, 1888).
An Act Making Appropriations for the Support of the Army for Fiscal Year Ending June Thirtieth, Eighteen Hundred and Eighty-Nine, and for Other Purposes. *US Statutes at Large*, December 1887 to March 1889 (September 22, 1888).
An Act Making Appropriations for the Support of the Army for Fiscal Year Ending June Thirtieth, Eighteen Hundred and Ninety-Five, and for Other Purposes. *US Statutes at Large*, August 1893 to March 1895 (August 6, 1894).
An Act Making Appropriations for the Support of the Army for Fiscal Year Ending June Thirtieth, Nineteen Hundred and Eleven. *US Statutes at Large*, March 1909 to March 1911 (March 23, 1910).
An Act Making Appropriations for the Support of the Army for Fiscal Year Ending June Thirtieth, Nineteen Hundred and Five, and for Other Purposes. *US Statutes at Large*, March 1903 to December 1905 (March 23, 1904).
An Act Making Appropriations for the Support of the Army for Fiscal Year

Ending June 30, 1920, and for Other Purposes. *US Statutes at Large*, May 1919 to March 1921 (July 11, 1919).

An Act Making Appropriations to Supply Urgent Deficiencies in Appropriations for Military and Naval Establishments on Account of War Expenses for the Fiscal Year Ending June Thirtieth, Nineteen Hundred and Seventeen, and for Other Purposes. *US Statutes at Large*, April 1917 to March 1919 (June 15, 1917).

An Act to Punish Acts of Interference with the Foreign Relations, the Neutrality, and the Foreign Commerce of the United States, to Punish Espionage, and Better to Enforce the Criminal Laws of the United States, and for Other Purposes. *US Statutes at Large*, April 1917 to March 1919 (June 15, 1917).

Headquarters of the Army, Adjutant Generals Office. General Order no. 23 (March 18, 1892).

Navy Department. General Order no. 128 (May 7, 1903).

———. General Order no. 372 (June 25, 1889).

———. General Order no. 544 (March 13, 1900).

Secretary of the Navy. General Order no. 292 (March 23, 1882).

US Congress. Congressional Record 19. 50th Cong., 1st sess., June 16, 1888.

———. Congressional Record 20. 50th Cong., 2nd sess., February 28, 1889.

———. Congressional Record 23. 52nd Cong., 1st sess., March 21, 1892.

———. Congressional Record 33. 56th Cong., 1st sess., April 16, 1900.

———. Congressional Record 33. 56th Cong., 1st sess., March 26, 1900.

———. Congressional Record 36. 57th Cong., 2nd sess., February 17, 1903.

———. Congressional Record 39. 58th Cong., 3rd sess., February 14, 1905.

———. Congressional Record 42. 60th Cong., 1st sess., April 10, 1908.

———. Congressional Record 48. 62nd Cong., 1st sess., June 8, 1912.

———. Congressional Record 52. 63rd Cong., 3rd sess., January 29, 1915.

———. Congressional Record 57. 65th Cong., 3rd sess., February 4, 1919.

———. Congressional Record 57. 65th Cong., 3rd sess., February 13, 1919.

———. Congressional Record 60. 66th Cong., 3rd sess., February 2, 1921.

———. Congressional Record 60. 67th Cong., 1st sess., April 29, 1921.

———. Congressional Record 62. 67th Cong., 4th sess., December 27, 1922.

———. Congressional Record 64. 67th Cong., 4th sess., February 5, 1923.

———. Congressional Record 64. 67th Cong., 4th sess., February 8, 1923.

———. Congressional Record 69. 70th Cong., 1st sess., March 12, 1928.

———. Congressional Record 72. 71st Cong., 2nd sess., January 11, 1930.

———. Congressional Record 72. 71st Cong., 2nd sess., January 20, 1930.

———. Congressional Record 75. 72nd Cong., 2nd sess., December 7, 1932.

———. Congressional Record 87. 77th Cong., 1st sess., June 11, 1941.

———. Congressional Record 91. 79th Cong., 1st sess., February 16, 1945.

US Department of the Navy. Annual Reports of the Secretary of the Navy, 1883–1945. Washington, DC: US Government Printing Office, 1883–1900.

US War Department. Annual Reports of the Secretary of War, 1892–1908. Washington, DC: US Government Printing Office, 1892–1908.

―――. Bulletin no. 74 (December 31, 1917).
―――. General Order no. 14 (February 9, 1918).
―――. General Order no. 40 (April 23, 1918).
―――. General Order no. 80 (August 26, 1918).

Newspaper and Magazines

"Aliens Parody Anthem: Sing 'Der Stern Spangled Banana' in N.Y. Saloon." *Washington Post*, April 2, 1918, 4.
"The American Legion: News: Local, State, National." *New York Tribune*, October 3, 1921, 4.
"Another Army Dispute: Secretary Elkins' Decision Concerning the Inspection of Militia." *North Platte Tribune*, May 29, 1892, 1.
"The Armies of Europe: Official Figures of Interest Compiled by the War Department." *Goodland Republic*, April 12, 1894, 1.
"The Army Bureau of Intelligence: Steps That Have Been Taken to Establish Such a Bureau." *Evening Star*, October 6, 1885, 1.
"Army Has Charts of Red Activities: Gen, Churchill Shows Senate Military Committee the Haunts in New York." *New York Times*, June 18, 1919, 19.
"Army and Navy Criticism Curbed by President, Church Group Says: Complaint over Naval Memorandum Asserting that Federal Council Is Aiding Communism Is Declared to Have Brought Order by Executive after Conference." *New York Times*, December 7, 1935, 1.
"Army and Navy Gossip: United States Navy." *Washington Post*, April 7, 1907, 20.
"Army and Navy News: Orders to Officers—A Naval Office of Intelligence—Other Matters." *New York Times*, March 26, 1882, 2.
"Assigned to the Bancroft: Commander Clover's Request for Sea Duty is Complied with." *Sun*, April 8, 1898, 1.
Associated Press. "Waiting the Message." *Los Angeles Herald*, April 10, 1898, 4.
Baldwin, Hanson W. "U.S. Alert to Spy Out Spies: Army and Navy Intelligence Staffs Keep Constant Vigil Against Foreign Prying." *New York Times*, July 19, 1936, E10.
Barkley, Frederick R. "Close Watch on Spies Revealed by Arrests: FBI, Army and Navy Act When Secret Agents Become a Real Menace." *New York Times*, July 6, 1941, E8.
Bartlett, John R. "Watching for the Enemy in the Spanish War." *Century Illustrated Magazine*, October 1901, 907.
"Bombs Made in Germany: U. S. Naval Bureau Identifies Infernal Machines as Imported Product." *Tonopah Daily Bonanza*, May 1, 1919, 1.
Branzel, Bruno. "That We May Live." *Sunday Star*, November 3, 1940, B-9.
"The Bureau of Naval Intelligence." *New York Times*, July 4, 1889, 4.
"A Busy Diplomatic Attaché." *Evening Star*, September 2, 1884, 1.
"Capt. Mahan's Duty: His Assignment will be Made Congenial in this City." *Evening Star*, April 10, 1895, 1.

"Censoring, Except Radio, Is Ended: All Military Suspension of Messages Discontinued." *Sun*, November 16, 1918, 8.
Churchill, Brigadier General Marlborough. "Credit for Bolshevist Disclosures." *New York Times*, October 5, 1918, 12.
"Col. Churchill New Censor: Power Consolidated Under Plans of General Staff Consolidation." *Washington Post*, June 22, 1918, 6.
Collon, Frances M. "Army Studies Alien Tongues." *New York Times*, October 17, 1943, E7.
"Commander Mason Dead." *Salt Lake Herald*, October 16, 1899, 1
"Diplomats Talk: Navy Department Prepares for the War." *Herald*, April 1, 1898, 1.
"Eyes of Our Army." *New York Times*, March 4, 1941, 22.
"Foiled Spies in Army: Intelligence Service Routed Germans, Churchill Says." *Washington Post*, June 18, 1919, 3.
"German Army Organization: A Valuable Work upon this Topic Issued at Washington." *North American*, May 24, 1894, 8.
"The Gossip Shop." *Bookman*, December 1924, 4.
Hoover, J. Edgar. "Is There a Spy Menace?" *Week Magazine*, July 14, 1940, 2.
"How We Abused the Loyalty of Our Foreign-Born." *New Ulm Post*, April 4, 1919.
"Interests President: He Discusses with Experts Progress of Naval War in the Far East." *Washington Post*, May 21, 1905, 13.
"Involve Naval Heads: Newport Charges Bring Daniels and Roosevelt into Case." *Washington Post*, March 3, 1920, 11.
Jenks, John E. "A Government Picture-Book." *Youth's Companion*, August 29, 1901, 419.
"Keep Watch on Spies: Gregory, Bielaski and Churchill Warn against Relaxation." *Washington Post*, November 10, 1918, 18.
"Keeping Tabs of Navies All Over the World: Not a Vessel Moving in the Remotest Seas Escapes the Vigilance of the Office of Naval Intelligence." *Washington Times*, June 23, 1895, 3.
Ladies' Home Journal, June 1903, 14.
"Look Now for Peace: Effect of Rojestvensky's Great Defeat." *Evening Star*, May 29, 1905, 1.
"More Germans to Be Interned: Ninety-One Taken Wednesday Night Are Searched and Examined." *New York Times*, September 28, 1917, 1.
"The Naval General Staff." *Sun*, March 22, 1900, 1.
"Navies of the Old World: How Our Government Obtains Information as to the Building of War-Ships." *Indianapolis Journal*, October 16, 1885, 1.
"Navies of the World: Capt. C.D. Sigsbee's Record of the Work Recently Done." *New York Times*, September 3, 1901, 8.
"Navy Guards against Spies." *Wilmington Morning Star*, November 12, 1940, 1.
"The Navy in Excitement: Lively Times in All Branches at the Department." *New York Times*, January 15, 1892, 1.

"Navy Intelligence Office." *Atchison Daily Globe*, February 3, 1899, 1.
"Navy Men Tighten Vigilance on Spies: Espionage Activity Always Increases in the Expansion Periods, Says Standley." *New York Times*, July 26, 1936, 27.
"New Naval Regulations." *Anaconda Standard*, December 11, 1898, 1.
"News of Army and Navy." *Washington Post*, May 5, 1918, 3.
"No Naval Spies Caught Here, Says Intelligence Bureau." *New York Tribune*, January 23, 1918, 4.
North American, editorial, June 27, 1884, 1.
"Not Satisfied with Its Work: Mr. Lamont to Overhaul the Bureau of Military Information." *New York Times*, January 12, 1894, 9.
"Not Unprepared for War: Coast Defenses in Better Condition than Supposed." *New York Times*, December 19, 1895, 1.
"On Pacifist List, but Serve Nation: Others Recorded in the 'Who's Who in Radicalism' Are Now in Jail." *New York Times*, January 26, 1919, 8.
Pinkerton, William M. "Foreign Spies Pit Cleverness against Four Big Agencies: F. B. I., G-2, O. N. I. and State Department's Special Agencies, Always on Alert. Spite Is Greatest Problem." *Sunday Star*, May 15, 1938, C-3.
"President Urges Fund to Fight Spies: Favors Large Increase in Army and Navy Agencies—Deplores Sale of FBI Story." *New York Times*, June 25, 1938, 1.
"Proposed Army War College: Probable That It Will Be Located in Washington." *Tazewell Republican*, August 22, 1901, 1.
"Put None but Americans on Guard!" *Washington Post*, May 31, 1917, 6.
"Quieter Yesterday: Less 'War' Excitement at the National Capitol." *Kansas City Journal*, March 14, 1898, 1.
"Rams and Big Guns: Observations of United States Naval Officers in the South American War." *Saint Louis Daily Globe-Democrat*, October 5, 1885, 14.
"Second in Naval Power: The United States is Near the Head of the List on Sea Power." *Minneapolis Journal*, March 24, 1903, 1.
"Senate Committee for Full Inquiry: Daniels Declares Admiral Sims Must Make Good His Allegations." *Richmond Times-Dispatch*, January 20, 1920, 1.
"Senate Will Probe Reds' Moves Here: Radical Speeches in Washington Theatre Inspire the Demand for Action." *New York Tribune*, February 5, 1919, 1.
"Shows Tonnage of Navies: Office of Naval Intelligence Gives Relative Rank of Powers." *Washington Post*, November 6, 1907, 4.
"Spain's Flotilla in a Gale: The Scattered Boats Put in at the Cape Verde Islands." *Sun*, April 3, 1898, 1.
"Spain's Navy: Two Strong Additions to Her Fighting Force." *Saint Paul Globe*, December 27, 1896, 1.
"Spain's Sea Strength: Col. Wagner Issues a Compilation of Her Available Naval Force—Speed and Armament." *New York Times*, April 3, 1898, 1.
"Spies and Thieves Barred from U. S. Office Buildings: Loss of State Secrets from State, War and Navy Departments Forces Officials to Adopt Strict Regulations Against Prowlers—Important Papers Stolen." *Washington Herald*, July 19, 1915, 1.

"The Spirit." *Evening Star*, comic strip, January 18, 1942, 2.
"Spy Suspect Is Seized Here in Secret Raid: Wilhelm Korthaus, Ostensibly Employed by German Dye Firm, Held." *New York Tribune*, March 12, 1918, 1.
"Thousands of Spies Are Here: Estimated that 100,000 Are in the United States Who Need Watching." *Ogden Standard*, February 19, 1917, 1.
Tower, Samuel A. "Intelligence Net to Be World-Wide: For First Time in History This Country Plans an Effective and Permanent Service." *New York Times*, August 3, 1947, E5.
"United States Now Second in Navy Strength: Building Program during War, Coupled with Germany's Surrender, Makes Us British Contender." *Pensacola Journal*, August 18, 1919, 1.
Wheeler, George M. "Necessity for a General Staff." *Cosmopolitan*, August 1898, 464.
"Working Day and Night: No Cessation of the Preparation for War." *Sun*, March 23, 1898, 1.
"572 Slackers Sought in D. C.: War Department Prepares to Round Up 100,000 throughout U.S." *Washington Herald*, July 27, 1920, 1A.

Motion Pictures
Adventures of the Flying Cadets. Directed by Lewis D. Collins and Ray Taylor. Universal Pictures, 1943.
The Border Wireless. Directed by William S. Hart. William S. Hart Productions, 1918.
Cipher Bureau. Directed by Charles Lamont. Franklyn Warner Productions, 1939.
Confessions of a Nazi Spy. Directed by Anatole Litvak. Warner Bros., 1939.
Espionage Agent. Directed by Lloyd Bacon. Warner Bros., 1939.
Huns and Hyphens. Directed by Lawrence Semon. Vitagraph Company of America, 1918.
Marie Galante. Directed by Henry King. Fox Film Corporation, 1934.
Mata Hari. Directed by George Fitzmaurice. Metro-Goldwyn-Mayer, 1931.
Mr. Moto's Last Warning. Directed by Norman Foster. Twentieth Century Fox, 1939.
Murder in the Air. Directed by Lewis Seiler. Warner Bros., 1940.
Navy Secrets. Directed by Howard Bretherton. W. T. Lackey Productions, 1939.
Rendezvous. Directed by William K. Howard. Metro-Goldwyn-Mayer, 1935.
Smashing the Spy Ring. Directed by Christy Cabanne. Columbia Pictures, 1938.
13 Rue Madeleine. Directed by Henry Hathaway. Twentieth Century Fox, 1947.

Novels
Eliot, Major George F. *Federal Bullets*. New York: William Caslon, 1936.
———. *The Navy Spy Murders*. New York: Dodge, 1937.
———. *The Purple Legion*. New York: William Caslon, 1936.

Hawkins, John. *Pilebuck.* New York: E. P. Dutton, 1943.
Marquand, John P. *No Hero.* Boston: Little and Brown, 1935.
Mason, Francis Van Wyck. *The Man from G-2.* New York: Reynal and Hitchcock, 1938.
White, Ared. *Agent B-7.* Boston: Houghton Mifflin, 1934.
———. *Seven Tickets to Singapore.* Boston: Houghton Mifflin, 1939.

Secondary Sources

Books

Abrahamson, James L. *America Arms for a New Century: The Making of a Great Military Power.* New York: Free Press, 1981.
Ambrose, Stephen E. *Upton and the Army.* Baton Rouge: Louisiana State University Press, 1964.
Barr, Ronald J. *The Progressive Army: U.S. Army and Command and Administration, 1870–1914.* New York: St. Martin's Press, 1998.
Bath, Alan H. *Tracking the Axis Enemy: The Triumph of Anglo-American Naval Intelligence.* Lawrence: University Press of Kansas, 1998.
Beaver, Daniel R. *Modernizing the American War Department: Change and Continuity in a Turbulent Era, 1885–1920.* Kent, OH: Kent State University Press, 2006.
Bidwell, Colonel Bruce W. *History of the Military Intelligence Division, Department of the Army General Staff: 1775–1941.* Frederick, MD: University Publications of America, 1986.
Clendenen, Clarence C. *Blood on the Border: The United States Army and the Mexican Irregulars.* London: Macmillan, 1969.
Deacon, Richard. *The Silent War: A History of Western Naval Intelligence.* London: Grafton, 1988.
Dorwart, Jeffery M. *History of the Office of Naval Intelligence 1865–1945.* Annapolis, MD: Naval Institute Press, 2019.
———. *The U.S. Navy's Intelligence Dilemma, 1919–1945: Conflict of Duty.* Annapolis, MD: Naval Institute Press, 1983.
Eisenhower, Dwight D. *Crusade in Europe.* New York: Doubleday, 1948.
Gage, Beverly. *The Day Wall Street Exploded: A Story of America in Its First Age of Terror.* New York: Oxford University Press, 2009.
Gilbert, James L. *World War I and the Origins of U.S. Military Intelligence.* Lanham, MD: Scarecrow Press, 2012.
Haber, Samuel. *Efficiency and Uplift: Scientific Management in the Progressive Era, 1890–1920.* Chicago: University of Chicago Press, 1964.
Hammond, Paul Y. *Organizing for Defense: The American Military Establishment in the Twentieth Century.* Princeton, NJ: Princeton University Press, 1961.
Hofstadter, Richard. *The Age of Reform: From Bryan to F. D. R.* New York: Knopf, 1955.

House, Jonathan M. *Military Intelligence: 1870–1991*. Research Guides in Military Studies 6. Westport, CT: Greenwood Press, 1993.
Jeffreys-Jones, Rhodri. *American Espionage: From Secret Service to CIA*. New York: Macmillan, 1977.
LaFeber, Walter. *The New Empire: An Interpretation of American Expansion 1860–1898*. Ithaca, NY: Cornell University Press, 1963.
Langer, William L., and S. Everett Gleason. *The Challenge to Isolation: 1937–1940*. New York: Harper and Brothers, 1952.
Karsten, Peter. *The Naval Aristocracy: The Golden Age of Annapolis and the Emergence of Modern American Navalism*. New York: Free Press, 1972.
May, Ernest R. *From Imperialism to Isolation: 1898–1919*. New York: Macmillan, 1964.
McGerr, Michael. *A Fierce Discontent: The Rise and Fall of the Progressive Movement in America*. New York: Oxford University Press, 2003.
Miller, Edward. *War Plan Orange: The U.S. Strategy to Defeat Japan, 1897–1945*. Annapolis, MD: Naval Institute Press, 1991.
Miller, Nathan. *Spying for America: The Hidden History of U.S. Intelligence*. New York: Paragon House, 1989.
Millett, Allan R. *Semper Fidelis: The History of the United States Marine Corps*. New York: Macmillan, 1980.
Millis, Walter. *Arms and Men: A Study of American Military History*. New York: Mentor Books, 1956.
Morison, Elting E. *Admiral Sims and the Modern American Navy*. Boston: Houghton Mifflin, 1942.
Nelson, Major General Otto L., Jr. *National Security and the General Staff*. Washington, DC: Infantry Journal Press, 1946.
O'Toole, G.J.A. *Honorable Treachery: A History of US Intelligence, Espionage, and Covert Action from the American Revolution to the CIA*. New York: Atlantic Monthly Press, 1991.
Prados, John. *Combined Fleet Decoded: The Secret History of American Intelligence and the Japanese Navy in World War II*. New York: Random House, 1995.
Prange, Gordon W. *At Dawn We Slept: The Untold Story of Pearl Harbor*. New York: McGraw-Hill, 1981.
Ransom, Henry H. *Central Intelligence and National Security*. Cambridge, MA: Harvard University Press, 1958.
Shulman, Mark R. *Navalism and the Emergence of American Sea Power, 1882–1893*. Annapolis, MD: Naval Institute Press, 1995.
Smith, Myron J., Jr. *Cloak-and-Dagger Bibliography: An Annotated Guide to Spy Fiction, 1937–1975*. Metuchen, NJ: Scarecrow Press, 1976.
Talbert, Roy. *Negative Intelligence, the Army and the American Left, 1917–1941*. Jackson: University Press of Mississippi, 1991.
Trask, David F. *The War with Spain in 1898*. New York: Macmillan, 1981.
Troy, Thomas F. *Donovan and the CIA: A History of the Establishment of the*

Central Intelligence Agency. Frederick, MD: University Publications of America, 1984.

Weigley, Russell F. *History of the United States Army*. New York: Macmillan, 1967.

———. *The American Way of War: A History of United States Military Strategy and Policy*. Bloomington: Indiana University Press, 1973.

Wiebe, Robert H. *The Search for Order: 1877–1920*. New York: Hill and Wang, 1967.

Wohlstetter, Roberta. *Pearl Harbor: Warning and Decision*. Stanford, CA: Stanford University Press, 1962.

Government Publications

Condit, Kenneth W., Major John H. Johnstone, and Ella W. Nargele. *A Brief History of Headquarters Marine Corp Staff Organization*. Washington, DC: Historical Division, United States Marine Corps, 1971.

Cummings, Captain Damon E. *Admiral Richard Wainwright and the United States Fleet*. Washington, DC: Government Printing Office, 1962.

Ferrier, Sergeant David J. *ONI and OSS in World War II*. Washington, DC: Navy and Marine Corps WWII Commemorative Committee, Navy Office of Information, 1995.

Finnegan, John Patrick. *Military History: A Picture History*, 2nd ed. Fort Belvoir, VA: US Army, 1992.

Finnegan, John Patrick, and Romana Danysh. *Military Intelligence*. Washington, DC: Center for Military History, United States Army, 1998.

Haydon, F. Stansbury. Review of *A History of the Military Intelligence Division, 7 December 1941–2 September 1945* by the Military Intelligence Division. US Army, January 1948, 1–14.

Kovach, Karen. *The Life and Times of MG Dennis E. Noland, 1872–1956: The Army's First G2*. Fort Belvoir, VA: History Office, Office of the Chief of Staff, US Army Intelligence and Security Command, 1998.

Powe, Marc B., and Edward E. Wilson. *The Evolution of American Military Intelligence*. Fort Huachuca, AZ: US Army Intelligence Center and School, 1973.

Periodicals or Book Chapters

Angevine, Robert G. "Mapping the Northern Frontier: Canada and the Origins of the US Army's Military Information Division, 1885–1898." *Intelligence and National Security* 16, no. 3 (September 2001): 121–145.

———. "The Rise and Fall of the Office of Naval Intelligence, 1882–1892: A Technological Perspective." *Journal of Military History* 62, no. 2 (April 1998): 291–312.

Bethel, Elizabeth. "The Military Information Division: Origin of the Intelligence Division." *Military Affairs* 11 (April 1947): 17–24.Bigelow, Captain Michael E. "Van Deman." *Military Intelligence* 16, no. 4 (December 1990): 38–40.

Bigelow, Lieutenant Colonel (ret.) Michael E. "A Short History of Army Intelligence." *Military Intelligence Professional Bulletin* 38, no. 3 (2012): 7–26.

Dean, Sidney E. "New Navy, New Power." *Naval History* 27, no. 1 (February 2013): 56–62.

Decker, Michael H., and William Mackenzie. "Birth and Early Years of Marine Corp Intelligence." *Marine Corps History* 5, no. 2 (Winter 2019): 39–53.

Decker, Major (ret.) Michael H. and Sergeant (ret.) William Mackenzie. "Marine Corp Intelligence, the Interwar Years." *Marine Corp Gazette* 103, no. 9 (September 2019): 10–13.

Ellicott, Captain J. M. "Theodorus Bailey Meyers Mason: Founder of the Office of Naval Intelligence." *U.S. Naval Institute Proceedings* 78, no. 3 (March 1952): 265–267.

Fishel, Edwin C. "Myths That Never Die." *International Journal of Intelligence and Counterintelligence* 2, no. 1 (January 1988): 27–58.

Franz, Manuel. "Preparedness Revisited: Civilian Societies and the Campaign for American Defense, 1914–1920." *Journal of the Gilded Age and the Progressive Era* 17, no. 4 (October 2018): 663–676.

Galambos, Louis. "Emerging Organizational Synthesis in Modern American History." *Business History Review* 44, no. 3 (Autumn 1970): 279–290.

Goguen, Randy C. "U.S. Navy Owes T.B.M. MASON." *Naval History* 19, no. 3 (June 2005): 26–31.

Jones, Phill. "The Office of Naval Intelligence: Phill Jones Charts How the ONI Contributed to the Birth of the New US Navy." *History Magazine* 12, no. 3 (February/March 2014): 30–31.

Linn, Brian M. "The American Way of War." *Magazine of History*, October 2008, 19–23.

Mahnken, Thomas G. "Gazing at the Sun: The Office of Naval Intelligence and Japanese Naval Innovation, 1918–1941." *Intelligence and National Security* 11, no. 3 (July 1996): 424–441.

Moseman, Scott A. "Truman and the Formation of the Central Intelligence Agency." *Journal of Intelligence History* 19, no. 2 (June 2020): 149–166.

Pfeiffer, David A. "Sage Prophet or Loose Cannon?: Skilled Intelligence Officer in World War II Foresaw Japan's Plans, but Annoyed Navy Brass." *Prologue Magazine* 40, no. 2 (Summer 2008): 1–14.

Shulman, Mark R. "The Rise and Fall of American Naval Intelligence, 1882–1917." *Intelligence and National Security* 8, no. 2 (April 1993): 214–226.

Swartz, Captain Peter M. "Looking Out Over the Promised Land: The U.S. Naval Institute Proceedings, 1880–1889." *U.S. Naval Institute Proceedings* 140, no. 6 (June 2014): 16–18.

Dissertations and Theses

Brereton, Todd R. "An Impractical Sort of Officer: The Army Career of Arthur L. Wagner, 1875–1905." PhD diss., Texas A&M University, 1994.

Crumley, Brian T. "The Naval Attaché System of the United States, 1882–1914." PhD diss., Texas A&M University, 2002.

Green, James R. "The First Sixty Years of the Office of Naval Intelligence." MA thesis, American University, 1963.

McGinty, Patrick E. "Intelligence and the Spanish American War." PhD diss., Georgetown University, 1981.

Nelson, Laurence M., III. "Innovation in Intelligence: An Analysis of U.S. Marine Corps Intelligence Modernization during the Occupation of Haiti, 1915–1934." MA thesis, Utah State University, 2017.

Powe, Marc B. "The Emergence of a War Department Intelligence Agency." MA thesis, Kansas State University, 1974.

Soybel, Phyllis L. "A Necessary Relationship: The Development of Anglo-American Cooperation in Naval Intelligence." PhD diss., University of Illinois at Chicago, 1997.

Votaw, John F. "United States Military Attachés, 1885–1919: The American Army Matures in the International Arena." PhD diss., Temple University, 1991.

Index

Adams, Emory S., 215–216
Adjutant Generals, 50–51, 63, 67, 85, 87, 105.
   Adams, Emory S., 215
   Ainsworth, Fred C., 100
   Breck, Samuel, 67
   Bridges, Charles H., 188
   Carter, William H., 86
   Corbin, Henry C., 71, 76, 98
   Drum, Richard C., 42–43, 112
   Ulio, James A., 246
   Wagner, Arthur L., 58
Agent B-7, 201
Ahern, A. P., 134–135
Aid for Information, 127, 130, 140, 146, 156
Aid for Operations of the Fleet, 103, 107
Aid for Personnel, 103
Ainsworth, Fred C., 100, 101
air intelligence, 176–177, 212, 215, 242, 269
Air Intelligence Staff, 244
Air Section, 176–177
Alger, Russell A., 67, 74, 85, 293n36
Allen, Ronald H., 225
Ambrose, Stephen E., 8
American–Britain Conversations, 212
American Civil Liberties Union, 196
American Federation of Labor, 180
American Intelligence Service, 244
American Jewish Conference, 166
American Protection League, 147–148, 312n7
anarchism, 153 *See also* anarchists
anarchists, 166. *See also* anarchism
Ancrum, William, 116
Anderson, Walter S., 209–211, 230
   analysis of information and, 224
   "Are We Ready?" and, 211
   "Are You Ready?" and, 209
   Atherton, Ray and, 332n73
   Basic War Plans and, 211

   chief of naval operations and, 210
   Department of the Navy and, 210–211, 332n71
   Department of State and, 216, 219
   Director of Naval Intelligence, 209–211, 216, 219, 224, 328–332n31
   District Intelligence Officers and, 210, 216, 222
   Federal Bureau of Investigation and, 216, 222
   Military Intelligence Division and, 216, 222
   mobilization and, 211
   as naval attaché, 209, 332n71
   naval attachés and, 209–210, 211–212, 220, 230, 328n29
   naval intelligence and, 209, 211
   naval observers and, 219, 230
   Navy General Board and, 209
   Office of Naval Intelligence and, 209–211, 216, 332n71
   "Principal Naval Intelligence Service Operating Plan (General)" and, 210–211
   Rainbow plans and, 219
   "Readiness of the Naval Establishment to Meet a Serious Emergency?" and, 211
   Sharp, F. D. and, 222
   Strategic Information Section and, 209
Andrew, Adolphus, 213
Angevine, Robert G., 44
Anglo–Venezuela Dispute, 62, 64
APL. *See* American Protection League
Armistice, 138, 141, 160, 170, 308n66
Army General School, 264
Army–Navy board, 65
Army War College, 101, 105–106, 127–129, 132, 134
   Army intelligence and, 81, 136
   assistant chief of staff for intelligence, G-2, and, 188

Army War College, *continued*
  creation of, 96
  general staff and, 299n35
  library of, 106
  Military Information Committee and, 100
  Military Information Division and, 98, 137
  military intelligence and, 302n89
  Military Intelligence Branch, 136
  Military Intelligence Division and, 188
  Military Intelligence Section and, 134
  purpose of, 96
  Second Division and, 88, 99–100, 299n37
  Third Division and, 96, 299n37
  War College Board and, 96
  war planning and, 85
Army War College Section, 102
Arthur, Chester A., 11, 12, 16, 24
Asiatic Squadron, 12, 62
Assistant Chief of Staff for Intelligence, G-2
  Bissell, Clayton, 246, 258, 263
  Churchill, Marlborough, 138
  Ford, Stanley H., 171, 317n86
  Heintzelman, Stuart, 162, 180
  Knight, Harry E., 188
  Lee, Raymond E., 243, 339n47
  Lincoln, Francis H., 188–189
  McCabe, E. R. Warner, 207, 214, 216
  Miles, Sherman, 207, 214, 231, 243, 331n63, 339n47
  Naylor, William K., 163
  Nolan, Dennis E., 118, 162, 215
  Reeves, James H., 163, 170–171
  Smith, Alfred T., 188
  Strong, George V., 214, 244
  Vandenberg, Hoyt S. and, 264, 266
  See also Director of Military Intelligence
Assistant Secretary of the Navy, 95, 139, 166
  Roosevelt, Franklin D., 115, 123, 125, 130, 139, 146, 166, 185, 221
  Roosevelt, Theodore, 57–58, 66–67, 73, 113, 185
  Roosevelt, Theodore, Jr., 174
  Soley, James R., 34
  Sullivan, John L., 122
  See also Secretary of the Navy
Assistant Secretary of State, 187, 205
Attorney General, 117, 153
Astor, Vincent, 221

Atherton, Ray, 249, 332n73
Attorney General, 117, 153, 155
Auxiliary Naval Force, 70
Aviation Intelligence Branch, 212–213

Babcock, John B., 38–39
Babcock, John W., 142–143
Babcock, J. V., 116, 193
Baker, Newton D., 134
  Army intelligence and, 147
  Churchill, Marlborough and, 168–169
  General Order no. 80 and, 137
  Military Intelligence Division and, 168–169
  Secretary of War, 133, 147, 168
  War College Division and, 133
Baldridge, Harry A., 185, 321n9
Baldwin, Hanson W., 201, 325n76
Baltimore, USS, 45
Barber, Francis M., 59, 74
Barker, A. S., 73
Barkley, Frederick R., 229
Bartlett, John R., 69–70, 71, 72, 75, 295n71
Basic War Plans, 211
Bayard, Thomas F., 49
Baxter, John, 202
Beach, W. D., 87, 88, 92–93, 99–100, 299n35
Beard, Charles, 195
Beardall, John R., 231
Beehler, William H., 22, 73, 296–297n91
Belknap, Reginald R., 132
Bell, J. Franklin, 99–101, 303n95
Bellamy, Ralph, 202
Benson, William S., 130–131
Berle, Adolf A.
  Anderson, Walter S. and, 216, 332n73
  Assistant Secretary of State, 205
  centralized intelligence agency and, 216
  on the chief of naval intelligence, 205
  Department of State and, 216, 249
  intelligence committee and, 216
  Joint Intelligence Committee and, 340n74
  military intelligence and, 340n74
  Military Intelligence Division and, 216
  Pearl Harbor and, 205
Berry, A. G., 19, 20, 25, 285n60
Bethel, Elizabeth, 285n60
Betts, Thomas J., 247

Biddle, John, 105
Bissell, Clayton, 246–247, 251, 263, 264, 343–344n14
Bliss, Tasker H., 42, 96, 129, 151
Blount, Lewis, 202
Bolivia, 9, 12
Bonaparte, Charles J., 84
Bond, James, 202, 225
Branch Intelligence Office, 131, 141
Branch Offices (Army), 214–215, 245, 340n59
Branzel, Bruno, 228
Breck, Samuel, 67
Breckinridge, Henry S., 123
Brereton, Todd R., 59
Bretherton, Howard, 227
Bridges, Charles H., 188
Bryan, William J., 54
Buck, William H., 73
Buckingham, Benjamin H., 33, 39–40, 286n8
Bureau of Aeronautics, 212–213
Bureau of Equipment, 18, 35, 48
Bureau of Insurgent Records in Manila, 72, 85. *See also* Military Information Division (The Philippines)
Bureau of Investigation, 147, 170. *See also* Federal Bureau of Investigation
    Department of Justice and, 170
    domestic security and, 148, 177
    media and, 150
    Military Intelligence Division and, 170
Bureau of Military Information, 7
Bureau of Navigation, 14, 20, 73, 82, 95
    Department of the Navy and, 8, 82
    library, 15
    naval attachés and, 39–40
    navalists, 19
    Office of Naval Intelligence and, 15, 16, 21, 24, 34, 47, 50, 69, 75, 83, 208
Bureau of Ordnance, 65, 73
Byrnes, James, 266

Cabinet Committee on Censorship, 237
Cagney, James, 267
Cámara, Manuel de la, 60
Canada
    Great Britain and, 44
    maps of, 48
    media and, 62
    Military Information Division and, 38, 44, 62, 287n17
    as rival, 31, 50
Carson, Ralph, 257
Carter, William H., 86, 87, 299n31
Cassard, Paul, 237
Cavalry, 4, 7
Central Intelligence Agency, 1, 4
    Army Intelligence and, 270
    Cold War and, 268
    creation of, 2, 160, 265, 267, 268, 269
    Department of the Army and, 270
    director of naval intelligence and, 268–269
    Federal Bureau of Investigation and, 267
    Joint Intelligence Committee and, 249
    media and, 268
    Military Intelligence Division and, 267, 269–270
    National Security Council and, 269–270
    Office of Naval Intelligence and, 267, 268
    Office of Strategic Intelligence and, 267–268
    Pearl Harbor and, 267
    strategic intelligence and, 267
Central Intelligence Group, 122, 266
centralized intelligence agency, 6, 9, 187. *See also* Central Intelligence Agency
    creation of, 259
    Department of the Navy and, 266
    Department of State and, 266
    Department of War and, 266
    director of naval intelligence and, 256–257
    domestic security and, 196
    Gestapo and, 265
    military intelligence and, 259
    Military Intelligence Division and, 259
    Office of Naval Intelligence and, 251, 256–257, 259
    reorganization and, 263
    secretary of state and, 266
    strategic military intelligence organizations and, 251
Chadwick, French E., 18, 112
    Bureau of Equipment chief, 35, 48
    Chief Intelligence Officer, 34–35, 40, 48, 112

Chadwick, French E., *continued*
  general staff and, 48–49
  naval attaché, 18, 34, 39–41, 112, 218, 283n22
  New York (USS) and, 112
  Office of Naval Intelligence and, 218
  public relations and, 35
  Proceedings and, 22, 48
Chaffee, Adna R., 92
Chambers, Washington I., 20–21, 23, 32
Chandler, Lloyd H., 16, 90
Chandler, William H., 16, 284n49
  directives, 16–17, 20, 21, 23, 24
  Office of Naval Intelligence and, 24
Charleston, USS, 59
Chief Intelligence Officer
  Bartlett, John R., 69
  Chadwick, French E., 34–35, 40
  Clover, Richardson, 58, 69, 82
  Davis, Charles H. Davis, 34, 46
  Mahan, Frederick A., 56
  Mason, Theodorus B. M., 16, 21, 25, 32, 71
  Potts, Templin M., 102
  Rodgers, Raymond P., 32, 34, 66, 84, 102
  Schroeder, Seaton, 84, 89–90
  Sigsbee, Charles D., 82–84, 94
  Singer, Frederic, 35, 47, 56, 59, 61, 64
  Soley, James R. and, 47
  Tracy, Benjamin F. and, 45
  Vreeland, Charles E., 102
  Wainwright, Richard, 56, 64, 66, 103, 166
  See also Chief of Naval Intelligence; Director of Naval Intelligence
Chief of Naval Intelligence, 205, 262, 268.
  See also Chief Intelligence Officer; Director of Naval Intelligence
Chief of Naval Operations, 44, 176, 209–210, 216, 219
  Benson, William S., 130
  Coontz, Robert E., 157
  Denfeld, Louis E., 268
  King, Ernest J., 236, 237
  Leahy, William D., 187, 197
  Stark, Harold R., 207, 210, 223–224, 237
Chief of Staff, 127, 132, 134, 138, 170, 210
  Bell, J. Franklin, 99
  Bliss, Tasker H., 129, 151
  Chaffee, Adna R., 92

Craig, Malin, 189
  MacArthur, Douglas, 198
  March, Peyton C., 136–137, 168
  Marshall, George C., 217, 244
  Pershing, John J., 162
  Second Division and, 92
  Scott, Hugh L., 128–130
  Strong, George V. and, 250
  Wood, Leonard, 101, 123
  Young, Samuel B. M., 87–88
Chile, 9, 12, 45–46, 64, 159
China, 66, 172, 177, 191, 193
Churchill, Marlborough, 117, 137–139, 149, 304n127
  American Expeditionary Forces and, 144
  Army intelligence and, 138, 160
  Assistant Chief of Staff for Intelligence, G-2, 138
  as chief censor, 149
  Bolshevism and, 168
  conference and, 161
  demobilization and, 157
  Department of War and, 139, 160–161
  Director of Military Intelligence, 117, 160, 170
  domestic security and, 149, 168
  general staff and, 149
  military intelligence and, 169
  Military Intelligence Division and, 137–138, 144, 157, 160, 161, 168–170, 308n65
  as military observer, 107
  New York Times and, 308n65
  Red Scare and, 170
Churchill, Winston, 107, 217, 219, 220
CIA. *See* Central Intelligence Agency
CIG. *See* Central Intelligence Group
CIO. *See* Chief Intelligence Officer
Cleveland, Grover, 11, 31, 49
Clover, Richardson, 61, 69, 75–76
  Bancroft (USS) and, 69
  card catalogue system, 71
  Chief Intelligence Officer, 58, 70, 82
  naval attachés and, 60, 75
  naval war board and, 73
  Office of Naval Intelligence and, 295n64
  Spanish-American War and, 76
CNO. *See* Chief of Naval Operations
COI. *See* Office of the Coordinator of Information

Cold War, 1, 4, 262, 268
Collon, Frances M., 257–258
Color plans, 193, 194
Colwell, John C., 33, 285n8
COMINCH. *See* Commander-in-Chief, US Fleet
Command and General Staff College, 129, 163
Commander-in-Chief, Pacific Fleet, 235
Commander-in-Chief, US Fleet
  chief of staff and, 250
  combat intelligence division and, 254
  Department of the Navy and, 237–238, 255
  director of naval intelligence and, 258
  dissolution of, 262
  general staff and, 238
  Joint Intelligence Collection Agencies and, 251
  Office of Naval Intelligence and, 236, 237, 251, 245, 254–256
  operational intelligence and, 235–236, 240, 255–256, 258
  Warner Report, 251
  war planning and, 237
Communist Party of America, 166, 194, 195
COMPACFLT. *See* Commander-in-Chief, Pacific Fleet
Coontz, Robert E., 157
Corbin, Henry C., 71, 76, 98, 297n94
Corcoran Court, 309n76
Corvall, Barry, 228
Counterintelligence Group, 239, 253
Coxe, Alexander B., 134–135, 137, 144
Craig, Malin, 189
Crosley, W. S., 104
Crowninshield, Arent S., 69, 73, 75–76
Crumley, Brian T., 18
Cuba, 54, 72, 93, 113
  maps of, 48, 63, 177
  Maine (USS) and, 82
  Military Information Division and, 38, 44, 62–63, 74, 77, 293n36
  naval intelligence and, 61
  Office of Naval Intelligence and, 61
  operational intelligence of, 64, 93
Cuban Revolution of 1895, 61
Culgoa, 74
Cummings, Damon E., 61

Daniels, Josephus, 131
  chief of naval operations and, 104
  Department of the Navy and, 145
  domestic security and, 145
  military preparedness and, 131
  Naval War College and, 126
  Navy General Board and, 126
  Office of Naval Intelligence and, 104, 156
  as a pacifist, 126
  Secretary of the Navy, 104, 126, 156, 167
  War Information Service and, 131
Darling, Charles H., 89
Davis, Charles H., Jr., 34, 46, 47, 50
Davis, Charles H., Sr., 34
DCI. *See* Director of Central Intelligence
Delimitation Agreement, 217
Denby, Edwin, 178
Denfeld, Louis E., 268
Dennis, Kay, 228
Department of the Air Force, 267
Department of the Army and, 270, 345n36
Department of Commerce, 175
Department of Defense, 270
Department of Justice, 146, 167, 201
  Army intelligence and, 201
  Bureau of Investigation, 170
  counterintelligence and, 171, 312n7
  domestic security and, 179
  Germany and, 311n108
  Military Intelligence Division and, 170, 324–325n66
  naval intelligence and, 201
  Office of Naval Intelligence and, 179
  See also Attorney General
Department of Naval Intelligence, 14
Department of the Navy
  Adjutant General's Office and, 99
  air intelligence and, 242
  budget of, 125, 140, 182
  Bureau of Navigation and, 8, 16
  censorship and, 132, 158
  centralized intelligence agency and, 266
  chief intelligence officer and, 56, 69, 103
  chief of naval operations and, 238
  Commander-in-Chief, US Fleet and, 237–238, 255
  communism and, 254
  counterintelligence and, 201
  demobilization and, 260

Department of the Navy, *continued*
  director of naval intelligence and, 167, 173, 185, 197, 211–212, 213, 235, 236, 237, 241
  domestic security and, 130, 184, 197, 223, 252, 262
  Duke of Windsor and, 121
  Federal Bureau of Investigation and, 213
  Geneva Naval Conference and, 159 and, 159
  Germany and, 223
  Great Depression and, 182
  isolationism and, 182
  Japan and, 173, 221
  London Naval Conference and, 191
  managerial revolution and, 32
  Manual of Organization Charts and, 242
  Marine Corps and, 127
  media and, 68, 178, 222
  military intelligence and, 201, 260–261, 268
  Military Intelligence Division and, 213
  mobilization and, 209
  naval attachés and, 18, 19, 39, 40, 41, 51, 90, 105, 156, 218, 263, 332n71, 333n83
  naval intelligence and, 105, 140, 196–197, 262–263, 268
  Naval War College and, 84
  Office of Naval Intelligence and, 16, 21, 34, 35, 55, 61, 65, 68, 69–70, 77, 80–81, 82–84, 89, 102, 105, 109, 110, 126, 135, 142, 144–146, 151, 158, 166, 175, 181, 184, 186, 188, 189–192, 207, 209, 223, 224–225, 226, 233, 235, 236, 238, 240, 255, 256, 257, 259, 261–263, 268, 270, 313n26
  Office of Strategic Services and, 209
  OP-16-x and, 193
  operational intelligence, 124, 225
  operational security and, 109
  Pearl Harbor and, 224
  Rainbow plans and, 209
  reorganization and, 103–105, 237
  Strategic Information Section and, 209
  strategic intelligence and, 235
  strategic military intelligence organizations and, 9, 10, 149
  War of the Pacific and, 12
  war planning, 44, 64, 109, 110, 124, 252

Warner Report and, 240
  War Plan Orange and, 193
  World War II and, 125, 257, 260–261
Department of Ordinance and Gunnery, 13
Department of State, 51, 53, 101, 174, 179
  Central Intelligence Group and, 266
  centralized intelligence agency and, 266
  Joint Intelligence Committee and, 248–249
  media and, 202
  military attaché and, 319–320n128–129
  Military Intelligence Division and, 216, 319–320nn128–129
  naval attachés and, 18, 175, 333n83
  relationship with the Office of Naval Intelligence and, 262, 268
  Russo-Japanese War and, 90
  secret service section and, 147
Department of the Treasury, 14–15, 40, 228, 248–249, 312n7. *See also* Secret Service
Department of War
  American Civil War and, 7
  Army intelligence and, 81, 88, 92–93, 129, 149, 188, 264
  Army War College and, 96, 129
  assistant chief of staff for intelligence, G-2, and, 194, 215, 236
  Branch Offices and, 214
  budget of, 125, 140, 182
  bureau chiefs and, 43
  centralized intelligence agency and, 266
  counterintelligence and, 171, 188, 201, 214, 264
  demobilization and, 138, 260, 263
  Department of Justice and, 171
  domestic security and, 130, 147, 171, 176, 184, 197, 252
  Evening Star and, 27
  expansionism and, 7
  General Mobilization Plan and, 176
  general orders and, 89, 99
  Great Depression and, 182
  Information Section and, 160
  isolationism and, 182
  managerial revolution and, 32
  Mexico and, 128
  military attachés and, 39, 41, 106, 128, 156
  Military Information Division and, 10,

20, 21, 26–28, 55, 63, 71–72, 74, 76, 80–81, 98
military intelligence and, 129, 160, 181, 201, 260–261, 264
Military Intelligence Branch and, 136, 307n50
Military Intelligence Division and, 149, 160, 162, 171, 181, 184, 188, 189, 192, 193–194, 197, 199, 204, 207, 214–215, 221, 226, 236, 243, 247, 257, 259, 264, 269–270, 314n38
Military Intelligence Section, 135, 144
Military Intelligence Service, 247
military morale mission and, 149
mobilization and, 162, 193–194, 209
National Defense Act of 1920 and, 163
negative intelligence and, 171
operational intelligence and, 77, 124
plant protection and, 307n50
Rainbow plans and, 209
Red Scare and, 197
reorganization of, 243–244, 264
Second Division and, 99
Second Section and, 101
society and, 200
strategic intelligence and, 244
strategic military intelligence organizations and, 9, 10, 149
War College Division and, 106
war planning and, 124, 193–194, 252
World War I and, 321n17
World War II and, 125, 257, 260–261
Dewey, George, 61–62, 74, 95, 97, 301n69
Dickman, Joseph T., 85
Director of Central Intelligence, 122, 186, 266, 268–269
Director of Military Intelligence, 138–139, 151, 155, 170
   Baker, Newton D. and, 168–169
   Churchill, Marlborough, 117, 137, 160, 170
   March, Peyton C. and, 137, 168–169
   Nolan, Dennis E., 87, 118, 160
   Van Deman, Ralph H. and, 137, 139, 168–169, 171
   See also Assistant Chief of Staff for Intelligence, G-2
Director of Naval Intelligence
   Anderson, Walter S., 209–211, 216, 219, 224, 328n31–32, 332n73

Baldridge, Harry A., 185
Ellis, Hayne, 185, 192, 195
Galbraith, William W., 159, 167
Hepburn, Arthur J., 159, 167
Holmes, Ralston H., 186–188, 191–192, 209
Inglis, Thomas B., 262
James, Jules, 211, 224
Johnson, Alfred W., 159, 175, 185, 189, 194
Kirk, Alan G., 121, 212–213, 224, 329n37
Long, Andrew, 158
McNamee, Luke, 158, 167, 174, 175
Niblack, Alfred P., 60, 119, 156–158, 172, 174
Oliver, James H., 103, 126, 139
Puleston, William D., 185–186, 191, 193, 195–197
Rodgers, Thomas S., 103–104
Schuirmann, Roscoe E., 241–242
Thebaud, Leo H., 186, 242–243, 255, 256
Train, Harold C., 122, 238–239, 329n39
Welles, Roger, Jr, 139, 145–146
Wilkinson, Theodore S., 213–214, 229, 252, 254
See also Chief Intelligence Officer; Chief of Naval Intelligence
disillusionment, 152, 153, 173, 180, 182, 184
Division of European Affairs, 333n83
Division of Operations and Training, 120, 164, 208
Division of Plans and Policies, 208
DNI. *See* Director of Naval Intelligence
Dodge Commission, 76
Donovan, William J., 251
   Army intelligence and, 265
   Central Intelligence Agency and, 249
   centralized intelligence agency and, 217, 249, 251, 265
   chief of naval operations and, 237
   Federal Bureau of Investigation and, 217, 265
   Gestapo and, 249, 265
   Great Britain and, 220
   Joint Intelligence Committee and, 237, 249
   military intelligence and, 218, 232, 236
   Military Intelligence Division and, 217, 258–259, 265
   Office of the Coordinator of Information and, 217, 233, 237

Donovan, William J., *continued*
  Office of Naval Intelligence and, 217, 233, 258–259
  Office of Strategic Services and, 236, 248, 249–250, 265
  strategic intelligence and, 233, 236
Dorsey, George E., 310n92
Dougherty, John A., 91
Driscoll, James, 199
Drum, Richard C., 36, 43. 112, 285n60
  Canada and, 50
  Evening Star and, 26
  Military Information Division and, 26–28, 36
Duke of Windsor, 121
Dunlop, Phil, 202
Dunn, John W., 138
Dyer, George C., 238
Dyer, George L., 60

Eisenhower, Dwight D., 183, 199–200, 249, 339n45, 339n53
Eisner, Will, 342n117
Eliot, George F., 197, 201, 323n62
Elkins, Stephen B., 37, 43, 50
Ellicott, John M., 13, 32, 42, 50
Ellis, Earl "Pete", 157, 164–165, 177–178, 315n48, 318–319n116
Ellis, Hayne, 185, 192–193, 195
Elton, Fox, 201
Emory, William H., 34, 41
empire, 54, 55, 77
  enablers of empire, 55, 66
  military progressives and, 80
  United Stated Navy and, 76, 95
  See also imperialism; imperialists
Endicott, William C., 27, 41, 285n60
"Estimate of the Situation for 1937," 196
"Estimate of the Situation for 1939," 197
"Estimates of the Situation and Base Development Plans," 172
European Squadron, 8, 12
exceptionalism, 2
expansion, 13, 69, 77. *See also* expansionists
expansionists, 12, 13, 54, 58, 75, 271. *See also* expansion

Far East Section/Division, 120, 190–192, 213–214, 226, 320n7

fascists, 197, 219, 222
"Father of Military Intelligence," 128, 198
FBI. *See* Federal Bureau of Investigation
Federal Bureau of Investigation, 208
  agents of, 257
  Army intelligence and, 201
  Central Intelligence Agency and, 267
  counterintelligence and, 216, 227–228, 253, 323n62
  Counterintelligence Group and, 252
  Department of the Navy and, 213
  director of, 222, 239, 253, 268–269
  director of navl intelligence and, 268–269
  District Intelligence Officers and, 216, 222
  domestic security and, 222, 228–229, 240, 253
  facilities of, 196
  media and, 202, 227–229, 257, 323n62, 335n115
  military attachés and, 253
  military intelligence and, 227
  Military Intelligence Division and, 222, 228
  naval attachés and, 253
  naval intelligence and, 201, 334n93
  relationship with Military Intelligence Division, 216–217, 222, 228–229, 252–253, 257
  relationship with Office of Naval Intelligence, 216–217, 222, 228–229, 240, 252–253, 257, 262, 268
  society and, 228
  Special Intelligence Service and, 253
Federal Council of Churches, 196
Feland, Logan, 120, 164–165, 177, 315n48, 315n50
First Division, 87, 100
First Section, 100–101
Fisher, Steve, 227
Fleming, Ian, 202, 225
Folger, William M., 45
Ford, Stanley H., 171, 198, 317nn86–87
Foreign Economic Administration, 251
Forrestal, James V., 212, 213, 263, 330n44
Foss, George E., 97, 98, 302n76
Foulk, George, 19, 111
Fowler, Dan, 323n62
Fox, Charles E., 50

Frankel, Samuel B., 225
Franz, Manuel, 123
free trade, 3, 30
Funston, Frederick, 63

Gade, John A., 159–160
Gage, Beverly, 79, 153
Galbraith, William W., 159, 167
Garbo, Greta, 200
Garrison, Lindley M., 107, 123
General Mobilization Plan and, 176
General Order No. 14, 136
General Order No. 23, 38, 43–44
General Order No. 40
General Order No. 80, 137
General Order No. 115, 88–89
General Order No. 116, 99
General Order No. 120, 87
General Order No. 292, 14, 15, 16, 24, 282n14
General Order No. 425, 108
General Order No. 544, 95
General Staff Act, 86
general staffs, 26, 65, 88, 102, 103, 110, 131, 138, 151, 208
  Army intelligence and, 163
  Army War College and, 299n35
  chief of staff and, 129, 245
  Commander-in-Chief, US Fleet and, 238
  creation of, 3, 22, 23, 35, 44, 48–49, 52, 80–81, 86–87, 92, 94–95, 103–104
  demobilizations and, 269
  divisions of, 137
  Europe and, 38, 88
  growth of, 160
  manning of, 129
  Marine Corps and, 164
  military attachés and, 106
  military intelligence and, 125, 160
  Military Intelligence Division and, 151, 188, 214, 236, 251, 269
  missions of, 105
  mobilization and, 162
  Naval War College and, 46
  Office of Naval Intelligence and, 238, 251
  Patch Board and, 263
  reorganizations of, 101, 128–129, 136, 137, 160, 162, 235
  War College Division and, 106

War Plans Division and, 236
  after World War II, 269
Geneva Naval Conference, 159
Germany, 89, 94, 108, 131–132, 146–147, 173, 179, 221
  blitzkrieg and, 220
  communists and, 219
  fascists and, 219
  France and, 210
  general staff and, 86
  Great Britain and, 210
  media and, 200–201, 202, 228
  military attachés and, 107
  naval attachés and, 193, 220
  Office of Naval Intelligence and, 62, 193, 223, 268, 311n108
  Operation Overlord ad, 256
  Office of Strategic Services and, 267
  propaganda and, 168
  Lusitania and, 126
  Spain and, 191
  spying and, 150, 168, 311n108
  and threat to domestic naval interests, 126
  U-boats and, 157
  Venezuela and, 83
  war declaration and, 132
  World War I and, 220
Gestapo, 249, 265
Ghormley, Robert L., 212, 220, 221, 333nn83–84
Gibbon, John H., 83
Gilbert, James L., 123, 346n12
Gilded Age, 5, 11, 27, 30
Gillis, Irvin van Gorder, 90
Gleason, S. Everett, 153, 182
Gleaves, Albert G., 9, 20, 25, 41
Godfrey, John H., 219, 220, 225
Gompers, Samuel, 180
Goodrich, Caspar F., 84, 97
Gordon, Bill, 200
Graf Spee, 223
Grant, Ulysses S., 16, 130
Great Britain, 62, 148, 215, 317n98
  American–Britain Conversations and, 212
  Canada and, 36, 44, 287n17
  Dunkirk and, 220
  Germany and, 210
  maps and, 48, 65

Great Britain, *continued*
  media and, 200
  military intelligence and, 130, 134
  naval attachés and, 209, 218
  naval intelligence and, 142, 219
  negative Intelligence, 135
  operational intelligence and, 219
  positive intelligence and, 135
  as sea power, 172, 173, 322n35
Great Depression, 182, 184, 188, 191, 195, 200, 208, 272
  Department of the Navy and, 182
  Department of War and, 182
  military intelligence and, 207
  Military Intelligence Division and, 156, 184, 204, 226–227
  New Deal and, 260
  Office of Naval Intelligence and, 156, 160, 184, 203, 226–227, 255
  World War II and, 234
Great War. *See* World War I
Great White Fleet, 91, 93
Greely, Adolphus W., 36–37
Green, James R., 206
Grew, Joseph C., 221
Gulf Oil, 240, 337n26

Hagen, Ole, 220
Haislip Board Report, 269–270
Haiti, 127, 165, 315n48
Hale, Eugene, 95
Hall, William Reginald, 139
Halsey, William F., Jr., 158
Harding, Warren G., 173
Hardy, Oliver, 150
Harrison, Benjamin, 31, 35, 45
Hawkins, John, 257
Hawkins, Ward, 257
Hayden, Edward E., 69
Heintzelman, Stuart, 162–163, 179, 314n40, 319n126
Henderson Robert, 248
Hepburn, Arthur J., 159, 167
Herbert, Hilary A.
  Naval War College and, 46
  Office of Naval Intelligence and, 47–48, 64, 66, 293–294n45
Hillenkoetter, Roscoe H., 186, 220
Hitler, Adolf, 191, 202, 210, 224–225, 332n76

Hofstadter, Richard, 30, 182
Holcomb, Thomas, 208
Holman, William S., 37, 287n23
Holmes, Ralston S., 186–188, 191–192, 209, 212, 329n35
Hooe Building, 160, 308n57
Hoover, Herbert, 183, 185, 189–190, 191, 194–195, 323n49
Hoover, J. Edgar, 229
  assistant chief of staff for intelligence, G-2, and, 253
  counterintelligence and, 228
  Department of State and, 197, 216
  director of naval intelligence and, 239, 253
  Federal Bureau of Investigation and, 216, 228, 239, 253, 265, 334n93
  media and, 228–229
  Military Intelligence Division and, 197, 216, 228, 253
  Nazis and, 253
  Office of Naval Intelligence and, 197, 228, 253, 328n32
  public relations and, 228
  Society and, 228
  Special Intelligence Service and, 253
Horne, Frederick, 239, 240, 249
Hough, Henry H., 159, 167
Howell, Glenn F., 194–195, 323nn39–42, 323–324nn48–49
Hughes, Charles E., 174, 180, 319–320nn128–129
Hunt, William H., 13, 15, 16, 24, 25

imperialism, 2, 3, 30, 54, 186. *See also* imperialist
imperialists, 54, 62. *See also* imperialism
Industrial Age, 12, 267, 271. *See also* Industrial Revolution; industrialization
industrialization, 30
  professionalization and, 26
  societies response to, 27, 46–47, 67, 79–80, 272
  See also Industrial Age; Industrial Revolution
Industrial Revolution, 3, 8, 10, 29, 54, 259. *See also* Industrial Age; industrialization

Industrial Workers of the World, 148, 166, 316n70
Ingersoll, Royal E., 213, 223–224, 230, 334n106
Inglis, Thomas B., 262, 268, 269
Intelligence Group, 239, 254
Intelligence Office, 215–216
internationalists, 11, 47, 123, 182, 234
International Naval Rendezvous and Review, 35
isolationism, 152, 153, 272
  Department of the Navy and, 182
  Department of War and, 182
  Office of Naval Intelligence and, 203
  See also isolationist
isolationists, 153, 155, 184, 185 189
  domestic security and, 271–272
  Japan and, 234
  Military Intelligence Division and, 271–272
  Office of Naval Intelligence and, 195, 271–272
  World War I and, 147
  See also isolationism
Italy, 35, 191, 322n35

James, Jules, 211, 212, 224
JANAID. *See* Joint Army-Navy Air Intelligence Division
JANIS. *See* Joint Army Navy Studies
Japan, 46, 66, 84, 95, 97, 108, 177–178, 185, 192, 206
  China and, 191, 193
  counterintelligence and, 221, 226
  diplomats and, 174, 231
  District Intelligence Officers and, 222
  doctrine of, 231
  Great White Fleet and, 91
  Imperial Navy and, 91, 175, 190, 322n35
  intelligence collection on, 167, 221
  intentions of, 120, 206, 230–231, 326–327n6
  invasion of Manchuria and, 191
  isolationists and, 234
  Joint Intelligence Committee and, 327n9
  London Naval Conference and, 190–191
  "Magic" and, 226
  Marianas Islands and, 89
  media and, 200
  military attaché and, 226
  military intelligence and, 203
  Military Intelligence Division and, 204, 229, 232, 243, 261, 327n9
  Mr. Moto and, 199, 227–228
  naval attachés and, 191, 221, 230
  naval intelligence and, 174, 197, 203, 230
  Office of Naval Intelligence and, 107, 165, 190, 193, 202, 229–231, 255, 261, 268, 300n46, 326–327n6, 327n9
  Open Door policy and, 172
  pacifists and, 234
  Pearl Harbor and, 203, 205, 214, 231–232, 261
  Philippines, the, and, 89, 243
  Russo-Japanese War and, 89, 91, 95, 231, 300n47
  Siberia and, 226
  sphere of influence and, 89, 175
  War Plan Orange and, 107–108, 177, 194, 235, 322n36
  Western Pacific and, 230
  World War II and, 322n36
Japanese American Internment Camps, 252, 341n97
Japanese Consulate, 194
JCS. *See* Joint Chiefs of Staff
Jeffreys-Jones, Rhodri, 155
JIC. *See* Joint Intelligence Committee
JICA. *See* Joint Intelligence Collection Agencies
JIS 89, 251
Johnson, Alfred W., 159, 175, 185, 189–190, 194, 318n104
Johnson, G. A., 177
Johnson, Luther A., 229
Johnston, Marbury, 83
Joint Army–Navy Air Intelligence Division, 265
Joint Army and Navy Board, 132
Joint Army Navy Studies, 248, 255
Joint Board, 218
Joint Chiefs of Staff, 247–248, 249, 250–251, 255, 265
Joint Intelligence Collection Agencies, 249, 251
Joint Intelligence Committee, 218, 250
  Central Intelligence Agency and, 249

Joint Intelligence Committee, *continued*
  chief of naval operations and, 237
  Department of State and, 248–249
  Department of Treasury and, 248–249
  Japan and, 327n9
  Joint Chiefs of Staff and, 248
  meetings of, 237
  Marine Corps M-2 and, 248–249
  military intelligence and, 249, 261, 340n74
  Military Intelligence Division and, 248–249, 254
  Office of the Coordinator of Information and, 237
  Office of Naval Intelligence and, 248–249, 254
  Office of Strategic Services and, 248–249
  Office of War Information and, 248–249
Joint Planning Committee, 218
Jones, Thaddeus W., 100

Kalbfus, Edward C., 193
Karmany, Lincoln, 35, 127, 164
Karsten, Peter, 14, 32
Kelly, Monroe, 220
Kelton, J. C., 37, 43, 51, 289–290n75
Kennedy, Joseph P., 220
Kilpatrick, Walter K., 187–188
Kimball, William W., 22, 55–58, 65, 291–292nn15–16
Kin, Peter, 195
King, Ernest J., 250
  Chief of Naval Operations, 236, 237
  combat intelligence division and, 254
  Commander-in-Chief, US Fleet, 236, 237, 254
  Department of the Navy and, 237
  Military Intelligence Division and, 250
  naval intelligence and, 240
  Office of Naval Intelligence and, 236, 250
  Operational intelligence and, 236
King, James W., 9, 10
Kirk, Alan G., 229, 332n78
  censorship and, 212
  as consultant, 212
  Department of the Navy and, 212, 223, 224–225, 332n71, 333nn83–84
  Department of State and, 333n83
  Director of Naval Intelligence, 121, 212–213, 224, 329n37

District Intelligence Officers and, 223
  domestic security and, 212, 222–223
  Federal Bureau of Investigation and, 222
  Germany and, 220, 332n76, 332–333n80
  Great Britain and, 219–220, 225, 328n24, 332n72, 332n77, 332–333n80, 333n84
  Joint Intelligence Committee and, 218
  Military Intelligence Division and, 222, 330n46
  naval attachés and, 121, 211–212, 219–220, 329n38, 333n83
  naval intelligence and, 220
  naval observers and, 224–225, 20
  Office of Naval Intelligence and, 212–213, 217, 223, 224–225, 330n45, 332n71
  Office of Public Relations and, 224
  British Admiralty's Operational Intelligence Centre and, 224
  secretary of the Navy and, 224
  strategic intelligence and, 212
Kittredge, Tracy B., 103
Knight, Harry E., 188
Knox, Dudley W., 116, 143
  Eclipse of American Seapower, The, and, 175
  Office of Naval Intelligence and, 104, 126, 131
  Office of Naval Records and, Library, 158
  Proceedings and, 104
  as a Taylorist, 104
  War Records Section and, 186
Knox, William F. "Frank", 212, 224, 225, 240, 338n33
Korea, 19, 111
Kroner, Hayes A., 231–232, 243–246
Kuhn, Joseph E., 129–130, 132–135

LaFeber, Walter, 54
Lamont, Daniel S., 38, 51
Langer, William L., 153, 182
Laurel, Stan, 150
Layton, Edwin T., 186
League of Nations, 153, 248
Leahy, William D., 187, 197, 210, 266
LeBreton, D. M., 176
Lee, Raymond E., 243–244, 339n47
Lee, W. G., 180
LeFeber, Walter, 54

Lejeune, John A., 164–165, 177–178, 315n48
Lemon Building, 87, 99, 114
Lend-Lease Act, 223, 224
Liggett, Hunter, 106–107
Limited National Emergency Order, 188, 189, 210, 214, 232
Lincoln, Francis H., 188–189, 321n15, 321n17
London Naval Conference, 189, 190, 191, 322n22
Long, Andrew, 157–158, 173–174
Long, John D., 57, 75–76, 95
  General Order no. 544 and, 95
  naval attachés and, 73, 75–76
  Naval War Board and, 69, 73
Luce, Stephen B.
  Bureau of Navigation and, 301n65
  general staff and, 23, 46, 94–95, 301n69
  as a military progressive, 94
  as a navalist, 94
  Naval War College and, 94, 301n65
  Office of Naval Intelligence and, 23, 50, 301n65
  Proceedings and, 22
  Unites States Naval Institute and, 94
  "War Schools" and, 23
Ludlow, William, 96
Ludlow Board, 96
Lusitania, 126

MacArthur, Arthur, 37
MacArthur, Douglas, 198
Macomb, Montgomery M., 107, 128–129
"Magic" intelligence, 226, 230, 231–232
Mahan, Alfred T., 57, 175
  chief intelligence officer and, 34
  Naval War College and, 23, 284n47
  Office of Naval Intelligence and, 34
Mahan, Frederick A., 56
Mahnken, Thomas C., 203
Maine, USS, 60, 63, 66, 72, 82
Major, Samuel I. M., 108
Manchukuo, 193. *See also* Manchuria
Manchuria, 191. *See also* Manchukuo
Mansfield, Joseph J., 317n98
March, Peyton C.
  Army intelligence and, 136, 149, 307–308n52
  as chief of staff, 136, 168
  General Order no. 80 and, 137
  general staff and, 136–137
  Intelligence Regulations, 1920 and, 161
  as military attaché, 42
  Military Intelligence Branch and, 137
  Military Intelligence Division and, 170
  War Plans Division and, 160
Marine Corps intelligence, 164–165, 181, 208–209
  growth of, 4, 127, 209
  Military Intelligence Section and, 164–165, 177, 181
  missions of, 2
  Office of Naval Intelligence and, 177
  war planning and, 209
Marquand, John P., 199, 227
Marsh, C. C., 89–90
Marshall, George C., 250
  as chief of staff, 217, 244
  Military Intelligence Division and, 232, 250
  Office of Naval Intelligence and, 250
  strategic intelligence and, 244
Mason, C. H., 169
Mason, Francis Van Wyck, 202
Mason, Theodorus B. M., 13, 14, 23, 25, 32, 111
  Bureau of Navigation and, 16
  death of, 71, 295n70
  Department of the Navy and, 24
  legacy of, 25–26
  managerial revolution and, 80
  as a naval aide, 16
  naval attachés and, 17, 111
  naval intelligence and, 111, 131, 134, 233
  as a navalist, 16, 22
  Office of Naval Intelligence and, 233
  Proceedings and, 22
  shipboard officers, 19
  United States Naval Academy and, 13, 21
Massachusetts Institute of Technology, 222
Masteller, Kenneth C., 138
May, Ernest R., 54
McCabe, E. R. Warner, 207, 214, 216
McCallum, Donald, 221
McClellan, George B., Jr., 301–302n71
McClellan, George B., Sr., 7
McCollum, Arthur H., 120, 186, 191, 226, 231

McCully, Newton A., 90, 108, 114, 299n39
McGerr, Michael, 79
McKeller, Kenneth, 179
McKinley, William, 54, 55, 57, 85
  maps and, 74
  Military Information Division and, 76
  Spain and, 61
McNamee, Luke, 158–159, 167, 174, 175, 178
McNarney, Joseph T., 176–177, 243–244, 249
Memorandum No. 64, 137
Merritt, Wesley, 72
Messersmith, George, 187
Mexican–American War, 6, 285n60
Mexico, 107–108
  Army intelligence and, 128
  Military Information Division and, 38, 44
  maps of, 48, 177
  military information committee and, 107
  naval war portfolio for, 108
  Punitive Expedition and, 128
  as rival, 31
  War College Division and, 106
  War Plan Green and, 194
Meyer, George von Lengerke, 103, 108, 109
MIB. *See* Military Intelligence Branch
MIC. *See* Military Intelligence Committee
MID. *See* Military Information Division
Miles, Nelson A., 64, 87, 293n36
Miles, Sherman, 229, 331n67
  Army intelligence and, 231
  Assistant Chief of Staff for Intelligence, G-2, 214, 231, 242, 331n63, 339n47
  counterintelligence and, 331n63
  data management and, 215
  Department of War and, 214–215
  domestic security and, 214–215, 331n63
  foreign intelligence and, 215
  general staff and, 215, 243
  Great Britain and, 214
  Joint Intelligence Committee and, 218, 261
  "Magic" and, 231
  as military attaché, 214
  military intelligence and, 217–218, 261
  Military Intelligence Division and, 207, 214–215, 218, 231, 232, 330n46, 331n63
  mobilization and, 214–215
  Office of Naval Intelligence and, 218
  rank of, 215
  secretary of the Navy and, 218
  secretary of war and, 218
  strategic military intelligence organizations and, 217–218
  war plans and, 215
  War Plans Division and, 215
military attachés, 39, 41–42, 43, 51, 59, 62–63, 86–87, 93, 96, 99, 101, 106–107, 124, 128, 144, 161, 288n43
  Army intelligence and, 176
  assistant chief of staff for intelligence, G-2, and, 208
  counterintelligence and, 226, 312n7
  creation of, 36, 41
  Department of State and, 319–320nn128–129
  Department of War and, 156
  expansion of, 51, 58, 136
  Federal Bureau of Investigation and, 253
  funding of, 58, 67, 76, 85, 98, 179–180, 200
  Japan and, 226
  media and, 227
  Military Information Division and, 136, 290n80
  military information section and, 127
  Military Intelligence Division and, 161, 179–180, 199–200, 218
  Military Intelligence Service and, 244
  missions of, 38–39
  naval attachés and, 226
  Russo-Japanese War and, 92–93
  second division and, 299n31
  Spanish-American War and, 72
  Special Intelligence Service and, 253
  strategic intelligence and, 264
  War College Division and, 105–107, 123
Military Information Committee, 101–102, 107
  Army intelligence and, 102
  creation of, 100
  Mexico and, 107
  military attachés and, 101
  Military Information Division and, 101
  missions of, 106
  operational intelligence and, 107

Second Section and, 100
War College Division and, 102
Military Information Division
  Adjutant General's Office and, 29, 87, 208
  becoming the Second Division, 87–88
  budget of, 58, 76, 85, 88
  Canada and, 62, 287n17
  creation of, 10, 20, 26–28, 112, 346n11
  Cuba and, 62–63, 72
  data management and, 37–38, 42–44, 62, 67, 85, 89, 123
  demobilization and, 75
  Department of War and, 50, 98
  foreign intelligence and, 44
  general staff and, 81, 84–85, 88, 92, 96
  General Staff Act and, 86
  growth of, 32, 53, 58, 271
  manpower of, 36, 72
  mapping and, 21, 35–36, 37–38, 42, 44, 48, 55–56, 59, 61–63, 72, 74, 77, 89, 92
  media and, 31, 51–52, 62, 67–69, 98–99
  military attachés and, 136, 290n80
  Military Information Division (The Philippines) and, 85–86
  missions of, 11, 27–28, 31, 36–37, 42–44, 50, 53, 55, 71–72, 80, 106, 136, 287n17
  monographs and, 44, 52
  operational intelligence and, 55, 72, 77
  over-regulations of, 78, 271
  Philippines and, 72
  Progressivism and, 271
  public relations and, 61, 89
  purpose of, 55, 74, 176
  reestablishment of, 136
  as reformists, 31, 38, 54
  relationship with Office of Naval Intelligence, 28, 32, 34, 38, 53, 69, 86, 112
  reorganization of, 37, 63, 80, 293n33
  reputation of, 36, 38–39, 42, 44, 48, 52, 56, 58, 76, 81, 85
  Second Division and, 93, 114, 299n29, 299n31
  society and, 11, 52, 55, 80, 98
  submersion of, 100, 102
  Spanish-American War and, 63, 81, 88, 292n27
  transferring to the Office of the Chief of Staff, 87
  war planning, 44, 49, 50, 55, 58–59, 61, 64–65, 85–86, 123
Military Information Division (The Philippines), 72, 85–86, 303n95
  Records in Manila
  See also Bureau of Insurgent
Military Information and Monographs Committee, 102
Military Information Section, 128, 135
  military attachés and, 127
  mission of, 127
  Pre-World War I organization, 101–102, 123
Military Intelligence Branch, 136
  creation of, 136
  and the Department of War, 136, 307n50
  Hooe Building and, 308n57
  Military Information Division and, 136
  missions of, 136, 138
  Monroe Courts and, 308n57
  Plant Protection and, 307n50
Military Intelligence Division
  air intelligence and, 269
  Air Section and, 176–177
  American Expeditionary Forces and, 144
  Army intelligence and, 214, 246, 263, 265, 270
  assistant chief of staff for intelligence, G-2, and, 188–189, 198, 214–215, 227, 235–236, 258–259, 263, 331n63
  Aviation Intelligence Branch and, 212–213
  Bolshevism and, 168
  Branch Offices and, 214–215, 245
  Bureau of Investigation and, 170
  censorship and, 149, 170, 215
  Central Intelligence Agency and, 267, 269–270
  Central Intelligence Group and, 266
  centralized intelligence agency and, 259
  chief of staff and, 128, 134, 226, 258, 270
  Color plans and, 194
  counterintelligence and, 171, 176, 184, 188, 201–202, 207, 214, 216–217, 218, 235, 253
  Counterintelligence Group and, 252–253
  creation of, 26–28, 123, 129–130, 137
  customers of, 176, 270

Military Intelligence Division, *continued*
  data management/information gathering and, 124, 164, 165, 170, 176, 181, 188, 192, 215, 226, 257, 265
  demobilization and, 138, 160, 161, 170, 176, 178, 199, 251, 252, 263, 269, 271–272
  Department of Justice and, 170, 171, 324–325n66
  Department of the Navy and, 213
  Department of State and, 216, 319–320nn128–129
  Department of War and, 148, 162, 171, 188, 192, 193–194, 197, 199, 204, 207, 214–215, 221, 226, 236, 243, 247, 257, 259, 264, 269–270, 314n38
  director of military intelligence and, 139
  domestic security and, 124, 126, 141, 149, 154, 155, 158, 162, 165, 168–171, 180, 183, 184, 188, 189, 197–198, 199, 202, 216, 222, 226, 228–229, 252–253, 257, 271–272
  evaluation and assessment function and, 184, 221, 244
  Federal Bureau of Investigation and, 222, 228
  foreign intelligence and, 151, 170, 232
  funding of, 125–126, 134, 151, 154, 155, 161, 162, 163, 168, 178–180, 181, 183, 199, 202–204, 232, 234, 249, 258, 272, 319n126
  general staff and, 151, 188, 214, 235, 236, 251, 269
  Great Depression and, 184, 204, 226–227
  growth of, 148, 207, 214–215, 227, 231, 232–233, 235, 245, 246, 271
  Haislip Board Report and, 269–270
  history of, 138
  Hooe Building and, 160
  Intelligence Branch and, 180
  Intelligence Office and, 215
  isolationist movement and, 271–272
  Japan and, 194, 204, 229, 232, 243, 261, 327n9
  Japanese American Internment Camps and, 341n97
  Joint Army Navy Studies and, 255
  Joint Intelligence Collection Agencies and, 249
  Joint Intelligence Committee and, 218, 248–249, 254
  "Magic" and, 226
  manning of, 154, 160, 176, 180, 183, 189, 199, 203, 214–215, 235, 243, 249, 258, 272
  Marine Corps intelligence and, 165
  media and, 168, 170, 185, 201–203, 218, 227, 229, 257–258, 268
  Mexico and, 194
  military attachés and, 161, 179–180, 199–200, 218, 231, 319–320nn128–129
  military intelligence and, 169, 192, 226, 270
  missions of, 2, 6, 124, 132, 137–138, 161, 163, 170–171, 172–173, 176, 181, 188, 189, 198, 202, 207, 232, 235, 247, 248, 249, 251, 252, 258, 261, 264–266, 269, 272
  mobilization and, 162, 188, 193–194, 207–208, 214, 226–227, 234, 272
  morale of, 214
  Munitions Building and, 248
  National Mall and, 160
  National Security Council and, 267
  nature of, 183
  naval attachés and, 175
  naval intelligence and, 160, 263
  negative intelligence and, 149, 171
  New Deal and, 205, 206, 232, 234, 272
  New York Times and, 308n65
  operational intelligence and, 124, 126, 141, 151, 258, 264–265, 269
  Pearl Harbor and, 232, 261
  Pentagon and, 257
  Positive Branch and, 180
  purpose of, 3, 237, 243, 267
  Red Scare and, 161, 168–171, 176, 197, 271–272
  relationship with Federal Bureau of Investigation, 216–217, 222, 228–229, 252–253, 257
  relationship with Military Intelligence Service, 244–247, 258, 264
  relationship with Office of Naval Intelligence, 140, 148–149, 158, 172–173, 187, 188, 214, 216–217, 222, 227–229, 236, 240, 242, 247–251, 253, 258, 262, 265, 270

relationship with Office of Strategic Services, 242, 245, 247, 249–250, 270
reorganization of, 160, 161, 162, 163–164, 189, 214, 235, 243, 245–247, 252, 264, 267
reputation of, 149, 161, 162, 171, 184, 189, 192, 201–202, 207, 216, 218, 235, 236, 261, 265, 309n68
secretary of the Army and, 270
secretary of defense and, 270
secretary of war and, 207, 218
society and, 124, 154, 168, 170, 176, 181, 182, 183, 198, 199, 228, 232, 257, 271
Special Intelligence Service and, 253
as spy-catchers, 124, 149, 154, 200, 261
strategic intelligence and, 184, 221, 236, 261, 263, 265–266, 269–270
strategic warning and, 206–208, 215, 229, 232
Taylorism and, 206
Turner, Richmond K. and, 254
war planning and, 125, 161, 184, 188, 193–194, 204, 207, 218, 236, 247
War Plans Division and, 194, 236, 243
War Plan Green and, 194
War Plan Orange and, 194
War Plan White and, 168, 170
World War I and, 126, 161, 271
World War II and, 215, 233, 234, 235, 247, 252, 257, 258, 269, 272
Military Intelligence Section (Army)
American Expeditionary Forces and, 144
Army War College and, 134
branch offices and, 147
censorship and, 134
chief of staff and, 134, 151
creation of, 133–134, 143
cryptology and, 135
Department of War and, 135
domestic security and, 148
foreign intelligence and, 143
funding of, 135
general staff and, 134
manning of, 135
media and, 150
missions of, 138, 147
relationship with Office of Naval Intelligence, 140, 147
reorganization of, 135–136

Military Intelligence Section (Marines), 120, 156, 164–165, 177, 181, 208
Military Intelligence Service
Army intelligence and, 246
American Intelligence Service and, 244
chief of staff and, 246
creation of, 243–244
Department of War and, 247
evaluation and assessment function and, 244
military attachés and, 244
Pentagon and, 245
relationship with Military Intelligence Division, 244–247, 258, 264
strategic intelligence and, 244
Military Intelligence Training Center, 263–264
military morale, 138, 149
military observers, 7, 93, 106–107, 135, 214, 227
military preparedness, 129, 130, 131, 271
military progressives, 80–81, 88, 123, 129, 153
professionalism and, 80
Taylorism and, 80, 100
war planning and, 80
See also military progressivism
military progressivism, 79–81, 87, 92, 186.
See also military progressive
Military Reservation Division, 27
Millis, Walter, 10, 29
Mills, Albert L., 106
Mills Building, 83, 102, 104
MIS. See Military Intelligence Section
Miscellaneous Branch, 27
Monroe Courts, 136, 308n57
Monroe Doctrine, 9, 61, 192
Moore, Samuel N., 230
Morgan, Daniel, 5
Mott, T. Bentley, 63, 92
Munitions Building, 248

National Archives, 267–268, 299n39
National Conference of Jews and Christians, 196
National Defense Act of 1916, 128–129
National Defense Act of 1920, 160, 162, 163, 321n18
National Intelligence Authority, 266

National Mall, 160, 218
National Security Act of 1947, 267
National Security Council
  Army Intelligence and, 270
  Central Intelligence Agency and, 269–270
  Department of the Army, 270
  formation of, 267
  military intelligence and, 267
  Military Intelligence Division and, 267
  missions of, 344n27
  National Security Act of 1947 and, 267
  Office of Naval Intelligence and, 267, 268
Naval Act of 1890, 50
naval aristocracy, 32, 55
naval attachés, 22, 39–41, 46, 57, 58, 59–61, 71, 86, 89, 105, 124, 132, 190–192, 218, 331n70
  creation of, 14, 17–19, 25
  Department of Commerce and, 175
  Department of the Navy and, 40, 47, 66, 73, 156, 263, 332n71
  Department of State and, 175
  Federal Bureau of Investigation and, 253
  funding of, 47, 76, 98, 140, 192, 263
  Germany and, 62, 220
  Great Britain and, 209, 218
  information gathering and, 140, 156, 187, 191
  Japan and, 91, 175, 191, 230
  Kelly, Monroe, 220
  manning of, 140, 214
  Marine Corps and, 127
  media and, 68
  military attachés and, 226
  Military Intelligence Division and, 175
  missions of, 39–41, 75
  Office of Naval Intelligence and, 142, 156, 173–174, 175, 209, 218, 221, 226, 254, 262, 302n78
  Philippines and, 62, 74
  Russo-Japanese War and, 90
  Sino–Japanese War and, 59
  Spanish-American War and, 70, 72–74
  Special Intelligence Service and, 253
  Union of Soviet Socialist Republics and, 191
  War Information Services and, 127
  Wilkinson, Theodore S. and, 230
  World War II and, 254
Naval Board, 61, 68, 74, 75. *See also* Navy General Board; Naval War Board
"Naval Department Organization" (article), 48
"Naval Intelligence" (article), 21, 29, 49
Naval Intelligence Division, 142, 225, 219
Naval Records and Library Branch, 186
Naval War Board, 69, 70, 73, 82, 94. *See also* Naval Board; Navy General Board
Naval War College, 45–47, 83–84, 95, 97, 203
  Aid for Operations of the Fleet and, 103
  analysis of information and, 176
  creation of, 10, 23–24
  Department of the Navy and, 84
  mobilization and, 126
  naval intelligence, 102
  naval war board and, 73
  Office of Naval Intelligence and, 45–46, 64–65, 77, 81, 84, 94, 102, 108, 193, 301n65
  war planning, 45–46, 73, 108
Naval War Plan, 107
naval war portfolio, 108
Navies of the World, The, 10
Navy Building, Main, 104, 121, 218, 269
Navy General Board, 84, 103–104, 108, 126, 224
  Aid for Operations of the Fleet and, 103
  "Are You Ready?" and, 209
  coastal defense and, 95
  creation of, 66, 94–95
  missions of, 95
  mobilization and, 126
  Office of Naval Intelligence and, 84, 91, 109
  war planning, 95, 108
  See also Naval Board; Naval War Board
Navy Intelligence School, 263, 268
Navy Subsidiary Demobilization Plan for Intelligence, 262
Naylor, William K., 163
Nazis, 191, 222, 253, 257
Negative Branch, 135, 138, 161–162, 168
negative intelligence, 134, 136, 138, 149, 171
Nelson, Otto L., Jr., 247

Index 381

New Deal, 182–183, 195, 203–204, 205, 208, 222, 232–233, 243, 272
　assistant chief of staff for intelligence, G-2, and, 235
　capitalism and, 205, 234, 272
　democracy and, 205
　directors of naval intelligence and, 184
　domestic security and, 229
　Great Depression and, 260
　military intelligence and, 184, 205, 227, 272
　Military Intelligence Division, 206, 232, 234, 235, 272
　Office of Naval Intelligence and, 232, 234, 272
　society and, 271
　Strategic intelligence and, 229
　strategic military intelligence organizations and, 236
New Empire: An Interpretation of American Expansion 1860–1898, The, 54
New Mexico (USS), 240
New York (USS), 112
NIA. *See* National Intelligence Authority
Niblack, Alfred P., 119, 156, 166–167, 309n77
　Army War College and, 172
　assistant secretary of the Navy and, 174
　Commander, United States Naval Forces in Europe, 157
　demobilization and, 156, 157
　Department of the Navy and, 119, 157, 166
　Director of Naval Intelligence, 119, 158
　domestic security and, 119, 156, 158, 165–166, 172, 313n19
　Foreign Branch and, 173
　foreign intelligence and, 156
　Germany and, 62
　Japan and, 173
　military intelligence and, 167
　Military Intelligence Division and, 166, 172–173, 313n20
　as naval attaché, 60, 73, 157, 165, 172
　on naval attachés, 18, 158, 172, 174, 317n94
　as a navalist, 119, 158
　naval intelligence and, 206
　Office of Naval Intelligence and, 119, 166, 172–173, 310n92, 315n52, 315n54, 317n94

Office of Naval Intelligence: Its History and Aims and, 157–158
　Red Scare and, 167, 172
Nichols, Neil B., 248
NID. *See* National Intelligence Division
Nimitz, Chester W., 211, 212
Noland, Dennis E., 87, 118
　Agent B-7 and, 201
　American Expeditionary Forces and, 118, 201
　Army War College and, 161
　Assistant Chief of Staff for Intelligence, G-2, 118, 162, 215
　Director of Military Intelligence, 160
　Department of War and, 215
　Intelligence Regulations, 1920 and, 161
　Military Information Committee and, 107
　military intelligence and, 161
　Military Intelligence Division and, 161, 215
　monographs and, 161
　Negative Branch and, 161–162
　operational intelligence and, 144
　positive intelligence, 144
　rank of, 215
　Second Division and, 87
　war plans and, 107
North Atlantic Squadron, 12, 50, 65
North, Hugh, 202
NSC. *See* National Security Council
Nulton, Louis M., 83
NWC. *See* Naval War College
Nye, Gerald P., 197

O'Brien (Democrat operative), 194–195, 323n49
Office of the Coordinator of Information, 217, 233, 237, 247
Office of Economic Warfare, 249
Office of Intelligence, 10, 14
Office of Naval Intelligence
　Advanced Changes to U.S. Navy Regulations of 1920 and, 263
　Aide for Operations of the Fleet and, 103
　air intelligence and, 212, 242, 265
　analysis of information and, 172, 176, 184, 190, 193, 203, 214, 221, 223–226, 233, 326–327n6, 327n13
　"Are We Ready?" and, 223

Office of Naval Intelligence, *continued*
  "Are You Ready?" and, 209
  Army Air Force and, 265
  Army intelligence and, 101, 140, 149, 268
  assistant chief of staff for intelligence, G-2, and, 252
  Aviation Intelligence Branch, 212–213
  Basic Post-War Plan No. 1 and, 262
  Basic Post-War Plan No. 75, 262
  Basic War Plans and, 211
  Belknap, Reginald R. and, 132
  Bolshevism and, 166
  Branch Intelligence Office and, 131
  Bureau of Navigation and, 208
  Cabinet Committee on Censorship and, 237
  censorship and, 109, 132, 140, 145, 187, 237
  Central Intelligence Agency and, 267, 268
  Central Intelligence Group and, 266
  centralized intelligence agency and, 251–252, 256–257, 259
  chief of naval operations and, 186, 223–224, 226, 236, 242, 254, 268
  China and, 191
  combat intelligence division and, 254
  Combat Intelligence Section and, 263
  Commander-in-Chief, US Fleet and, 236, 237, 240, 251, 254–256, 258, 262
  communism and, 255
  Communist Party of America and, 194
  Corcoran Court and, 309n76
  counterintelligence and, 126, 144, 147, 196–197, 201, 202, 207, 216–217, 218, 230, 235, 241–242, 253
  creation of, 10, 14–15, 26, 76
  Cuba and, 61
  data management/information gathering and, 39, 42, 45, 68, 72, 84, 89, 103, 104, 105, 109, 124, 145, 156, 160, 171–172, 181, 183, 187, 190, 192, 195, 199, 203, 208, 223, 235, 238, 241–242, 253–254, 257, 269
  demobilization, 75, 156, 158, 178, 184, 203, 241–243, 251, 252, 262, 271272
  Department of Justice and, 179
  Department of the Navy and, 29, 61, 82–83, 110, 126, 135, 142, 144–145, 158, 166, 181, 186, 188, 190–192, 207, 209, 223–225, 226, 233, 235, 236, 238, 240, 255, 256, 257, 259, 263, 268, 270
  directors of naval intelligence and, 158, 159, 178, 206, 208, 211, 223, 237–238, 257, 258–259, 261–262
  disillusionment and, 184
  District Intelligence Offices and, 256
  District Intelligence Officers and, 237
  as Division of Naval Intelligence, 104, 242
  domestic security and, 105, 124–125, 132, 140, 141, 145–146, 148, 150, 154, 155–157, 165, 167–168, 172, 174, 178–180, 183–184, 185, 187, 189, 194–195, 197, 199, 202, 213, 216–217, 221–223, 228–229, 233, 235, 237–238, 240, 242, 252–253, 257, 258, 261–262, 269, 271–272
  "Estimate of the Situation for 1937" and, 196
  "Estimate of the Situation for 1939" and, 197
  Evening Star and, 26
  Far East Section/Division and, 120, 320n7
  Federal Council of Churches and, 196
  Fleet Problem and, 192
  foreign intelligence, 151, 173–174, 225, 262
  funding of, 125–126, 135, 140, 151, 154, 155, 157, 163, 175, 178, 181, 182–183, 185, 186, 196, 199, 202, 203, 209, 211, 232, 234, 249, 262, 272, 302n78
  general staff and, 52, 95, 104, 238, 251
  Germany and, 62, 193, 223, 268, 311n108
  Great Depression and, 160, 184, 203, 226–227, 255
  Great White Fleet and, 93
  growth of, 4, 21, 32, 53, 82, 109, 110, 132, 139, 141, 148, 151, 185, 187, 232, 271
  history of, 158, 172
  Information Section and, 178
  investigations of, 146, 150
  isolationism and, 203
  isolationists and, 195, 271–272
  Japan and, 91, 95–96, 107, 185, 190, 193, 203, 229–231, 255, 261, 268, 300n46, 326–327n6, 327n9

Japanese American Internment Camps and, 252
Joint Intelligence Collection Agencies and, 249, 251
Joint Intelligence Committee and, 218, 248–249, 253
Lend-Lease Act and, 223
London Naval Conference and, 189, 191
library, 15, 20
managerial revolution and, 271
manning of, 75, 82–83, 119, 126, 130, 135, 141, 143, 145, 154, 173, 183, 186–188, 190, 192, 199, 203, 209, 211, 213, 234, 238, 240, 241, 242, 249, 252, 262, 272
Marine Corps and, 127, 164–165, 177
media and, 24, 31, 46, 51–52, 67–69, 71, 97–98, 150, 172, 185, 196, 199, 201–203, 218, 227, 229, 257, 267–268, 302n78, 323n62
military intelligence and, 181, 192, 203, 226, 267, 268
military progressives and, 81
missions of, 2, 11, 15, 16–17, 25, 28, 31, 34–35, 39, 45, 47, 53, 55, 77, 80, 84, 94, 96, 103–104, 105, 107, 109, 124, 126, 132, 140–141, 145, 156, 163, 172–173, 175, 176, 178–179, 181, 186–187, 189, 207–208, 211, 212, 214, 221, 224, 229, 232, 238, 240, 241–242, 248, 249, 252, 254–256, 260, 263, 266, 269, 270, 272, 286n65
mobilization and, 187–188, 208, 210, 226–227, 234, 272
morale of, 35, 47, 104, 185, 213–214, 225
nadir of, 109
National Security Council and, 267, 268
nature of, 183
naval attachés and, 18–19, 40, 74, 142, 156, 158, 173–174, 175, 209, 218, 221, 226, 254, 262, 302n78, 317n94
naval board and, 68, 73
Naval Intelligence Division and, 225
naval observers and, 107, 214, 226
Naval Records and Library Branch and, 186
Naval War Board and, 69, 94
Naval War College and, 46, 56, 77, 81, 94, 102, 108, 193, 301n65
Naval Intelligence Division and, 142

Navy Building, Main and, 269
Navy Intelligence School and, 268
Navy Subsidiary Demobilization Plan and, 262
New Deal and, 232, 234, 272
Office of Public Relations and, 224
OP-16-B, 186
OP-20-G and, 235
OP-23, 262
OP-32, 263
operational intelligence and, 45–46, 55, 60, 77, 124, 126, 141–142, 151, 157, 203, 225, 230, 235–236, 237, 239–240, 252, 254, 255–256, 258, 262, 268–269, 305n5
Operation Overlord and, 256
pacifists and, 195, 221
Pearl Harbor and, 224, 232, 236, 237, 253–254, 261
Pentagon and, 239, 257, 269
plant protection and, 141, 145–146, 148, 187, 212
Progressivism and, 271
protection of, 24, 49, 57, 89, 99
public relations and, 29, 31, 34–35, 38, 42, 47, 53, 55–56, 61, 76, 89, 103, 109, 165, 177, 224, 346n6
purpose of, 3, 21, 55, 90, 97, 107, 179, 237, 267
as reformists, 31, 54, 56, 84
Red Scare and, 158, 172, 184, 271–272
relationship with Department of State, 262, 268
relationship with Federal Bureau of Investigation, 216–217, 222, 228–229, 240, 252–253, 257, 262, 268
relationship with MID, 28, 32, 38, 53, 69, 86, 140, 148–149, 158, 172–173, 187, 188, 214, 216–217, 222, 228–229, 236, 240, 242, 247–251, 253, 258, 262, 265, 270
relationship with Military Intelligence Section (Army), 140, 147
relationship with Military Intelligence Section (Marines), 208
relationship with Office of Strategic Services, 242, 247, 249–250, 270
reorganizations and, 80, 103, 104, 126, 131, 210, 239–240, 250–251, 262, 267

384 *Index*

Office of Naval Intelligence, *continued*
   reputation of, 21, 25, 33–35, 48–49, 56, 60, 81–82, 83, 89, 103, 109–110, 126, 146, 149, 151, 158, 178–179, 184, 192, 196, 201–202, 207, 218, 225, 227, 235, 237, 255, 258, 261, 330n45
   Russo-Japanese War and, 97
   secretary of the Navy and, 207, 218, 224, 268
   Sino–Japanese War and, 192
   society and, 11, 55, 71, 80–81, 97, 124, 145, 154, 172, 175, 181, 183, 213, 228, 232, 241, 252, 257, 269, 271
   Spanish-American War and, 69–70, 72–74, 81, 82, 109, 234–235
   Special Intelligence Service and, 253
   as spy-catchers, 124, 132, 149, 154, 261
   State, War, and Navy Building and, 15
   strategic intelligence and, 142, 172, 174, 184, 203, 221, 233, 236, 254, 256, 261, 265–266, 269, 270
   as strategic military intelligence organization, 206, 261, 269
   strategic warning and, 203, 206–207, 213, 229, 231, 237
   Union of Soviet Socialist Republics and, 255, 262, 268
   United States Naval Institute and, 22, 23, 56
   Warner Report and, 240
   war planning, 23–24, 29, 31, 34–35, 38–39, 42, 44–46, 52–53, 55–56, 57, 61, 64–65, 66, 72–73, 82, 92, 93–97, 103, 105, 107–109, 110, 125, 126, 143, 171–172, 175, 184, 190, 192–193, 195, 207, 218, 225, 255, 269, 327n7
   War Plan Orange and, 108–109, 193
   War Plans Division and, 104–105, 172, 178, 187, 221, 223–224, 226, 253
   Washington Naval Conference and, 173
   World War I and, 105, 126, 139, 141, 146, 150, 151, 172, 252, 271
   World War II and, 210, 233, 234–235, 241–242, 247, 252–254, 257, 258, 272
Office of Naval Operations, 104
Officer Procurement Act of 1947, 268
Office of Strategic Services, 236, 250–251
   Army intelligence and, 250
   Central Intelligence Agency and, 267
   Central Intelligence Group and, 266
   Department of the Navy and, 209
   Germany and, 267
   Joint Chiefs of Staff and, 247
   Joint Intelligence Committee and, 248–249
   media and, 267
   military intelligence and, 249
   naval intelligence and, 250
   relationship with Military Intelligence Division and, 242, 245, 247, 249–250, 270
   relationship with Office of Naval Intelligence, 242, 247, 249–250, 270
   Strategic Information Section and, 209
   strategic intelligence and, 236, 265, 270
   strategic military intelligence organizations and, 234
Office of War Information, 248–249
Oliver, James H., 105, 127, 131
   Department of the Navy and, 131
   Director of Naval Intelligence, 104, 126, 139
   military preparedness and, 130
   naval attachés, 105
   Navy General Board, 126
   Office of Naval Intelligence and, 130, 146
ONI. *See* Office of Naval Intelligence
Operational Intelligence Section, 239
Operation Plan 712, "Advanced Base Force Operations in Micronesia," 177–178
OPNAV, 262. *See also* Chief of Naval Operations
OSS. *See* Office of Strategic Services
Outhwaite, Joseph H., 37, 287n23
Overman, Lee S. and, 306–307n33
overregulation, 3, 99, 271

Pacific Squadron, 9, 12, 45
Padgett, Lemuel, 98
Palmer, A. Mitchell, 117, 153, 155, 166, 168–169
Palmer, Leigh C., 146
Panama Canal, 89, 149, 192, 200, 230
Pan-American, 222
Paris Peace Conference, 139
Patch, Alexander M., 263. *See also* Patch Board; Patch-Simpson Board
Patch Board, 263. *See also* Patch, Alexander M.; Patch-Simpson Board

Patch-Simpson Board, 264. *See also* Patch, Alexander M.; Patch Board
Patterson, Robert B., 264
Pearl Harbor
  Army intelligence and, 206
  assistant chief of staff for intelligence, G-2, and, 252, 253
  attack on, 206, 224, 231, 232, 236, 261
  Central Intelligence Agency and, 267
  Department of the Navy and, 224
  director of naval intelligence and, 252, 253
  hearings on, 261
  intelligence failures of, 229
  Japan and, 203, 205, 232, 261
  military intelligence and, 269
  Military Intelligence Division and, 232
  Office of Naval Intelligence and, 224, 232, 236, 237
  Strategic Military intelligence Organizations and, 208
Pentagon, 239, 245, 257, 266, 269
Perry, James DeWolf, 166
Pershing, John J., 138, 163
  American Expeditionary Forces and, 143, 162, 308n66
  assistant chief of staff for intelligence, G-2, and, 162
  Chief of Staff, 162
  Department of War and, 308n66
  general staff and, 321n18
  as military attaché, 42
  Military Information Division and, 143
  Military Intelligence Division and, 138, 151, 162, 314n40
  reorganization and, 162
  Second Division and, 87
Peru, 9, 12
Philippines, 149, 230
  Bureau of the Insurgents Records Office and, 85
  Japan and, 89, 243
  maps of, 48
  Military Information Division, 77, 85
  Spanish-American War and, 70–71, 72, 74
Phillips, Warren B., 222
Phony War, 210–211
Pinkerton, William M., 202, 325–326n78
plan of campaign, 46, 91, 108
Plan Dog, 223
Planning and Training Section, 187–188
Poindexter, Miles, 179, 319n121
Poor, Charles L., 83
Populism, 30
Positive Branch, 135, 138, 161, 162, 180
positive intelligence, 134, 136, 138, 144
Potts, Templin, 19, 102, 108, 109
Powhatan (USS), 9
Preparedness Movement, 123, 127
Preparatory Commission, 248
Price, Byron J., 237
Printing Law of 1895, 76
Proceedings, 304n109
  Chadwick, French E. and, 48
  contributors to, 13, 22, 23
  Knox, Dudley W. and, 104
  Rodgers, Raymond P. and, 33
  Rogers, Charles and, 21
Proctor, Redfield, 43
professionalism, 4, 75, 80. *See also* professionalization
professionalization, 2, 3, 26, 92. *See also* professionalism
progressive, 31, 80, 83, 100, 173
Progressive Era, 3, 59, 75, 78, 80–81, 86, 110
  Army intelligence and, 100, 102
  end of, 153
  See also Progressive; Progressivism
Progressives, 79–80, 103, 104. *See also* Progressive Era; Progressivism
Progressivism, 2, 79
  definition of, 3, 79, 271
  Military Information Division and, 271
  military progressivism and, 79
  Office of Naval Intelligence and, 271
  Taylorism and, 205
  See also Progressive; Progressive Era
Puerto Rico, 48, 74
Puleston, William D.
  as anti-communist, 191, 195
  centralized intelligence agency and, 196
  counterintelligence and, 197
  Director of Naval Intelligence, 185–186, 191, 193, 195–197
  District Intelligence Officers and, 196
  domestic security and, 185, 193, 195–197, 199

Puleston, William D., *continued*
  "Estimate of the Situation for 1937" and, 196
  Federal Bureau of Investigation and, 196
  information-gathering and, 199
  isolationists and, 197
  Japan and, 191, 196
  Military Intelligence Division and, 196
  Naval War College and, 193
  Navy General Board and, 193
  Nazism and, 191
  Office of Naval Intelligence and, 186, 196, 199
  pacifists and, 197
  strategic military intelligence organizations and, 195
  Union of Soviet Socialist Republics and, 191
  war planning and, 186, 193
  War Plans Division and, 193
Pullman, Raymond W., 133
Punitive Expedition, 128

Radford, William, 8–9
Rainbow plans, 209, 219, 221
Rainbow V, 223
Ramsay, Francis M., 9
Randall, Samuel J., 41
Rathom, John R., 166
Reagan, Ronald, 228, 335n116
reconnaissance, 5, 6, 7, 33, 49, 93
Reddles, William L., 164
Red Scare, 117, 152, 153, 155, 161, 165
  after, 155, 176, 195, 197
  Army intelligence and, 171
  assistant chief of staff for intelligence, G-2 and, 178
  definition of, 153
  director of naval intelligence and, 178
  domestic security and, 271–272
  end of, 154
  Military Intelligence Division and, 161, 168–171, 176, 184, 271–272
  Office of Naval Intelligence and, 158, 165, 172, 184, 271–272
  society and, 154, 169
Reeves, James H., 163–164, 170–171, 176, 316n82
Renard, Edward, 228

Robinett, Paul M., 217, 335n129
Rodgers, Christopher R. P., 9, 12, 14, 33
Rodgers, Raymond, 32–33, 109
  Bureau of Navigation and, 84
  Chief Intelligence Officer, 32, 34, 41, 42, 49, 51–52, 67, 84, 102
  as naval attaché, 33, 40–41, 60
  naval attaché reporting and, 91
  as a navalist, 84
  Naval War College and, 45, 91, 94, 102
  Navy Codebook and, 92
  Navy General Board and, 91
  Proceedings and, 33
  United States Naval Institute and, 33
  and war planning, 45
Rodgers, Thomas S., 103, 104
Rogers, Charles, 19, 21–22, 29, 49
Roosevelt, Franklin D.
  Acting Secretary of the Navy, 156, 166
  Aid for Information and, 156
  assistant chief of staff for intelligence, G-2, and, 207
  Assistant Secretary of the Navy, 115, 123, 125, 130, 139, 185, 221
  counterintelligence and, 183, 202, 207, 216, 326n80
  death of, 255, 265
  Department of the Navy and, 130, 209
  Department of War and, 209
  director of naval intelligence and, 139, 207, 211
  district intelligence officer and, 156
  domestic security and, 209, 216–217, 221
  efficiency measures and, 250
  Federal Bureau of Investigation and, 216–217
  Great Britain and, 219, 220–221
  intelligence committee and, 216
  as an internationalist, 182
  isolationists and, 182
  Japan and, 185
  Japanese American Internment Camps and, 252
  Limited National Emergency Order and, 188, 189, 210, 214, 232
  media and, 326n80
  military intelligence and, 207, 217–218
  Military Intelligence Division and, 202, 207, 216–217, 236

Military Intelligence Section and, 140
mobilization and, 209
National Conference of Jews and
    Christians and, 196
naval intelligence and, 115, 125, 166
New Deal and, 182, 234
Office of the Coordinator of Information
    and, 247
Office of Naval Intelligence and, 125,
    130, 146, 183, 185, 196, 202, 207,
    216–217, 221–222, 231, 233, 236, 237
Office of Strategic Services and, 115, 236,
    247
President, 182, 185, 207, 208, 211, 221,
    234, 247, 265
Rainbow plans and, 209
strategic intelligence and, 208, 233, 236
strategic military intelligence
    organizations and, 115, 217–218, 226
Union of Soviet Socialist Republics and,
    255
unlimited national emergency and, 224
World War I and, 221
World War II and, 115
Roosevelt, Theodore
    Assistant Secretary of the Navy, 57, 66,
        73, 113, 185
    chief intelligence officer and, 57–58, 89
    Great White Fleet and, 91
    as lieutenant colonel, 69
    military preparedness and, 123
    naval attachés and, 60, 66
    naval intelligence and, 113
    naval war board and, 73
    as a navalist, 30, 57, 91, 113
    Office of Naval Intelligence and, 67, 80,
        89–91, 102, 103, 113, 185
    Panama Canal and, 89
    President, 80, 92, 93–94, 95, 97, 103
    Russo-Japanese War and, 91
    strategic military intelligence
        organizations and, 113
    war planning and, 66
Roosevelt, Theodore, Jr., 174
Root, Edwin A., 98
Root, Elihu, 85–87, 92, 98–99
    General Orders and, 87
    General Staff and, 8–87, 96
    Military Information Division, 86, 88, 96

as Progressive, 85, 88
Secretary of War, 85–86, 98, 123
as a Taylorist, 85
Roullard, George D., 225
Rowen, Andrew S., 64
Russell, John H., 104, 126–127, 164
Russia, 89–90, 97, 106, 200, 300n47
Russo-Japanese War, 89–91, 95, 97, 105, 114,
    300n47

Sam, Vilbrun Guillaume, 127
Santiago de Cuba, Battle of, 77
Sargent, Nathan, 40, 288n32
Scherer, Lloyd C., 72, 74
Schofield, Frank H., 116
Schofield, John M., 37, 86
School of Application for Infantry and
    Cavalry, 10
Schroeder, Seaton, 33, 97
    Chief Intelligence Officer, 84
    Japan and, 89
    naval attachés and, 89–90
    Naval War College and, 84
    Proceedings and, 22
Schuirmann, Roscoe E., 241–242, 251, 254,
    256
Schwan, Theodore, 52, 92
scientific management, 127
Scott, Hugh L., 128, 129, 130, 133–134
Scott, Winfield, 7
Second Division, 87–88, 93, 100
    Army War College, 88, 99, 299n37
    creation of, 87–88
    Cuba and, 93
    Department of the Navy and, 93
    Department of the War and, 93, 99
    general staff and, 88
    Japan and, 93
    Lemon Building and, 87, 114
    manpower of, 93
    mapping and, 93
    military attachés and, 87, 99–100
    Military Information Committee and, 100
    Military Information Division and, 87,
        114, 299n29
    missions of, 87, 92, 96, 99
    nature of, 88
    submersion of, 93, 99–101
    Office of Naval Intelligence and, 93

Second Division, *continued*
  Third Division and, 89, 97, 98, 100, 299n37
  topography and, 87
  war planning and, 87, 96
Second Section, 100–101
Secretary of the Army, 270
Secretary of Defense, 270
Secretary of the Navy
  Bonaparte, Charles J., 84
  Chandler, William H., 16
  Daniels, Josephus, 104, 126, 132, 156, 167
  Darling, Charles H., 89
  Denby, Edwin, 178
  Forrestal, James V., 263
  Herbert, Hilary A., 46, 47, 56, 65, 293–294n45
  Hunt, William H., 13
  Knox, William F., 212, 224, 240
  Long, John D., 57, 65–66, 75, 95
  Meyer, George von L., 103, 109
  Roosevelt, Franklin D., 156
  Swanson, Claude A., 197
  Tracy, Benjamin F., 34, 45–47, 50
  Welles, Gideon, 34
  Whitney, William C., 40, 49
Secretary of State
  Bayard, Thomas F., 49
  Byrnes, James and, 266
  Hughes, Charles E., 174, 180
  Stimson, Henry L., 190
Secretary of War
  Alger, Russell A., 63, 65, 67, 74, 85
  Baker, Newton D., 133, 137, 147, 168–169
  Elkins, Stephen B., 37, 50
  Endicott, William C., 42, 285n60
  Garrison, Lindley M., 107, 123
  Lamont, Daniel S., 38, 51
  Proctor, Redfield, 43
  Root, Elihu, 8, 85–87, 123
  Stimson, Henry, 123, 232
  Weeks, John W., 180
Secret Service, 14, 147, 148, 312n7. *See also* Department of the Treasury
Seiler, Lewis, 228
Semon, Lawrence, 150
Senate Document No. 388, 83
Shafter, William R., 64, 113
Shallenberger, Ashton C., 179

Sharpe, George H., 7
Sherman, William T., 7–8, 10, 26
"Shore Leave," 227
Shulman, Mark R., 47, 90, 346n6
Sicard, Montgomery, 73
Signal Corps, 28, 37, 58
Sigsbee, Charles D., 82–83, 89, 94–6, 298n95, 302n76
Simpson, Edward, 9
Simpson, W. A., 87, 298n26
Simpson, William H., 263. *See also* Patch Board; Patch-Simpson Board
Sims, William S., 116, 142–143
  death of, 186
  Department of the Navy and, 142
  foreign intelligence and, 143
  mobilization and, 157
  as naval attaché, 58, 59–61, 73–74, 142, 186
  naval intelligence and, 142, 157, 186
  Naval Intelligence Division and, 141
  navalist, 141
  Office of Naval Intelligence and, 22, 131, 141–142, 157, 186, 315n54
  operational intelligence and, 143, 235
  as shipboard intelligence officer, 33, 59
  Spain and, 292nn20–21, 296n77
  United States Naval Forces Operating in European Waters and, 116, 141
  World War I and, 157, 235
Singer, Frederic, 56
  Chief Intelligence Officer, 35, 47, 56, 59, 64
  Spanish naval assets and, 61
  war planning and, 64
Sino–Japanese War (1895), 59
Sino–Japanese War (1937), 191–192
Slocum, Stephen L., 130
Smith, Alfred T., 188, 198, 324–325n66
Smith, Myron J., 320n4
Smith-Hutton, Henri H., 221
Socialist Party, 166
Solbert, O. N., 180
Soley, James R., 34, 45, 47, 288n39
Souers, Sidney W., 122, 266
South Atlantic Squadron, 12
Southerland, William H. H., 50
Spanish Army, 63, 74
Spanish Navy, 73–74

assets of, 60, 61, 69
construction and, 68
defeat of, 77
morale of, 61
ship movements and locations, 60–61, 68, 73, 77, 295n61, 296n77
squadrons of, 60, 73
Special Activities Branch, 211
Special Intelligence Section, 230
Special Intelligence Service, 253
Special Naval Observer, 221
spy-catchers, 137
   Army intelligence and, 257
   director of naval intelligence as, 203
   military intelligence as, 183, 227, 228
   Military Intelligence Division as, 124, 149, 154, 200, 261
   naval intelligence as, 179
   Office of Naval Intelligence as, 124, 149, 154, 261
   society and, 195
   strategic military intelligence organizations as, 202, 229
Stafford, David A., 208–209
Stafford, William H., 325n73
Stalin, Josef, 255
Stark, Harold R., 224, 334n99
   Chief of Naval Operations, 207, 209, 223, 237
   Department of the Navy and, 213
   director of naval intelligence and, 230
   Joint Intelligence Committee and, 213
   naval intelligence and, 207
   Office of Naval Intelligence and, 225–226, 253
   Pearl Harbor and, 253
   War Plans Division and, 207, 226
   Wilkinson, Theodore S. and, 213, 230
Star Wars defense program, 335n116
Stephens, W. D., 220
Stevenson, Archibald E., 168
Stimson, Henry L., 123, 190, 232
Strategic Information Section, 209
strategic intelligence, 38, 48, 170–171, 192, 215, 217, 218, 244, 247–248, 260, 270
   Army intelligence and, 270
   assistant chief of staff for intelligence, G-2, and, 263
   attachés and, 178

Central Intelligence Agency and, 267
Central Intelligence Group and, 266
Congress and, 40
Department of the Navy and, 235
Department of War and, 244
directors of naval intelligence and, 235
domestic security and, 158, 178, 229
duties of, 2
foreign intelligence and, 174
Marine Corps and, 164
military attachés and, 264
military intelligence and, 258–259, 265, 271
Military Intelligence Division and, 77, 184, 221, 236, 261, 263, 265–266, 269–270
Military Intelligence Service and, 244
missions of, 109, 126, 133, 158, 221
naval intelligence and, 236
New Deal and, 229
Office of Naval Intelligence and, 142, 172, 174, 184, 203, 221, 236, 254, 256, 261, 265, 266, 269, 270
Office of Strategic Services and, 236, 247, 265, 270
publications of, 49
role in American Civil War and, 7
strategic warning and, 221
war planning and, 158
World War I and, 127
World War II and, 212
strategic military intelligence organizations
   before Pearl Harbor, 208
   centralized intelligence agency and, 251
   counterintelligence and, 251
   creation of, 10–11, 14, 16, 28, 265
   data management, 61
   demobilization and, 156
   director of naval intelligence and, 261
   domestic security and, 110
   funding of, 184–185
   growth of, 32, 47, 78, 86, 110, 151
   customers of, 19
   Department of the Navy and, 9, 11, 149
   Department of War and, 9, 11, 149
   directors of naval intelligence and, 261
   foreign intelligence and, 55
   managerial revolution and, 29
   manning of, 184–185, 257

strategic military intelligence organizations, *continued*
  Marine Corps and, 35, 120, 155, 165, 208
  Military Intelligence Section and, 134
  Military Intelligence Section (Marines), 208
  military progressivism and, 81
  missions of, 17, 32, 38, 43, 54, 55, 80, 195, 259, 261, 270
  nature of, 4
  New Deal and, 236
  Office of Naval Intelligence and, 206, 261, 269
  Office of Strategic Services and, 234
  operational intelligence and, 55–56, 141, 233
  operations of, 22
  protection of, 80
  recognition of, 29, 67
  reputation of, 184–185
  society and, 24, 55, 67, 98, 110, 154, 199, 270–271
  Spanish-American War and, 56, 77, 233
  spy-catchers and, 202, 229
  war planning and, 53, 54, 55
  World War I and, 183, 233
  World War II and, 258
strategic warning, 140
  Army intelligence and, 208
  military intelligence and, 208
  Military Intelligence Division and, 206–208, 215, 229, 232
  naval intelligence and, 237
  Office of Naval Intelligence and, 203, 206–207, 213, 229, 231, 237
  strategic intelligence and, 221
  World War II and, 259
Strauss, Lewis, 194–195
Strong, George V., 340n63
  Army intelligence and, 246, 250
  Assistant Chief of Staff for Intelligence, G-2, 214, 244
  chief of staff and, 250
  director of naval intelligence and, 249
  evaluation and assessment function and, 244
  general staff and, 246
  Joint Intelligence Collection Agencies and, 249
  military intelligence and, 330n48
  Military Intelligence Division and, 214, 244–245, 250
  Military Intelligence Service and, 244–246
  Office of Economic Warfare and, 249
  Office of Naval Intelligence and, 250
  Office of Strategic Services and, 250
  Preparatory Commission and, 248
  Reorganizations and, 245–246
  strategic intelligence and, 244, 245
  strategic military intelligence organizations, 246
Stuart, Edwin R., 92
Sullivan, John L., 122
Swanson, Claude A., 197, 303n105
Swartz, Peter M., 12, 282n4
Sweeney, Walter C., 102, 125, 163, 176

tactical intelligence, 64, 97, 133, 143, 170, 264–265
Taft, William H., 80, 103, 105, 130
Taylor, Daniel M., 36, 42, 50, 287n17
Taylor, Frederick C., 79. *See also* Taylorism; Taylorist
Taylor, Henry C., 64, 95
Taylorism, 88, 208
  definition of, 3
  Joint Intelligence Committee and, 218
  Military Intelligence Division and, 206
  military progressives and, 80, 100
  Progressives and, 79
  Progressivism and, 205
  See also Taylor, Frederick C.; Taylorist
Taylorist, 104, 155, 183, 235, 239. *See also* Taylor, Frederick C.; Taylorism
Tennessee (USS), 32
"That We May Live," 228
Thebaud, Leo H.
  centralized intelligence agency and, 262
  chief of naval operations and, 242
  Communism and, 255
  demobilization and, 242–243
  Director of Naval Intelligence, 186, 242–243, 255, 256
  JIS 89 and, 251
  naval attachés and, 255
  naval intelligence and, 339n43

Office of Naval Intelligence and, 242–243, 251, 255, 256, 258, 261–262
  operational intelligence and, 256, 258
  Union of Soviet Socialist Republics and, 255
Third Agency Rule, 223
Third Division, 87–89
  Army intelligence and, 88
  Army War College and, 96, 299n37
  Second Division and, 89, 97, 98, 100, 299n37
  war planning and, 96
  War College Division, 99
Thompson, Edgar, 143
Topete, Pascual Cervera y, 60
topographic engineers, 4, 6
Townshend, Richard W., 41
Tracy, Benjamin F., 34, 45, 46–47, 50, 289n71
Train, Harold C., 122
  chief of naval operations and, 238–239
  Commander-in-Chief, US Fleet and, 254
  Counterintelligence Group and, 239
  Department of the Navy and, 238, 240
  Department of State and, 249
  Director of Naval Intelligence, 122, 238–239, 329n39
  Great Britain and, 239
  Intelligence Group and, 239
  Joint Intelligence Collection Agencies and, 249
  naval attachés and, 239, 337n21
  naval intelligence and, 250
  Office of Naval Intelligence and, 238–241, 254, 256, 337n26, 338n34
  Office of Strategic Services and, 249–250
  operational intelligence and, 240, 256
  Pentagon and, 239
  personality of, 239
  Preparatory Commission and, 248
  reorganizations and, 239–240
  Roosevelt, Franklin D. and, 239
  Russia and, 239
  Warner Report and, 240
Trask, David F., 78
Truman, Harry S.
  Advanced Changes to U.S. Navy Regulations of 1920 and, 263

  Central Intelligence Group and, 266
  centralized intelligence agency and, 265–266
  director of central intelligence and, 266
  Gestapo and, 265
  National Intelligence Authority and, 266
  National Security Act of 1947 and, 267
  Office of Naval Intelligence and, 263
  Office of Strategic Services and, 265
  Patch-Simpson Board and, 264
  Potsdam Conference and, 255
  President, 265
  secretary of the Navy and, 266
  secretary of state and, 266
  secretary of war and, 266
  strategic intelligence and, 266
Turner, Richmond K.
  on analysis of information and, 225
  chief of naval operations and, 224
  Department of the Navy and, 213
  director of naval intelligence and, 223–224
  Director of War Plans Division, 206, 223–225
  information-gathering and, 253
  Japan and, 226, 334n106
  Joint Intelligence Committee and, 253
  Military Intelligence Division and, 253
  naval attachés and, 226
  naval observers and, 226
  Office of Naval Intelligence and, 206, 223–226, 253–254, 326n6
  Pearl Harbor and, 253
  Russia and, 226
  War Plans Division and, 120, 207, 223–224, 226
  World War II and, 253
Twining, Nathan C., 116

Ulio, James A., 246
Union of Soviet Socialist Republics, 191, 224, 254–255, 262, 265, 268
United States Infantry and Cavalry School, 49
United States Naval Academy, 13, 40, 157
United States Naval Forces Operating in European Waters, 141–142
United States Naval Institute, 13, 14, 22–23, 33, 46

Upton, Emory, 21, 26, 27, 31
  American way of war and, 154
  Armies of Asia and of Europe, 10
Upton, Emory, *continued*
  as progressive, 31
  managerial revolution and, 79

Van Buren, Donald C., 169, 316n70
Van Deman, Ralph H., 99–100, 130, 132–136, 147–149, 151, 181, 197–198
  American Expeditionary Forces and, 147, 308n66
  American Protection League and, 147–148
  Army intelligence and, 128–129, 140, 168
  Army War College and, 299n37
  assistant chief of staff for intelligence, G-2, and, 198
  Bolshevism and, 168
  chief of staff and, 307n35
  communists and, 198
  counterintelligence and, 85, 139, 147–148, 171, 197–198
  death of, 198
  Department of War and, 144, 198, 308n66
  director of military intelligence and, 137, 139, 168–169, 171
  domestic security and, 133, 143–144, 147–148, 331n63
  as "Father of Military Intelligence," 128, 198
  foreign intelligence and, 143
  general staff and, 93, 137, 151
  Germany and, 310n97
  "Historical Sketch" and, 128
  Japanese American Internment Camps and, 341n97
  manning and, 135
  maps and, 62–63
  military attachés and, 128–129, 136
  Military Information Committee and, 100
  Military Information Division and, 58, 128
  Military Information Division (The Philippines) and, 85
  military intelligence and, 306n17
  Military Intelligence Branch and, 136
  Military Intelligence Division and, 129, 134, 136, 198, 203
  Military Intelligence Section, 134, 143–144, 147–148, 151
  Office of Naval Intelligence and, 147
  operational intelligence and, 143
  Paris Peace Conference and, 139
  Philippines, the, and, 85
  reassignment of, 137, 144
  Second Division and, 93, 299n37
  Spanish-American War and, 72, 74
  State, War, and Navy Building and, 292–293n29
  Third Division and, 299n37
  War College Division and, 128, 136
  Washington Post and, 136–137
Vandenberg, Hoyt S., 264–265, 266
VCNO. *See* Vice Chief of Naval Operations.
Versailles Treaty, 191, 193
Vice Chief of Naval Operations, 239, 241
Vincent, Thomas M., 39, 62
Virginia, USS, 84
Volkmar, William J., 28, 35–36, 42, 287n17
Vreeland, Charles E., 102

Wagner, Arthur L., 63, 69, 74, 77
  Canada and, 44
  Cuba and, 62, 64
  mapping and, 62–63, 74
  Military Information Division and, 39, 49, 58–59, 62–63, 293n33, 295n64
  Naval War College, 65
  Office of Naval Intelligence and, 65
  operational intelligence and, 64
  reorganizations and, 293n33
  The Security of Service and Information, 49, 58
  tactical intelligence and, 113
  war planning and, 49, 74
Wainwright, Richard, 61, 82
  Bureau of Navigation and, 65
  Bureau of Ordnance and, 65
  Chief Intelligence Officer, 56–57, 103, 166
  Maine, (USS) and, 62, 66
  Naval War College and, 57, 64–65, 66–67
  Proceedings and, 22
  Spanish-American War and, 103
  war planning and, 64–65, 66

Walker, John G., 14, 17, 19, 34, 111
  Bureau of Navigation and, 11
  Canada and, 50
  Chicago, Burlington, & Quincy Railroad, 9
  Chief of Bureau of Navigation, 9
  Department of the Navy and, 111
  naval attachés and, 17–18, 39
  naval intelligence and, 233
  navalist, 15, 16
  Office of Naval Intelligence, 21, 25, 34, 49–50, 57, 111, 233
  Powhatan (USS), 9
War College Board, 86, 96
War College Committee, 100
"War College Department Manual," 134
War College Division, 102, 105–106, 127, 129, 132, 134, 136
  Army intelligence and, 102
  Department of War and, 106
  funds of, 88, 101–102, 135
  general staff and, 106
  manning of, 129
  mobilization and, 107
  Mexico and, 106
  military attachés and, 105–106, 123
  Military Intelligence Committee and, 102
  reorganization of, 102, 133
  Second Section, 100
  Third Division and, 99
  Wotherspoon, William and, 99
"The War Department Basic Plan for the Post-War Military Organization," 264
War of 1812, 5–6, 57, 231
Ward, Harry F., 196
Ward, Henry H., 73
War Information Service, 126, 131
Warner, Rawleigh, 240, 250, 337n26. *See also* Warner Report
Warner Report, 240, 250–251. *See also* Warner, Raleigh
War of the Pacific, 9, 12, 13, 32
"The War of the Pacific Coast South America between Chile and the Allied Republics of Peru and Bolivia, 1879–81," 13
War Plan Black, 108
War Plan Green, 194
"War Plan Mobilization Plan, 1923," 163

War Plan Orange, 177, 231
  Department of the Navy and, 193
  director of naval intelligence and, 235
  Japan and, 107, 177, 194, 235, 322n36
  Military Intelligence Division and, 194
  Office of Naval Intelligence and, 107–109, 192, 193
  World War II and, 322n36
War Plan for Photographs, xx
War Plans Division (Army), 160, 162, 243–244
  general staff and, 236
  Military Intelligence Division and, 194, 236, 243
War Plans Division (Navy)
  analysis of information and, 176, 207, 223–224
  chief of naval operations and, 172, 225, 20
  creation of, 104
  director of, 178
  director of naval intelligence and, 184, 190
  information-gathering and, 253
  Office of Naval Intelligence and, 104–105, 172, 178, 187, 221, 223–224, 253
  strategic intelligence and, 172
  World War II and, 253
"War Plans—Division of Naval Intelligence," 185
War Plans Section (Navy), 171
War Plan White, 168, 170
"War Schools," 23
"War with Spain, 1896, General Considerations of the War, the Results desired, and the Consequent Kind of Operations to be Undertaken," 65
Wars of German Unification, 8, 10, 17, 26
Washington, George, 5
Washington Barracks, 99
Washington Naval Conference, 173–174
Washington Naval Treaty, 191
Watergate, 195
WCD. *See* War College Division
Weeks, John W., 180, 319–320nn128–129
Weigley, Russell F., 130, 236
Welles, Gideon, 34
Welles, Roger, Jr., 140–141, 145–146, 156
  Branch Intelligence Offices and, 141
  Department of the Navy and, 145
  Director of Naval Intelligence, 139
  domestic security and, 139, 143, 144

Welles, Roger, Jr., *continued*
  health of, 145
  Information gathering and, 140
  Military Intelligence Section and, 140
  naval attachés and, 140
  Office of Naval Intelligence and, 140, 144, 310n92
  secretary of the Navy and, 140, 150
  war planning and, 172
Western Pacific Fleet, 74
Wheeler, George M., 293n42
White, Ared, 201, 227
White, George A., 201
Whitney, H. H., 64
Whitney, William C., 40, 49
Whittlesey, Humes H., 69, 91, 139
"Who's Who in Pacifism and Radicalism," 168
Wiebe, Robert H., 77, 282n2
Wilkinson, Theodore S., 230–231
  chief of naval operations and, 230, 237, 254
  Department of the Navy and, 229–230, 237–238
  Director of Naval Intelligence, 213–214, 229, 252, 243
  domestic security and, 237, 252
  Joint Intelligence Committee and, 213, 237
  military intelligence and, 213
  reputation of, 213, 237
  Office of the Coordinator of Information and, 237
  Office of Naval Intelligence and, 213–214, 229–230, 237–238, 254
  operational intelligence and, 237
  Special Intelligence Section and, 229
  War Plan Division and, 230
Williams, Dion, 164
Williams, Robert, 37–38, 44
Wilson, Edward E., 206
Wilson, Woodrow, 103, 105, 123, 126, 131
  Army intelligence and, 80
  Department of the Navy and, 109
  military intelligence and, 125
  naval attachés and, 230
  naval observers and, 230
  Office of Naval Intelligence and, 80
  as a pacifist, 109
  peace conference and, 139
  Preparedness Movement and, 126
  as president, 220
  war planning and, 109
Winthrop, Beekman, 108
Withers, Grant, 227
Wohlstetter, Roberta, 206
Wood, Leonard, 101, 106, 123
"Work and Activities of the Military Intelligence Division, General Staff," 138
Wotherspoon, William, 99–101, 107
Wray, Fay, 227
Wright, M. Fisher, 19
W. T. Lackey Productions, 227

Yale University, 193
Yardley, Herbert O., 135
Yarnell, Harry E., 116, 171
yellow journalism, 68
Young, Samuel B. M., 88
Young Turks, 32

Zacharias, Ellis M., 119, 156, 181, 248, 256, 337n21
  counterintelligence and, 260
  Counterintelligence Group and, 239, 252
  Department of the Navy and, 119, 238, 240, 313n26
  director of naval intelligence and, 119, 122, 238–240, 255, 313n26, 336n5, 338n33
  domestic security and, 252
  Far East Section/Division and, 190–191, 320n7
  insubordination of, 240
  Intelligence Group and, 239
  Japan and, 238, 337n19, 338n33
  Military intelligence and, 236
  naval intelligence and, 119, 154, 236, 238, 241, 250, 320n7
  New Mexico (USS) and, 240
  Office of Naval Intelligence and, 159, 206, 236, 238–240, 242, 254, 255, 258, 313n26, 320n7, 336n5
  operational intelligence and, 239–240, 254, 255–256, 258
  Operational Intelligence Section and, 239
  Reorganizations and, 240
  strategic intelligence and, 236
  Taylorist, 239

www.ingramcontent.com/pod-product-compliance
Lightning Source LLC
Chambersburg PA
CBHW021507040925
32098CB00007B/37/J